T0248875

New Frontiers in Artificial Intelligence

New Frontiers in Artificial Intelligence

Edited by Jeremy Rogerson

MURPHY & MOORE

www.murphy-moorepublishing.com

Murphy & Moore Publishing,
1 Rockefeller Plaza,
New York City, NY 10020, USA

Copyright © 2022 Murphy & Moore Publishing

This book contains information obtained from authentic and highly regarded sources. Copyright for all individual chapters remain with the respective authors as indicated. All chapters are published with permission under the Creative Commons Attribution License or equivalent. A wide variety of references are listed. Permission and sources are indicated; for detailed attributions, please refer to the permissions page and list of contributors. Reasonable efforts have been made to publish reliable data and information, but the authors, editors and publisher cannot assume any responsibility for the validity of all materials or the consequences of their use.

Trademark Notice: Registered trademark of products or corporate names are used only for explanation and identification without intent to infringe.

ISBN: 978-1-63987-386-9

Cataloging-in-Publication Data

New frontiers in artificial intelligence / edited by Jeremy Rogerson.
   p. cm.
Includes bibliographical references and index.
ISBN 978-1-63987-386-9
1. Artificial intelligence. 2. Fifth generation computers. 3. Neural computers. I. Rogerson, Jeremy.
Q335 .N49 2022
006.3--dc23

For information on all Murphy & Moore Publications
visit our website at www.murphy-moorepublishing.com

 MURPHY & MOORE

Contents

Preface

The main aim of this book is to educate learners and enhance their research focus by presenting diverse topics covering this vast field. This is an advanced book which compiles significant studies by distinguished experts in the area of analysis. This book addresses successive solutions to the challenges arising in the area of application, along with it; the book provides scope for future developments.

The simulation of human intelligence in machines which are programmed to think and act like humans is referred to as artificial intelligence. It is based on the proposition that the natural intelligence displayed by humans and animals, that encompasses the elements of consciousness and emotions, can be defined in a way such that machines can mimic it. The major approaches which govern the development of artificial intelligence are cybernetics and brain simulation, sub-symbolic, symbolic, and statistical approaches. Artificial intelligence finds widespread application for a variety of purposes such as self-driving cars, medical diagnosis, image recognition, search engines, energy storage and online advertising. Some of the common challenges associated with this field are reasoning, planning, learning, knowledge representation, perception, natural language processing, social intelligence and general intelligence. This book unfolds the innovative aspects of artificial intelligence which will be crucial for the progress of this field in the future. It elucidates new techniques and their applications in a multidisciplinary manner. As this field is emerging at a fast pace, this book will help the readers to better understand the concepts of artificial intelligence.

It was a great honour to edit this book, though there were challenges, as it involved a lot of communication and networking between me and the editorial team. However, the end result was this all-inclusive book covering diverse themes in the field.

Finally, it is important to acknowledge the efforts of the contributors for their excellent chapters, through which a wide variety of issues have been addressed. I would also like to thank my colleagues for their valuable feedback during the making of this book.

Editor

Local gradient pattern - A novel feature representation for facial expression recognition

M. Shahidul Islam

Department of Computer Science, School of Applied Statistics, National Institute of Development Administration, Bangkok, Thailand.

*Corresponding author: suva.93@grads.nida.ac.th (M.Shahidul Islam)

Abstract

Many researchers adopt Local Binary Pattern for pattern analysis. However, the long histogram created by Local Binary Pattern is not suitable for a large-scale facial database. This paper presents a simple facial pattern descriptor for facial expression recognition. Local pattern is computed based on local gradient flow from one side to another side through the center pixel in a 3x3 pixels region. The center pixel of that region is represented by two separate two-bit binary patterns, named as Local Gradient Pattern (LGP) for the pixel. LGP pattern is extracted from each pixel. Facial image is divided into 81 equal sized blocks and the histograms of local LGP features for all 81 blocks are concatenated to build the feature vector. Experimental results prove that the proposed technique along with Support Vector Machine is effective for facial expression recognition.

Keywords: *Facial Expression Recognition, Local Feature Descriptor, Pattern Recognition, CK+, LIBSVM.*

1. Introduction

Facial expression is very important in daily interactions. It adds some more meaning to the verbal communication. Facial expression contributes 55% to the meaning of the communication whereas verbal expression contributes only 7% [1]. Therefore, a developing automatic facial expression recognition system has become a research issue in computer vision. Few important applications of this system are video surveillance for security, driver state monitoring for automotive safety, educational intelligent tutoring system (ITS), clinical psychology, psychiatry and neurology, pain assessment, image and video database management, and lie detection. Due to these applications, it attracts much attention of the researchers in the past few years [2]. Most of the facial expression recognition systems (FERS) available in the market are based on the Facial Action Coding System (FACS) [3] which involves more complexity due to facial feature detection and extraction procedures. Shape based models have problem with on plane face transformation. Gabor wavelets [4] are very popular but the feature vector length is huge and has a computational complexity.

Another appearance-based approach, LBP-local binary pattern [5], which is adopted by many researchers also has disadvantages, for example: (a) it produces long histograms, which slows down the recognition speed, and (b) Under some certain circumstances, it misses the local feature, as it does not consider the effect of the center pixel. To overcome all the above problems, this paper proposed a novel appearance-based local feature descriptor LGP - Local Gradient Pattern, which has a tiny feature vector length of 8. Appearance based methods are less dependent on initialization and can encode patterns from either local or full facial area. However, appearance features do not generalize across individuals, as they encode specific appearance information. Ahonen *et al.* [6] implemented a facial expression recognition system using Local Binary Pattern. LBP was first proposed by Ojhala *et al.*, [5] in 1996 for texture analysis. Slowly it has become popular, due to its unique power to differentiate textures using local 8-bit binary pattern. An LBP value from a local 3x3 pixels region is computed using the following equation (1).

$$LBP(i,j) = \sum_{p=1}^{P} 2^{p-1} * f(g_c - g_p) \qquad (1)$$

$$f(x) = \begin{cases} 0 & x < 0 \\ 1 & x \geq 0 \end{cases}$$

Where g_c and g_p are the gray color intensity of the center pixel (i, j) and p neighboring pixel respectively. A detailed example of obtaining LBP value is shown in Figure 1.

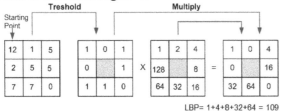

Figure 1. Example of obtaining LBP value.

Zhao et al. [7] applied both facial dynamics and Local Binary Pattern on the Three-Orthogonal-Planes (LBP-TOP) and Volume Local Binary Patterns (VLBP) to combine motion and appearance. Xiaohua et al. [8] also used LBP-TOP on eyes, nose and mouth separately. They formulated an equation to find the weight for those areas. An extension to the original LBP operator called LBP$_{RIU2}$ was proposed in [9]. A binary pattern differs from different angles. According to LBP$_{RIU2}$, these entire eight directional pattern would be counted as a single bin. For example, an LBP pattern 00000001 can be seen as 00000010 from 45-degree angle; therefore, they will be counted in the same bin. Although LBP features achieved high accuracy rates for facial expression recognition but it is time consuming due to its long feature dimension. Ojansivu et al. [10] proposed LPQ (Local Phase Quantization), another appearance-based facial feature extraction method that is blur insensitive. Yang et al. [11] used a local binary pattern and local phase quantization together and achieved very good result in case of person independent environment. Li et al (2012) used RI-LPQ (rotation invariant Local Phase Quantization) along with SRC (Sparse Representation-based Classification) classifier and obtained better accuracy than LBP. Kabir et al. [12] proposed LDPv (Local Directional Pattern - Variance) by computing weight from local region

using local variance and applying it to the feature vector. He used support vector machine, as a classifier and found his method to be effective for facial expression recognition.

The proposed feature representation method captures crucial texture information from local 3x3 pixels area. The referenced pixel is surrounded by eight pixels. Each of these 8 pixel's gray color intensity is used to build two 2-bit binary patterns. It is robust to monotonic gray-scale changes caused, for example, by illumination variations as it uses the magnitude of color difference instead of direct gray value. The feature vector length is only 8, which is suitable for large-scale dataset. In comparison with LBP [5] or LPQ[10], the proposed method performs better both in time and classification accuracy.

The rest of the paper is organized to explain the proposed local feature representation method in section 2, proposed framework in section 3, data collection and experimental setup in section 4, results and analysis in section 5 and conclusion in section 6.

2. Methodology - Local Gradient Pattern

The proposed representation method is based on facial color gradient differences of a local 3x3 pixels region (see Figure 2).

a1	b1	a2
b4	C	b2
a4	b3	a3

Figure 2. Local 3x3 pixels region

The representations operate on gray scale facial images. The pixel C in Figure 2 is represented by two 2-bit binary patterns e.g., pattern-1 and pattern-2 as shown in Figure 3. a1 to a4 and b1 to b4 represents the gray color intensity of the corresponding pixels. Bit-1 for Pattern-1 is 0 if $a1 \leq a3$ else it is 1. Similar way other bits are also calculated using the formula shown in Figure 3. Pattern-1 can have $2^2=4$ different combinations e.g., 00, 01, 10 and 11. Therefore four bins are needed to represent pattern-1. Similarly, another four bins are needed for pattern-2 (see Figure 4).

This new representation is called LGP. An LGP is computed for each pixel of the image. An example of obtaining LGP is shown in Figure 5.

Therefore, for the pixel '25', both bin-3 and bin-6 will be increased by one.

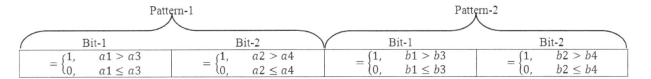

Figure 3. Single pixel representation using two separate patterns

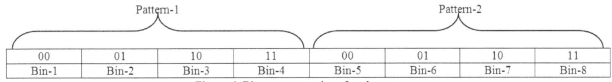

Figure 4. Bin representations for the patterns

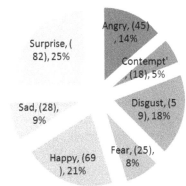

Figure 5. Example of obtaining LGP

3. Proposed Framework for Facial Expressions Recognition

The framework consists of the following steps:

I. For each of training images, convert it to gray scale if in a different format.

II. Detect the face in the image, resize it to 180x180 pixels and divide it into equal sized 20x20 pixels block.

III. Compute feature value for each pixel using LGP.

IV. Construct the histogram for each of 81 blocks.

V. Concatenate the histograms of each block to get the feature vector for the whole image.

VI. Build a multiclass Support Vector Machine for face expression recognition using feature vectors of the training images.

VII. Do step 1 to 5 for each of testing images and use the Multiclass Support Vector Machine from step 6 to identify the face expression of the given testing image.

4. DATASET and Experimental setup

The extended Cohn-Kanade dataset (CK+) [13] is used for experiments to evaluate the effectiveness of the proposed method. In CK+, there are 326 peak facial expressions from 123 subjects. Seven emotion categories are there. They are 'Anger', 'Contempt', 'Disgust', 'Fear', 'Happy', 'Sadness' and 'Surprise'.

Figure 6 shows the numbers of instances for each expression in the CK+ dataset. No subject with the same emotion has been collected more than once.

All the facial images in the dataset are posed and they are taken in a controlled environment. Some samples from the dataset are shown in Figure 7.

Figure 6. CK+ Dataset, 7 class expressions, number of instances of each expression and percentage.

Figure 7. Cohn-Kanade (CK+) sample dataset

The steps of face detection, preprocessing and feature extraction are illustrated in Figure 8. *fdlibmex* library, free code available for Matlab is used for face detection. The library takes a gray color image as input and returns the frontal face. The returned face is square in size and the resolution varies from 170x170 to 190x190. Therefore, all the detected faces are normalized to 180x180 pixels dimension for the experimental purpose. The face is then masked using an elliptical shape as shown in Figure 9.

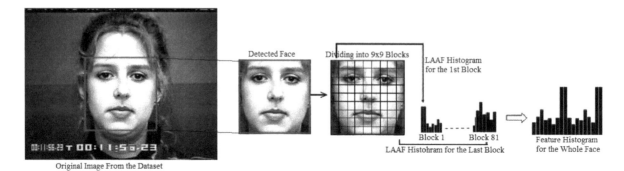

Original Image From the Dataset

Figure 8. Steps of Facial Feature Extraction

Figure 9. Elliptical shaped cropped sample faces from CK+ dataset.

The input face is divided into several equal sized blocks, because a block can give more location information. In the experiment, the 180x180 sized face is equally divided into 9x9=81 blocks of 20x20 pixels each. An LGP is extracted for each pixel from each block. Concatenating feature histograms of all the blocks produces a unique feature vector for the given image. In the experiments, a non-overlapping ten-fold cross validation is applied. LIBSVM [14], a multiclass support vector machine is used for classification. 90% of 326 images (90% from each expression) are used in each fold as the training input and the remaining 10 % of images are used as testing.

Ten rounds of this experiment are conducted and the average confusion matrix is reported. The kernel parameters for the classifier are set to: s=0 for SVM type C-Svc, t=1 for polynomial kernel function, c=100 is the cost of SVM, g= 1/ (length of feature vector), b=1 for a probability estimation. This setting of LIBSVM is found to be suitable for CK+ dataset with seven classes of data.

5. Experimental results and analyses

The feature vector length and feature dimension for 81 blocks are compared with some other methods in Table 1.

Face dimension, block dimension and the number of blocks are calculated before experiments. According to Table 2 and Table 3, the number of blocks considered for further experiments is

9x9=81. Combinations like 9x8, 8x9, 6x9, 9x6, 8x10, 10x8 are also tried but 9x9=81 is found to be the best among all combinations.

The confusion matrix for LGP is shown in

Table 4. Confusion matrix makes it easy to see if the system is confusing two classes or not.

Table 1. Feature Vector Dimension of proposed methods and some other popular methods.

Method	Feature vector Length	Feature vector Dimension used in our experiment	
LBP (Local Binary pattern)[5]	256	256x9x9	=20736
LPQ (Local Binary pattern)[10]	256	256x9x9	=20736
LDPv (Local Directional Pattern Variance)[12]	56	56x9x9	=4536
LGP (Proposed Method)	8	8x9x9	=648

Table 2. Block Dimension vs. Classification Accuracy

Blocks	Block Dimension (Pixels)	Classification Accuracy (%) LGP
6x6	30x30	88.52%
9x9	20x20	91.90%
10x10	18x18	90.75%
12x12	15x15	89.42%
15x15	12x12	89.34%
18x18	10x10	89.71%

Table 3. Face Dimension vs. Classification Accuracy

Face Dimension (Pixels)	Blocks	Classification Accuracy (%) LGP
240x240	12x12	89.28%
220x220	11x11	89.10%
200x200	10x10	89.80%
180x180	9x9	91.90%
160x160	8x8	89.25%
140x140	7x7	89.63%

Table 4. Confusion matrices for FERS using LGP (Accuracy= 91.9%)

C :		Actual						
		Angry	Contempt	Disgust	Fear	Happy	Sad	Surprise
prediction	Angry	**84.4**	4.4	4.4	0.0	0.0	6.7	0.0
	Contempt	5.6	**83.3**	0.0	5.6	0.0	0.0	5.6
	Disgust	4.9	0.0	**93.4**	1.6	0.0	0.0	0.0
	Fear	4.0	8.0	4.0	**60.0**	12.0	0.0	12.0
	Happy	0.0	0.0	0.0	0.0	**100.0**	0.0	0.0
	Sad	7.1	3.6	7.1	3.6	0.0	**78.6**	0.0
	Surprise	1.2	0.0	0.0	0.0	0.0	0.0	**98.8**

From the confusion matrix, it is clear that the most confusing expression classes are anger, contempt, fear and sad. The highest accuracy for class anger is obtained by the proposed method i.e., LGP. It should be noted that the results are not directly comparable due to different experimental setups, different versions with different emotion labels, preprocessing methods, and the number of instances used, but they still point out the discriminative power of each approach. **Error! Reference source not found.** compares LGP with some other static analysis methods in terms of the number of sequences and classification accuracy. An LGP clearly outperforms the others in almost all cases. It takes 0.0057 second to extract features from face of 180x180 resolutions, which cannot be compared with other methods, as feature extraction time is not cited in their papers.

Table 6 shows that proposed texture based expression recognition is better than previous texture based methods and compares favorably with state-of-the-art procedures using shape or shape and texture information combined.

Table 5. Comparison with Different Approaches, Number of expression classes=7 and non-dynamic.

Author	Number of subjects (Dataset)	Number of sequences	Classification accuracy (%)
LGP	123(CK+)	326	92%
[15]	123(CK+)	327	90%
[16]	96(--)	320	88%
[17]	90(--)	313	87%
[18]	123(CK+)	327	87%
[19]	123(CK+)	327	82%

Table 6. Results comparison, using different methods on (CK+/CK) dataset with seven main facial expressions. S: shape based method, T: texture based method. An. = Anger, Co. = Contempt, Di. = Disgust, Fe. =Fear, Ha. =Happy, Sa. =Sad, Su. =Surprise, Ne.=Neutral)

Method	T/S	Dataset	An.	Co.	Ne.	Di.	Fe.	Ha.	Sa.	Su
*LGP	T	CK+	84%	83%	-	93%	60%	100%	79%	99%
*LBP	T	CK+	79%	94%	-	97%	72%	100%	79%	99%
*LPQ	T	CK+	62%	67%	-	78%	52%	93%	43%	96%
LDPv	T	CK	79%	-	90%	93%	93%	100%	92%	99%

*Experiments using LGP, LBP and LPQ are conducted using same experimental setup.

6. Conclusion

The proposed method in this paper achieved classification accuracy of 92%, which is better than other available methods in the person dependent environment. It computes the feature pattern for a single pixel using the gray color value differences of its surrounding pixels, which is independent of grayscale change caused by monotonic illumination changes. The facial region is divided into 81 equal sized blocks and histogram of LGP codes computed for each block is concatenated to build the feature vector, which uniquely represents the face. The best thing is that it has a very tiny feature vector length. Therefore, the method is suitable for a large-scale dataset consists of high dimensional photos. The classification accuracy obtained using multiclass support vector machine (LIBSVM) outperforms

most of the appearance-based methods proposed in the last few decades. In future, some boosting algorithm can be incorporated with the classifier. Face alighment is also a big issue for classification. In CK+ dataset, pictures are taken in a controlled environment. Thus, it is not natural and also the instances for different classs of expressions are not equal. Experiments on equally distributed data might increase the accuracy level.

References
[1] Mehrabian, A. (1968). Communication without words. Psychological today, 2, 53-55.

[2] Zeng, Z., Pantic, M., Roisman, G. I., & Huang, T. S. (2009). A survey of affect recognition methods: Audio,

visual, and spontaneous expressions. Pattern Analysis and Machine Intelligence, IEEE Transactions on, 31(1), 39-58.

[3] Tong, Y., Liao, W., & Ji, Q. (2007). Facial action unit recognition by exploiting their dynamic and semantic relationships. Pattern Analysis and Machine Intelligence, IEEE Transactions on, 29(10), 1683-1699.

[4] Zhang, Z., Lyons, M., Schuster, M., & Akamatsu, S. (1998, April). Comparison between geometry-based and gabor-wavelets-based facial expression recognition using multi-layer perceptron. InAutomatic Face and Gesture Recognition, 1998. Proceedings. Third IEEE International Conference on (pp. 454-459). IEEE.

[5] Ojala, T., Pietikäinen, M., & Harwood, D. (1996). A comparative study of texture measures with classification based on featured distributions. Pattern recognition, 29(1), 51-59.

[6] Ahonen, T., Hadid, A., & Pietikainen, M. (2006). Face description with local binary patterns: Application to face recognition. Pattern Analysis and Machine Intelligence, IEEE Transactions on, 28(12), 2037-2041.

[7] Zhao, G., & Pietikainen, M. (2007). Dynamic texture recognition using local binary patterns with an application to facial expressions. Pattern Analysis and Machine Intelligence, IEEE Transactions on, 29(6), 915-928.

[8] Expression recognition in videos using a weighted component-based feature descriptor. In Image Analysis (pp. 569-578). Springer Berlin Heidelberg.

[9] Ojala, T., Pietikainen, M., & Maenpaa, T. (2002). Multiresolution gray-scale and rotation invariant texture classification with local binary patterns. Pattern Analysis and Machine Intelligence, IEEE Transactions on, 24(7), 971-987.

[10] Ojansivu, V., & Heikkilä, J. (2008). Blur insensitive texture classification using local phase quantization. In Image and Signal Processing (pp. 236-243). Springer Berlin Heidelberg.

[11] Yang, S., & Bhanu, B. (2012). Understanding discrete facial expressions in video using an emotion avatar image. Systems, Man, and Cybernetics, Part B: Cybernetics, IEEE Transactions on, 42(4), 980-992.

[12] Kabir, H., Jabid, T., & Chae, O. (2012). Local Directional Pattern Variance (LDPv): A Robust Feature Descriptor for Facial Expression Recognition. The International Arab Journal of Information Tecnology,9(4), 382-391.

[13] Lucey, P., Cohn, J. F., Kanade, T., Saragih, J., Ambadar, Z., & Matthews, I. (2010, June). The extended Cohn-Kanade dataset (CK+): A complete dataset for action unit and emotion-specified expression. In Computer Vision and Pattern Recognition Workshops (CVPRW), 2010 IEEE Computer Society Conference on (pp. 94-101). IEEE.

[14] Chang, C. C., & Lin, C. J. (2011). LIBSVM: a library for support vector machines. ACM Transactions on Intelligent Systems and Technology (TIST), 2(3), 27.

[15] Littlewort, G., Whitehill, J., Wu, T., Fasel, I., Frank, M., Movellan, J., & Bartlett, M. (2011, March). The computer expression recognition toolbox (CERT). In Automatic Face & Gesture Recognition and Workshops (FG 2011), 2011 IEEE International Conference on (pp. 298-305). IEEE.

[16] Shan, C., Gong, S., & McOwan, P. W. (2005, September). Robust facial expression recognition using local binary patterns. In Image Processing, 2005. ICIP 2005. IEEE International Conference on (Vol. 2, pp. II-370). IEEE.

[17] Bartlett, M. S., Littlewort, G., Fasel, I., & Movellan, J. R. (2003, June). Real Time Face Detection and Facial Expression Recognition: Development and Applications to Human Computer Interaction. In Computer Vision and Pattern Recognition Workshop, 2003. CVPRW'03. Conference on (Vol. 5, pp. 53-53). IEEE.

[18] Jeni, L. A., Lőrincz, A., Nagy, T., Palotai, Z., Sebők, J., Szabó, Z., & Takács, D. (2012). 3D shape estimation in video sequences provides high precision evaluation of facial expressions. Image and Vision Computing, 30(10), 785-795.

[19] CL, S. N., Jha, S. S., Das, P. K., & Nair, S. B. (2012). Automatic Facial Expression Recognition Using Extended AR-LBP. In Wireless Networks and Computational Intelligence (pp. 244-252). Springer Berlin Heidelberg.

2

An indirect adaptive neuro-fuzzy speed control of induction motors

M. Vahedi[*], M. Hadad Zarif and A. Akbarzadeh Kalat

Faculty of Electrical & Robotic Engineering, Shahrood University of Technology, Shahrood, Iran.

Corresponding author: vahedi.mojtaba@gmail.com (M.Vahedi).

Abstract

This paper presents an indirect adaptive system based on neuro-fuzzy approximators for the speed control of induction motors. The uncertainty including parametric variations, the external load disturbance and unmodeled dynamics is estimated and compensated by designing neuro-fuzzy systems. The contribution of this paper is presenting a stability analysis for neuro-fuzzy speed control of induction motors. The online training of the neuro-fuzzy systems is based on the Lyapunov stability analysis and the reconstruction errors of the neuro-fuzzy systems are compensated in order to guarantee the asymptotic convergence of the speed tracking error. Moreover, to improve the control system performance and reduce the chattering, a PI structure is used to produce the input of the neuro-fuzzy systems. Finally, simulation results verify high performance characteristics and robustness of the proposed control system against plant parameter variation, external load and input voltage disturbance.

Keywords: *Induction Motor; Indirect Adaptive Control; Neuro-fuzzy Approximators; Uncertainty Estimation; Stability Analysis; Reconstruction Error.*

1. Introduction

In the last few decades, the speed control of induction motors (IMs) has been the focus of widespread researches [1-6]. However, the closed loop control system stability has not been guaranteed in most of these researches. Moreover, the asymptotic convergence of the speed tracking error is very important in most industrial applications and should be mathematically guaranteed. To solve this problem, many Lyapunov based control algorithms for IMs have been presented in the literature [7-9]. However, these researches have focused on the position control of induction servo motors and the boundedness of fluxes and currents has not been guaranteed. Recently, a speed control system with stability analysis has been presented based on the sliding mode control [10]. In that research, boundedness of fluxes and currents is guaranteed using some limiters. However, the proposed control law contains the sign function which may cause the undesirable chattering phenomenon. Thus, presenting a continuous control law with stability analysis is required. Model based control approaches, such as feedback linearization, are

very popular and attractive. However, they are not suitable for IMs due the variations of the external load disturbance. To enhance the performance of feedback linearization and overcome uncertainties including parametric uncertainty, un-modeled dynamics and external disturbances, considerable researches have been carried out in the field of adaptive and robust control [11-16]. Adaptive control can overcome parametric uncertainty [17], while robust control can compensate both parametric and nonparametric uncertainty. In order to design an adaptive control law, the structure of the system dynamics should be available. In other words, the regressor vector should be known. Thus, conventional adaptive control laws may not be successful for complicated systems with unknown dynamics. Although robust control can overcome nonparametric uncertainties, but the upper bound of uncertainties should be known [18]. Overestimation of this bound will increase the amplitude of the control signal and consequently may damage the system. On the other hand, underestimation of this bound will deteriorate the system performance by increasing the tracking error [19,20]. Moreover, in some robust control approaches, such as sliding mode control, the control law is discontinuous which may result in the chattering phenomenon [21].

In order to improve the performance of adaptive or robust controllers, many researchers have applied artificial intelligence. Various neural networks and fuzzy systems are widely used in adaptive and robust control [22-26] due to their universal approximation property. These researches can be considered as different efforts made toward common objectives which are estimation and compensation of uncertainty. Generally, adaptive neuro-fuzzy approaches can be classified into two main groups: direct and indirect. In direct approaches, an adaptive neuro-fuzzy system is designed to approximate the ideal control law, while in indirect methods, first the unknown nonlinear dynamics of the systems are identified and then a control input is generated based on the universal approximation theorem [27]. According to this theorem, neuro fuzzy systems can approximate any nonlinear functions with arbitrary small approximation error. An adaptive fuzzy speed control of IMs is presented in [22] in which the gains of the sliding mode controller are adjusted by a fuzzy system and the centers of fuzzy sets are updated by an adaptation law: the gain adjustment to compensate the uncertainty and the centers updating to reduce the control effort chattering. A multivariable adaptive fuzzy speed controller for IMs is proposed in [23] where the approximation of the nonlinear parameters in the feedback linearization control law is based on fuzzy logic. The advantage of this paper in comparison with previous related works is that it does not need any prior knowledge of plant dynamics. In [24], an adaptive speed control using a neural network representing the feedback linearization law has been presented. Also an error compensator is added in order to compensate the approximation error between the neural network and the feedback linearization law. In [25] adaptive neuro-fuzzy systems for speed control of IM have been represented. In the designed neuro-fuzzy scheme, neural network techniques have been used to choose a proper rule base, which has been achieved by using the back propagation algorithm. This integrated approach improves the system performance, efficiency, reliability, cost effectiveness and dynamism of the designed controller. Zerikat and Hekroun [26] have improved an adaptive speed control of a hybrid fuzzy neural network for a high performance IM drive to increase the performance and robustness

of the IM drive under nonlinear loads and parameter variations.

In this paper, a novel speed controller for IMs has been presented. The control law is proposed based on feedback linearization technique. Two neuro-fuzzy systems have been designed to estimate the unknown nonlinear functions required in the control law. As mentioned before, many speed control approaches for induction motors have been presented in the literature without stability analysis. The contribution of this paper is presenting a rigorous mathematical stability analysis for neuro-fuzzy speed control of induction motors. The adaptation laws for training the parameters of neuro-fuzzy estimators are derived from the stability analysis in which the boundedness of fluxes and currents has been guaranteed. In order to guarantee the asymptotic convergence of the speed tracking error and improve the control system performance, the reconstruction errors of neuro-fuzzy systems have been compensated using a robustifying term in the control law. Recently, some algorithms have been proposed in the literature for the compensation of the reconstruction error. These algorithms result in discontinuous control laws due to the existence of the sign function, which may increase the possibility of the chattering phenomenon [28-33]. As an advantage over these approaches, this paper presents a continuous robustifying term. Moreover, simulation results show that the proposed controller represents acceptable robustness against variations of the external load disturbance. In addition the controller is capable of fast disturbance rejection due to the undesirable effects from the input voltage.

This paper is organized as follows; Section 2 describes the IM model. Section 3 presents the proposed control law and stability analysis. Simulation results are given in section 4 and finally, section 5 concludes the paper.

2. Induction motor model

The fifth-order model of an IM under the assumptions of equal mutual inductances and linear magnetic circuit is given by:

$$\frac{di_{sa}}{dt} = -a_0 i_{sa} + a_1 \psi_{ra} + a_2 \omega \psi_{rb} + a_3 u_{sa} \tag{1-a}$$

$$\frac{di_{sb}}{dt} = -a_0 i_{sb} + a_1 \psi_{rb} - a_2 \omega \psi_{ra} + a_3 u_{sb} \tag{1-b}$$

$$\frac{d\psi_{ra}}{dt} = -\frac{R_r}{L_r} \psi_{ra} - n_p \omega \psi_{rb} + \frac{R_r}{L_r} M i_{sa} \tag{1-c}$$

$$\frac{d\psi_{rb}}{dt} = -\frac{R_r}{L_r} \psi_{rb} + n_p \omega \psi_{ra} + \frac{R_r}{L_r} M i_{sb} \tag{1-d}$$

$$\frac{d\omega}{dt} = \frac{n_p M}{JL_r}(\psi_{ra}i_{sb} - \psi_{rb}i_{sa}) - \frac{T_L}{J} \qquad (1\text{-}e)$$

where, u_s, i, T_L, and ψ indicate stator voltage input to the machine, current, external load torque, and flux linkage respectively; the subscripts r and s stand for rotor and stator; (a,b) denote the components of a vector with respect to a fixed stator reference frame and, $\sigma = 1 - (M^2/L_sL_r)$,

$a_0 = (M^2R_r + L_r^2R_s)/(\sigma L_sL_r^2)$, $\qquad a_3 = 1/(\sigma L_s)$
$a_1 = (MR_r)/(\sigma L_sL_r^2)$, $a_2 = (n_pM)/(\sigma L_sL_r)$, [34-37].

3. The proposed control scheme
Consider the following general form of nonlinear systems
$$\dot{x}_n = f_1(X) + g(X)u \qquad (2)$$
in which $f_1(X)$ and $g(X)$ are unknown nonlinear functions and X is the state variable vector defined as $X = [x_1 \quad x_2 \quad \dots \quad x_n]^T$. According to (1), it is clear that $X = [i_{sa} \quad i_{sb} \quad \psi_{ra} \quad \psi_{rb} \quad \omega]^T$ is the state vector of this system. The time derivative of (1-e) is
$$\ddot{\omega} = h(X,t) + g(X,t)u \qquad (3)$$
in which u is the input voltage amplitude of stator and $h(X,t)$ and $g(X,t)$ are
$$h(X,t) = b_0(i_{sa}\psi_{ra} + i_{sb}\psi_{rb})$$
$$+ b_1(i_{sa}\psi_{rb} - i_{sb}\psi_{ra}) + b_2|\psi_r|^2 \qquad (4)$$
$$g = c_0\frac{\sqrt{3}}{3}\psi_{ra}(\sin(\alpha t - \frac{2\pi}{3}) - \sin(\alpha t + \frac{2\pi}{3}))$$
$$- c_1(2\sin(\alpha t) - \sin(\alpha t - \frac{2\pi}{3}) - \sin(\alpha t + \frac{2\pi}{3})) \qquad (5)$$
in which $|\psi_r|^2 = \psi_{rb}^2 + \psi_{ra}^2$, $b_0 = -(n_p^2 M\omega)/(JL_r)$,
$b_1 = \frac{R_r n_p M}{JL_r^2} + a_0\frac{a_2}{Ja_3}$, $\qquad b_2 = -n_p^2 M^2\omega/(\sigma JL_sL_r^2)$,
$c_0 = \frac{n_p M}{\sigma JL_sL_r}$ and $c_1 = \frac{n_p M\psi_{rb}}{3\sigma JL_sL_r}$. Based on feedback linearization, consider the following control law:
$$u = \frac{\ddot{\omega}_d + k_d\dot{e} + k_pe - h(X,t)}{g(X,t)} \qquad (6)$$
in which $e = \omega_r - \omega$ is the speed tracking error and k_p, k_d are design parameters. So for implementation of the control law, the acceleration signal $\dot{\omega}$ is required and because this feedback is contaminated with noise, the performance of control system is deteriorated. In order to reduce the system order and remove the acceleration feedback we can rewrite the (3) as follows

$$\ddot{\omega} = h(X,t) + g(X,t)u + \dot{\omega} - \dot{\omega} \qquad (7)$$
which can be shown in form (2) as:
$$\dot{\omega} = f(X,t) + g(X,t)u \qquad (8)$$
in which $f(X,t) = h(X,t) + \dot{\omega} - \ddot{\omega}$ and $g(X,t)$ are unknown nonlinear functions. Based on feedback linearization, consider the following proposed control law:
$$u = \frac{-\hat{f}(X,t) + \dot{\omega}_r + k_pe + k_l\int edt + u_r}{\hat{g}(X,t)} \qquad (9)$$
in which $\dot{\omega}_r$ is the derivative of reference speed ω_r, $e = \omega_r - \omega$ is the speed tracking error, k_p, k_d are design parameters, $\hat{f}(X,t)$ and $\hat{g}(X,t)$ are the neuro-fuzzy estimations of $f(X,t)$ and $g(X,t)$, and u_r is the robustifying control term to compensate the reconstruction errors of the neuro-fuzzy systems $\hat{f}$ and $\hat{g}$. The structure of the speed control system is illustrated in figure 1 in which V_{dist} is the undesirable disturbance of the input voltage.

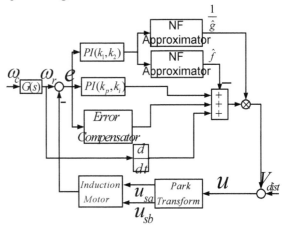

Figure 1. The structure of proposed control system.

In figure 2 the signal propagation in each layer of neuro-fuzzy estimators is illustrated. In this figure $S = [s_1 \quad s_2 \quad \cdots \quad s_n]^T$ is the input variable vector and $\mu_i^j(s_i) = \exp[-(s_i - m_i^j)^2/(\sigma_i^j)^2]$ is the Gaussian membership function, in which m_i^j ($i = 1,\dots n$ and $j = 1,\dots,N$) is the mean of the Gaussian function in the jth term of the ith input variable s_i, and σ_i^j is its corresponding standard deviation. In this paper each input variable has two linguistic fuzzy sets as negative and positive thus, N is set to 2. Also in the kth node in the rule layer ($k = 1,\dots,p$), the fuzzy AND operation determines the output by multiplying the input signals as $\xi_k(S) = \prod_{i=1}^n w_{ji}^k\mu_i^j(s_i)$ where w_{ji}^k is unity weights between the membership layer and the rule layer, and p is the number of rules.

$$y_o = \sum_{k=1}^{p} \theta_{ok} \xi_k(S)$$ is one of the overall outputs that

is the summation of its inputs by considering related weights θ_{ok} way to comply with the journal paper formatting requirements is to use this document as a template and simply type your text into it.

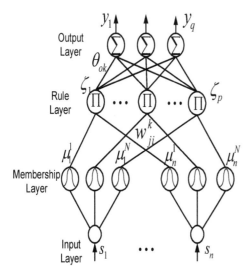

Figure 2. The structure of the neuro-fuzzy approximators.

In this paper, $\hat{f}(X,t)$ and $\hat{g}(X,t)$ are estimated using two neuro-fuzzy systems. The input of each system is given by the PI structure shown in figure 1. This filter is very common in the speed control of electrical motors and often improves the tracking performance of the controllers. The input-output relation of this filter is described by

$s(t) = k_1 e(t) + k_2 \int_0^t e(\tau) d\tau$ in which k_1 and k_2 are

positive tuning parameters. In this paper, the input and output of neuro-fuzzy systems are scalars. Thus, we can write the output of neuro-fuzzy approximators as follows:

$$y = \theta^T \xi \tag{10}$$

where, $\theta = [\theta_1, \theta_2]^T$ is the consequent adjustable parameter vector and $\xi = [\xi_1, \xi_2]^T$. From (8), the closed loop equation is given by

$$\dot{\omega}_r - \dot{\omega} = \dot{\omega}_r - f(X,t) - g(X,t)u \tag{11}$$

Substituting u from (9) into (11) yields

$$\dot{e} + k_p e + k_I \int e = (\hat{f} - f) + (\hat{g} - g)u - u_r \tag{12}$$

According to (10), it follows from (12) that

$$\dot{e} = -k_p e - k_I \int e \, dt + (\hat{\theta}_f - \theta_f)^T \xi \tag{13}$$
$$+ (\hat{\theta}_g - \theta_g)^T \eta u - u_r$$

By defining $E = \left[\int e \, dt \quad e \right]^T$, we have:

$$\dot{E} = AE + B\left\{ (\hat{f} - f) + (\hat{g} - g)u - u_r \right\} \tag{14}$$

in which $A = \begin{bmatrix} 0 & 1 \\ -k_I & -k_p \end{bmatrix}$ and $B = \begin{bmatrix} 0 \\ 1 \end{bmatrix}$. Suppose that

$f^* = \theta_f^{*T} \xi$ and $g^* = \theta_g^{*T} \eta$ are the best approximations of f and g. Therefore,

$$\dot{E} = AE + B\left\{ \hat{f} - f^* + (\hat{g} - g^*)u + \varepsilon - u_r \right\} \tag{15}$$

where, $\varepsilon = \left[f^* - f \right] + \left[g^* - g \right] u$ is the reconstruction error (approximation error). According to the universal approximation theorem, ε is bounded as $|\varepsilon| < \rho$ and it is assumed that ρ is a positive known constant. By defining $\tilde{\theta}_f = \hat{\theta}_f - \theta_f^*$ and $\tilde{\theta}_g = \hat{\theta}_g - \theta_g^*$

$$\dot{E} = AE + B\left\{ \tilde{\theta}_f^T \xi + \tilde{\theta}_g^T \eta u_I + \varepsilon - u_r \right\} \tag{16}$$

Theorem 1. Considering the nonlinear system (8) and the control law (9), if the following conditions are met, the internal signals in the control system are bounded and the tracking error converges to zero asymptotically:

$$\dot{\hat{\theta}}_f = -\gamma_1 E^T PB\xi \tag{17}$$

$$\dot{\hat{\theta}}_g = -\gamma_2 E^T PB\eta u \tag{18}$$

Proof. Consider the following positive definite function

$$L = \frac{1}{2} E^T PE + \frac{1}{2\gamma_1} \tilde{\theta}_f^T \tilde{\theta}_f + \frac{1}{2\gamma_2} \tilde{\theta}_g^T \tilde{\theta}_g \tag{19}$$

The time derivative of (19) is:

$$\dot{L} = \frac{1}{2} \left(E^T A^T + \left\{ \xi^T \tilde{\theta}_f + u\eta^T \tilde{\theta}_g + \varepsilon - u_r \right\} \right) PE$$
$$+ \frac{1}{2} \left(E^T P \left(AE + b(\tilde{\theta}_f^T \xi + \tilde{\theta}_g^T \eta u + \varepsilon - u_r) \right) \right) \tag{20}$$
$$+ \frac{\tilde{\theta}_f^T \dot{\hat{\theta}}_f}{\gamma_1} + \frac{\tilde{\theta}_g^T \dot{\hat{\theta}}_g}{\gamma_2}$$

According to the Lyapanove equation $A^T P + PA = -Q$. Since the matrix A is a Hurwitz matrix, we can use this equation and simplify (20) as

$$\dot{L} = E^T PB \left(\tilde{\theta}_f^T \xi + \tilde{\theta}_g^T \eta u + \varepsilon - u_r \right)$$
$$+ \frac{\tilde{\theta}_f^T \dot{\hat{\theta}}_f}{\gamma_1} + \frac{\tilde{\theta}_g^T \dot{\hat{\theta}}_g}{\gamma_2} - \frac{1}{2} E^T QE \tag{21}$$

In other words

$$\dot{L} = \frac{-1}{2} E^T QE + \left(E^T PB\tilde{\theta}_f^T \xi + \frac{\tilde{\theta}_f^T \dot{\hat{\theta}}_f}{\gamma_1} \right)$$
$$+ \left(E^T PB\tilde{\theta}_g^T \eta u + \frac{\tilde{\theta}_g^T \dot{\hat{\theta}}_g}{\gamma_2} \right) + E^T PB\varepsilon \tag{22}$$
$$- E^T PB u_r$$

Using (17) and (18), (22) can be simplified as

$$\dot{L} = \frac{-1}{2}E^T QE + E^T PB\varepsilon - E^T PBu_r \quad (23)$$

Since $|\varepsilon| < \rho$ it follows from (23) that

$$\dot{L} \le \frac{-1}{2}E^T QE + |E^T PB|\rho - E^T PBu_r \quad (24)$$

Define $z = E^T PB$ thus

$$\dot{L} \le \frac{-1}{2}E^T QE + |z|\rho - zu_r \quad (25)$$

According to [18] we can propose the robustifying term as

$$u_r = \frac{z\rho}{|z| + \lambda e^{-\beta t}} \quad (26)$$

in which λ and β are constant positive scalars, so

$$\dot{L} \le \frac{-1}{2}E^T QE + |z|\rho - \frac{z^2\rho}{|z| + \lambda e^{-\beta t}} \quad (27)$$

After some manipulations, we can write

$$\dot{L} \le \frac{-1}{2}x^T Qx + \rho\frac{|z|\lambda e^{-\beta t}}{|z| + \lambda e^{-\beta t}} \quad (28)$$

Since $\quad \forall a > b > 0 : \frac{ab}{a+b} < b < a \quad$ we have

$$\frac{|z|\lambda e^{-\beta t}}{|z| + \lambda e^{-\beta t}} \le \lambda e^{-\beta t}, \text{ therefore}$$

$$\dot{L} \le \frac{-1}{2}E^T QE + \rho\lambda e^{-\beta t} \quad (29)$$

According to [18], (29) indicates that speed tracking error asymptotically converges to zero. To ensure the boundedness of internal dynamics of IM including i_{ra}, i_{rb}, ψ_{sa} and ψ_{sb}, according to (1) we can write

$$\dot{X}_1 = AX_1 + v(t) \quad (30)$$

in which

$$X_1 = [i_{sa}\, i_{sb}\, \psi_{ra}\, \psi_{rb}]^T \quad (31)$$

$$v(t) = \left[\frac{1}{\sigma L_s}u_{sa} \quad \frac{1}{\sigma L_s}u_{sb} \quad 0 \quad 0\right]^T \quad (32)$$

and A is given in (33). Since the eigenvalues of A are negative, the state vector X_1 in $\dot{X}_1 = AX_1$ is exponentially stable. Moreover, the control law (9) is bounded. Thus, the vector $v(t)$ is bounded. Consequently, the system (30) can be considered as a stable linear system with bounded inputs.

$$A = \begin{bmatrix} -a_0 & 0 & \frac{MR_r}{\sigma L_s L_r^2} & \frac{n_p M}{\sigma L_s L_r}\omega \\ 0 & -a_0 & -\frac{n_p M}{\sigma L_s L_r}\omega & \frac{MR_r}{\sigma L_s L_r^2} \\ \frac{R_r M}{L_r} & 0 & -\frac{R_r}{L_r} & -n_p\omega \\ 0 & \frac{R_r M}{L_r} & n_p\omega & -\frac{R_r}{L_r} \end{bmatrix} \quad (33)$$

4. Simulation results

To make the superiority of the proposed method more obvious, its performance is compared with the controller designed in [23]. In Simulation 1 the proposed neuro-fuzzy control algorithm has been tested and Simulation 2 presents the performance of the adaptive fuzzy MIMO controller [23].

4.1. Simulation 1

Consider a three-phase standard IM with parameters given in the table 1.

Table 1. Rated parameters of case study induction motor.

P	Power	3 (KW)
f	Frequency	60 (Hz)
V	Rated voltage	380 (V)
I	Rated current	6.9 (A)
n_p	Number of pole pairs	2
R_s	Stator resistance	1.115 (Ω)
R_r	Rotor resistance	1.083 (Ω)
L_s	Stator inductance	0.005974 (H)
L_r	Rotor inductance	0.005974 (H)
M	Mutual inductance	0.2037 (H)
J	Total inertia	0.02 (kgm2)

To test the control system robustness against the thermal variation of motor parameters and external load disturbance, it is assumed that

$$\begin{aligned} R_s &= R_{s0}(1 + 0.2\sin(t)) \quad \Omega \\ R_r &= R_{r0}(1 + 0.2\cos(t)) \quad \Omega \\ L_s &= L_{s0}(1 + 0.1\sin(t)) \quad H \\ L_r &= L_{r0}(1 + 0.1\cos(t)) \quad H \end{aligned} \quad (34)$$

and

$$T_L = \begin{cases} 2\ N.M & t < 12 \\ 8\ N.M & 12 \le t \le 17 \\ 3\ N.M & t > 17 \end{cases} \quad (35)$$

In this paper, in order to examine the speed regulation capability in response to sudden variations of the speed command, ω_c has been defined the summation of the constant value 155 and a square wave (altitude = 10, frequency = 0.1 Hz). Also by using a proper reference model the transient response of the speed control system has been regulated. Finally, in order to verify the ability of the proposed control law in rejecting input voltage disturbances, the following voltage disturbance has been inserted to u.

$$v_{dist} = \begin{cases} 15\,V & 8 \le t \le 9 \\ 0\;\;V & otherwise \end{cases} \qquad (36)$$

The initial values of θ_f and θ_g in neuro-fuzzy systems have been set to 1. Moreover, the learning rates of adaptation laws (13), (14), the proportional gain K_p and K_I in (5) have been selected as $\gamma_1 = 1000$, $\gamma_2 = 0.1$, $K_p = 20$ and $K_I = 100$. Also λ and β in (22) have been set to 1 and 0.1 respectively. The upper bound of the reconstruction error has been assumed as $\rho = 1$.

The tracking performance of the proposed control scheme and the speed tracking error are illustrated in figure 3, figure 4 and figure 5.

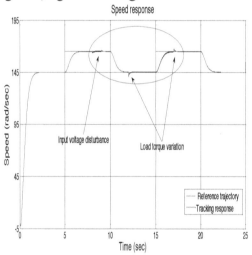

Figure 3.The tracking performance of the proposed control scheme.

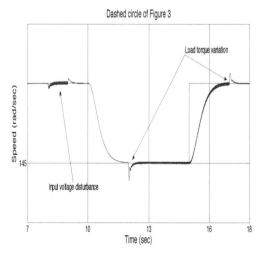

Figure 4. Dashed circle of the Figure 3 is zoomed.

As shown in these figures, the asymptotic convergence of the motor speed to the command signal is satisfying in terms of fast external load disturbance rejection and robustness against motor parameter variation and undesirable disturbances

of the input voltage. Finally the control effort is presented in figure 6.

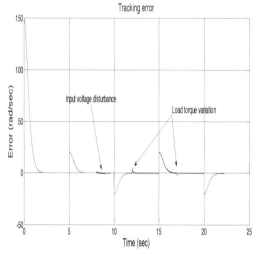

Figure 5.asymptotic convergence of tracking error.

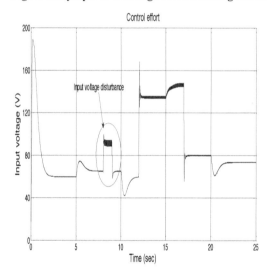

Figure 6. The control effort.

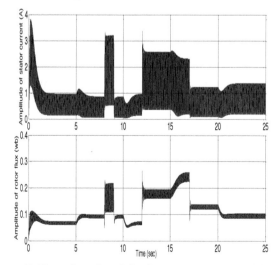

Figure 7. The value of modules for stator current and flux in the control system.

Moreover, as illustrated in this figure, the motor voltage is under the maximum permitted voltage.

In addition, based on table 1 the amplitude of stator current $\sqrt{i_{sa}^2 + i_{sb}^2}$ must be less than 6.9 A. Also the flux upper limit can be computed by multiplying flux density to pole cross section that achieved 0.48 so in this machine the $\sqrt{\psi_{ra}^2 + \psi_{rb}^2}$ value must be less than or equal 0.48. In the meantime, figure 7 shows bounded closed-loop signals for the proposed control system.

4.2. Simulation 2

In this simulation, the adaptive fuzzy MIMO control presented in [23] is used for the speed control of the IM model described in Simulation 1. The reference model, external load torque, and input voltage disturbances are the same as Simulation 1. The tracking performance of this control scheme is illustrated in figure 8 and figure 9. As shown in figure 9, this control approach fails in rejecting the external load torque and input voltage disturbances. However, as shown in figure 4, the proposed method completely eliminates the effect of these disturbances. It should be noted that the adaptive fuzzy MIMO method [23], requires feedbacks from all state variables and also the acceleration signal is used, while the proposed controller needs just the speed feedback. Moreover, there are six uncertain functions which should be estimated in the adaptive fuzzy MIMO method. In order to estimate each function, 243 fuzzy rules are needed. However, the neuro-fuzzy approach presented in this paper is much simpler and less computational. In addition, the non-singularity of the estimated input gain matrix in [23] is a critical condition which can be violated easily and make the control system unstable. Another superiority of the proposed controller is compensating the reconstruction error of the neuro-fuzzy estimator which has improved the performance of the controller. The cost function $J = \int_0^{30} e^2(t)dt$ has been defined for quantitative comparisons. In the proposed method $J = 3.137$ while the method presented in [23] results in $J = 6.457$.

5. Conclusion

Speed control of induction motors is very important in many industrial applications such as pump actuators, milling machines and elevators. In this paper an indirect adaptive system for the speed control of IMs is presented in which the uncertainty including parametric variations, the external load disturbance and unmodeled dynamics is estimated and compensated by designing two neuro-fuzzy systems with online training approaches based on Lyapunov stability analysis. In order to guarantee the asymptotic convergence of the speed tracking error and improve the control system performance, the reconstruction errors of neuro-fuzzy systems is compensated using a robustifying term in the control law. Finally, high performance characteristics and robustness of the proposed control system against plant parameter variation, external load and input voltage disturbances are verified by the simulation results.

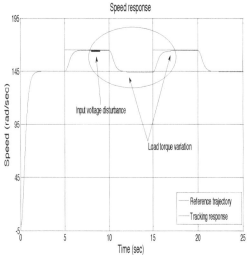

Figure 8. The tracking performance of the adaptive fuzzy MIMO method [23].

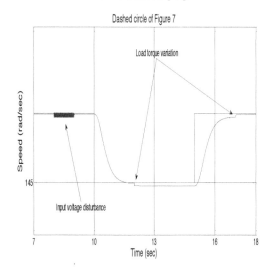

Figure 9. Dashed circle of the Figure 8 is zoomed.

References

[1] Kim, G. S., Ha, I. J. & Ko, M. S. (1992). Control of induction motors for both high dynamic performance and high power efficiency. IEEE Tran Ind Electron, vol. 39, pp. 323–333.

[2] Bodson, M., Chiasson, J. & Novotnak, R. (1994). High-performance induction motor control via input–output linearization. IEEE Contr Syst Mag, vol. 14, pp. 25–33.

[3] Liaw, C. M., Kung, Y. S. & Wu, C. M. (1991). Design and implementation of a high-performance field-oriented induction motor drive. IEEE Trans Ind Electron, vol. 38, pp. 275-282.

[4] Takahashi, I. & Noguchi, T. (1986). A new quick-response and high-efficiency strategy of an induction motor. IEEE Trans Ind Appl, vol. l, pp. 820-827.

[5] Nash, JN. (1997). Direct torque control, induction motor vector control without an encoder. IEEE Trans Ind Appl, vol. 33, pp. 333-341.

[6] Buja, G. (1998). A new control strategy of the induction motor drives: The direct flux and torque control. IEEE Ind Electron Newslett, vol. 45, pp. 14–16.

[7] Wang, W. J. & Chen, J. Y. (2005). Passivity-based sliding mode position control for induction motor drives. IEEE Trans Energy Convers, vol. 20, pp. 316-321.

[8] Shiau, L. G & Lin, J. L. (2001). Stability of sliding-mode current control for high performance induction motor position drives. In: IEE Proceedings of Electric Power Applications, pp. 69 -75.

[9] Barambones, O. & Alkorta, P. (2011). An Adaptive Sliding Mode Position Control for Induction Motor Drives. In: International Conference on Computer as a Tool, EUROCON, Lisbon, Portugal, pp. 1-4.

[10] Barambonesa O., Alkortab, P., & Gonzalez de Durana, J. M. (2014). A real-time estimation and control scheme for induction motors based on sliding mode theory. Journal of the Franklin Institute, vol. 351, pp. 4251-4270.

[11] Alonge, F. & Raimondi, T. (1995). Indirect adaptive speed control of induction motor systems based on model reference identifiers. In: Proceedings of the 1995 IEEE IECON 21st International Conference on, pp. 1035-1040.

[12] Lin, Y. C., Fu, L. C. & Tsai, C. Y. (1999). Nonlinear sensorless indirect adaptive speed control of induction motor with unknown rotor resistance and load. In: American Control Conference, San Diego, CA: USA, pp. 2168-2172.

[13] Halbaoui, K., Boukhetala, D. & Boudjema, F. (2008). New robust model reference adaptive control for induction motor drives using a hybrid controller. In: Power Electronics, Electrical Drives, Automation and Motion, SPEEDAM 2008, Ischia, Italy, pp. 1109-1113.

[14] Behzad, H., Khorashadizadeh, S., & Kalat, A. A. (2011). A robust adaptive method to control the crushing mill machine. In Control, Instrumentation and Automation (ICCIA), 2011 2nd International Conference on (pp. 547-551). IEEE.

[15] Fateh, M. M., & Khorashadizadeh, S. (2012). Optimal robust voltage control of electrically driven robot manipulators. Nonlinear Dynamics, vol. 70, no. 2, pp. 1445-1458.

[16] Li, j. & Zhong, Y. (2012). Robust speed control of induction motor drives employing first-order auto-disturbance rejection controllers. In: Industry Applications Society Annual Meeting, IAS, Las Vegas, NV: USA, 1-7.

[17] Astrom, K. J. & Wittenmark, B. (1994). Adaptive Control. 2nd ed. Prentice Hall.

[18] Khorashadizadeh, S., & Fateh, M. M. (2014). Robust task-space control of robot manipulators using Legendre polynomials for uncertainty estimation. Nonlinear Dynamics, vol. 79, no. 2, pp. 1151-1161.

[19] Fateh, M. M., Ahmadi, S. M. & Khorashadizadeh, S. (2014). Adaptive RBF Network Control for Robot Manipulators. Journal of AI and Data Mining, vol. 2, no. 2, pp. 159-166.

[20] Fateh, M. M. & Azargoshasb, S., & Khorashadizadeh, S. (2014). Model-free discrete control for uncertain robot manipulators using a fuzzy estimator. COMPEL: The International Journal for Computation and Mathematics in Electrical and Electronic Engineering, vol. 33, no. 3, pp. 1051-1067.

[21] Slotine, J. J. & Li, W. (1991). Applied nonlinear control. Prentice Hall.

[22] Agamy, M. S., Yousef, H. A. & Sebakhy, O.A. (2004). Adaptive fuzzy variable structure control of induction motors. In: Electrical and Computer Engineering. Canadian Conference on, Niagara Falls: Canada, pp. 89-94.

[23] Yousef, H. A. & Wahba, M. A. (2009). Adaptive fuzzy mimo control of induction motors. Expert Syst Appl. vol. 36, pp. 4171-4175.

[24] Fateh, M. M., & Khorashadizadeh, S. (2012). Robust control of electrically driven robots by adaptive fuzzy estimation of uncertainty. Nonlinear Dynamics, vol. 69, no. 3, pp. 1465-1477.

[25] Kusagur, A., Kodad, S. F. & Sankar, Ram, B. V. (2012). Modelling & Simulation of an ANFIS controller for an AC drive. World J of Model Simul, vol. 8, pp. 36-49.

[26] Zerikat, M. & Hekroun, S. (2008). High performance speed tracking of IM using an adaptive fuzzy NN control. Int J Sci Tech Autom Control Comp Eng IJ-STA Special Issue, pp. 516-531.

[27] Wang, L. X. (1994). Adaptive fuzzy systems and control: Design and stability analysis. Englewood Cliffs, NJ: Prentice Hall Inc.

[28] Shahnazi, R., ModirShanechi, H. & Pariz, N. (2008). Position Control of Induction and DC Servomotors: A Novel Adaptive Fuzzy PI Sliding Mode Control. IEEE Trans Energy Convers, vol. 23, pp. 138-147.

[29] Lin, C. M. & Hsu, C. F. (2004). Adaptive fuzzy sliding mod control of inductions servomotor systems. IEEE Trans Energy Convers, vol. 19, pp. 362-368.

[30] Khorashadizadeh, S., & Fateh, M. M. (2013). Adaptive fourier series-based control of electrically driven robot manipulators. In Control, Instrumentation, and Automation (ICCIA), 2013 3rd International Conference on (pp. 213-218). IEEE.

[31] Fard, M. B., & Khorashadizadeh, S., (2015), Model free robust impedance control of robot manipulators using fourier series expansion. In AI & Robotics (IRANOPEN), (pp. 1-7). IEEE

[32] Khorashadizadeh, S., & Fateh, M. M., (2015), uncertainty estimation in robust tracking control of robot manipulators using the Fourier series expansion, Robotica, In press.

[33] Khorashadizadeh, S., Fateh, M. M., & Azargoshasb S., (2014), Compensating the reconstruction error of fuzzy estimator in robust model-free control of electrically driven robot manipulators, 14th Iranian Conference on Fuzzy Systems, pp. 99-104.

[34] Fitzgerald, AE. & Kingsley, C. J. (2002). Electric Machinery. 6th ed. New York, NY, USA: McGraw-Hill.

[35] Krause, P. C. & Wasynczuk, O. (2002). Analysis of Electric Machinery and Drive Systems. 2nd edition. New York, NY, USA, McGraw-Hill.

[36] Leonhard, W. (2001). Control of Electrical Drives. 3rd ed. Berlin, Germany: Springer

[37] Krause, P. C. & Thomas, C. H. (1965). Simulation of symmetrical induction machinery. IEEE Trans Power Ap Syst, vol. 84, pp. 1038-1053.

3

Formal approach on modeling and predicting of software system security: Stochastic petri net

H. Motameni

Department of Computer Engineering, Sari Branch, Islamic Azad University, Sari, Iran

*Corresponding author: motameni@iausari.ac.ir (H.Motameni)

Abstract

To evaluate and predict component-based software security, a two-dimensional model of software security is proposed by Stochastic Petri Net in this paper. In this approach, the software security is modeled by graphical presentation ability of Petri nets, and the quantitative prediction is provided by the evaluation capability of Stochastic Petri Net and the computing power of Markov chain. Each vulnerable component is modeled by Stochastic Petri net and two parameters, Successfully Attack Probability (SAP) and Vulnerability Volume of each component to another component. The second parameter, as a second dimension of security evaluation, is a metric that is added to modeling to improve the accuracy of the result of system security prediction. An isomorphic Markov chain is obtained from a corresponding SPN model. The security prediction is calculated based on the probability distribution of the MC in the steady state. To identify and trace back to the critical points of system security, a sensitive analysis method is applied by derivation of the security prediction equation. It provides the possibility to investigate and compare different solutions with the target system in the designing phase.

Keywords: *Software Security, Vulnerability, Stochastic Petri Net, Markov Chain, Sensitivity Analysis.*

1. Introduction

Security has been identified as a major stumbling block in the realization of highly trustworthy software systems [1]. Modeling and predicting software security in design phase provides the possibility of investigation and comparisons of different solutions of target systems. Petri Net is a formal method which is based on mathematical theories. Petri Net is useful for modeling and analysis of systems with parallelization, synchronization and conflict quality [2,3,4]. Stochastic Petri Net is extended from Petri Net where each is associated with a random variable. SPNs combine the powers of Petri Net and Markov chain processes.

In this paper, an advanced approach is suggested to develop the modeling and predicting software security with SPN in design phase. Vulnerability volume of each component to another component is a new parameter that is added to security modeling by SPN.As a result, we improve the accuracy of security in software system prediction. After modeling system security by SPN, The reachable graph is obtained from SPN; The Markov Chain corresponding reachable graph can be extracted and Markov chain calculation is performed. Finally, sensitivity analysis is launched on prediction equation of each component. Sensitivity analysis result can be used to identify the security bottlenecks and trace back to vulnerability points.

This paper is organized as follows: Section 2 discusses the related work. Issues related to stochastic Petri Nets are presented in section 3. Security modeling based on SPN is introduced in section 4. In section 5, an advanced approach is presented to modeling software security with SPN. Sensitivity analysis of software security model is proposed in section 6. A case study is provided in section 7. Section 8 concludes this paper.

2. Related works

Reliability and security analysis has received much attention over the past decades. There have been some attempts to quantify the security of software system by means of Tiger Team Penetration practices, where a group of experts sit together and try to break in by exploiting any weakness it might possess. However this practice is subjective to the kind of people consisting of the Tiger Team and thus is non-reproducible [5]. There have been some approaches which focus on the process which is adopted while the software is being developed to access the security of final product [5]. One example of this is the SSECMM or Systems Security Engineering Capability Maturity Model. However, branching the software to be secured by evaluating its development process has not found much popularity. This is because even after following the best practices, there is scope of some weakness present in the final product, which would not be uncovered, until it is rigorously tested for its vulnerabilities.

To improve the trustworthiness of software design, formal Threat-Driven approach is represented and explores explicit behaviors of security threats as the mediator between security goals and applications of security features. Security crisis was modeled through Petri net-based aspects [6].

Architecture-based software reliability analysis has been especially investigated by researchers such as surveyed by Gokhale [7]. In that literature, the architecture-based techniques are classified into two path- and state-based categories. For the accuracy and other reasons, state-based approaches are usually adopted [7]. Markov model has been adapted in most previous state-based approaches [1,5,8,9,10].

Some disadvantages are inevitable in using Markov models as modeling tools. First, Markov models lack the abilities to represent parallelism, synchronization, confliction and preemption. Second, they support limited analysis capabilities. Last but not least, a system modeled by a Markov model is hard to extend. The Markov Chain structure changes greatly for even a small change to the system design [1].

In the recent approach, Stochastic Petri Nets have been used for system reliability modeling [11]. It eliminates the difficulty in construction of Markov Chain. Also, Petri nets retain much of the character of the system, such as parallelism, synchronization, confliction and preemption. Furthermore, Petri nets enable us to present system activities in hieratically graphical models so they are recommended to be appropriate state-based models for modeling and quantifying non-functional properties [12].

Sensitivity analysis is provided an approach to investigate influence of changes in different parameters. Gokhail et al. [13] developed an equation to analyze the sensitivity of the reliability. Yang et al. [14] introduced modeling, prediction and sensitivity analysis of a component and Nianhua et al. [1] proposed a combination of components in sequence, parallel, loop and selection style. This paper developed modeling and prediction of software system security with SPN and increased software security prediction.

3. Stochastic petri nets

Petri net is a 5-tuple [15], $PN = (P, T, I, O, M_0)$, where P is a finite set of places and T is a finite set of transitions. $P \cap T = \varnothing$ and $P \cup T = \varnothing$. I is input function where $I = (T * P) = \{0,1\}$, if there is an arc from p to t then $I(t, p) = 1$, so p is an input place for t. O is output function where $O = (T * P) = \{0,1\}$, if there is an arc from t to p then $O(t, p) = 1$, so p is an output place for t. $M_0: P \rightarrow \{1,2,...\}$ is initial marking. A transition is enable if each of its input places contains at least one token.

Stochastic Petri net or SPN [16] is a 6-tuple $(P, T, I, O, M_0, \lambda)$ where P, T, I, O and M_0 has the same meaning of a Petri net and λ is set of average firing rate of transitions.

4. Security modeling based on SPN

Suppose that in component based system, each software component contains vulnerability which can be compromised and failure can be repaired by some techniques. Vulnerability is a potential weakness which can be compromised. A component security modeling method based on SPN is proposed in [14]. A software system may contain combination of such component in series, parallel, loop or selection styles. Security modeling and prediction of a system with combination of these styles was proposed in [1].

5. Advanced approach to software security modeling based on SPN

The only parameter of software security modeling and prediction which is proposed in [1] is a successful attack probability of each component whereas there are some other parameters that can be effective in quantitatively prediction of software security. Two components with the same successfully attack probability may have different vulnerability level over whole system. This issue isn't considered in the proposed method by [1].

Vulnerability volume of a component over whole software system is such a parameter which was ignored. This parameter effect is obvious in series and parallel styles of components. Vulnerability measure of one component depends on the type of software system. Software security prediction equations have to be rewritten by adding this variable. In this case, we will add Vulnerability volume of a component toward others components, namely, it must be investigated how much each component influences in the security of whole software system. To calculate system tolerance, successfully attack probability of a component must multiply by the ratio of its efficiency in the system security.

5.1. SPN model of a component

Probability density functions for normal execution, attack and repair action in a component are shown by λ_{i1}, λ_{i2} and λ_{i3} respectively. Figure 1, referenced from [14], demonstrates a model of a component represented by SPN where t_i^e represents the normal behavior of the component with execution rate of λ_{i1}. t_i^e Represents an attack on the component I. Its rate is λ_{i2}. P_i^b is start place. A token appearing in the place t_i^f denotes that the component i has been compromised so a recovery action should be taken, such as rebooting. The transition t_i^r represents the recovery action with the rate of λ_{i3}. t_i^s indicates successfully execution of component.

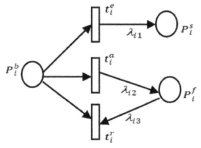

Figure 1. Security component model based on SPN.

5.2. Sequence components model based on SPN

In sequence model, components are executed in sequential manner. Only a single component is executed at instant of time. Figure 2 shows two components in sequence manner.

The probability of successful attack in a sequence model composed of n components is in (1):

$$\prod_{i=1}^{n}[(\mu_i) * (SAP_i)] \tag{1}$$

Where SAP_i is the successful attack probability of component i and μ_i is a new parameter, the vulnerability volume of component i over whole system, that is addition parameter to modeling.

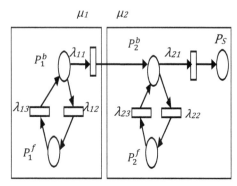

Figure 2. Sequence components model based on SPN.

The probability of successful execution without compromise in a sequence model composed of n components is in (2):

$$\prod_{i=1}^{n}[(1 - \mu_i) * (1 - SAP_i)] \tag{2}$$

5.3. Parallel components model based on SPN

A parallel model is usually used in a concurrent execution environment to improve performance. An example of this model is depicted in figure 3.

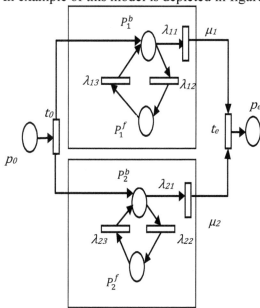

Figure 3. Parallel components model based on SPN.

The probability of successful attack in a parallel model composed of n components is in (3):

$$max_{i=1}^{n}[(\mu_i) * (SAP_i)] \tag{3}$$

The probability of successful execution without compromise in a parallel model composed of n components is in (4):

$$1 - max_{i=1}^{n}[(\mu_i) * (SAP_i)] \tag{4}$$

5.4. Loop component model based on SPN

A loop model is used in an iterative execution environment, in which a component is executed iteratively for some times. Figure 4 indicates an example of this model. The transition t_{loop} in figure 4 activates the iterated component.

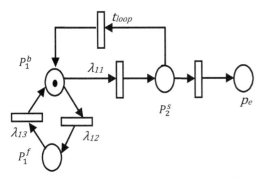

Figure 4. Loop component model based on SPN.

The probability of successful attack in a loop model is in (5):

$$\prod_{i=1}^{n} [(\mu) * (SAP)] \qquad (5)$$

The probability of successful execution without compromise in a loop model is in (6):

$$\prod_{i=1}^{n} [(1 - \mu) * (1 - SAP)] \qquad (6)$$

5.5. Selection component model based on SPN
In a selection model, components are executed with conflict. Only one component can be executed according to the selection condition. The probability of the system successfully compromised or executing in a selection model is equal to the selected component. If component i is selected, the probability of successful attack to system is calculated by (7):

$$[(\mu_i) * (SAP_i)] \qquad (7)$$

The probability of successful execution without compromise in selection model is in (8):

$$(1 - \mu_i) * (1 - SAP_i) \qquad (8)$$

5.6. Software security prediction evaluation
In [1, 14], an approach was presented for successfully attack probability by intruder to software system is security metric in steady state. SAP is computed by adding probability of system states that contain one token. The higher the SAP, the greater the probability the software system can be promised.

Quantifying the SAP on a component consists of following three steps.

- Construct an isomorphic MC from the SPN model;
- Evaluate the SPN steady state probability distribution based on the MC;
- Evaluate the SAP based on the steady state probability distribution of the SPN model.

Due toless memory regarding the exponential distribution of firing delays, SPN models are

isomorphic to Continuous Time Markov Chains [1]. The method in [14] is used to evaluate the steady state probability distribution of reachable states. The method of evaluating compromised probability for a single component has appeared in [14]. A failure place in an SPN model is represented as $p_{fr}, r = 1, 2, \ldots, k$. Thus, the SAP can be evaluated as (9):

$$SAP = \sum_{j=1}^{n} \sum_{r=1}^{k} P[M_j(p_{fr}) \geq 1] \qquad (9)$$

$P[M_j(p_{fr}) \geq 1]$ indicates places of probability p_{fr} that contain at least one token in steady state. Thus, tolerance capacity of a component toward attack is represented in (10).

$$TP = 1 - SAP = 1 - \sum_{j=1}^{n} \sum_{r=1}^{k} P[M_j(p_{fr}) \geq 1] \qquad (10)$$

So we can compute the security of hierarchal software system.

6. Sensitivity analysis
Sensitivity analysis is useful for software optimization in the early design phase [8]. It is difficult to study some model parameters in design phase. Sensitivity analysis can investigate change effects in parameters over quantitative analysis results. Successfully attack probability is computed by derivation over these variables [1] in (11).

$$\frac{d(SAP(\lambda_1, \ldots, \lambda_{|T_t|}))}{d\lambda_i} = \frac{d\sum_{j=1}^{n} \sum_{r=1}^{k} P[M_j(p_{fr}) \geq 1]}{d\lambda_i} \qquad (11)$$

Equation (11) is a sensitivity analysis of security prediction for one component. According to the new parameter that is added to modeling, sensitivity analysis can be computed for new parameter, as follow:

$$\frac{d(SAP)}{d\mu} = \frac{d\sum_{j=1}^{n} \sum_{r=1}^{k} P[M_j(p_{fr}) \geq 1]}{d\mu} \qquad (12)$$

7. Case study
To evaluate the new approach, first the security modeling and prediction evaluation of a single component is illustrated, and then the evaluation for a software system including different components in different styles and in different levels of hierarchical can be calculated based on the result of each single component.

7.1. A single component modeling
Figure 5 shows a single software security critical component based on SPN. The transition t_2 represents an intrusion to component. The resume action is shown by transition t_3.

Existence of a token in place P_2 represents compromised state caused by an intrusion. Transition t_1 shows a successful execution of the component. To evaluate the prediction values using MC techniques, transition t_4 is added.

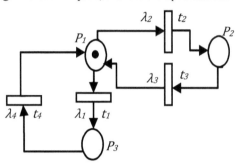

Figure 5. SPN model for evaluating security of a component.

7. 2. Extracting reachable graph

The reachable markings, shown in table 1, are obtained from figure 5.

Table 1. Reachable marking obtained figure 5.

Marking	P_1	P_2	P_3
M_1	1	0	0
M_2	0	1	0
M_3	0	0	1

Reachable graph is specified by reachable marking and isomorphism SPN model. Isomorphic Markov chain with SPN model in figure 7 is equivalent with reachable graph of figure 6.

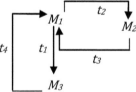

Figure 6. Reachable graph for SPN model.

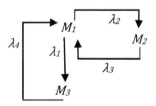

Figure 7. Markov chain isomorphic to SPN model.

7.3. Evaluating security prediction

Matrix Q regarding to Markov chain is as (13):

$$Q = \begin{matrix} M_1 \\ M_2 \\ M_3 \end{matrix} \begin{bmatrix} -(\lambda_1 + \lambda_2) & \lambda_2 & \lambda_1 \\ \lambda_3 & -\lambda_3 & 0 \\ \lambda_4 & 0 & -\lambda_4 \end{bmatrix} \quad (13)$$

Suppose that $Y = (P(M_1), P(M_2), P(M_3))$. Thus we can get (14):

$$\begin{cases} YQ = 0 \\ P(M_1) + P(M_2) + P(M_3) = 1 \end{cases} \quad (14)$$

The calculated result for the probability distribution at steady state is shown (15):

$$\begin{cases} P(M_1) = \dfrac{\lambda_3\lambda_4}{\lambda_3\lambda_4 + \lambda_2\lambda_4 + \lambda_1\lambda_3} \\ P(M_2) = \dfrac{\lambda_2\lambda_4}{\lambda_3\lambda_4 + \lambda_2\lambda_4 + \lambda_1\lambda_3} \\ P(M_3) = \dfrac{\lambda_1\lambda_3}{\lambda_3\lambda_4 + \lambda_2\lambda_4 + \lambda_1\lambda_3} \end{cases} \quad (15)$$

A token in M_2 indicates that the software component is compromised by an intrusion. According to (9), we can get (16):

$$SAP = P(M_2) = \frac{\lambda_2\lambda_4}{\lambda_3\lambda_4 + \lambda_2\lambda_4 + \lambda_1\lambda_3} \quad (16)$$

By adding vulnerability volume of a component, over whole software system, namely μ, we can rewrite (16) as follow in (17):

$$\mu \times SAP = \frac{\mu\lambda_2\lambda_4}{\lambda_3\lambda_4 + \lambda_2\lambda_4 + \lambda_1\lambda_3} \quad (17)$$

7.4. Sensitivity analysis

Sensitivity analysis of this component is calculated by derivation of (17)

$$\left| \frac{d(\mu \times SAP)}{\mu} \right| = \frac{\lambda_2\lambda_4}{\lambda_3\lambda_4 + \lambda_2\lambda_4 + \lambda_1\lambda_3} \quad (18)$$

Because in a software system with a single component, vulnerability volume over whole system, μ, is equal to 1 so onlythe impact of changes of t_1, t_2 and $t_3$to SAP are considered. We have the followings:

$$\left| \frac{d(\mu \times SAP)}{d\lambda_1} \right| = \frac{\mu\lambda_2\lambda_3\lambda_4}{(\lambda_3\lambda_4 + \lambda_2\lambda_4 + \lambda_1\lambda_3)^2} \quad (19)$$

$$\left| \frac{d(\mu \times SAP)}{d\lambda_2} \right| = \frac{\mu(\lambda_3\lambda_4^2 + \lambda_1\lambda_3\lambda_4)}{(\lambda_3\lambda_4 + \lambda_2\lambda_4 + \lambda_1\lambda_3)^2} \quad (20)$$

$$\left| \frac{d(\mu \times SAP)}{d\lambda_3} \right| = \frac{\mu\lambda_2\lambda_4(\lambda_1 + \lambda_4)}{(\lambda_3\lambda_4 + \lambda_2\lambda_4 + \lambda_1\lambda_3)^2} \quad (21)$$

$$\left| \frac{d(\mu \times SAP)}{d\mu} \right| = \frac{\lambda_2\lambda_4(\lambda_1 + \lambda_4)}{(\lambda_3\lambda_4 + \lambda_2\lambda_4 + \lambda_1\lambda_3)^2} \quad (22)$$

When the value of λ_i, $i = 1, 2, 3, 4$, is assigned, the sensitivity caused by them can be calculated by $(19) - (22)$. The transition t_4 is used for the facility of the steady state computation. The execution time is very short. So the value for λ_4 is very large. Suppose that λ_4 equals to 1,000,000. Let $\lambda_3 = 6$, $10 \leq \lambda_1 \leq 30$ and $1 \leq \lambda_2 \leq 10$. Figure 8 shows the probability distribution of SAP for different normal execution and attack rates. It shows that the probability of the component being in the compromised state increases with an increasing attack efficiency in the steady state.

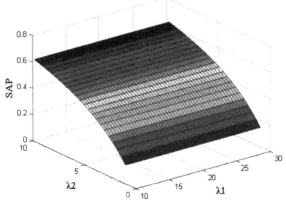

Figure 8. Relationship between normal execution rate λ_1, attack rate λ_2 and SAP.

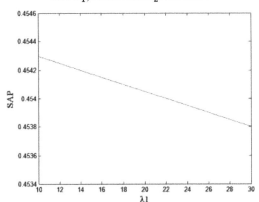

Figure 9. Relationship between normal execution rate λ_1 and SAP.

Suppose that $\lambda_1 = 15$. Let $0 \leq \lambda_2 \leq 10$ and $0 \leq \lambda_3 \leq 15$. Figure 9 shows that the probability of the component being in the compromised state in steady state decreases with an increased resume in rate λ_3. It increases rapidly with increasing the attack rate λ_2.

Although accuracy improvement by advanced modeling and predicting software security is obvious with a new parameter; however, it is difficult to quantitatively express the improvement of a new method, but as it was mentioned in new approach, software system security is evaluated from new dimensioned that was ignored in recent approach. These two new approaches are compared in table 2.

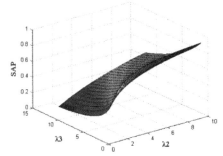

Figure 10. Relationship between the attack rate λ_2, resume rate λ_3 and SAP.

8. Conclusion

This paper proposes the two-dimensional method to model and predict software security based on stochastic Petri nets. The main contributions of the paper can be summarized as follows:

• An advanced method for security of software system based on Stochastic Petri net with added metric is proposed. A software system is modeled in view of the new metric, parallelization, synchronization and confliction characteristics of a component-based system can be easily modeled by stochastic Petri nets, while Markov Chains are absent of the abilities to represent these characteristics.

• Vulnerability volume of a component is added as a new parameter of system, and security prediction equations are rewritten. Thus, adding a new dimension of security in software system increases the accuracy of software security evaluation.

• A sensitivity analysis method is applied which provides a mean to identify and trace back to the critical components for security enhancement. It also provides the probability to investigate and compare different solutions to the target system before realization. We will work on the following open issues in the future:

- Modeling and predicting software system security based on stochastic Petri net by just vulnerability measure as a parameter.
- Advanced modeling and prediction of software system security with UML.
- Implementing the system by Petri net tools and Markov chain simulation to evaluate the security of software system.

Table 2. Advanced modeling and prediction with SPN vs. modeling and prediction suggested by [1].

Evaluating software system security approach	Stochastic Petri net	Advanced security modeling
Number of parameters for security modeling	1	2
Number of parameters for sensitivity analysis	1	2
Parameter/s	Successfully attack probability	Successfully attack probability, vulnerability measure
Accuracy measure	High	Higher

References

[1] Yang, N., Yu, H., Qian, Z., & Sun, H. (2012). Modeling and quantitatively predicting software security based on stochastic Petri nets. Mathematical and Computer Modelling, vol. 55, no. 1, pp. 102–112.

[2] Yang, N., Yu, H., Sun, H., & Qian, Z. (2010). Modeling UML Sequence Diagrams Using Extended Petri Nets. International Conference on Information Science and Applications. ICISA2010. IEEE Computer Society, pp. 596–603.

[3] Murata, T. (1989). Petri nets: Properties, analysis and applications. Proceedings of the IEEE, vol. 77, no. 4, pp. 541–580.

[4] Dempsey, J. R., Davis, G. W. A., Crossfield, A. S., & Williams, W. C. (1964). Program Management in Design and Development. SAE Technical Paper.

[5] De Miguel, M. A., Briones, J. F., Silva, J. P., & Alonso, A. (2008). Integration of safety analysis in model-driven software development. Software, IET, vol. 2, no. 3, pp. 260-280.

[6] Xu, D., & Nygard, K. E. (2006). Threat-driven modeling and verification of secure software using aspect-oriented Petri nets. Software Engineering, IEEE Transactions on, vol. 77, no. 4, pp. 265–278.

[7] Bode, E., Herbstritt, M., Hermanns, H., Johr, S., Peikenkamp, T., Pulungan, R., & Becker, B. (2009). Compositional dependability evaluation for STATEMATE. Software Engineering, IEEE Transactions on, vol. 35, no. 2, pp. 274–292.

[8] Sharma, V. S., & Trivedi, K. S. (2007). Quantifying software performance, reliability and security: An architecture-based approach. Journal of Systems and Software, vol. 80, no. 4, pp. 493–509.

[9] Wang, W.-L., Pan, D., & Chen, M.-H. (2006). Architecture-based software reliability modeling. Journal of Systems and Software, vol. 79, no. 1, pp. 132–146.

[10] Madan, B. B., Goševa-Popstojanova, K., Vaidyanathan, K., & Trivedi, K. S. (2004). A method for modeling and quantifying the security attributes of intrusion tolerant systems. Performance Evaluation, vol. 56, no. 1, pp. 167–186.

[11] Ammar, H. H., Huang, Y., & Liu, R. (1987). Hierarchical models for systems reliability, maintainability, and availability. Circuits and Systems, IEEE Transactions on, vol. 34, no. 6, pp. 629–638.

[12] Gokhale, S. S. (2007). Architecture-based software reliability analysis: Overview and limitations. IEEE Transactions on Dependable and Secure Computing, no.1, pp. 32–40.

[13] Gokhale, S. S., & Trivedi, K. S. (2002). Reliability prediction and sensitivity analysis based on software architecture. In Software Reliability Engineering, 2002. ISSRE 2003. Proceedings. 13th International Symposium on (pp. 64–75). IEEE.

[14] Yang, N., Yu, H., Sun, H., & Qian, Z. (2010). Quantifying software security based on stochastic Petri nets. Journal of Computational Information Systems, vol. 6, no. 9, pp. 3049–3056.

[15] Balbo, G. (2001). Introduction to stochastic Petri nets. In Lectures on Formal Methods and PerformanceAnalysis (pp. 84–155). Springer.

[16] Florin, G., Fraize, C., & Natkin, S. (1991). Stochastic Petri nets: Properties, applications and tools. Microelectronics Reliability, vol. 31, no. 4, pp. 669–697.

4

Improving the performance of UPQC under unbalanced and distortional load conditions: A new control method

R. Ghanizadeh[*] and M. Ebadian

Department of Electrical & Computer Engineering, University of Birjand, Birjand, Iran.

*Corresponding author: r_ghanizadeh@birjand.ac.ir (R. Ghanizadeh).

Abstract

This paper presents a new control method for a three-phase four-wire Unified Power Quality Conditioner (UPQC) to deal with the problems of power quality under distortional and unbalanced load conditions. The proposed control approach is the combination of instantaneous power theory and Synchronous Reference Frame (SRF) theory which is optimized by using a self-tuning filter (STF) and without using load or filter currents measurement. In this approach, load and source voltages are used to generate the reference voltages of series active power filter (APF) and source currents are used to generate the reference currents of shunt APF. Therefore, the number of current measurements is reduced and system performance is improved. The performance of proposed control system is tested for cases of power factor correction, reducing source neutral current, load balancing and current and voltage harmonics in a three-phase four-wire system for distortional and unbalanced loads. Results obtained through MATLAB/SIMULINK software show the effectiveness of proposed control technique in comparison to the conventional p-q method.

Keywords: *Power Quality, Unified Power Quality Conditioner, Voltage Harmonic Mitigation, Current Harmonic Mitigation, Source Neutral Current Mitigation.*

1. Introduction

Among the main problems of power quality in the three-phase four-wire systems are the current harmonics, load unbalance, exceeding neutral current, voltage harmonic, voltage sag and voltage swell. Poor power quality causes low power factor, low efficiency and overheating of transformers and so on [1]. Furthermore, in distribution systems, the total load of system is rarely balanced, and this increases the neutral current in three-phase four-wire systems. Since the fundamental component of current and current components of higher frequencies exist in the neutral current, their passing through the neutral wire causes it to overheat [2]. By using more complicated and more advanced softwares and hardwares in control systems, power quality has become one of the most important issues for electronic engineers. Thus, to deal with the problem of power quality, numerous standards have been presented by various standard organizations e.g. IEEE519 standard. Ideally, the current and voltage waveforms are in phase,

power factor is equal to unity and consumed reactive power is equal to zero. Under such conditions, active power could be transmitted with maximum efficiency [3]. Passive filters were used in the past to deal with power quality problems. However, their limitations including fixed compensation, possibility of occurrence of resonance with the source impedance and problems of tuning passive filter parameters caused the research on active filters and hybrid filters to start [4-6]. UPQC is one of the best solutions for simultaneous compensation of voltage and current problems [6,7]. UPQC was introduced for the first time in 1998 by Fujita and Akagi [7]. The structure of UPQC is similar to that of unified power flow controller (UPFC) used in transmission systems and its main goal is to control power flow in the fundamental frequency [8], whereas UPQC is used in distribution systems for performing duties of series and shunt APFs simultaneously. On the other hand, distribution network may have DC components or harmonics and may be unbalanced. Therefore, UPQC must carry out parallel and series compensation under such conditions [9]. The shunt and series APFs of UPQC are linked to each other by a dc-link. In UPQC, unlike UPFC, the series APF is connected to the source side and the shunt APF is connected to the load side. The shunt APF is used to compensate current distortions and to supply load reactive power [7]. Thus, the shunt APF of UPQC acts as a current source which injects the compensation current into the network. The series APF is used to compensate voltage fluctuations and so it can act as voltage source which injects the compensation voltage into the network through a series transformer.

In the past few years, several control strategies have been presented in literature for determining the voltage and current reference signals. Some of the most common strategies include p-q-r theory [10], improved single-phase p-q theory [11], synchronous reference frame (SRF) theory [12], symmetric component transformation [13], Icosφ theory [14,15] and some other innovative control methods[16,17]. In [18], the one-cycle control approach (without calculating the reference) is used for controlling a three-phase four-wire UPQC. Among the these control methods, the most important and common control methods are p-q and SRF theories and so far some research have been done to modify these two control theory [19-22]. However, these two strategies based on balanced three phase systems can be used for single phase systems [23,24]. In Some research, these two control methods combined for better performance of UPQC [25,26].

One of the important parts in both these strategies is PLL determining automatically the system frequency and the phase angle of fundamental positive-sequence component of three phase generic input signal [27]. In order to improve performance of UPQC under distorted and unbalanced voltage waveforms, some research have been done to modify PLL circuit [19,20]. As the application of artificial neural network and fuzzy inference systems is growing in power electronics, an ANN-based controller is designed for current control of shunt active filter [28]. The performance of fuzzy logic controller and ANN controller is compared [29].

In this paper, the proposed control method which is the combination of instantaneous power theory and synchronous reference frame (SRF) theory is optimized by using a STF and without using load or filter currents measurement. The performance of proposed system is tested by using MATLAB/SIMULINK software in cases such as

power factor correction, reducing source neutral current, load balancing and reducing current and voltage harmonics in a three-phase four-wire system for distortional and unbalanced loads. Results obtained from simulation show the power and effectiveness of proposed control method in comparison to the conventional p-q method.

2. UPQC
The UPQC improves power quality, because of its capability in removing harmonics and simultaneous compensation of voltage and current. Almost all papers about UPQC show that it could be used for solving all the power quality problems. Figure 1 shows the basic structure of UPQC consisting of shunt and series APFs. The shunt APF is used for absorbing current harmonics, compensating reactive power and regulating dc-link voltage. The main purpose of using series APF is removing voltage harmonics of the source. Furthermore, series APF is capable of compensating voltage unbalance and compensating harmonics at the point of common coupling in consumer side [28].

3. Proposed control method
3.1. STF
Hong-Sock studied integral in the synchronous reference frame and showed that:

$$V_{xy}(t)=e^{j\omega t}\int e^{-j\omega t}U_{xy}(t)dt \qquad (1)$$

where, U_{xy} and V_{xy} are instantaneous signals respectively before and after the integration in the synchronous reference frame [30]. Applying the Laplace transform on (1), the equation of the transfer function $H(s)$ is expressed as:

$$H(s)=\frac{V_{xy}(s)}{U_{xy}(s)}=\frac{s+j\omega}{s^2+\omega^2} \qquad (2)$$

In order to obtain self-tuning filter (STF) with a cutoff frequency from the transfer function H(s), a constant parameter k is introduced [31]. Thus, by the use of parameter k, a function H(s) can be written as follows:

$$H(s)=\frac{V_{xy}(s)}{U_{xy}(s)}=\frac{k(s+k)+j\omega_n}{(s+k)^2+\omega_n^2} \qquad (3)$$

By adding a constant parameter k to H(s), the amplitude of the transfer function is limited and equal to the amplitude of frequency component (ω_n). In addition, the phase delay is zero for cutoff frequency. By replacing the input signals $U_{xy}(s)$ by $x_{\alpha\beta}(s)$ and the output signals $V_{xy}(s)$ by $\hat{x}_{\alpha\beta}(s)$, the following expressions can be obtained:

$$\hat{x}_\alpha=(\frac{k}{s}[x_\alpha(s)-\hat{x}_\alpha(s)]-\frac{\omega_n}{s}.\hat{x}_\beta(s)) \qquad (4)$$

$$\hat{x}_\beta = (\frac{k}{s}[x_\beta(s) - \hat{x}_\beta(s)] - \frac{\omega_n}{s} \cdot \hat{x}_\alpha(s)) \qquad (5)$$

where, ω_n is desired output frequency, and k is the filter gain. The higher the value of k, the higher the accuracy of extracting the desirable component is. Also, when the value of *k* decreases, the transient duration increases. $x_{\alpha\beta}(s)$, and $\hat{x}_{\alpha\beta}(s)$ may also be either voltage or current signals, respectively before and after filtering. Therefore, by using a STF, the fundamental component of distortional signals can be obtained without changing the amplitude and phase delay. According to (4) and (5), block diagram of STF is shown in figure 2 [31].

Figure 3 shows the frequency response of the STF versus different values of the parameter *k* for fc=50Hz. At 50Hz, the phase angle of bode diagram is null, which means that the two input and output signals are in phase either k. Also the phase shift for the other frequencies is shown. On the other hand, it is observed from figure 3 showing that $|H(s)| = 0\,dB$ at $f_c=50Hz$. The rate of amplitude changes for the other frequencies is shown in figure 3.

One of the feature of STF is that despite extreme unbalance between two input signals, the STF will create always two equal magnitude sine-waves according to following equation:

$$\frac{x_\alpha(s) + x_\beta(s)}{2} = \hat{x}_\alpha(s) = \hat{x}_\beta(s) \qquad (6)$$

This feature is a disadvantage of STF for generating reference load voltages under unbalance voltage condition. To overcome this problem, d-q theory is used for control of series APF.

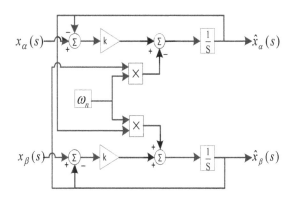

Figure 2. The block diagram of STF.

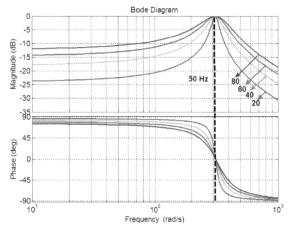

Figure 3. Bode diagram for the STF versus pulsation for different values of the parameter k (fc=50Hz).

3.1. Reference voltage signal generation of the series APF

The proposed control method has been used for solving all the problems related to the power quality including source voltage harmonics, unbalanced voltages, voltage sag and swell. In the proposed approach, by using (7), first the measured voltages of source are transferred to the d-q-o coordinates. Under harmonic voltage conditions, instantaneous voltages of source (v_{sq} and v_{sd}) contain two components; harmonic and mean component, the latter contains the positive sequence. Furthermore, when the voltage unbalance exists, the zero sequence voltage (v_{so}) of source also emerges.

$$\begin{bmatrix} v_{So} \\ v_{Sd} \\ v_{Sq} \end{bmatrix} = \sqrt{\frac{2}{3}} \begin{bmatrix} \frac{1}{\sqrt{2}} & \frac{1}{\sqrt{2}} & \frac{1}{\sqrt{2}} \\ \sin(\omega t) & \sin(\omega t - \frac{2\pi}{3}) & \sin(\omega t + \frac{2\pi}{3}) \\ \cos(\omega t) & \cos(\omega t - \frac{2\pi}{3}) & \sin(\omega t + \frac{2\pi}{3}) \end{bmatrix} \begin{bmatrix} v_{Sa} \\ v_{Sb} \\ v_{Sc} \end{bmatrix} \qquad (7)$$

As it is stated in (8) and (9), the source voltages in d-q-o coordinates contains harmonic and mean components. In order to compensate for harmonic and unbalance voltages, a negative and zero sequence of voltage set to zero and the

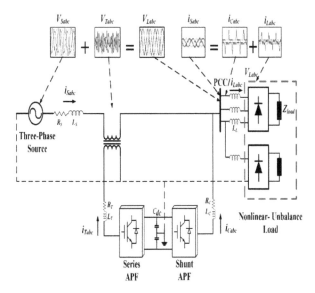

Figure 1. The basic structure of unified power quality conditioner (UPQC).

fundamental component of voltage in d axes ($\hat{v}_{Sd}$) are separated from harmonic components by the LPF. Therefore, the load reference voltage is obtained by (10):

$$v_{Sd} = \hat{v}_{Sd} + \tilde{v}_{Sd} \tag{8}$$

$$v_{Sq} = \hat{v}_{Sq} + \tilde{v}_{Sq} \tag{9}$$

$$\begin{bmatrix} v^*_{La} \\ v^*_{Lb} \\ v^*_{Lc} \end{bmatrix} = \sqrt{\frac{2}{3}} \begin{bmatrix} \dfrac{1}{\sqrt{2}} & \sin(\omega t) & \cos(\omega t) \\ \dfrac{1}{\sqrt{2}} & \sin(\omega t - \dfrac{2\pi}{3}) & \cos(\omega t - \dfrac{2\pi}{3}) \\ \dfrac{1}{\sqrt{2}} & \cos(\omega t - \dfrac{2\pi}{3}) & \cos(\omega t + \dfrac{2\pi}{3}) \end{bmatrix} \begin{bmatrix} 0 \\ \hat{v}_{Sd} \\ 0 \end{bmatrix} \tag{10}$$

The three phase reference load voltages (V^*_{Labc}) are compared to the distortional voltages of source side (V_{Sabc}) and the errors are processed by the PWM controller and required signals for IGBT switches of the series APF are generated.

The voltage sag or swell compensation may include absorbing/injecting real power from/to supply line. Therefore, real powers of series and shunt APFs must be balanced. In order to make the dc-link voltage fixed, the absorbed and injected real powers by series and shunt APFs must be equal to injected and absorbed powers by shunt APF, respectively [27]. The series APF control is shown in figure 4.

3.1. Reference current signal generation of the shunt APF

The shunt APF is used for compensating harmonics, load unbalance and reactive power generated by nonlinear load. The p-q theory is used to control the shunt APF. In this theory, voltages and currents are transferred to α-β-o coordinates by (11) and (12):

$$\begin{bmatrix} i_{S0} \\ i_{S\alpha} \\ i_{S\beta} \end{bmatrix} = \sqrt{\frac{2}{3}} \begin{bmatrix} \dfrac{1}{\sqrt{2}} & \dfrac{1}{\sqrt{2}} & \dfrac{1}{\sqrt{2}} \\ 1 & -\dfrac{1}{2} & -\dfrac{1}{2} \\ 0 & \dfrac{\sqrt{3}}{2} & -\dfrac{\sqrt{3}}{2} \end{bmatrix} \begin{bmatrix} i_{Sa} \\ i_{Sb} \\ i_{Sc} \end{bmatrix} \tag{11}$$

$$\begin{bmatrix} v_{S0} \\ v_{S\alpha} \\ v_{S\beta} \end{bmatrix} = \sqrt{\frac{2}{3}} \begin{bmatrix} \dfrac{1}{\sqrt{2}} & \dfrac{1}{\sqrt{2}} & \dfrac{1}{\sqrt{2}} \\ 1 & -\dfrac{1}{2} & -\dfrac{1}{2} \\ 0 & \dfrac{\sqrt{3}}{2} & -\dfrac{\sqrt{3}}{2} \end{bmatrix} \begin{bmatrix} v_{Sa} \\ v_{Sb} \\ v_{Sc} \end{bmatrix} \tag{12}$$

The current transferred to the Clark's system enter the STF which is set to the fundamental frequency. The STF output currents will be the fundamental components ($\hat{i}_{s\alpha}$ and $\hat{i}_{s\beta}$) which will

contain the fundamental components of active and reactive powers. To fully compensate for the reactive power, the fundamental component of reactive power obtained from (13) must be subtracted as a current component from current fundamental components.

Considering the switching loss (P_{Loss}), voltage fluctuation would be a good index showing that these fluctuations could be converted into a current by using a proportional-integral (PI) controller. This current must be injected into a main axis. Hence, For DC voltage regulation, voltage of dc-link is compared with reference voltage (V^*_{DC}), and then is injected to into the main axis by PI and it doesn't need any external supply.

On the other hand, when the load is unbalanced, there will be current in neutral wire. the total power of zero sequence component will be obtained from (14). To decrease the neutral current, the total zero sequence power must be supplied by shunt APF and this index must also be injected into main axis. As it is stated in (15), if it is needed to fully compensate for both the zero sequence component and reactive power, $i'_{s\alpha}$ and $i'_{s\beta}$ are the reference injected currents which must be injected into α-β axes. As it is stated in (16) and (17), by injecting these currents into α-β axes, the reference currents $i^*_{s\alpha}$ and $i^*_{s\beta}$ for shunt APF are obtained. Then, the reference currents in abc coordinates are calculated by (18).

$$\hat{q} = \hat{i}_\beta \hat{v}_{S\alpha} - \hat{i}_\alpha \hat{v}_{S\beta} \tag{13}$$

$$p_0 = v_{S0} i_{S0} \tag{14}$$

$$\begin{bmatrix} i'_{S\alpha} \\ i'_{S\beta} \end{bmatrix} = \frac{1}{\hat{v}_{S\alpha}^2 + \hat{v}_{S\beta}^2} \begin{bmatrix} \hat{v}_{S\alpha} & -\hat{v}_{S\beta} \\ \hat{v}_{S\beta} & \hat{v}_{S\alpha} \end{bmatrix} \begin{bmatrix} p_{Loss} + p_0 \\ -\hat{q} \end{bmatrix} \tag{15}$$

$$i^*_{S\alpha} = \hat{i}_{S\alpha} + i'_{S\alpha} \tag{16}$$

$$i^*_{S\beta} = \hat{i}_{S\beta} + i'_{S\beta} \tag{17}$$

$$\begin{bmatrix} i^*_{Sa} \\ i^*_{Sb} \\ i^*_{Sc} \end{bmatrix} = \sqrt{\frac{2}{3}} \begin{bmatrix} 1 & 0 \\ -\dfrac{1}{2} & \dfrac{\sqrt{3}}{2} \\ -\dfrac{1}{2} & \dfrac{-\sqrt{3}}{2} \end{bmatrix} \begin{bmatrix} i^*_{S\alpha} \\ i^*_{S\beta} \end{bmatrix} \tag{18}$$

The reference currents, i^*_{sa}, i^*_{sb} and i^*_{sc} are calculated to compensate neutral currents, reactive and harmonic currents in the load. These reference source currents are compared to measured currents of the source and errors resulted from this comparison are received by a hysteresis band controller to produce required switching signals of shunt APF. The shunt APF control is shown in figure 4.

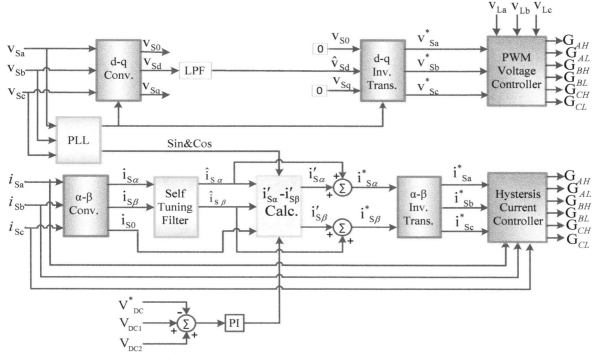

Figure 4. The block diagram of proposed control method for UPQC.

4. Simulation results

In this study, the proposed control method for UPQC which is used for compensating distortional and unbalanced load currents under the conditions of distortional and unbalanced source voltages are evaluated by MATLAB software. The load used in simulations is a combination of a three-phase rectifier load and a single-phase rectifier load. The single-phase rectifier load is used to create load unbalance in phase 'a'. Also, the source voltage contains odd harmonics up to the order of 17. Furthermore, the third harmonic and its multiples are not considered in simulations, because the third harmonic and its multiples will be compensated by the connections of transformers and often there is no need to compensate for them by the series APF. Passive filters with R and C are used to remove the switching ripples in voltage and current waveforms. The values of simulated parameters are given in table 1.

4.1. The performance of UPQC in load balancing, power factor correction and current and voltage harmonics compensation

The responses of UPQC in load balancing, power factor correction and current and voltage harmonics compensation are shown in figure 5. Figure 5(a) shows the harmonic voltages before compensation. It could be seen from figure 5(c) that by injecting compensating for voltage into system, the series APF of UPQC removes source

voltage harmonics and creates sinusoidal voltages for the load. Voltages injected by the series APF are shown in figure 5(b). As voltage harmonics is removed by the series APF, load voltage THD decreases from 11.25% to 1.47%. Voltage harmonics spectrums before and after compensation are shown in figure 6(a) and figure 6(b), respectively. On the other hand, figure 5(d) shows the load harmonic and unbalanced current before compensation. It could be seen from figure 5(f) that by injecting compensating currents for system, the shunt APF makes the source current sinusoidal and balanced and decreases source current THD from 28.27% to 2.36%. The currents injected by shunt APF into the network are shown in figure 5(e). Also, the current harmonic spectrum of phase 'a' of the source before and after compensation, are shown in figure 6(c) and figure 6(d), respectively. It could be seen from figure 5(g) that the current through neutral wire before compensation is equal to 26.6 A. When the neutral compensating for current is injected by the shunt APF, the neutral current of source decreases to zero. The neutral compensating for current injected by shunt APF and source neutral current are shown in figure 5(h) and figure 5(i), respectively. As UPQC enters the circuit, the whole reactive power of load is supplied by shunt APF and voltages and currents of source become in phase and the load just derives reactive power from source. Figure 5(k) shows the reactive power derived from the source which has an amplitude equal to zero.

Table 1. System parameters [19].

	Parameters		Value
Source	Voltage	V_{Sabc}	380V
	Frequency	f	50Hz
Load	3-Phase ac Line Inductance	L_{abc}	2mH
	1-Phase ac Line Inductance	L_{La1}	1mH
	3-Phase dc Inductance	L_{dc3}	10mH
	3-Phase dc Resistor	R_{dc3}	100 Ω
	1-Phase dc Resistor	R_{dc1}	50 Ω
	1-Phase dc Capacitor	C_{dc1}	240µf
dc-link	Voltage	V_{dc}	700V
	Capacitor	C_1/C_2	2200µF
Shunt APF	Ac Line Inductance	L_{Cabc}	1mH
	Filter Resistor	R_{Cabc}	5 Ω
	Filter Capacitor	C_{Cabc}	4.7µF
	Hysteresis Band	h	0.5A
Series APF	Ac Line Inductance	L_{Sabc}	0.6mH
	Filter Resistor	R_{Sabc}	5 Ω
	Filter Capacitor	C_{Sabc}	26µF
	Switching Frequency	f_{PWM}	15kH
STF	Factor k In STF Block	k	60

4.1. Performance of UPQC during a sudden increase of load

In this section, to investigate the dynamic response of UPQC and to see how it enters the circuit, first it is assumed that UPQC is not in the circuit. As it could be seen from figure 7 (a) and figure 7(c), source contains unbalanced and harmonic voltages and load derives unbalanced and harmonic currents from the source. At t=0.1s, the UPQC enters the circuit and shunt and series APFs start the compensation. Figure 7 (b) shows that when UPQC enters the circuit, series APF immediately injects compensating voltages into the network and makes the load voltages sinusoidal.

Also, figure 7(d) shows the currents generated by shunt APF which makes the currents derive from the network balanced and sinusoidal. The performance of UPQC in compensating for the neutral current of source and load reactive power

is shown in figure 7(f) and figure 7(h), respectively.

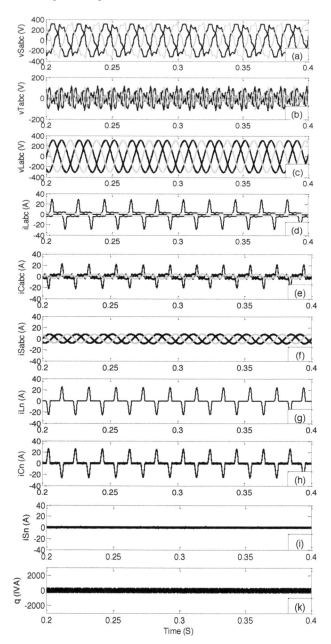

Figure 5. Simulation results for the proposed control approach for: (a) source distortional voltages, (b) voltages injected by transformer (c) load voltages (d) unbalanced and nonlinear load currents (e) currents injected by compensator (f) source currents (g) load neutral current (i) neutral current injected by compensator (h) instantaneous reactive power.

In order to show the UPQC performance during a sudden change in the load, when system is operating, the load is suddenly increased at t=0.2s. As it is shown in figure 7, in addition to compensating for load unbalance, supplying reactive power and compensating for harmonics, the UPQC controller gets a new static state after the load change.

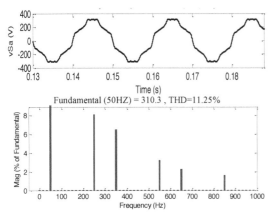

Figure 6(a). Load voltage and its harmonic spectrum before compensation.

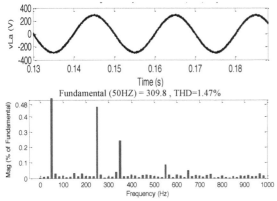

Figure 6(b). Load voltage and its harmonic spectrum after compensation.

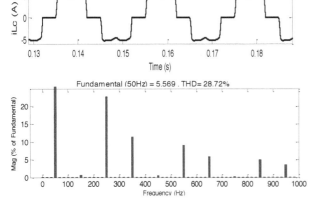

Figure 6(c). Load current and its harmonic spectrum before compensation.

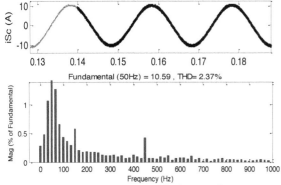

Figure 6(d). Load current and its harmonic spectrum after compensation.

Furthermore, figure 7(i) shows that a slight change in dc-link voltage occurs at the moment that the load change (0.2s) which is immediately controlled by the dc-link voltage controller and the dc-link voltage returns to its previous value.

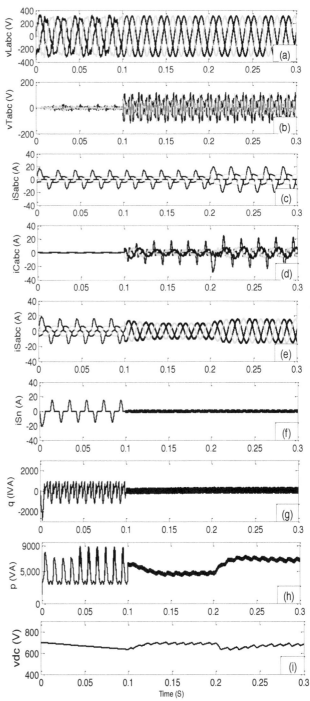

Figure 7. The results of UPQC performance while operating. (a) load voltages, (b) voltages injected by the series transformers (c) load currents (d) source currents (e) the injected compensating currents (f) source neutral current (g) instantaneous reactive power (h) instantaneous active power (i) dc link voltage.

4.2. Comparison to the convention methods

Conventional techniques published so far in the literature have more computational burden. On the other hand, the proposed method is a simple approach for effectively compensating current and voltage harmonics, reactive power and load balancing. Other advantages of this approach is the reduction of number of current and voltage measurements for controlling the shunt and series APFs. In the proposed method, to control the shunt APF, we just need to measure the source current whereas in conventional techniques, it is necessary to measure the currents of load, source and shunt APF. In the proposed control method, it is not necessary to measure neither the currents of shunt APF or the voltages of series APF which have fast variations. In order to compare the proposed approach with conventional p-q method, the results obtained from both these techniques are compared in table 2.

Table 2. % THD of the supply currents and load voltages.

Supply currents/load voltage	Without UPQC	UPQC with proposed method	UPQC with conventional p-q method
%THD in current in Phase a	28.72%	2.36%	3.04%
%THD in load voltage	11.25%	1.47%	2.23%

The simulation results obtained by using conventional p-q method are shown in figure 8. Figure 8(a) shows the source harmonic voltages before compensation. It could be seen from figure 8(c) that by injecting compensating voltages into system, the series APF of UPQC generates sinusoidal load voltages and decreases the load voltage THD from 11.25% to 2.23% whereas in the proposed control method, the load voltage THD is decreased from 11.25% to 1.47 %. The voltages injected by the series APF are shown in figure 6(b). On the other hand, figure 8(f) shows that, by injecting compensating currents for network, the UPQC shunt APF compensates load unbalance and load current harmonics and also decreases the source current THD from 28.72 % to 3.04 %, whereas in the proposed control method, source current THD is decreased from 28.72 % to 2.23%.

The load harmonic and unbalanced currents and shunt APF injected currents are shown in figure 8(d) and figure 8(e), respectively. Figure 8(i) shows that the source neutral current is decreased to zero by the shunt APF of UPQC. It could be seen from figure 8(k) that reactive power is fully

compensated by shunt APF. Simulation results show that the proposed control technique outperforms conventional p-q control theory.

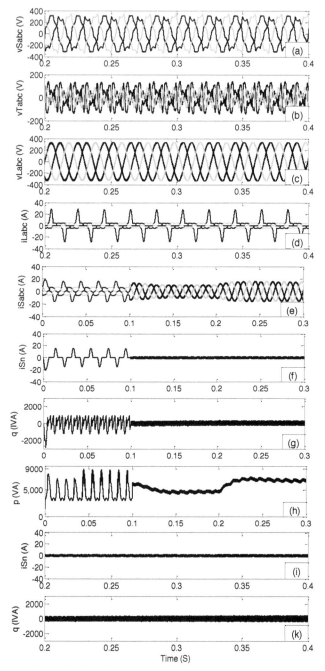

Figure 8. Simulation results for conventional p-q method: (a) distortional unbalanced voltages of the source (b) voltages injected by the transformer (c) load voltages (d) unbalanced and nonlinear load currents (e) currents injected by the compensator (f) source currents (g) load neutral current (h) neutral current injected by compensator (i) source neutral current (h) instantaneous reactive power.

4. Conclusion

In this paper, the performance of the proposed control method for a three-phase four wire UPQC was investigated. Simulation results show the capability of proposed control approach in dealing with the problems of power quality such as load balancing, load reactive power compensation, and current and voltage harmonics compensation under voltage unbalance conditions. In the proposed control method, to control the shunt APF, we just need to measure source current while in conventional methods currents of load, source and shunt APF must be measured. Therefore, the number of current measurements is decreased in the proposed approach. Simulation results show that under conditions of unbalanced and nonlinear load current, this method not only decreases the effects of load distortion and unbalance in the power system, but also improves the power factor. Meanwhile, whenever the source voltages are distortional and unbalanced, the series APF provides sinusoidal voltages for loads. Also, in this research, it is shown that the UPQC simultaneously compensates voltage and current problems and it has the best compensation features even during the emergence of unbalanced components in the three-phase four-wire electrical systems. Simulation results reveal that the proposed control technique has better compensation performance than conventional p-q control theory.

References

[1] Gunther, E. W. & Mehta, H. (1995). A Survey of Distribution System Power Quality. IEEE Transactions on Power Delivery, vol. 10, no. 1, pp. 322-329.

[2] Gun Lee, G., Albu, M. M. & Heydt, G. T. (2004). A Power Quality Index Based on Equipment Sensitivity, Cost and Network Vulnerability. IEEE Transactions on Power Delivery. vol. 19, no. 3, pp. 1504-1510.

[3] Ewald, F. & Mausoum, M. A. S. (2008). Power Quality in Power Systems and Electrical Machines. Elsevier, Academic Press, London, UK.

[4] Singh, B., Al-Haddad, K. & Chandra, A. (1999). A Review of Active Filters for Power Quality Improvement. IEEE Transactions on Industrial Electronics, vol. 46, no. 5, pp. 960-971.

[5] Akagi, H. (1996). New Trends in Active Filters for Power Conditioning. IEEE Transactions on Industry Applications, vol. 32, no. 6, pp. 1312-1322.

[6] Fang, Z., Akagi, H. & Nabae, A. (1990). A New Approach to Harmonic Compensation in Power Systems-a Combined System of Shunt Passive and Series Active Filters. IEEE Transactions on Industry Applications, vol. 26, no. 6, pp. 983-990.

[7] Fujita, H. & Akagi, H. (1998). The Unified Power Quality Conditioner: the Integration of Series and Shunt-Active Filters. IEEE Transactions on Power Electronics, vol. 13, no. 2, pp. 315- 322.

[7] Senand, K. K. & Stacey, E. J. (1998). UPFC-

Unified Power Flow Controller: Theory, Modeling, and Applications. IEEE Transactions on Power Delivery. vol. 13, no. 4, pp. 1453- 1460.

[9] Han, B., Bae, B., Kim, H. & Baek, S. (2006). Combined Operation of Unified Power-Quality Conditioner with Distributed Generation. IEEE Transactions on Power Delivery, vol. 21, no. 1, pp. 330 -338.

[10] Zhili, T., Xun, L., Jian, C., Yong, K. & Shanxu, D. (2006). A Direct Control Strategy for UPQC in Three-Phase Four-Wire System. 5th International Conference on Power Electronics and Motion Control. Shanghai, China, 2006.

[11] Khadkikar, V. & Chandra, A. (2009). A Novel Structure for Three-Phase Four-Wire Distribution System Utilizing Unified Power Quality Conditioner (UPQC). IEEE Transactions on Industry Applications, vol. 45, no. 5, pp. 1897- 1902.

[12] Xun, L., Guorong, Z., Shanxu, D. & Jian Chen, C. (2007). Control Scheme for Three-Phase Four-Wire UPQC in a Three-Phase Stationary Frame. Annual Conference of the IEEE on Industrial Electronics Society. Taipei, Taiwan, 2007.

[13] Ghosh, A., Jindal, A. K. & Joshi, A. (2004). A Unified Power Quality Conditioner for Voltage Regulation of Critical Load Bus. IEEE Power Engineering Society General Meeting, 2004.

[14] Bhuvaneswari, G. & Nair, M. G. (2008). Design, Simulation, and Analog Circuit Implementation of a Three-Phase Shunt Active Filter Usingthe ICosΦ Algorithm. IEEE Transactions on Power Delivery, vol.23, no.2, pp.1222- 1235.

[15] Yash, P., Swarup, A. & Singh, B. (2012). A Novel Control Strategy of Three-phase, Four-wire UPQC for Power Quality Improvement, Journal of Electrical Engineering & Technology, vol. 1, no. 1, pp. 1- 8.

[16] Teke, A., Saribulut, L. & Tumay, M. (2011). A Novel Reference Signal Generation Method for Power-Quality Improvement of Unified Power-Quality Conditioner, IEEE Transactions Power Delivery, vol.26, no. 4, pp.2205- 2214.

[17] Abardeh, M. H & Ghazi, R. (2010). A New Reference Waveform Estimation Strategy for Unified Power Quality Conditioner (UPQC). IEEE International Energy Conference & Exhibition. Manama, Bahrain,2010.

[18] Guozhu, C., Yang, C. & Smedley, K. M. (2004). Three-Phase Four-Leg Active Power Quality Conditioner Without References Calculation. Nineteenth Annual IEEE Applied Power Electronics Conference and Exposition, 2004.

[19] Kesler, M. & Ozdemir, E. (2011). Synchronous-Reference-Frame-Based Control Method for UPQC under Unbalanced & Distorted Load Conditions. IEEE Transactions on Industrial Electronics, vol. 58, no.9, pp. 3967- 3975.

[20] Teke; A., Meral, M.E., Cuma, M. U., Tumay, M. & Bayindir, K. C. (2013). OPEN Unified Power Quality Conditioner with Control Based on Enhanced Phase Locked Loop. Generation, Transmission and Distribution, vol. 7, no. 3, pp. 254- 264.

[21] Viji, A. J. & Sudhakaran, M. (2012). Generalized UPQC System with an Improved Control Method Under Distorted and Unbalanced Load Conditions. International Conference on Computing, Electronics and Electrical Technologies. Kumaracoil, 2012.

[22] Da Silva, C. H., Pereira, R. R., Da Silva, L. E. B., Lambert-Torres, G., Bose, B. K. & Ahn, S. U. (2010). A Digital PLL Scheme for Three-Phase System Using Modified Synchronous Reference Frame. IEEE Transactions on Industrial Electronics, vol. 57, no. 11, pp. 3814- 3821.

[23] Correa, J. M., Farret, F. A. & Simoes, M. G. (2005). Application of a Modified Single-Phase P-Q Theory in the Control of Shunt and Series Active Filters in a 400 Hz Microgrid. 36th IEEE Power Electronics Specialists Conference, Recife, Brazil, 2005.

[24] Da Silva, S. A. O., Barriviera, R., Modesto, R. A, Kaster, M. & Goedtel, A. (2011). Single-Phase Power Quality Conditioners with Series-Parallel Filtering Capabilities, IEEE International Symposium on Industrial Electronics. Gdansk, 2011.

[25] Viji, A. J. & Sudhakaran, M. (2012). Flexible 3P4W System Using UPQC with Combination of SRF and P-Q Theory Based Control Strategy. 22nd

Australasian Universities Power Engineering Conference. Bali,2012.

[26] Kesler, M. & Ozdemir, E. (2010). A Novel Control Method for Unified Power Quality Conditioner (UPQC) Under Non-Ideal Mains Voltage and Unbalanced Load Conditions. 25th Annual IEEE Applied Power Electronics Conference and Exposition. Palm Springs, CA, 2010.

[27] Akagi, H., Watanabe, E. & Aredes, M. (2007). Instantaneous Power Theory and Applications to Power Conditionin. New Jersey, John Wiley & Sons.

[28] Kinhal, V. G, Agarwal, P. & Gupta, H. (2011). Performance Investigation of Neural-Network-Based Unified Power-Quality Conditioner. IEEE Transactions on Power Delivery, vol. 26, no. 1, pp. 431- 437.

[29] Dinesh, L., Srinivasa, S. & Mallikarjuna Rao, N. (2012). Simulation of Unified Power Quality Conditioner for Power Quality Improvement Using Fuzzy Logic and Neural Networks. Innovative Systems Design and Engineering, pp.3, no. 3, pp. 36- 47.

[30] Song, H., Park, H. & Nam, K. (1999). An Instantaneous Phase Angle Detection Algorithm Under Unbalanced Line Voltage Condition. 30th Annual IEEE Power Electronics Specialists Conference, Charleston, SC. 1999.

[31] Abdusalam, M., Poure, P., Karimi, S. & Saadate, S. (2009). New Digital Reference Current Generation for Shunt Active Power Filter Under Distorted Voltage Conditions. Electric Power Systems Research, vol. 79, no. 10, pp. 759- 765.

5

Adaptive fuzzy pole placement for stabilization of non-linear systems

A. Karami-Mollaee

Department of Electrical & Robotic Engineering, Shahrood University of Technology, Shahrood, Iran.

*Corresponding author: akarami@shahroodut.ac.ir (A. Karami-Mollaee).

Abstract
A new approach is proposed for the pole placement of non-linear systems using the state feedback and fuzzy system. We use a new online fuzzy training method in order to identify and obtain a fuzzy model for an unknown non-linear system using only the system input and output. Then we linearize this identified model at each sampling time to have an approximate linear time-varying system. In order to stabilize the linear system obtained, we first choose the desired time-invariant closed-loop matrix, and then a time-varying state feedback is used. The behavior of the closed-loop non-linear system is regarded as a linear time-invariant (LTI) system. Therefore, the advantage of the proposed method is the global asymptotical exponential stability of unknown non-linear systems. Due to the high speed convergence of the proposed adaptive fuzzy training method, the closed-loop system is robust against uncertainty in system parameters. Finally, a comparison is made with the boundary layer sliding mode control (SMC).

Keywords: *Fuzzy Identification, Pole Placement, Non-linear Control, Switch Reluctance Motor, Sliding Mode Control.*

1. Introduction
Control of non-linear systems is still a challenging area in the literature of control system theory, and some efforts have been made to study this subject [1]. However, most of them can be only applied to a certain class of non-linear systems. For instance, feedback linearization is only applicable to a class of non-linear systems that meet the involutivity condition and can be transformed to the companion form [1]. Many other methods have some limitations. For example, chattering is the most important problem in the sliding mode control (SMC) [2]. An intelligent approach such as the fuzzy systems and neural networks can help us solve these problems and limitations [3-6].

In addition, many efforts have been made to extend the linear control schemes to non-linear systems. On such a method is gain-scheduling control, which is designed based on a finite number of linearized models at each operating point [7,8], also called multiple-model adaptive control (MMAC) [8]. In [7], a MMAC neural network method is used to control non-linear systems. This method is expensive in terms of training and computation, and moreover, its stability has not been proved [17]. Another simple method in linear controller design is pole placement. When all of the state variables of a system are completely controllable, the closed-loop poles of the system can be placed in arbitrary locations on the phase plane using the state feedback with appropriate gains [1,9]. Some efforts have been directed toward computational methods of finding a feedback gain, and many numerical algorithms have been proposed [10-13]. In these methods, the minimal numerical operations are at least proportional to the cube of the system dimension [13]. To eliminate these time-consuming computations, neural networks have been proposed [14-16]. For example, in [10,15], the Sylvester equation has been solved using the recurrent neural networks. In all of these methods, stability of the closed-loop system has not been proved. In [17], a method for pole placement of non-linear systems has been presented based on the recurrent neural network, and the stability of the closed-loop system has been proved. However, the plant model has been assumed to be known. In [19], a method has been presented using the Takagi–Sugeno (TS) fuzzy systems based on the linear matrix inequality (LMI). Thus this approach cannot be online, i.e. first of all, LMI should be solved. The proposed approach in [20] is based upon solution of the Diophantine equations. However, the stability of the closed-loop non-linear system has not been proved. The approach mentioned in [20] is only for discrete-time dynamic plants. Other methods have been suggested in [18-20].

In this work, we proposed a method for pole placement of non-linear systems using the fuzzy systems, which eliminate the time-consuming computations of MMAC. We assumed that the non-linear system model was unknown, and that the system states were not accessible. Closed-loop stability was also proved. Since the non-linear plant model was unknown, we first identified its model using a fuzzy system, and then this identified model was linearized at any time to obtain a linear time-varying system. As shown in [1,17], the eigenvalues were not the stability criteria for the linear time-varying systems. Thus we applied a time-varying state feedback to this time-varying linear system such that the closed-loop linear system was time-invariant at any time.

The rest of this paper has been organized into six sections. The system model and problem formulation are described in section 2. In section 3, we present the system identification procedure. In section 4, linearization of the non-linear system and state feedback are explained. Finally, in section 5, we discuss the simulation and comparison results to verify the theoretical concepts presented in the previous sections. The conclusion is given in section 6.

2. Problem formulation

The eigenvalues are not the criteria used for the stability of linear time-varying systems [1,17]. For example, consider the following matrix:

$$A(t) = \begin{bmatrix} -1+1.5\cos^2(t) & 1-1.5\sin(t)\cos(t) \\ -1-1.5\sin(t)\cos(t) & -1+1.5\sin^2(t) \end{bmatrix} \quad (1)$$

For any t, the eigenvalues are $\lambda_{1,2} = -0.25(1 \pm j\sqrt{7})$. However, the linear system $\dot{x} = A(t)x$ is not stable. To overcome this problem, we proposed a new approach, which was depicted in figure 1. We first chose a fixed closed-loop matrix A_{cl}, and then calculated the feedback gain at each sampling time for the linearized identified model of non-linear system. Consider the following single input non-linear system:

$$\dot{x}_i = x_{i+1} : i = 1,2,\ldots,n-1$$
$$\dot{x}_n = f(x,u) \quad (2)$$
$$y = x_1$$

such that y is the measurable system output, $x = [x_1, x_2 \ldots, x_n]^T$ is the inaccessible vector state, and u is the input control signal. Note that the function $f(x,u)$ is unknown. The other form of this equation is as follows:

$$\dot{x} = Ax + Bg(x,u)$$
$$y = C^T x \quad (3)$$

where:

$$g(x,u) = f(x,u) + \sum_{i=1}^{n} a_i x_i \quad (4)$$

and:

$$A = \begin{bmatrix} 0 & 1 & 0 & \cdots & 0 \\ 0 & 0 & 1 & \ddots & \vdots \\ \vdots & \vdots & \ddots & \ddots & 0 \\ 0 & 0 & \cdots & 0 & 1 \\ -a_1 & -a_2 & \cdots & -a_{n-1} & -a_n \end{bmatrix}, B = \begin{bmatrix} 0 \\ 0 \\ \vdots \\ 0 \\ 1 \end{bmatrix}, C = \begin{bmatrix} 1 \\ 0 \\ \vdots \\ 0 \\ 0 \end{bmatrix} \quad (5)$$

Assume that a_i is such that A is a Hurwitz matrix, and that the pair (A,B) is controllable, and (A,C) is observable.

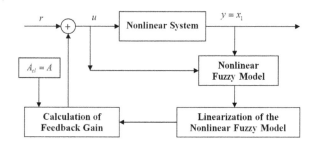

Figure 1. Structure of the proposed approach.

3. System identification

According to the fuzzy theorems, the Gaussian fuzzy basis functions (GFBF) can approximate any real continuous function with arbitrary accuracy. This means that GFBF has a universal approximation property [4]. Due to the approximation capability of GFBF, there exists an ideal weight vector w with arbitrary large enough dimension m such that the system (3) can be written as follows:

$$\dot{x} = Ax + Bg$$
$$g = w^T \xi(x,u) + \varepsilon_x \quad (6)$$
$$y = C^T x$$

where, ε_x is an arbitrary small reconstruction error with bound B_ε, i.e. $|\varepsilon_x| < B_\varepsilon$. Moreover, $\hat{w} \in R^m$ is the weight vector estimate of fuzzy rules, and $\xi(.): R^{n+1} \to R^m$ is the Gaussian membership function (GMF) vector. Based on (6), to estimate the non-linear function $g(x,u)$, a singleton fuzzifier with product inference engine and a defuzzifier as weight sum of each output rule is used.

Now, the following estimator could be proposed:

$$\dot{\hat{x}} = A\hat{x} + B\left(\hat{w}^T \xi(\hat{x},u) + k_x(y - \hat{y})\right) + T(y - \hat{y}) \quad (7)$$

where, $\hat{x} = [\hat{x}_1, \hat{x}_2 ..., \hat{x}_n]^T$ is the identified model state vector, and matrix A and observer gain vector $T \in R^{n \times 1}$ are chosen such that $A_s = A - TC^T$ is stable, i.e. for any symmetric positive definite matrix Q, there exists a symmetric positive definite matrix P satisfying the following Lyapunov equation:

$$A_s^T P + P A_s = -Q \quad (8)$$

By subtracting (7) from (6), we obtain:

$$\begin{aligned}\dot{\tilde{x}} &= A\tilde{x} + B\left(w^T \xi(x,u) + \varepsilon_x\right) \\ &\quad - B\left(\hat{w}^T \xi(\hat{x},u) + k_x(y-\hat{y})\right) - T(y-\hat{y})\end{aligned} \quad (9)$$

in which $\tilde{x}(t) = x(t) - \hat{x}(t)$ and $\tilde{w} = w - \hat{w}$ are the state and parameter estimation errors.

$$\begin{aligned}\dot{\tilde{x}} &= A_s\tilde{x} + B\left(w^T\xi(x,u) - \hat{w}^T\xi(\hat{x},u)\right. \\ &\qquad\qquad \left. - k_x(y-\hat{y}) + \varepsilon_x\right) = \\ A_s\tilde{x} &+ B\left(-k_x(y-\hat{y}) + \varepsilon_x - w^T\xi(\hat{x},u)\right. \\ &\qquad\quad \left. + w^T\xi(\hat{x},u) - k_x(y-\hat{y}) + \varepsilon_x\right) = \\ A_s\tilde{x} &+ B\left(\tilde{w}^T\hat{\xi} + w^T\tilde{\xi} - k_x(y-\hat{y}) + \varepsilon_x\right)\end{aligned} \quad (10)$$

such that: $\tilde{\xi} = \xi - \hat{\xi}$, $\xi = \xi(x,u)$, and $\hat{\xi} = \xi(\hat{x},u)$.

Theorem 1: Using the following adaptive weight law:

$$\dot{\hat{w}} = k_w \hat{\xi} \tilde{y} - 4k_e k_w |\tilde{y}| \hat{w} \quad (11)$$

the estimation error $\tilde{x}(t)$ converges to zero if $k_x \to \infty$. k_w and k_e are the arbitrary positive scalar constants, and $\tilde{y} = y - \hat{y}$.

Proof: Consider the following Lyapunov function:

$$V(t) = \frac{1}{2}\tilde{x}^T P \tilde{x} + \frac{1}{2k_w}\tilde{w}^T \tilde{w} \quad (12)$$

Taking the derivative of $V(t)$ yields:

$$\dot{V}(t) = \frac{1}{2}\dot{\tilde{x}}^T P\tilde{x} + \frac{1}{2}\tilde{x}^T P\dot{\tilde{x}} + \frac{1}{k_w}\tilde{w}^T\dot{\tilde{w}} \quad (13)$$

Substituting (8) and (10) in the above equation follows that:

$$\begin{aligned}\dot{V}(t) &= -\frac{1}{2}\tilde{x}^T Q\tilde{x} + \tilde{x}^T PB(w^T\tilde{\xi} + \varepsilon_x) \\ &\quad - k_x\tilde{x}^T CC^T\tilde{x} + \tilde{w}^T\left(\frac{1}{k_w}\dot{\tilde{w}} + \hat{\xi}B^T P\tilde{x}\right)\end{aligned} \quad (14)$$

Using the equality $\dot{\tilde{w}} = -\dot{\hat{w}}$, and tuning law (11) in the above equation leads to:

$$\begin{aligned}\dot{V}(t) &= -\frac{1}{2}\tilde{x}^T Q\tilde{x} + \tilde{x}^T PB(w^T\tilde{\xi} + \varepsilon_x) \\ &\quad - k_x\tilde{x}^T CC^T\tilde{x} + 4k_e|\tilde{y}|\tilde{w}^T\hat{w}\end{aligned} \quad (15)$$

Now consider the logical assumptions that the actual weight w is norm bounded, and, moreover, the activation functions ξ and $\hat{\xi}$ in (7) are chosen such that their norm be bounded also (see (32)) i.e. $\|w\| \le B_w$ and $\|\xi\| \le B_\xi$ or $\|\hat{\xi}\| \le B_\xi$. Therefore, we can write: $|w^T\tilde{\xi} + \varepsilon| \le 2B_w B_\xi + B_\varepsilon$. Here, considering the properties of the positive definite matrices Q and P, and using $\hat{w} = w - \tilde{w}$, the above equation yields:

$$\begin{aligned}\dot{V}(t) &\le -\left(0.5\underline{\sigma}(Q) + k_x\right)\|\tilde{x}\|^2 \\ &\quad + \bar{\sigma}(PB)(2B_w B_\xi + B_\varepsilon)\|\tilde{x}\| \\ &\quad - 4k_e\left(\|\tilde{w}\|^2 - B_w\|\tilde{w}\|\right)|\tilde{y}|\end{aligned} \quad (16)$$

Now, we define $B_{\tilde{x}}$ as follows:

$$\begin{aligned}B_{\tilde{x}} &= \frac{\bar{\sigma}(PB)(2B_w B_\xi + B_\varepsilon) + k_e B_w^2\|C\|}{0.5\underline{\sigma}(Q) + k_x} \\ &= \frac{\bar{\sigma}(PB)(2B_w B_\xi + B_\varepsilon) + k_e B_w^2}{0.5\underline{\sigma}(Q) + k_x}\end{aligned} \quad (17)$$

where, $\bar{\sigma}$ and $\underline{\sigma}$ denote the maximum and minimum singular values, respectively. Therefore:

$$\begin{aligned}\dot{V}(t) &\le -\left(0.5\underline{\sigma}(Q) + k_x\right)\left(\|\tilde{x}\| - B_{\tilde{x}}\right)\|\tilde{x}\| \\ &\quad - 4k_e\left(\|\tilde{w}\| - \frac{1}{2}B_w\right)^2|\tilde{y}|\end{aligned} \quad (18)$$

or:

$$\dot{V}(t) \le -\left(0.5\underline{\sigma}(Q) + k_x\right)\left(\|\tilde{x}\| - B_{\tilde{x}}\right)\|\tilde{x}\| \quad (19)$$

Take: $\omega(t) = \left(0.5\underline{\sigma}(Q) + k_x\right)\left(\|\tilde{x}\| - B_{\tilde{x}}\right)\|\tilde{x}\|$, and suppose: $\|\tilde{x}\| > B_{\tilde{x}}$. Then one can write: $\dot{V} \le -\omega(t) \le 0$, and from (12), one can write $V(t) > V(0)$. Therefore, $\tilde{x}$, $\tilde{\xi}$, and $\tilde{w}$ are bounded when $\|\tilde{x}\| > B_{\tilde{x}}$. Moreover, it is easy to show that $\ddot{V}$ is bounded when $\|\tilde{x}\| > B_{\tilde{x}}$ because it is clear that $\ddot{V}$ is also dependent on $\tilde{x}$, $\tilde{\xi}$ and

$\tilde{w}$ i.e. $\dot{V}(t)$ is uniformly continuous. Integration of $\dot{V} \leq -\omega(t) \leq 0$ from zero to t yields:

$$0 \leq \int_0^t \omega(\tau)d\tau \leq \int_0^t \omega(\tau)d\tau + V(t) \leq V(0) \qquad (20)$$

when $t \to \infty$, the above integral exists, and is less than or equal to $V(0)$. Since $V(0)$ is positive and finite, according to the Barbalat's lemma [1], we have:

$$\lim_{t\to\infty} \omega(t) = \lim_{t\to\infty} (0.5\underline{\sigma}(Q) + k_x)\left(\|\tilde{x}\| - B_{\tilde{x}}\right)\|\tilde{x}\| = 0 \qquad (21)$$

Since $(0.5\underline{\sigma}(Q) + k_x)$ is greater than zero, (21) implies decreasing $\|\tilde{x}\|$ until it reaches $B_{\tilde{x}}$, whose result is $\lim_{t\to\infty}\|\tilde{x}\| = B_{\tilde{x}}$.

This guarantees that $B_{\tilde{x}}$ is the lower bound of $\|\tilde{x}\|$, and it is clear that $\lim_{k_x\to\infty} B_{\tilde{x}} = 0$. Then $\|\tilde{x}\|$ or $\tilde{x}$ will converge to zero if $k_x \to \infty$. The result of this theorem can be written as:

$$\lim_{\substack{k_x\to\infty \\ t\to\infty}} \tilde{x} = 0 \qquad (22)$$

4. State feedback

According to (7) and due to the convergence of fuzzy system based on (22), we have:

$$\dot{\hat{x}} = A\hat{x} + B\hat{w}^T \xi(\hat{x}, u) \qquad (23)$$

Using (4) and (23), we can write:

$$\dot{\hat{x}}_n = \hat{w}^T \xi(\hat{x}, u) - \sum_{i=1}^n a_i x_i \qquad (24)$$

Then an approximate instantaneous linear model is as follows [17]:

$$\dot{\hat{x}}_n = \sum_{i=1}^n \left(\hat{w}^T \frac{\partial \xi(\hat{x}, u)}{\partial \hat{x}_i} - a_i\right)\hat{x}_i + \left(\hat{w}^T \frac{\partial \xi(\hat{x}, u)}{\partial u}\right)u + H.O.T \qquad (25)$$

where, $H.O.T$ is the higher order terms in the Taylor series, which can be considered as the perturbation, and can be neglected [1,17]. Note that this linear system is not time-invariant because the gain vector w varies with time, and as we aforementioned, the eigenvalues are not the criteria for stability.

Then we should apply a state feedback such that the closed system is linear time-invariant (LTI). To this end, we used the following state feedback:

$$u(t) = k(t)\hat{x}(t) + r(t) = \sum_{i=1}^n k_i(t)\hat{x}_i(t) + r(t) \qquad (26)$$

$$k(t) = [k_1(t), k_2(t), \ldots, k_n(t)]$$

where, $r(t)$ is the new input control signal. Then:

$$\dot{\hat{x}}_n =$$

$$\sum_{i=1}^n \left(\hat{w}^T \frac{\partial \xi(\hat{x}, u)}{\partial \hat{x}_i} - a_i\right)\hat{x}_i + \left(\hat{w}^T \frac{\partial \xi(\hat{x}, u)}{\partial u}\right)\left(\sum_{i=1}^n k_i(t)\hat{x}_i(t) + r(t)\right) =$$

$$\sum_{i=1}^n \left(\hat{w}^T \frac{\partial \xi(\hat{x}, u)}{\partial \hat{x}_i} - a_i + \hat{w}^T \frac{\partial \xi(\hat{x}, u)}{\partial u} k_i(t)\right)\hat{x}_i + \left(\hat{w}^T \frac{\partial \xi(\hat{x}, u)}{\partial u}\right)r(t) \qquad (27)$$

We choose:

$$k_i(t) = -\left(\hat{w}^T \frac{\partial \xi(\hat{x}, u)}{\partial \hat{x}_i}\right)\bigg/\left(\hat{w}^T \frac{\partial \xi(\hat{x}, u)}{\partial u}\right) \qquad (28)$$

Then:

$$\dot{\hat{x}}_n = \sum_{i=1}^n (-a_i)\hat{x}_i + \left(\hat{w}^T \frac{\partial \xi(\hat{x}, u)}{\partial u}\right)r(t) \qquad (29)$$

or:

$$\dot{\hat{x}} = A\hat{x} + Gr \qquad (30)$$

where, A is as (5), and:

$$G = \begin{bmatrix} 0 & 0 & \cdots & 0 & \hat{w}^T \frac{\partial \xi(\hat{x}, u)}{\partial u} \end{bmatrix}^T \in R^n \qquad (31)$$

5. Simulation and comparison results

In the following examples, the proposed method is applied to a non-linear non-affine system to show the effectiveness of this approach. Consider the following one-phase model of switch reluctance motor (SRM) [21].

$$\dot{x}_1 = x_2$$

$$\dot{x}_2 = \frac{N_r^2 \psi_s}{J h^2(x_1)} \frac{dh(x_1)}{dx_1}\left\{1 - [1 + u h(x_1)]e^{-u h(x_1)}\right\} - \frac{T}{J} \qquad (32)$$

$$h(x_1) = L_a + L_u \sin(x_1)$$

where, x_1 is the electrical angular position, x_2 is the mechanical angular velocity, u is the stator current (input control signal), T is the load torque, ψ_s is the flux linkage, J is the total rotor and load inertia, N_r is the number of rotor poles, and L_u and L_u are the values for inductance at the aligned and un-aligned positions, respectively. In this work, the SRM parameters werechosen as:

$N_r = 4$, $J = 0.07\,Kg.m^2$, $\psi_s = 0.1\,Wb$, $L_a = 180\,mH$, $L_u = 8\,mH$, and $T = 0.5\,N.M$.

The simulations were performed using MATLAB, with a sample time of 0.001. For the fuzzy system, we chose a GMF vector with three inputs $(\hat{x}_1, \hat{x}_2, u)$ and eleven rules as follow:

$$\xi_i(\hat{x}_1, \hat{x}_2, u) = \exp\left(-\left(\sqrt{\hat{x}_1^2 + \hat{x}_2^2 + u^2} - (6-i)\right)^2\bigg/6\right) \qquad (33)$$

where, $i = 1, 2, \ldots, 11$. The output of defuzzifier is $\hat{g}$, and the fuzzy network tuning parameters were chosen as $k_w = 5$, $k_x = 100$ and $k_e = 30$. The other parameters were chosen as:

$$A = \begin{bmatrix} 0 & 1 \\ -9 & -8 \end{bmatrix}, T = \begin{bmatrix} 1 \\ 1 \end{bmatrix} \tag{34}$$

The initial conditions for the weight vector were chosen as $w(0) = [0,0,\ldots,0]^T$, and, moreover, $x(0) = [x_1(0), x_2(0)]^T = [2,1]^T$, and $r(t)$ is as a pulse function shown in figure 2. Figures 3 till 13 show the simulation results. We can see that the behavior of the closed-loop systems is as a linear system. Figures 3, 4 and 5 show the non-linear model of $f(x,u)$ and its fuzzy estimation. From figure 5, we can see the accuracy and precision of the proposed adaptive fuzzy system in estimation of the non-linear systems. Figures 6, 7 and 8 shows the input control signal of SRM and as we can see, its initial value is not large and has no oscillation. Figures 9 and 10 show the system states and their estimation. Finally, figures 11 and 12 demonstrate the behavior of the fuzzy systems. In these figures, the adaptive weight vectors are shown, i.e. the outputs of (11). In figure 13, the outputs of fuzzy membership are shown, i.e. the outputs of (33).

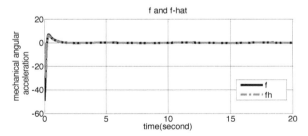

Figure 2. Reference input.

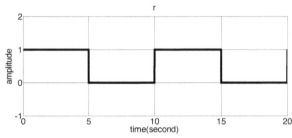

Figure 3. Non-linear system and its fuzzy estimation.

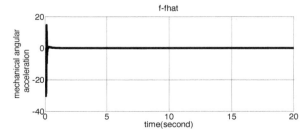

Figure 4. Difference between non-linear system and its fuzzy estimation.

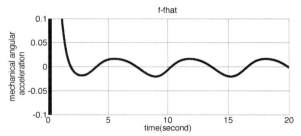

Figure 5. Difference between non-linear system and its fuzzy estimation.

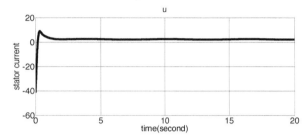

Figure 6. Input control signal of non-linear system.

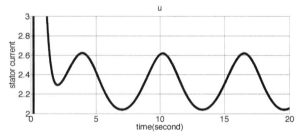

Figure 7. Input control signal of non-linear system.

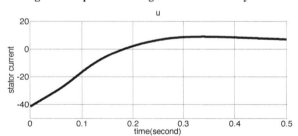

Figure 8. Input control signal of non-linear system.

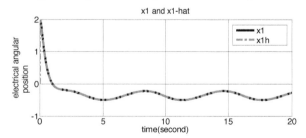

Figure 9. First state and its estimation.

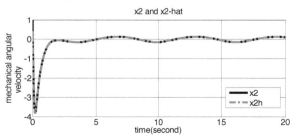

Figure 10. Second state and its estimation.

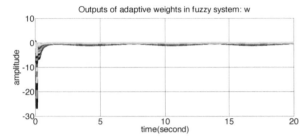

Figure 11. Adaptive weight of fuzzy system.

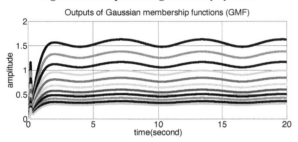

Figure 12. Adaptive weight of fuzzy system.

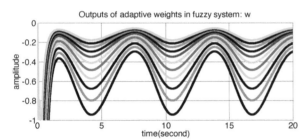

Figure 13. Output of Gaussian membership functions.

In order to compare the proposed method with the boundary layer sliding mode control (SMC), the following estimation of the sliding surface was defined:

$$\hat{s} = \sum_{i=1}^{n} \lambda_i \hat{x}_i, \lambda_n = 1 \qquad (35)$$

The coefficients $\lambda_i : i = 1,2,\ldots,n$ should be chosen so that the following polynomial is Hurwitz:

$$P^{n-1} + \lambda_{n-1}P^{n-2} + \lambda_{n-2}P^{n-3} + \ldots + \lambda_2 P + \lambda_1 = 0 \qquad (36)$$

The input control signal can be calculated using the following reaching law [1,2]:

$$\dot{\hat{s}} = -k\, sat(\hat{s}/\varphi) \qquad (37)$$

whose result is:

$$u = \left(\hat{w}^T \frac{\partial \xi(\hat{x},u)}{\partial u} \right)^{-1} \left(-k\, sat(\hat{s}/\varphi) - \sum_{i=1}^{n-1}\lambda_i \hat{x}_i \right.$$

$$\left. - \sum_{i=1}^{n} \left(\hat{w}^T \frac{\partial \xi(\hat{x},u)}{\partial \hat{x}_i} - a_i \right) \hat{x}_i \right) \qquad (38)$$

For the stability of the closed-loop system, the inequality $k > |H.O.T|$ should be satisfied [1,2,22]. However, the problem is that the terms $H.O.T$ are unknown. To solve this problem, a large k should be chosen, which leads to chattering [2,22].

For SRM, (38) leads to:

$$u = \left(\hat{w}^T \frac{\partial \xi(\hat{x},u)}{\partial u} \right)^{-1} \left(-k\, sat(\hat{s}/\varphi) - \lambda_1 \hat{x}_1 - \hat{x}_2 \right.$$

$$\left. - \left(\hat{w}^T \frac{\partial \xi(\hat{x},u)}{\partial \hat{x}_1} - a_1 \right) \hat{x}_1 - \left(\hat{w}^T \frac{\partial \xi(\hat{x},u)}{\partial \hat{x}_2} - a_2 \right) \hat{x}_2 \right) \qquad (39)$$

We chose the parameters as $\lambda_1 = 2, k = 5, \varphi = 0.1$. Figures 14 to 20 show the simulation results.

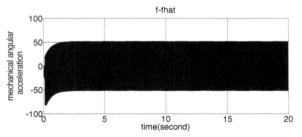

Figure 14. Non-linear system and its fuzzy estimation.

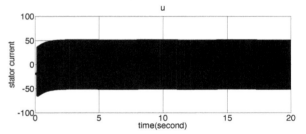

Figure 15. Difference between non-linear system and its fuzzy estimation.

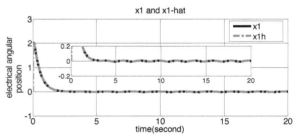

Figure 16. Input control signal of non-linear system.

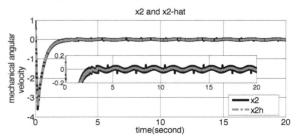

Figure 17. First state and its estimation.

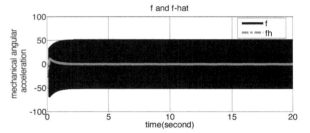

Figure 18. Second state and its estimation.

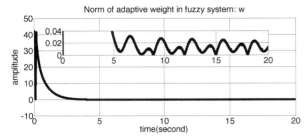

Figure 19. Norm of adaptive weights of fuzzy system.

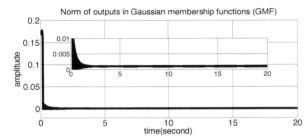

Figure 20. Norm of output of Gaussian membership functions.

We can see the effect of chattering in SMC, while the results in the state feedback are smooth. Another SMC drawback is its large value of input control signal, while the input control signal in state feedback is small and without chattering (compare Figures 6 and 16). We know that the convergence in both SMC and state feedback is asymptotical [1]. From figures 9, 10 and 17, 18, we can see that the only advantage of SMC is its faster convergence. In this example, the convergence time in SMC is about 2 seconds but in state feedback, it is about 4 seconds.

6. Conclusion

In this work, a new approach was proposed for the state feedback of unknown non-linear systems, which could lead to global asymptotical exponential stability. To have the unknown plant model, a fuzzy system was used, and an online adaptive training method was proposed using only the output system. In comparison with the existing approach, we first chose the closed-loop matrix, and then calculated the state feedback. Then the behavior of the closed-loop non-linear system is as a linear time invariant (LTI) system. Another advantage of the proposed method is its robustness against uncertainty in system parameters because the gain vector is computed online, and any drift and perturbation in parameters of the system affect this gain directly. This approach is simple in concept and realization. Finally, the proposed state feedback was compared with the boundary layer sliding mode control.

References

[1] Slotine, J.-J. E. & Li, W. (1991). Applied nonlinear control. Prentice-Hall.

[2] Lee, H. & Utkin, V.-I. (2007). Chattering suppression methods in sliding mode control systems. Elsevier, Annual Review in Control, vol. 31, pp. 179-188.

[3] Norgaard, M., Ravn, O., Poulsen, N. K. & Hansen, L. K. (2001). Neural network for modeling and control of dynamic systems. Springer, New York.

[4] Tanaka, K. & Wang, H. O. (2001). Fuzzy control systems design and analysis. John Wily, Canada.

[5] Alibakhshi, F., Teshnehlab, M., Alibakhshi, M. & Mansouri, M. (2015). Journal of AI and Data Mining (JAIDM), vol. 3, no. 2, pp. 141-147.

[6] Fateh, M. M., Ahmadi, S. M. & Khorashadizadeh, S. (2014). Journal of AI and Data Mining (JAIDM), vol.2, no. 2, pp. 159-166.

[7] Ahmed, M. S. & Tasaddug, I. A. (1994). Neural-net control for nonlinear plants: design approach through linearization. IEE Proceeding of Control Theory Application, vol. 141, no. 5, pp. 315-332.

[8] Watanabe, K. (1992). Adaptive estimation and control, partitioning approach. Prentice-Hall, Englewood Cliffs, Nj.

[9] Chi-Tsong, C. (1999). Linear system theory and design. Oxford University Press, Oxford.

[10] Bhattacharyya, S. P. & de Souza, E. (1982). Pole assignment via Sylvester's equation. Elsevier, System and Control Letters, vol. 1, no. 4, pp. 261-263.

[11] Carotenuto, L., Franze, C. & Muraca, P. (2001). New computational procedure to the pole placement problem by static output feedback. IEE Preceding 20010771, pp. 466-471.

[12] Lee, T. H., Wang, Q. G. & Koh, E. K. (1994). An iterative algorithm for pole placement by output feedback. IEEE Transaction on Automatic Control, vol. 39, no. 3, pp. 565-568.

[13] Shafai, B. & Bhattacharyya, S. P. (1988). An algorithm for pole placement in high order multivariable systems. IEEE Transaction on Automatic Control, vol. 33, pp. 870-876.

[14] Wang, J. & Wu, G. (1995). Recurrent neural network for synthesizing linear control systems via pole assignment. International Journal of System Science, vol. 26, no. 12, pp. 2369-2382.

[15] Zhang, Z., Jiang, D. & Wang, J. (2002). A recurrent neural network for solving Sylvester equation with time-varying coefficient. IEEE Transaction on Neural Network, vol. 13, no. 5, pp. 1053-1063.

[16] Zhang, Z. & Wang, J. (2002). Global exponential stability of recurrent neural network for synthesizing linear feedback control systems via pole assignment.

IEEE Transaction on Neural Network, vol. 13, no. 3, pp. 633-644.

[17] Karami-Mollaee, A. & Karami-Mollaee, M. R. (2006). A new approach for instantaneous pole placement with recurrent neural networks and its application in control of nonlinear time-varying systems. Elsevier, System and Control Letters, vol. 55, no. 5, pp. 385-395.

[18] Zhu, Q. M. & Guo, L. Z. (2002). A pole placement controller for non-linear dynamic plants. Journal of Systems and Control Engineering, vol. 216, no. 6, pp. 467-476.

[19] Toulottea, P.-F., Delprata, S., Guerraa, T.-M. & Boonaert, J. (2008). Vehicle spacing control using robust fuzzy control with pole placement in LMI region. Elsevier, Engineering Applications of Artificial Intelligence, vol. 21, no. 5, pp. 756–768.

[20] Marinescu, B. (2010). Output feedback pole placement for linear time-varying systems with application to the control of nonlinear systems. Elsevier, Automatica, vol. 46, no. 9, pp. 1524–1530.

[21] Xu, J.-X. & Tan, Y. (2002). On the P-type and Newton-type ILC schemes for dynamic systems with non-affine-in-input factors. Elsevier, Automatica, vol. 38, pp. 1237-1242.

[22] Karami-Mollaee, A., Pariz, N. & Shanechi, H. M. (2011). Position control of servomotors using neural dynamic sliding mode. Transactions of the IEEE/ASME (American Society of Mechanical Engineering), Journal of Dynamic Systems, Measurement and Control, vol. 133, no. 6, pp. 141-150.

6

Query expansion based on relevance feedback and latent semantic analysis

M. Rahimi*, M. Zahedi

School of Computer and IT, Shahrood University of Technology, Shahrood, Semnan, Iran.

Corresponding author: Marziea.rahimi@shahroodut.ac.ir (M. Rahimi).

Abstract
Web search engines are one of the most popular tools on the Internet, which are widely used by experienced and inexperienced users. Constructing an adequate query, which represents the best specification of users' information need to the search engine is an important concern of web users. Query expansion is a way to reduce this concern and increase user satisfaction. In this paper, a new method of query expansion is introduced. This method, which is a combination of relevant feedback and latent semantic analysis, finds the relative terms to the topics of user original query based on relevant documents selected by the user in relevant feedback step. The method is evaluated and compared with the Rocchio relevant feedback. The results indicate the capability of the method to better representation of user's information need and increasing significantly user satisfaction.

Keywords: *Query expansion, latent semantic analysis, relevant feedback.*

1. Introduction

The World Wide Web is a collection of vast amount of unlabeled, high dimensional and dynamic data. Web search engines as a quick and simple way to access to these data are widely used by experienced and inexperienced users. Most of the conventional search engines work based on text queries. Users enter some number of words as a query and search engine try to find documents related to the query. Therefore, success of the search process is greatly dependent on the user query; however, users enter broad or inadequate queries in most cases, which lead to retrieve irrelevant documents and user's dissatisfaction because of web search or intended information area inexperience. Users often enter topics of the intended information area and do not provide search engine with the other terms related to the topic.Query expansion is a method for reduction of this problem. Query expansion is the process of supplying the original user's queries with additional suitable terms. Many methods have been proposed for query expansion. These methods can be divided in two categories - global and local. Thesaurus based query expansion [1, 2, 3] is a type of global methods. Each term on the query is expanded with its synonyms or related terms from the thesaurus. This type of methods because of expanding query by synonyms can significantly decrease precision especially in case of ambiguous query terms. Another problem of the thesaurus based methods is constructing and maintenance of a thesaurus. These processes are very expensive and time consuming. In case of such vast and dynamic spaces as the World Wide Web, these problems become more serious and effective. Based on these issues, thesaurus based methods are often used in special technology domains like medical technology.

Relevant feedback is a local method claimed to be most successful method between query reformulating methods. This method can be explained by steps below, which can go through one or more iterations.

- The user submits an initial query.
- Search engine returns an initial set of results.
- The user marks some of these results as relevant or optionally nonrelevant.

- The system produces a better specification of user information need based on the user relevance feedback.
- Search engine returns the revised results based on the new specification.

Some algorithms are proposed to implement relevant feedback in [4, 5]. These algorithms show that relevant feedback can significantly improve precision and recall. The method is based on this idea that despite the user inability to issue an adequate and suitable query for information need, it is easy for him/her to judge a particular document for relevant but in a web search engine, it is difficult to encourage people to judge resulted documents [6].

As mentioned earlier, query expansion is the process of supplying the original users' queries with additional suitable terms. There are two key elements for applying a query expansion method; resource from which the expanding terms is chosen and the algorithm employed for choosing these terms [7]. In this paper, resource is the set of relevant documents selected by the user in relevant feedback process and the algorithm is based on latent semantic analysis.

The proposed method tries to choose the suitable words from relevant documents selected by the user based on latent semantic analysis and then this method is evaluated on the Google search engine and is compared to the Rocchio relevant feedback.

1.1. Latent Semantic Analysis

Latent semantic analysis (LSA) is a mathematical technique for uncovering the underlying topic structure of documents. LSA is one of the most important methods for semantic retrieval [8]. It has been employed for the first time for information retrieval by Deerwester et al in 1990 [9] as an efficient technique to deal with polysemy and synonymy problem in information retrieval and quickly become popular. It is a widely used technique in knowledge discovery and representation, cognitive science, machine learning and many other areas. Some recent applications of LSA are topic detection [10], text summarization [11], FAQ retrieval [12] and text clustering. Wei and Park use LSA along with genetic algorithm for text clustering. In this work, LSA is employed to reduce feature space so as to be appropriate for application of genetic algorithm [13]. Research [14] similarly uses LSA for dimensionality reduction. This work uses back-propagation neural networks for text categorization and for reducing the problem of slow training speed of this method, employs the LSA's capability of

reducing dimensionality along with improving performance. Cohen et al employ LSA to construct a semantic space in which semantic associations between psychiatric terms are uncovered and these associations are used to segment and extract clinical concepts from psychiatric narrative [15]. Another recent paper introduces a method with combination of LSA and hidden Markov model for topic segmentation. In this paper, LSA is used for calculating similarity of a vocabulary term and a given topic term. These measurements then use as HMM emission probabilities [16].

LSA is not an artificial intelligence program; instead, it uses singular value decomposition (SVD) which is a matrix-analytical method to find base components space. Let X be a rectangular m by n matrix, SVD decomposes it into 3 matrixes as below:

$$X = USV^T$$

Where S is an n by n diagonal matrix containing singular values of X and U is an m by n matrix, whose columns are right singular vectors of X. V^T is an n by n matrix rows of which are left singular vectors of X. These singular vectors are taken geometrically as coordinates of the new n dimensional space. Singular values and their associated singular vectors are sorted in descending order of significance.

In information retrieval, X is term-document matrix, and each row of which is a term and each column is a document. Each entry of this matrix like x_{ij} indicates the weight of term i in document j. Weights are calculated based on TF-IDF.

2. Proposed method

According to many researches about web users' behavior, most users in the Web issue queries in the length of one term. The average of query length is 2 to 3 terms [17, 18]. These short queries can easily lead to conflict and inappropriate results. On the other hand, experienced users provide search engines with longer queries [19] and successful searches are performed with longer queries than unsuccessful searches. Query expansion with adding some appropriate terms to the initial user query can assist search engines to improve search performance and user satisfaction.

The proposed method consists of three steps: 1) User initial search, 2) User relevance feedback and 3) Query expansion. In the first step, user issue the initial query based on his/her knowledge and needed information. In the relevant feedback step, the user selects 5 relevant documents from the results of an initial search. As mentioned earlier, users often search topics of the domains of their information need and ignore the other related terms of the domain. A relevant document collection can be used to extract other terms, which can be useful in producing more relevant results. The relevant document collection can be considered as a context for the original query terms. Each word in natural languages has several meanings and it is the context that determines which meaning of the word should be considered. A whole document is not a suitable choice for the context. Because a document consists of several topics and two words or terms are in the same context if they appear within a close neighborhood. Therefore, each document is divided into several windows in identical lengths. For preserving the sequence relationship of the words of the two successive windows, each window overlaps half of its next window.

The vector space model is applied to each window and a term-window matrix is constructed. LSA is applied to the matrix and $U \times S$ is calculated. Now, in the semantic space, the projected terms should be clustered. Each cluster is called topic cluster.

As mentioned earlier, latent semantic analysis uses SVD to decompose the term-document matrix X into three matrices U, S and V. Columns of U and V are singular vectors of X, which can be taken as dimensions of the semantic (topic) space. Each row of U associates with a term of vocabulary and $Y = U \times S$ is the projection of term by document matrix X in the topic space. Each dimension can be looked as a topic and each entry of matrix Y like y_{ij} is the importance of term i in topic j. With assigning each query to the topic, which has most influence in, some cluster of terms are constructed which specify each topic and are called as topic clusters.

The original user query is tokenized and stop words are removed to construct the set $q0$. Let C_j be a topic cluster and $q0_i$ be a member of set $q0$. And let EQ be an empty set.

$$q_{opt} = \{t_i \,|\, q0_i \in C_j \,\&\, t_i \in C_j\}$$

For each term $q0_i$ from vocabulary, t_i it is a member of vocabulary, and C_j is the topic cluster which q0$_i$ is assigned, and then all members of C_j are added to EQ. In some cases, the number of EQ's member may be large. In such cases, it is necessary to select some terms from EQ as extensions of original query. The global weights of terms is suitable for this aim i.e. m words with largest Global weights are selected to add to the original query. Global weight of each term is the number of selected relevant documents, which the term appears in.

2.1. Evaluation

The aim of the query expansion is increasing users' satisfaction. In many papers, precision and recall are used to evaluate the proposed information retrieval system. Precision is calculated at standard recall levels and then the precision-recall curve is interpolated. This procedure is performed for each test query and then the average is calculated over the test set of queries. Precision is the proportion of retrieved relevant documents over the whole retrieved documents and recall is the proportion of relevant retrieved documents over the whole relevant documents.

We cannot properly evaluate the users' satisfaction by this measure. One of the key elements of users' satisfaction is the rank of relevant documents in the resulted list. Users want to reach the best relevant document as soon as possible while browsing on the result pages is a boring and time consuming activity, which leads to dissatisfaction. Precision and recall do not consider this key element.

Another issue about the precision and recall is invisibility of not retrieved documents of the users to judgment. Some evaluation methods free of these problems has been introduced by researchers. One of these methods is binary preferences (Bpref) introduced by Beer and Moens in 2004 [20] as below:

$$Bpref = \frac{1}{R}\sum_r 1 - \frac{|N_r|}{R}$$

Where R is the number of relevant documents, N_r is a member of first R irrelevant documents ranked higher than the relevant document r.

For evaluating an information retrieval technique on the web, the number of result pages, which is considered, must be identified. The number of result pages viewed by the users is investigated in much research. Some research reveals that most users view only the first result page of the search engine. Jansen et al in an investigation on Excite search engine in 2000 found that 58 percent of users view only the first result page [21]. 19 percent view first two pages and 10 percent view the first three pages of result pages. Jansen and Spink in their research on search engine in 2003 appeared that 54 percent of users view first page, 19.3 percent first and second pages of result pages [22]. This percentage for research of Jansen et al which is performed on AltaVista search engine in 2005 are 72 percent for first page and 13 percent for first two pages [23]. Based on the above research, most users view only first and second pages of result pages. Therefore, the evaluation of user satisfaction on a search engine is taken into account in this paper.

3. Experimental result

Table 1. Example of proposed method's results

Original query	Expanded query by the proposed method	Bpref
Rose hybridization	Rose hybridization roses plants varieties cross process	0.5
Photography	Photography digital camera home articles techniques light	0.91
Owl wings	Owl wings feathers wing air sound prey	0.87

From the retrieved documents, five relevant documents are selected by the users in relevant feedback step. The LSA is applied on these relevant documents; expansion terms are selected and returned to the user. The user judges resulted documents of expanded query as the initial query results and Bpref is calculated for each new query. Results of the evaluation for some sample queries are reported in Table 1.

Rocchio algorithm [4] is the Standard relevant feedback algorithm. Refined query in this algorithm is calculated as below

$$q_m = \alpha q_0 + \beta \frac{1}{|D_r|} \sum_{d_j \in D_r} d_j - \gamma \frac{1}{|D_{nr}|} \sum_{d_j \in D_{nr}} d_j$$

Where α, β, γ are constant values attached to each term as its weight, d_j is a retrieved document, D_r is

The proposed method has been evaluated on a test set of queries issued by participated users. Users are asked for issuing their initial queries and then judgment of resulted documents on the first two result pages as relevant or irrelevant. Bpref is calculated based on this judgment for each query.

the set of selected relevant documents and D_{nr} is the set of selected irrelevant documents.

This algorithm can run more than one time but as reported in the literature, the most effective iteration is the first and other iterations do not improve the results significantly. This algorithm is implemented and has been applied on each test query. The user has judged results and Bperf has been calculated for each query. The results are reported in Table 2.

The average of Bpref on the test queries issued by the users is calculated for initial queries, Rocchio-resulted queries and produced queries of the proposed method. These values are displayed in Table 3 for comparison.

Table 2. Example of Rocchio method's results

Original query	Expanded query by the Rocchio method	Bpref
Rose hybridization	Rose hybridization roses plant seeds seed garden	0.64
Photography	Photography digital photos tips photo camera px	0.33
Owl wings	Owl wings Knoxville comments feathers owls published	0.75

Table 3. Mean Bpref for results of the considered methods

Method	Without query expansion	Query expansion by the proposed method	Query expansion by the Rocchio method
Bpref	0.43	0.76	0.59

Bpref value for the proposed method is the most. This method significantly improves user satisfaction. This improvement is dependent on improving both precision and ranking of relevant documents as shown in Table 4 for a sample query. In an equal condition with the proposed method i.e. equal number of selected relevant documents in relevant feedback step and equal number of expansion terms, cannot improve Bpref.

With more selected relevant documents, Rocchio algorithm may produce better results, but the

relevant feedback step is time consuming and very boring for the impatient web users and selecting the larger number of documents intensifies the problem. Rocchio algorithm despite increment of precision and recall theoretically, does not provide any guarantee to higher rank the relevant documents than irrelevant ones. On the web, user satisfaction is highly dependent on showing more relevant documents first. Proposed terms by the Rocchio algorithm are more general terms and lead to a broader query while the proposed method select more special terms and therefore a narrower query and better-ranked results. Difference between the proposed method and the Rocchio method results has tested for statistical significance by the paired t-test. The proposed method passed the test in the 95% level of significance.

The proposed algorithm does not necessarily select terms, which are more frequent. This algorithm selects the terms, which have similar frequency pattern to the user initial query terms in the selected relevant set of documents. For term selection, this method brings into account the number of relevant documents, which the word is appeared in too and as showed by the results, this method produce narrower queries and increases user satisfaction.

Table 4. An example of effect of the considered method on search results relevancy evaluated by the users

	Relevancy		
Method	Original	Rocchio	Proposed method
Query	Photography	Photography digital photos tips photo camera px	Photography digital camera home articles techniques light
Rank			
1	0	1	1
2	0	0	1
3	1	0	1
4	0	0	1
5	1	1	1
6	0	0	1
7	0	1	1
8	0	1	1
9	1	0	1
10	0	0	0
11	1	0	0
12	0	0	0
13	0	1	0
14	0	1	0
15	0	0	1
16	1	1	1
17	0	0	1
18	0	0	0
19	1	1	0
20	0	1	1
# Of relevant	6	9	12
Bpref	0.2	0.33	0.91

4. Conclusion

A new method of the query expansion has been introduced which analyzes frequency patterns of terms in the relevant documents selected by users from retrieved documents on an initial search based on users' original query. Based on this analysis, some topic clusters are constructed and the number of terms with the largest global weights is selected for adding to the original query. Resulted queries are evaluated based on Bpref measure which consider ranking of the retrieved documents along with the number of retrieved relevant documents for assessing users' satisfaction. The proposed method is compared to the Rocchio relevant feedback. This comparison shows that the proposed method produces queries more relevant to the user's information need and causes the lager number and higher ranking of the relevant documents. Therefore this method improves the user satisfaction significantly with little number of selected relevant documents.

References should be aligned with the journal style!!!

References

[1] Mandala R., Tokunaga T., Tanaka H., (2000). Query expansion using heterogeneous thesauri, Information Processing & Management, Volume 36, Issue 3, 1 May, Pages 361-378.

[2] Zazo A. F., Figuerola C. G., Alonso Berrocal J. L., Rodríguez E., (2005). Reformulation of queries using similarity thesauri, Information Processing & Management, Volume 41, Issue 5, September, Pages 1163-1173.

[3] Rocchio J., Relevance feedback in information retrieval. In: Salton G, ed. (1971). The Smart Retrieval System - Experiments in Automatic Document Processing", Prentice-Hall, Englewood Cli_s, NJ.pp. 313-323.

[4] Christopher D. Manning, Prabhakar Raghavan, Hinrich Schütze, (2009). An Introduction to Information Retrieval, Cambridge University Press.

[5] Efthimis E., (2010). Query Expansion. In Williams, Martha E. (Ed.), "Annual Review of Information Systems and Technologies (ARIST)", v31, pp 121-187.

[6] Valle-Lisboa J. C., Mizraji E., (2007). The uncovering of hidden structures by Latent Semantic Analysis", Information Sciences, Volume 177, Issue 19, 1 October, Pages 4122-4147

[7] Deerwester, S., Dumais, S. T., Landauer, T. K., Furnas, G. W., & Beck, L. (1998). Improving information retrieval with latent semantic indexing. In Proceedings of the 51st annual meeting of the American society for information science, Vol. 25 (pp. 36–40).

[8] Masafumi Hamamoto, Hiroyuki Kitagawa, Jia-Yu Pan, Christos Faloutsos, (2005). A Comparative Study of Feature Vector-Based Topic Detection Schemes",Proceeding WIRI '05 Proceedings of the International Workshop on Challenges in Web Information Retrieval and Integration.

[9] Jen-Yuan Yeh, Hao-Ren Ke, Wei-Pang Yang, and I-Heng Meng, (2005). Text summarization using a trainable summarizer and latent semantic analysis", Information Processing & Management Volume 41, Issue 1, January, Pages 75-95.

[10] Harksoo Kim, Hyunjung Lee, Jungyun Seo, (2007). A reliable FAQ retrieval system using a query log classification technique based on latent semantic analysis, Information Processing & Management Volume 43, Issue 2, March, Pages 420-430.

[11]- Wei Song, Soon Cheol Park, (2009). Genetic algorithm for text clustering based on latent semantic indexing", Computers & Mathematics with Applications, Volume 57, Issues 11-12, June, Pages 1901-1907.

[12] Bo Yu, Zong-ben Xu, Cheng-hua Li, (2008). Latent semantic analysis for text categorization using neural network", Knowledge-Based Systems, Volume 21, Issue 8, December, Pages 900-904.

[13] Trevor Cohen, Brett Blatter, Vimla Patel, (2008). Simulating expert clinical comprehension: Adapting latent semantic analysis to accurately extract clinical concepts from psychiatric narrative, Journal of Biomedical Informatics, Volume 41, Issue 6, December, Pages 1070-1087.

[14] Filip Ginter, Hanna Suominen, Sampo Pyysalo, Tapio Salakoski, (2009). Combining hidden Markov models and latent semantic analysis for topic segmentation and labeling: Method and clinical application", International Journal of Medical Informatics, Volume 78, Issue 12, December, Pages e1-e6.

[15] Silverstein, C., Henzinger, M., Marais, H. and Moricz, M. (1999). Analysis of a very large web search engine query log. SIGIR Forum, 33(1), 6-12.

[16] Aula, A. (2003). Query Formulation in Web Information Search" Proc. IADIS WWW/Internet 2003, 403-410.

[18]- Buckley, C. and Voorhees, E. (2004). Retrieval evaluation with incomplete judgements", In Proceedings of SIGIR.

[19] Freund, L. & Toms, E.G. (2006). Enterprise search behavior of software engineers. Proc. SIGIR, 645-646

[20] Buckley, C. and Voorhees, E. (2004). Retrieval evaluation with incomplete judgements. In Proceedings of SIGIR.

[21] Bernard J. Jansen, Amanda Spink, Tefko Saracevic, (2000). Real life, real users, and real needs: a study and analysis of user queries on the web, Information Processing & Management Vol. 36, Issue 2, 1 March, Pages 207-227.

[22] Jansen BJ, Spink A. (2003). An Analysis of Web Documents Retrieved and Viewed. Fourth International Conference on Internet Computing; 2003; Las Vegas, Nevada. p. 65-9.

[23] Bernard J. Jansen, Amanda Spink, Jan Pedersen, (2005). A Temporal Comparison of AltaVista Web Searching, Journal of the American Society for Information Science & Technology, Vol. 56, No. 6, pp. 559-570.

7

Feature extraction of hyperspectral images using boundary semi-labeled samples and hybrid criterion

M. Imani and H. Ghassemian[*]

Faculty of Electrical and Computer Engineering, Tarbiat Modares University, Tehran, Iran.

[*]Corresponding author: ghassemi@modares.ac.ir (H. Ghassemian).

Abstract

Feature extraction is a very important preprocessing step for classification of hyperspectral images. The linear discriminant analysis (LDA) method fails to work in small sample size situations. Moreover, LDA has a poor efficiency for non-Gaussian data. LDA is optimized by a global criterion. Thus, it is not sufficiently flexible to cope with the multi-modal distributed data. In this work, we propose a new feature extraction method, which uses the boundary semi-labeled samples for solving small sample size problems. The proposed method, called the hybrid feature extraction based on boundary semi-labeled samples (HFE-BSL), uses a hybrid criterion that integrates both the local and global criteria for feature extraction. Thus, it is robust and flexible. The experimental results with one synthetic multi-spectral and three real hyperspectral images show the good efficiency of HFE-BSL compared to some popular and state-of-the-art feature extraction methods.

Keywords: *Feature Extraction, Hyperspectral Image, Boundary Samples, Hybrid Criterion, Classification.*

1. Introduction

Hyperspectral imaging has many applications in different fields [1,2]. Analysis of hyperspectral images has a lot of challenges. For instance, due to the impact of the sensor's instantaneous field-of-view and the diversity of the land-cover classes, the presence of mixed pixels is possible. By converting the abundance map into a higher resolution image, the subpixel mapping technique can specify the spatial distribution of different categories at the subpixel scale. In [47], an adaptive subpixel mapping method based on a maximum a posteriori (MAP) model and a winner-take-all class determination strategy has been proposed to improve the accuracy of the subpixel mapping. Classification is one of the most important tasks in a hyperspectral image analysis. The objective of the hyperspectral image classification is to associate each pixel with a proper label [3, 4]. Increasing the spectral bands provided by the hyperspectral imaging technology has brought new potentials and challenges to data analysis. Classification can be done supervised or unsupervised. The unsupervised classification methods are used to solve the site labeling problems without the need for labeled samples. An unsupervised artificial immune classifier has been proposed in [48], which possesses biological properties such as clonal selection, immune network, and immune memory in addition to nonlinear classification properties. Hyperspectral images provide a valuable source of spectral information for class discrimination with lots of details [5]. On the other hand, in order to fully utilize the information contained in the increased features, a large number of training samples is required for the supervised classification of hyperspectral images. Unfortunately, obtaining the training samples is generally expensive and difficult. When the number of training samples is small compared to the number of features, the Hughes phenomenon occurs [6].

Parametric classifiers such as the maximum likelihood (ML) classifier model the probability density functions for individual classes. So, they are often ineffective for the classification of high dimensional data. In order to mitigate the curse of dimensionality and degrade the small sample size problem, there are various ways such as the use of semi-supervised classifiers [8], and non-parametric classifiers such as kernel-based classifiers [9], for example, support vector machines (SVMs). Another solution to cope with the large number of spectral bands in hyperspectral images is feature reduction. Feature reduction has three main advantages: improvement in classification accuracy, decreasing the computational cost and better understanding of data [11].

In general, feature reduction methods can be categorized into two groups: feature selection and feature extraction [12-14]. A full review of feature reduction methods has been provided in [15]. In general, a feature extraction algorithm provides a feature subset richer than that obtained using a feature selection technique with a higher cost [16]. Some feature selection methods have been represented in [17-19]. In [49], the authors have been proposed a stochastic search strategy inspired by the clonal selection theory in an artificial immune system, where dimensionality reduction is formulated as an optimization problem that searches an optimum with less number of features in a feature space.

Our main focus in this paper is on the feature extraction. The feature extraction methods are divided into two general groups: the supervised ones and the unsupervised ones. There are a variety of methods mentioned for feature extraction in the literature [20-26]. The most popular supervised feature extraction method is linear discriminant analysis (LDA) [27]. Generalized discriminant analysis (GDA) is the nonlinear extension of LDA [28]. LDA requires a much number of training samples for an accurate estimation of the scatter matrices. Thus, it has no good efficiency in small sample size situations. To cope with this problem, there are different approaches. The first approach is the use of unsupervised methods. The unsupervised feature extraction methods require no training samples [29-31]. However, unsupervised feature extraction methods do not consider the class separability, and so, may not be sufficiently appropriate for feature extraction in the classification applications. The second approach for feature extraction, in small sample size situation, is the use of non-parametric feature extraction methods [32-35]. Some feature extraction methods such as decision boundary feature extraction [36] and supervised feature extraction methods based on neural networks [37] need a large training set, and so, they are not efficient methods in small sample size situations. The third approach to cope with the small sample size problem is the semi-supervised approach that uses the ability of both

the labeled and unlabeled samples. Semi-supervised discriminant analysis (SDA) has been introduced in [38]. In the SDA method, the labeled samples are used to maximize the discriminating power, while the unlabeled samples are used to maximize the locality preserving power. Some other feature extraction and classification methods to solve the small sample size problem have been proposed in [50]-[53].

LDA is optimized by the global criterion where similarities are measured by distances between the samples and the sample mean vector. Global criterion-based methods such as LDA may perform poorly with multi-modal distributed data. In other words, they only work well with uni-modal distributed samples. In our proposed feature extraction method, the local criterion is added to the global criterion for a discriminant analysis. In the local criterion, similarities are measured by distances between the neighboring pairs. In comparison with the global criterion, the local criterion can treat well with multi-modal distributed data and make it more flexible than the global one. However, the local criterion-based algorithm has a weaker robustness than the global one. The local criterion-based algorithm is more complex than the global one, and hence, more prone to overfitting. In general, the global criterion-based feature extraction method has a stronger robustness and a weaker flexibility, while the local one has a stronger flexibility and a weaker robustness.

In this paper, we use a hybrid criterion that is a combination of the global and local criteria for providing the advantages of both of them. As mentioned earlier, LDA has some difficulties such as the following ones:

- Because of the singularity problem, it does not have good performance in small sample size situations.
- The good performance of LDA is dependent on the Gaussian assumption of data because LDA is optimized by the global criterion, which is robust and non-flexible.

To cope with the difficulties of LDA, we propose a few solutions together. To solve the small sample size problem, we propose to use the high confidence semi-labeled samples. There are three types of samples in an image data. Some samples are labeled-samples, where their labels are obtained by doing field operations or thought of experts. Most samples are unlabeled, and so, it is not specified which class they belong to. The third group is semi-labeled samples.

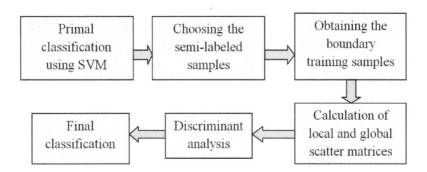

Figure 1. Block diagram of proposed method (HFE-BSL).

These samples are without label before classification. However, their class label is determined after a primal classification. The label of a semi-labeled sample can be correct or incorrect. We add the semi-labeled samples to the original training samples. Then, a useful subset composed of boundary training samples is selected from among a new training set for feature extraction and final classification. The use of this extended training set with relatively high confidence increases the discrimination ability, and so, improves the classification accuracy. To deal with multi-modal data, we combine the local criterion with the global one to provide robustness and flexibility. Using the hybrid criterion, the discriminant analysis works well for more general distributed data. SVM is an appropriate classifier for hyperspectral images [39-42], used effectively in this paper. The novelties of the proposed feature extraction method in this paper are briefly represented as follow:

1) Using SVM as a primal classifier to obtain high confidence semi-labeled samples.

2) Obtaining the boundary training samples.

3) Using a hybrid criterion in the discriminant analysis to obtain both advantages of the local and global criteria.

The remainder of this paper is organized as what follows: The proposed feature extraction method is introduced in section 2. The experimental results are given in section 3. Finally, section 4 concludes the paper.

2. Proposed method
In this section, we introduce the proposed method, hybrid feature extraction based on boundary semi-labeled samples (HFE-BSL). A block diagram of the proposed method is illustrated in Figure 1. We use SVM in three different sections in this paper:

1) SVM as a primal classifier for obtaining high confidence semi-labeled samples.

2) Applying SVM to the new training set (original training plus semi-labeled samples) to obtain SVs and use them as boundary training samples.

3) SVM as a final classifier for obtaining the final classification map (any other classifier can also be used to provide the final classification map).

2.1 Support vector machine
At first, we consider two class linearly separable states. Let $x_i \in \mathbb{R}^d, i = 1, 2, \dots, N_t$ be the training set where d is the number of bands or dimensions of the dataset, and N_t denotes the number of overall training samples. These training samples belong to either of the classes w_1, and w_2. The corresponding class labels are denoted as $y_i \in \{\mp 1\}$. The goal is to design a hyperplane $g(x) = w^T x + w_0$ that classifies all training sample correctly and leaves the maximum margin from both classes. The following quadratic optimization problem has to be solved:

$$\min J\left(w, w_0\right) = \frac{1}{2}\|w\|^2 \; subject\,to\; y_i\left(w^T x_i + w_0\right) \ge 1, \quad (1)$$

$$i = 1, 2, \dots, N_t$$

In order to solve this optimization problem, the Lagrangian function is defined as:

$$L\left(w, w_0, \lambda\right) = \frac{1}{2} w^T w - \sum_{i=1}^{N_t} \lambda_i \left[y_i \left(w^T x_i + w_0\right) - 1\right] \quad (2)$$

where λ is a vector consisting of the Lagrange multipliers, λ_i. The Lagrange multipliers are zero or positive. Feature vectors (x_i) that are associative with non-zero Lagrange multipliers $(\lambda_i \neq 0)$ are known as support vectors (SVs). SVs lie on either of the two separating hyperplanes: $w^T x + w_0 = \mp 1$. In other words, SVs are a subset of training samples that are located at the boundary between classes. Therefore, SVs can be considered as boundary training samples, and thus, they are a useful subset of training samples for class discrimination. To allow some training errors for generalization, the slack variables and the associated regularization parameter can be used for non-separable classes. If data cannot be linearly separated, the kernel trick is used to project data into a higher dimensional feature space.

2.2 Production of semi-labeled samples

In the first step of HFE-BSL, we obtain the high confidence semi-labeled samples. Semi-labeled samples are samples whose labels are not known at first and are determined after an initial classification. The collection of reliable training samples is very expensive in terms of time and finance, and it is not common to exploit large ground truth information. To address this issue, the kernel methods such as SVMs have been widely used due to their insensitivity to the curse of dimensionality. They have a high ability to perform with limited training sets, and so they can significantly help in addressing ill-posed problems based on limited training samples. Therefore, in this work, we use SVM for the determination of high confidence semi-labeled samples.

After an initial classification, using original training samples, we randomly choose n_{sl} semi-labeled samples in each class. To have the fair behavior with all classes, we select the same number of semi-labeled samples from all classes. Moreover, to obtain a more classification accuracy, it is appropriate to select much number of semi-labeled samples. To reach this purpose, the maximum number of semi-labeled samples that can be selected is obtained as follows:

$$n_{sl} = \min_{i=1,\ldots,c} n_i \qquad (3)$$

where n_i is the number of samples to which the class i label is assigned in the primary classification.

2.3 Obtaining boundary training samples

After production of semi-labeled samples with relatively high confidence in the first step, we add them to the original training samples. Let n_t be the number of original training samples and $n_{ct} = n_{sl} + n_t$ denote the number of new training samples (original training samples plus semi-labeled samples). To increase the classification accuracy, we only use a useful subset of new training samples that play an important role in class discrimination. This useful subset consists of the training samples that are located at the

boundary between classes. We train SVM using a new training set, consisting of the original and semi-labeled samples, to obtain SVs from them. In linear SVM, SVs are the samples that are located at the separating hyperplanes: $w^T x + w_0 = \mp 1$. In non-linear SVM, SVs are located within margins where $0 \le y_i(w^T x_i + w_0) < 1$ or in the opposite margins where $y_i(w^T x_i + w_0) < 0$. However, the use of SVs as boundary training samples increases the class discrimination. The obtained training subset, composed of SVs, is used for calculation of between-class and within-class scatter matrices in the discriminant analysis.

2.4 Discriminant analysis with hybrid criterion

After obtaining the boundary training samples, we use them for calculation of global and local scatter matrices as follows:

$$S_w^g = \sum_{k=1}^{c} \left(\sum_{i=1}^{n_k} \left(x_{i,k} - m_k \right) \left(x_{i,k} - m_k \right)^T \right) \qquad (4)$$

$$S_b^g = \sum_{k=1}^{c} n_k \left(m_k - m \right) \left(m_k - m \right)^T \qquad (5)$$

$$S_w^l = \sum_{k=1}^{c} \left(\sum_{i=1}^{n_k} \left(\sum_{x_+ \in N_{k_1}^+(x_{i,k})} \left(x_{i,k} - x_+ \right) \left(x_{i,k} - x_+ \right)^T \right) \right) \qquad (6)$$

$$S_b^l = \sum_{k=1}^{c} \left(\sum_{i=1}^{n_k} \left(\sum_{x_- \in N_{k_2}^-(x_{i,k})} \left(x_{i,k} - x_- \right) \left(x_{i,k} - x_- \right)^T \right) \right) \qquad (7)$$

where, S_w^g, S_b^g, S_w^l, and S_b^l are the global within-class, global between-class, local within-class, and local between-class scatter matrices, respectively. n_k denotes the number of boundary training samples, or SVs, in the kth class, m_k is the mean of SVs in kth class, m is the mean of entire SVs and $x_{i,k}$ is the ith SV in the kth class. $N_{k_1}^+(x_{i,k})$ is the set of k_1 nearest neighbours of $x_{i,k}$ that have the same class label as $x_{i,k}$, $N_{k_2}^-(x_{i,k})$ is the set of k_2 nearest neighbours of $x_{i,k}$ that have different class labels, and x_+ and x_- denote the element of $N_{k_1}^+(x_{i,k})$ and $N_{k_2}^-(x_{i,k})$, respectively. We define the hybrid within-class scatter matrix $\left(S_w^h \right)$ and the hybrid between-class scatter matrix $\left(S_b^h \right)$ as follow:

$$S_w^h = \alpha S_w^g + \left(1 - \alpha \right) S_w^l \qquad (8)$$

$$S_b^h = \alpha S_b^g + \left(1 - \alpha \right) S_b^l \qquad (9)$$

where $\alpha \in [0,1]$ is a non-negative parameter for providing a trade-off between the global and local terms. $\alpha = 1$ is equivalent to the traditional LDA (that includes just the global information). Moreover, by considering $\alpha = 0$, just the local information is included in the discriminant analysis. A favorable compromise between robustness and flexibility can be gained by choosing a proper value for the parameter α. An appropriate value for α can be found by searching over the nonnegative values in $[0,1]$. The projection matrix of HFE-BSL is composed of the eigenvectors $S_w^{h^{-1}} S_b^h$.

3. Experimental results

We used one synthetic multi-spectral dataset and three real hyperspectral images in our experiments. The objective of the experiments with the synthetic data is assessment and characterization of the proposed method in a fully controlled environment, whereas the objective of the experiments with real datasets is to compare the performance of the proposed method with other methods in the literature. A synthetic image with 80×120 pixels was generated. The synthetic scene has eight classes that contain linear mixtures of a set of spectral signatures randomly selected from a digital spectral library compiled by U.S. Geological Survey (USGS), which is available online in "http://speclab.cr.usgs.gov/spectral-lib.html". The USGS library contains spectral plots for nearly 500 materials in the 400-2500 nm spectral range, where the bands have been convolved to the number of bands available for Airborne Visible Infra-Red Imaging Spectrometers (AVIRIS) that comprises 224 spectral bands.

The first real hyperspectral dataset is the Indian pines image that was acquired by AVIRIS. This agriculture image consists of 145×145 pixels and 16 classes, 10 classes of it which were chosen for our experiments. This image comprises 224 spectral bands in the wavelength range from 0.4 to 2.5 μm, nominal spectral resolution of 10 nm, and spatial resolution of 20 m by pixel. The water absorption bands were then deleted, resulting in 200 bands. The second dataset is the University of Pavia that was acquired by Reflective Optics System Imaging Spectrometer (ROSIS). This urban image contains 9 classes and 610×340 pixels, with a spatial resolution of 1.3 m per pixel. The number of spectral bands in the original recorded image is 115 (with a spectral range from 0.43 to 0.86 μm). 12 noisy bands were removed, and the remaining 103 bands were used for the experiments. The Salinas scene is the third dataset used, which was acquired by AVIRIS. It was taken at low altitude with a pixel size of 3.7 m. It

consists of 16 classes and 512×217 pixels. It contains 224 spectral bands from 0.4 to 2.5 μm, with a nominal spectral resolution of 10 nm. In this dataset, 20 water absorption bands were removed and 204 bands remained. In this section, we evaluated the efficiency of HFE-BSL in comparison with LDA, SDA, and GDA. We used some measures for the classification evaluation. Accuracy and reliability are defined as follow:

$$ACC_i = \frac{\gamma_i}{A} \tag{10}$$

$$REL_i = \frac{\gamma_i}{B} \tag{11}$$

where, ACC_i and REL_i are the accuracy and reliability of the ith class, respectively. γ_i is the number of testing samples that are correctly classified, A is the total testing samples of class i, and B is the total samples labeled as class i. We used the average accuracy (AA), overall accuracy (OA), and average reliability (AR) for evaluation of the classification accuracy, which are calculated as follow:

$$AA = \frac{1}{c} \sum_{i=1}^{c} ACC_i \tag{12}$$

$$AR = \frac{1}{c} \sum_{i=1}^{c} REL_i \tag{13}$$

$$OA = \frac{\sum_{i=1}^{c} \gamma_i}{D} \tag{14}$$

where, D is the total number of testing samples. We used four classifiers to obtain the final classification maps: SVM, ML, 1-nearest-neighbor (1NN), and distance-weighted discrimination (DWD) [7], [10]. We implemented SVM with the radial basis function (RBF) kernel. The use of RBF kernel is a common choice, because it has less numerical difficulties, and it is easy to be tuned. In addition, the RBF kernel is a universal kernel and includes the other valid kernels as particular cases. We used the Library for Support Vector Machines (LIBSVM) tool for the implementation of SVM [43]. The one-against-one multi-class classification algorithm was used in the experiments. The SVM parameters were set as follow: the penalty parameter C was tested between $[10-1000]$ with a step size increment of 20, and γ parameter of the RBF kernel was tested between $[0.1-2]$ with a step size increment of 0.1. The best values were obtained using a 5-fold cross-validation approach.

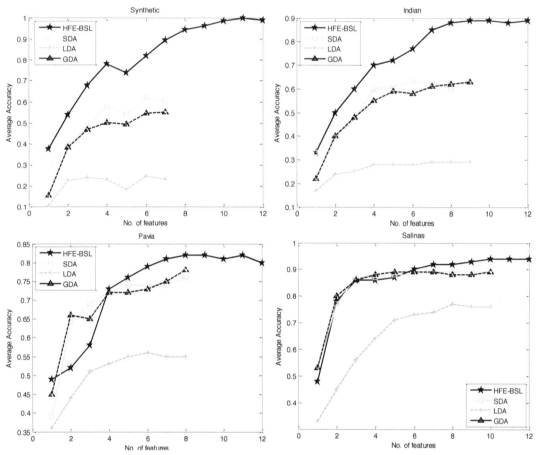

Figure 2. Classification accuracy versus number of extracted features using SVM classifier and 16 training samples.

The training samples were chosen randomly from the entire of the scene, and the remaining samples were used as the testing data. Due to the random selection of training samples, each experiment was repeated 10 times, and the average results were reported. The same training samples were used for all methods to obtain a fair comparison. We considered $\alpha = 0.5$ in our experiments to have both the robustness and flexibility as the same. The classification accuracies versus the number of extracted features, obtained by the SVM classifier and 16 original training samples, for synthetic, Indian, Pavia and Salinas datasets are shown in Figure 2. The accuracies and reliabilities for each class of Indian dataset obtained by the SVM classifier, 9 extracted features and 16 original training samples are represented in Table 1. Moreover, the average accuracy, average reliability, overall accuracy, and execution time for all the compared methods are reported in this table. This type of table, obtained by 16 original training samples, is given for Pavia with 8 extracted features (see Table 2) and for Salinas with 10 extracted features (see Table 3). The comparison of execution times, which are reported in Tables 1-3, show that the proposed method has more computation time than the other feature extraction methods. This is

expected, because the proposed method uses the SVM classifier at least two times: the first time, to obtain the initial classification map for providing the semi-labeled samples, and the second time, to obtain SVs as boundary samples. The ground truth map (GTM) and the classification maps of synthetic (with 7 extracted features), Indian (with 9 extracted features), Pavia (with 8 extracted features), and Salinas (with 10 extracted features) are shown in Figures 3-6, respectively.

The classification results obtained using different classifiers (SVM, ML, 1NN, DWD) with feature extracted by HFE-BSL, LDA, SDA, GDA and also using the original features (without feature extraction) are reported in Table 4. This table provides the highest average classification accuracies achieved by four classifiers and 16 original training samples. The numbers in the parentheses represent the number of features achieving the highest average accuracies in the experiments. For example the entry in the first column and the second row of Table 4, 92.34 ± 1.08 (6), means that the highest classification accuracy, which is obtained by the HFE-BSL feature extraction method and ML classifier, is provided by 6 extracted features and is equal to 92.34 with a standard deviation of 1.08.

Table 1. Accuracies and reliabilities obtained for each class of Indian dataset using 9 extracted features and 16 training samples.

	Class		HFE-BSL		SDA		LDA		GDA	
No	Name of class	# samples	Acc.	Rel.	Acc.	Rel.	Acc.	Rel.	Acc.	Rel.
1	Corn-no till	1434	0.83	0.77	0.56	0.45	0.19	0.30	0.62	0.49
2	Corn-min till	834	0.85	0.60	0.41	0.48	0.33	0.16	0.39	0.44
3	Grass/pasture	497	0.99	0.93	0.89	0.49	0.29	0.39	0.73	0.45
4	Grass/trees	747	0.99	0.98	0.68	0.77	0.36	0.18	0.74	0.80
5	Hay-windrowed	489	1.00	1.00	0.92	0.97	0.49	0.74	0.98	1.00
6	Soybeans-no till	968	0.82	0.69	0.62	0.58	0.34	0.17	0.63	0.43
7	Soybeans-min till	2468	0.61	0.89	0.60	0.69	0.08	0.40	0.49	0.75
8	Soybeans-clean till	614	0.92	0.76	0.42	0.48	0.23	0.11	0.45	0.46
9	Woods	1294	0.92	1.00	0.80	0.92	0.25	0.60	0.70	0.86
10	Bldg-Grass-Tree-Drives	380	1.00	0.80	0.41	0.44	0.31	0.18	0.58	0.44
	Average Accuracy and Average Reliability		0.89	0.84	0.63	0.63	0.29	0.32	0.63	0.61
	Overall Accuracy		0.92		0.83		0.61		0.82	
	Execution Time (s)		42.71		37.60		0.86		12.01	

Table 2. Accuracies and reliabilities obtained for each class of Pavia dataset using 8 extracted features and 16 training samples.

	Class		HFE-BSL		SDA		LDA		GDA	
No	Name of class	# samples	Acc.	Rel.	Acc.	Rel.	Acc.	Rel.	Acc.	Rel.
1	Asphalt	6631	0.83	0.89	0.70	0.88	0.25	0.63	0.69	0.90
2	Meadows	18649	0.71	0.90	0.69	0.84	0.52	0.87	0.61	0.87
3	Gravel	2099	0.71	0.57	0.61	0.46	0.44	0.26	0.72	0.50
4	Trees	3064	0.95	0.82	0.70	0.59	0.80	0.62	0.85	0.65
5	Painted metal sheets	1345	1.00	1.00	0.99	0.92	0.96	1.00	0.99	0.98
6	Bare Soil	5029	0.74	0.43	0.61	0.41	0.72	0.25	0.67	0.36
7	Bitumen	1330	0.85	0.60	0.93	0.49	0.29	0.17	0.89	0.46
8	Self-Blocking Bricks	3682	0.61	0.73	0.64	0.70	0.24	0.40	0.62	0.69
9	Shadows	947	1.00	1.00	1.00	1.00	0.71	0.61	1.00	0.97
	Average Accuracy and Average Reliability		0.82	0.77	0.76	0.70	0.55	0.53	0.78	0.71
	Overall Accuracy		0.89		0.80		0.73		0.82	
	Execution Time (s)		57.94		46.35		1.53		16.83	

Table 3. Accuracies and reliabilities obtained for each class of Salinas using 10 extracted features and 16 training samples.

	Class		HFE-BSL		SDA		LDA		GDA	
No	Name of class	# samples	Acc.	Rel.	Acc.	Rel.	Acc.	Rel.	Acc.	Rel.
1	Brocoli_green_weeds_1	2009	1.00	1.00	0.94	1.00	0.96	0.98	0.90	0.99
2	Brocoli_green_weeds_2	3726	1.00	1.00	0.99	0.96	0.95	0.98	0.98	0.93
3	Fallow	1976	1.00	1.00	0.86	0.85	0.63	0.62	0.96	0.87
4	Fallow_rough_plow	1394	1.00	0.99	0.99	0.98	0.81	0.89	1.00	0.85
5	Fallow_smooth	2678	0.99	1.00	0.93	0.90	0.68	0.76	0.96	0.97
6	Stubble	3959	1.00	1.00	0.96	1.00	0.91	1.00	0.97	1.00
7	Celery	3579	1.00	1.00	0.99	0.97	0.95	1.00	0.99	0.94
8	Grapes_untrained	11271	0.53	0.62	0.54	0.73	0.50	0.68	0.52	0.70
9	Soil_vineyard_develop	6203	0.98	0.99	0.96	0.98	0.65	0.94	0.99	0.99
10	Corn_senesced_green_weeds	3278	0.98	0.96	0.79	0.81	0.82	0.38	0.79	0.89
11	Lettuce_romaine_4weeks	1068	1.00	1.00	0.86	0.80	0.80	0.94	0.84	0.96
12	Lettuce_romaine_5 weeks	1927	1.00	0.99	0.99	0.82	0.56	0.54	0.99	0.91
13	Lettuce_romaine_6 weeks	916	1.00	1.00	1.00	0.67	0.72	0.48	1.00	0.74
14	Lettuce_romaine_7 weeks	1070	1.00	1.00	0.84	0.92	0.68	0.72	0.84	0.58
15	Vineyard_untrained	7268	0.49	0.40	0.68	0.51	0.58	0.46	0.66	0.51
16	Vineyard_vertical_trellis	1807	1.00	1.00	0.90	0.98	0.91	1.00	0.82	0.95
	Average Accuracy and Average Reliability		0.94	0.93	0.89	0.87	0.76	0.77	0.89	0.86
	Overall Accuracy		0.95		0.91		0.84		0.91	
	Execution Time (s)		73.66		51.11		3.05		21.71	

In addition to SDA, which is a popular semi-supervised feature extraction method, we compared our semi-supervised proposed method with two state-of-the-art semi-supervised feature extraction methods: semi-supervised local discriminant analysis (SELD) [45] and semi-supervised probabilistic principal component analysis (S^{2}PPCA) [46]. The aim of SELD is to find a projection for preserving the local neighborhood information and maximizing the class discrimination of the data. In the SELD method, an unsupervised method (from the class of local linear feature extraction methods such as neighborhood preserving embedding (NPE)) and a supervised method (LDA) are combined without any tuning parameters.

GTM   HFE-BSL   SDA

LDA   GDA

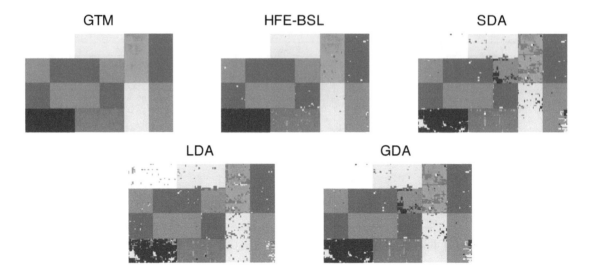

Figure 3. GTM and classification maps for synthetic dataset (16 training samples and 7 extracted features are used).

GTM   HFE-BSL   SDA

LDA   GDA

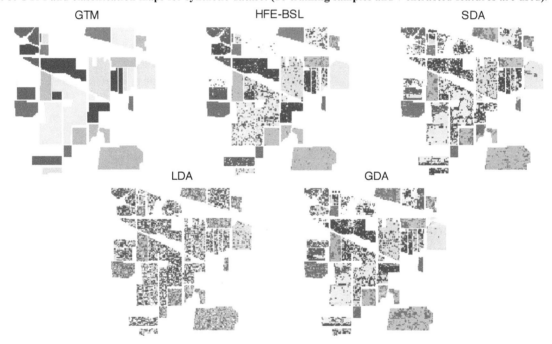

Figure 4. GTM and classification maps for Indian dataset (16 training samples and 9 extracted features are used).

GTM   HFE-BSL   SDA   LDA   GDA

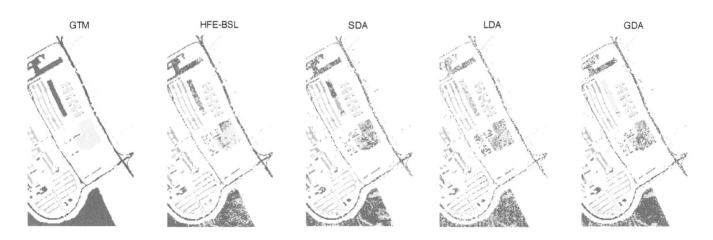

Figure 5. GTM and classification maps for Pavia dataset (16 training samples and 8 extracted features are used).

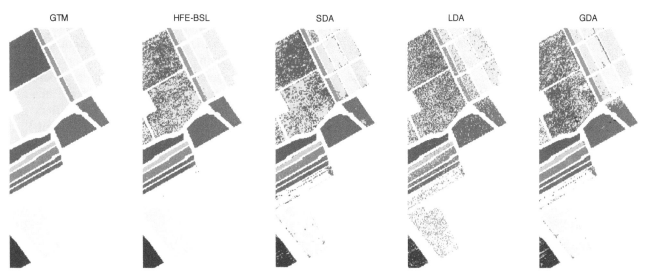

Figure 6. GTM and classification maps for Salinas dataset (16 training samples and 10 extracted features are used).

Table 4. Mean and standard deviation of highest average classification accuracies (numbers in parentheses represent number of features achieving highest average accuracies in experiments).

Dataset	Classifier	HFE-BSL	SDA	LDA	GDA	Original features
Synthetic	SVM	94.21±0.43 (7)	83.34±0.76 (6)	58.12±2.01 (7)	82.13±2.52 (5)	84.32±0.76 (224)
	ML	92.34±1.08 (6)	79.12±1.52 (4)	58.03±3.01 (4)	80.09±2.67 (5)	---
	1NN	93.12±0.98 (6)	80.91±0.92 (7)	59.02±1.05 (6)	81.72±2.60 (6)	84.05±1.07 (224)
	DWD	94.11±0.86 (7)	83.78±0.59 (7)	59.15±2.23 (7)	82.01±1.93 (7)	85.21±0.85 (224)
Indian	SVM	89.40±1.14 (9)	63.12±1.02 (6)	28.92±2.45 (7)	63.15±2.90 (9)	65.23±0.63 (200)
	ML	85.37±1.87 (6)	61.83±2.14 (5)	21.36±3.51 (4)	65.11±2.82 (6)	---
	1NN	87.26±1.51 (7)	64.44±1.18 (5)	25.33±2.38 (8)	63.72±2.45 (6)	61.08±3.10 (200)
	DWD	89.53±1.32 (8)	62.97±1.21 (5)	33.15±2.57 (9)	63.13±2.15 (9)	64.75±0.75 (200)
Pavia	SVM	82.39±0.78 (8)	76.29±0.81 (8)	55.65±1.98 (6)	78.38±2.06 (8)	76.13±0.76 (103)
	ML	79.21±2.01 (4)	78.20±1.93 (4)	55.41±2.61 (5)	73.64±1.64 (6)	---
	1NN	81.04±1.52 (6)	72.79±1.93 (7)	57.43±2.14 (8)	71.17±3.11 (4)	71.49±1.72 (103)
	DWD	81.22±1.49 (5)	74.54±1.03 (8)	59.25±1.86 (7)	78.68±2.01 (7)	77.11±1.13 (103)
Salinas	SVM	93.76±1.13 (10)	89.12±0.77 (7)	76.83±1.98 (8)	89.02±2.43 (5)	87.26±0.84 (204)
	ML	88.47±1.46 (6)	89.61±2.35 (9)	76.13±2.02 (5)	87.02±1.69 (4)	---
	1NN	91.45±1.24 (5)	89.28±1.88 (5)	77.03±1.76 (6)	89.88±1.94 (12)	86.36±2.03 (204)
	DWD	92.45±1.31 (4)	90.03±1.52 (9)	77.74±1.06 (10)	90.45±1.62 (4)	88.43±0.91 (204)

The supervised and unsupervised methods are not linearly combined. In other words, instead of using both the labeled and unlabeled samples together, at first, the samples were divided into two sets: labeled and unlabeled. Then, the labeled samples were employed through the supervised method only, and the unlabeled ones were employed through the unsupervised, locality preserving method only. Thus, the local neighborhood information is preserved inferred from unlabeled samples, while the class discrimination of the data is maximized inferred from the labeled samples. The supervised probabilistic principal component analysis (SPPCA) is the extension of the probabilistic PCA (PPCA) which incorporates the label information into the projection. In addition to the inter-covariance between the inputs and outputs, SPPCA takes into account the intra-covariance of both. S^2PPCA incorporates both the labeled and unlabeled information into the projections. Both SPPCA and S^{2}PPCA use an expectation maximization algorithm to generate the mapping. The experimental results for these methods compared to the others are reported in Table 4.

Moreover, we used the McNemars test to assess the statistical significance of differences in the classification results. The McNemars test is based upon the standardized normal test statistic [44]:

$$Z_{12} = \frac{f_{12} - f_{21}}{\sqrt{f_{12} + f_{21}}} \tag{15}$$

The number of samples correctly by classifier 1 and incorrectly by classifier 2 is denoted by f_{12}. The difference in the accuracy between the classifiers 1 and 2 is said to be statistically significant if $|Z_{12}| > 1.96$. The sign of Z_{12} indicates whether classifier 1 is more accurate than classifier 2 ($Z_{12} > 0$) or vice versa ($Z_{12} < 0$). The results of the McNemars tests for different cases with 16 original training samples are shown in Table 5.

For example, in table (Indian/SVM classifier/9 extracted features), $|Z_{14}| > 0$, means that HFE-BSL is superior to GDA and also because $|Z_{14}| = 37.23 > 1.96$, this difference is significant from the statistical view point.

Because of the singularity of within-class scatter matrix in small sample size situation, LDA had the worst efficiency. The use of kernel trick and the use of semi-supervised approach improved the classification accuracy of GDA and SDA, respectively. One sees from the results obtained that HFE-BSL can provide the highest classification accuracy compared to the other feature extraction methods. Note that the rank of between-class scatter matrix (S_b) is limited in the LDA, GDA, and SDA methods. Thus, these methods can be extract maximum $c - 1$ features. In the proposed method, HFE-BSL, local between-class scatter matrix (S_b^l) has a non-parametric form, and thus, its rank is not limited to the number of classes. Therefore, the rank of the hybrid between-class scatter matrix (S_b^h) is also not limited. Thus, the HFE-BSL method can extract more than $c - 1$ features. In what following, we represent the classification accuracies by SVM, 1NN, and ML trained by original training samples as a baseline. When we use only the original training samples (without any semi-labeled samples) in the proposed method, we name it hybrid feature extraction (HFE). We assessed the effect of training sample size on the classification accuracy. The

classification results were obtained using $n_t = 5, 10, 15, 20$, where n_t is the number of original available training samples. The classification accuracies achieved by different numbers of original training samples, different feature extraction methods, and different classifiers are reported in Tables 6, 7, 8, and 9 for the synthetic, Indian, Pavia, and Salinas datasets respectively.

The most important results can be reviewed as follow:

- The HFE-BSL method provided better classification results compared to the LDA, GDA, SDA, SELD, and S^{2}PPCA methods in terms of classification accuracy (average accuracy, average reliability, and overall accuracy).
- The higher classification accuracy of HFE-BSL compared to other methods was significant from the statistical view point.
- More accurate classification maps (with less noise) were obtained using HFE-BSL.
- The efficiency of the HFE-BSL method was assessed using 4 different classifiers: SVM (a kernel-based learning machine with low sensitivity to the training sample size), ML (a parametric classifier with high sensitivity to the training sample size), NN (a simple nonparametric classifier), and DWD (which avoids data piling, and can give improved generalizability).
- The better performance of HFE-BSL compared to other methods is shown in different numbers of extracted feature and also in different numbers of training samples.

The main advantages of the proposed method can be represented as follow: HFE-BSL uses the ability of SVM, which is a state-of-the-art classifier for high dimensional data with low sensitivity to the training set size, to obtain the semi-labeled samples with high confidence. HFE-BSL uses a rich and useful subset of semi-labeled samples, i.e., boundary samples, to increase the class discrimination. Moreover, the HFE-BSL method can simultaneously provide robustness and flexibility to deal with multi-modal data using both the global and local information for estimation of scatter matrices. The disadvantage of HFE-BSL is its more computation time than the competitor methods such as LDA, GDA, and SDA. This increased elapsed time is due to using SVM at least two times (the first time to obtain the initial classification map for providing the semi-labeled samples, and the second one to obtain SVs as boundary samples).

Table 5. Statistical significance of differences in classification (Z). Each case in table represents Z_{rc}, where r is row and c is column (all tables obtained by 16 training samples).

Indian/SVM classifier/9 extracted features			
	HFE-BSL	SDA	LDA	GDA
HFE-BSL	0	33.50	73.27	37.23
SDA	-33.50	0	52.51	4.72
LDA	-73.27	-52.51	0	-50.13
GDA	-37.23	-4.72	50.13	0

Indian/ML classifier/6 extracted features			
	HFE-BSL	SDA	LDA	GDA
HFE-BSL	0	19.25	55.24	12.41
SDA	-19.25	0	43.17	-5.80
LDA	-55.24	-43.17	0	-46.97
GDA	-12.41	5.80	46.97	0

Indian/1NN classifier/7 extracted features			
	HFE-BSL	SDA	LDA	GDA
HFE-BSL	0	9.23	50.52	9.14
SDA	-9.23	0	45.06	1.62
LDA	-50.52	-45.06	0	-43.37
GDA	-9.14	-1.62	43.37	0

Indian/DWD classifier/8 extracted features			
	HFE-BSL	SDA	LDA	GDA
HFE-BSL	0	44.65	71.30	43.17
SDA	-44.65	0	41.79	-1.06
LDA	-71.30	-41.79	0	-41.70
GDA	-43.17	1.06	41.70	0

Pavia/SVM classifier/8 extracted features			
	HFE-BSL	SDA	LDA	GDA
HFE-BSL	0	2.12	50.51	6.96
SDA	-2.12	0	52.06	8.53
LDA	-50.51	-52.06	0	-46.80
GDA	-6.96	-8.53	46.80	0

Pavia/ML classifier/4 extracted features			
	HFE-BSL	SDA	LDA	GDA
HFE-BSL	0	6.71	57.59	20.10
SDA	-6.71	0	54.35	14.09
LDA	-57.59	-54.35	0	-45.72
GDA	-20.10	-14.09	45.72	0

Pavia/1NN classifier/6 extracted features			
	HFE-BSL	SDA	LDA	GDA
HFE-BSL	0	14.68	59.05	15.78
SDA	-14.68	0	51.92	2.82
LDA	-59.05	-51.92	0	-48.08
GDA	-15.78	-2.82	48.08	0

Pavia/DWD classifier/5 extracted features			
	HFE-BSL	SDA	LDA	GDA
HFE-BSL	0	56.28	106.58	60.73
SDA	-56.28	0	60.71	8.36
LDA	-106.58	-60.71	0	-53.18
GDA	-60.73	-8.36	53.18	0

Salinas/SVM classifier/10 extracted features			
	HFE-BSL	SDA	LDA	GDA
HFE-BSL	0	6.22	46.25	0.27
SDA	-6.22	0	42.14	-5.47
LDA	-46.25	-42.14	0	-45.60
GDA	-0.27	5.47	45.60	0

Salinas/ML classifier/6 extracted features			
	HFE-BSL	SDA	LDA	GDA
HFE-BSL	0	0.53	53.31	1.91
SDA	-0.53	0	37.45	-20.98
LDA	-53.31	-37.45	0	-56.59
GDA	-1.91	20.98	56.59	0

Salinas/1NN classifier/5 extracted features			
	HFE-BSL	SDA	LDA	GDA
HFE-BSL	0	14.93	55.41	19.03
SDA	-14.93	0	46.12	4.06
LDA	-55.41	-46.12	0	-43.53
GDA	-19.03	-4.06	43.53	0

Salinas/DWD classifier/4 extracted features			
	HFE-BSL	SDA	LDA	GDA
HFE-BSL	0	45.18	73.63	45.51
SDA	-45.18	0	44.32	0.42
LDA	-73.63	-44.32	0	-44.19
GDA	-45.51	-0.42	44.19	0

4. Conclusion

We proposed a new feature extraction method in this paper. This method, called HFE-BSL, uses the ability of high confidence semi-labeled samples to cope with the small sample size problems. HFE-BSL uses a useful subset of training samples composed of boundary training samples for increasing the classification accuracy. The proposed feature extraction method combines both the global and local criteria for calculation of scatter matrices in discriminant analysis.

Thus, HFE-BSL is robust and flexible. The experiments carried out using four hyperspectral images indicated the good efficiency of the proposed approach in comparison with some popular and state-of-the-art feature extraction methods in small sample size situations.

The proposed method just uses the rich spectral information and does not consider the valuable spatial information. In the future works, we will try to use the spatial information contained in a neighborhood window to increase the reliability and accuracy of the semi-labeled samples. It is expected that the use of both the spectral and spatial information improves the classification performance.

Table 6. Highest average classification accuracies and their corresponding standard deviations achieved using SVM, ML, 1NN and DWD classifiers with features extracted by HFE-BSL, HFE, SDA, LDA, GDA, and using original features for synthetic dataset. Number in parenthesis represents number of features achieving highest accuracies in experiments.

Feature extraction	Classifier	n_t (the number of original training samples)			
		$n_t = 5$	$n_t = 10$	$n_t = 15$	$n_t = 20$
HFE-BSL	SVM	91.12±0.47(7)	93.31±0.49(7)	94.78±1.05(6)	95.12±0.97(7)
	ML	86.05±1.13(5)	89.54±1.09(5)	90.87±1.67(4)	91.92±1.83(6)
	1NN	89.35±0.98(6)	92.68±0.88(8)	93.38±0.90(9)	93.84±0.64(6)
	DWD	92.13±1.21(8)	93.22±1.32(7)	93.75±1.99(7)	94.98±1.36(7)
HFE	SVM	80.45±0.54(4)	86.46±0.72(6)	90.54±1.01(7)	93.53±1.13(7)
	ML	78.87±1.87(5)	83.65±2.08(5)	89.76±2.54(6)	90.64±1.05(6)
	1NN	80.36±0.99(7)	85.74±1.62(7)	90.34±1.43(7)	92.87±0.98(7)
	DWD	81.07±1.45(7)	86.33±0.86(6)	90.67±1.53(7)	92.54±2.32(7)
SDA	SVM	82.43±1.32(5)	86.18±0.53(5)	89.34±1.02(6)	91.20±1.83(4)
	ML	80.64±1.09(6)	84.56±0.1.76(7)	87.76±1.50(4)	90.67±1.09(4)
	1NN	82.76±2.07(7)	85.76±2.31(6)	88.98±1.09(5)	90.86±1.32(6)
	DWD	83.11±1.98(7)	85.85±1.96(6)	89.54±1.11(7)	91.09±0.98(7)
LDA	SVM	62.13±2.43(6)	74.21±2.11(7)	78.65±1.14(6)	85.52±2.15(7)
	ML	55.09±3.07(7)	68.64±3.011(6)	72.64±2.01(7)	81.98±2.64(7)
	1NN	57.87±2.87(6)	66.38±2.09(6)	73.87±3.73(6)	83.98±3.03(6)
	DWD	61.09±3.08(70	73.65±3.43(7)	77.98±2.52(6)	84.87±2.65(5)
GDA	SVM	80.32±1.98(7)	86.18±1.16(6)	89.14±2.06(5)	90.67±0.86(5)
	ML	79.04±0.98(5)	86.24±2.03(7)	88.24±3.04(6)	89.19±0.98(4)
	1NN	81.09±2.06(6)	87.76±1.07(6)	89.32±2.09(6)	89.02±1.09(6)
	DWD	81.63±1.84(6)	87.02±1.36(7)	89.01±2.76(5)	90.28±0.99(7)
Original features	SVM	82.14±1.94(224)	87.68±1.15(224)	88.02±0.65(224)	90.16±1.53(224)
	ML	---	---	---	---
	1NN	82.35±2.09(224)	87.98±2.35(224)	89.42±1.63(224)	88.75±1.67(224)
	DWD	82.76±2.15(224)	88.87±1.95(224)	89.33±1.23(224)	90.34±1.97(224)

Table 7. Highest average classification accuracies and their corresponding standard deviations achieved using SVM, ML, 1NN and DWD classifiers with features extracted by HFE-BSL, HFE, SDA, LDA, GDA, and using original features for Indian dataset. Number in parenthesis represents number of features achieving highest accuracies in experiments.

Feature extraction	Classifier	n_t (the number of original training samples)			
		$n_t = 5$	$n_t = 10$	$n_t = 15$	$n_t = 20$
HFE-BSL	SVM	86.43±0.42(10)	89.12±0.51(7)	89.11±1.13(8)	89.47±1.01(11)
	ML	79.74±1.34(5)	81.25±1.23(5)	85.20±1.72(6)	84.17±2.05(6)
	1NN	82.29±0.98(7)	84.57±1.49(6)	86.94±1.64(12)	87.35±2.17(5)
	DWD	87.03±0.65(6)	88.97±0.49(6)	89.23±2.01(9)	89.41±0.93(8)
HFE	SVM	48.34±0.76(4)	57.61±0.64(6)	63.34±1.04(6)	73.87±1.06(8)
	ML	44.67±1.97(3)	51.28±1.42(5)	60.81±1.21(6)	71.13±1.29(5)
	1NN	46.23±2.03(7)	52.09±0.75(6)	62.43±0.99(8)	72.74±0.63(5)
	DWD	49.23±0.76(8)	58.04±0.74(6)	62.97±1.41(9)	74.09±0.89(6)
SDA	SVM	58.37±1.08(5)	64.43±1.31(6)	69.75±0.78(6)	73.66±1.41(5)
	ML	51.73±3.02(6)	57.86±2.34(5)	61.81±2.02(4)	69.76±1.76(6)
	1NN	56.22±2.42(8)	63.03±1.98(7)	67.38±1.07(6)	72.79±1.48(7)
	DWD	58.24±0.69(6)	65.11±1.24(6)	70.01±2.01(9)	74.04±0.91(6)
LDA	SVM	23.34±1.02(4)	24.94±1.03(6)	26.69±1.76(7)	26.76±1.53(6)
	ML	22.15±3.44(3)	23.36±2.13(5)	19.05±4.01(5)	25.87±1.98(5)
	1NN	23.11±2.32(7)	23.96±1.67(7)	24.67±2.54(8)	26.13±2.64(5)
	DWD	25.14±.098(6)	24.89±0.94(6)	26.50±2.01(7)	26.37±1.03(7)
GDA	SVM	48.73±0.75(8)	55.29±2.25(9)	62.33±1.11(9)	65.27±2.32(9)
	ML	45.55±2.66(6)	53.93±1.76(4)	65.09±2.92(5)	62.36±3.51(6)
	1NN	47.38±2.45(5)	55.19±3.74(6)	63.14±2.54(6)	64.87±1.65(5)
	DWD	47.87±1.45(7)	55.65±1.72(6)	64.34±1.77(7)	64.97±1.39(7)
Original features	SVM	59.49±0.56(200)	61.69±1.52(200)	65.18±0.71(200)	70.13±0.92(200)
	ML	---	---	---	---
	1NN	51.33±2.36(200)	55.49±1.68(200)	60.68±2.93(200)	68.48±1.68(200)
	DWD	60.02±0.87(200)	60.94±1.42(200)	65.83±0.92(200)	70.32±0.98(200)

Table 8. Highest average classification accuracies and their corresponding standard deviations for Pavia dataset. Number in parenthesis represents number of features achieving highest accuracies in experiments.

Feature extraction	Classifier	n_t (the number of original training samples)			
		$n_t = 5$	$n_t = 10$	$n_t = 15$	$n_t = 20$
HFE-BSL	SVM	79.31±0.52(7)	80.71±0.14(6)	82.28±0.69(8)	82.34±1.11(10)
	ML	72.36±1.20(5)	76.04±0.72(4)	78.94±1.93(4)	79.12±0.98(4)
	1NN	78.62±0.67(7)	79.55±0.49(8)	80.76±1.38(6)	81.02±1.05(6)
	DWD	80.02±0.86(8)	80.54±0.34(7)	81.98±1.03(7)	82.62±1.04(9)
HFE	SVM	55.21±2.42(4)	71.31±0.79(5)	73.23±0.67(7)	75.19±1.38(8)
	ML	48.49±3.01(4)	64.36±1.83(5)	67.74±1.53(6)	70.45±1.90(3)
	1NN	50.72±2.37(6)	68.48±2.25(7)	71.64±2.16(8)	73.62±2.65(7)
	DWD	56.76±1.74(8)	71.01±2.02(8)	72.84±1.46(7)	75.24±1.36(8)
SDA	SVM	71.03±1.41(8)	74.32±0.83(8)	76.02±0.93(7)	77.18±0.48(6)
	ML	68.84±2.06(6)	72.57±0.1.57(7)	74.86±2.01(5)	78.95±0.94(5)
	1NN	68.42±1.89(7)	70.03±1.03(6)	71.90±1.92(7)	76.77±1.05(7)
	DWD	71.34±1.72(7)	73.95±1.03(6)	76.15±1.09(8)	77.13±0.68(7)
LDA	SVM	34.09±2.08(5)	36.04±1.09(6)	52.53±2.10(7)	56.44±1.98(7)
	ML	25.91±2.22(3)	28.48±2.28(5)	51.96±2.52(5)	53.72±3.64(4)
	1NN	27.38±1.54(7)	31.41±1.37(6)	55.23±1.97(8)	54.16±2.46(8)
	DWD	36.33±2.02(7)	36.92±2.01(5)	54.09±1.72(7)	55.65±2.21(6)
GDA	SVM	70.06±1.93(7)	73.23±1.36(6)	78.02±1.93(8)	81.68±1.21(7)
	ML	65.17±2.17(5)	68.10±3.07(3)	72.85±1.54(5)	77.41±1.63(6)
	1NN	66.92±0.89(5)	69.26±2.96(4)	71.09±2.99(4)	76.08±0.99(4)
	DWD	70.32±2.01(6)	73.32±1.35(6)	77.98±1.02(5)	82.01±1.72(5)
Original features	SVM	68.11±0.76(103)	71.48±0.82(103)	74.01±0.69(103)	76.83±0.56(103)
	ML	---	---	---	---
	1NN	67.73±1.19(103)	69.34±1.56(103)	70.31±1.62(103)	71.61±1.03(103)
	DWD	68.03±0.82(103)	72.34±0.72(103)	73.98±1.02(103)	76.74±0.88(103)

Table 9. Highest average classification accuracies and their corresponding standard deviations for Salinas dataset. Number in parenthesis represents number of features achieving highest accuracies in experiments.

Feature extraction	Classifier	n_t (the number of original training samples)			
		$n_t = 5$	$n_t = 10$	$n_t = 15$	$n_t = 20$
HFE-BSL	SVM	90.34±0.25(12)	92.26±0.52(11)	93.69±1.07(10)	93.32±1.03(13)
	ML	82.25±0.76(9)	84.47±1.95(7)	87.74±1.44(7)	88.41±2.08(8)
	1NN	88.84±0.49(8)	89.90±0.64(6)	90.87±1.37(5)	91.27±1.21(4)
	DWD	91.03±0.43(11)	91.34±0.67(10)	92.62±1.72(8)	92.74±0.99(12)
HFE	SVM	76.67±0.23(5)	83.12±0.47(10)	88.49±1.11(9)	92.53±0.97(9)
	ML	70.67±0.68(5)	78.25±1.83(9)	84.05±1.36(7)	86.67±2.25(10)
	1NN	73.24±0.52(6)	80.83±0.72(9)	86.67±1.48(8)	90.47±1.08(7)
	DWD	77.54±0.88(7)	83.01±0.52(10)	87.76±1.05(9)	91.98±0.43(6)
SDA	SVM	83.66±1.08(7)	87.58±0.39(7)	89.01±0.65(6)	92.48±0.97(5)
	ML	79.74±2.08(13)	85.41±2.05(12)	88.98±2.46(9)	89.99±1.12(10)
	1NN	80.25±0.89(8)	84.12±1.82(9)	88.69±2.13(4)	89.24±1.32(7)
	DWD	83.21±0.97(10)	86.23±2.04(10)	89.32±0.76(5)	92.83±0.76(8)
LDA	SVM	60.04±2.03(6)	72.33±1.96(9)	76.82±1.94(8)	84.55±2.05(7)
	ML	58.17±3.05(6)	69.47±2.44(7)	75.23±1.79(5)	83.62±3.46(9)
	1NN	62.27±1.97(6)	73.08±1.99(6)	77.00±1.63(6)	85.28±2.64(7)
	DWD	61.45±2.53(7)	73.01±2.03(9)	77.32±0.93(9)	84.98±2.05(10)
GDA	SVM	79.09±2.04(8)	86.28±1.26(6)	88.98±2.56(5)	90.49±0.89(5)
	ML	76.52±3.21(3)	84.51±2.42(11)	86.43±1.67(4)	88.37±1.83(10)
	1NN	77.21±1.65(10)	87.24±1.58(10)	89.22±1.85(11)	90.53±1.62(13)
	DWD	80.08±1.82(9)	86.83±1.62(9)	89.25±0.94(10)	91.02±2.11(12)
Original features	SVM	80.27±0.94(204)	85.68±1.05(204)	86.02±0.87(204)	89.16±1.94(204)
	ML	---	---	---	---
	1NN	81.14±1.27(204)	82.41±1.38(204)	85.62±2.17(204)	87.19±0.84(204)
	DWD	81.13±1.11(204)	84.56±0.86(204)	87.03±0.68(204)	89.32±1.73(204)

References

[1] Wu, D., & Sun, D. (2013). Advanced applications of hyperspectral imaging technology for food quality and safety analysis and assessment: A review — Part II: Applications. Innovative Food Science & Emerging Technologies, vol. 19, pp. 15-28.

[2] Gao, J., Li, X., Zhu, F., & He, Y. (2013). Application of hyperspectral imaging technology to discriminate different geographical origins of Jatropha curcas L. seeds. Computers and Electronics in Agriculture, vol. 99, pp. 186-193.

[3] Bazi, Y., & Melgani, F. (2010). Gaussian Process Approach to Remote Sensing Image Classification. IEEE Transactions on Geoscience and Remote Sensing, vol. 48, no. 1, pp. 186–197.

[4] Zhong, Y., & Zhang L. (2012). An Adaptive Artificial Immune Network for Supervised Classification of Multi-/Hyperspectral Remote Sensing Imagery. IEEE Transactions on Geoscience and Remote Sensing, vol. 50, no. 3, pp. 894–909.

[5] Landgrebe, D. A. (2003). Signal Theory Methods in Multispectral Remote Sensing, Hoboken, NJ: Wiley.

[6] Hughes, G. F. (1998). On the mean accuracy of statistical pattern recognition. IEEE Transactions on Information Theory, vol. IT-14, no. 1, pp. 55–63.

[7] Hall, P., Marron, J. S., & Neeman, A. (2005). Geometric representation of high dimension, low sample size data. Journal of the Royal Statistical Society: Series B, vol. 67, Part 3, pp. 427-444.

[8] Jackson, Q., & Landgrebe, D. A. (2001). An adaptive classifier design for high dimensional data analysis with a limited training data set. IEEE Transactions on Geoscience and Remote Sensing, vol. 39, no. 12, pp. 2664–2679.

[9] Camps-Valls, G., & Bruzzone, L. (2005). Kernel-based methods for hyperspectral image classification. IEEE Transactions on Geoscience And Remote Sensing, vol. 43, no. 6, pp. 1351–1362.

[10] Marron, J. S., Todd. M. J., & Ahn, J. (2007). Distance-Weighted Discrimination. Journal of the American Statistical Association, vol. 102, no. 480, pp. 1267-1271.

[11] Dhanjal, C., Gunn, S. R., & Shawe-Taylor, J. (2009). Efficient Sparse Kernel Feature Extraction Based on Partial Least Squares. IEEE Transactions on Pattern Analysis and Machine Intelligence, vol. 31, no. 8, pp. 1347-1361.

[12] Hosseini, S. A., & Ghassemian, H. (2015). Rational function approximation for feature reduction in hyperspectral data. Remote Sensing Letters, vol. 7, no. 2, pp. 101–110.

[13] Imani, M., & Ghassemian, H. (2015). High-Dimensional Image Data Feature Extraction by Double Discriminant Embedding. Pattern Analysis and Applications, DOI 10.1007/s10044-015-0513-z.

[14] Imani, M., & Ghassemian, H. (2016). Binary coding based feature extraction in remote sensing high dimensional data. Information Sciences, vol. 342, pp. 191-208.

[15] Jia, X., Kuo, B.C., & Crawford, M. (2013). Feature Mining for Hyperspectral Image Classification. Proceedings of the IEEE, vol. 101, no. 3, pp. 676-697.

[16] Maji, P., & Garai, P. (2013). Fuzzy–Rough Simultaneous Attribute Selection and Feature Extraction Algorithm. IEEE Transactions on Cybernetics, vol. 43, no. 4, pp. 1166-1177.

[17] Li, S., Qiu, J., Yang, X., Liu, H., Wan, D., & Zhu, Y. (2014). A novel approach to hyperspectral band selection based on spectral shape similarity analysis and fast branch and bound search. Engineering Applications of Artificial Intelligence, vol. 27, pp. 241-250.

[18] Esfandian, N., Razzazi, F., & Behrad, A. (2012). A clustering based feature selection method in spectro-temporal domain for speech recognition. Engineering Applications of Artificial Intelligence, vol. 25, no. 6, pp. 1194-1202.

[19] Dernoncourt, D., Hanczar, B., & Zucker, J.-D. (2014). Analysis of feature selection stability on high dimension and small sample data. Computational Statistics and Data Analysis, vol. 71, pp. 681–693.

[20] Liao, T. W. (2010). Feature extraction and selection from acoustic emission signals with an application in grinding wheel condition monitoring. Engineering Applications of Artificial Intelligence, vol. 23, no. 1, pp. 74-84.

[21] Zhang, Z., Tian, Z., Duan, X., & Fu, X. (2013). Adaptive kernel subspace method for speeding up feature extraction. Neurocomputing, vol. 113, pp. 58-66.

[22] Imani, M., & Ghassemian, H. (2015). Ridge regression-based feature extraction for hyperspectral data. International Journal of Remote Sensing, vol. 36, no. 6, pp. 1728–1742.

[23] Yu, G., & Kamarthi, S. V. (2010). A cluster-based wavelet feature extraction method and its application. Engineering Applications of Artificial Intelligence, vol. 23, no. 2, pp. 196-202.

[24] Li, B., Wang, C., & Huang, D. (2009). Supervised feature extraction based on orthogonal discriminant projection. Neurocomputing, vol. 73, pp. 191-196.

[25] Cariou, C., Chehdi, K., & Le Moan, S. (2011). BandClust: An Unsupervised Band Reduction Method for Hyperspectral Remote Sensing. IEEE Geoscience and Remote Sensing Letter, vol. 8, no. 3, pp. 565-569.

[26] Vicient, C., Sánchez, D., & Moreno, A. (2013). An automatic approach for ontology-based feature extraction from heterogeneous textualresources. Engineering Applications of Artificial Intelligence, vol. 26, no. 3, pp. 1092-1106.

[27] Fukunaga, K. (1990). Introduction to Statistical Pattern Recognition, 2nd Ed, New York: Academic.

[28] Baudat, G., & Anouar, F. (2000). Generalized discriminant analysis using a kernel approach. Neural Computing, vol. 12, no. 10, pp. 2385–2404.

[29] Zortea, M., Haertel, V., & Clarke, R. (2007). Feature Extraction in Remote Sensing High-Dimensional Image Data. IEEE Geoscience and Remote Sensing Letter, vol. 4, no. 1, pp. 107 - 111.

[31] Yin, J., Gao, C., & Jia, X. (2012). Using Hurst and Lyapunov Exponent for Hyperspectral Image Feature Extraction. IEEE Geoscience and Remote Sensing Letter, vol. 9, no. 4, pp. 705 - 709.

[33] Yin, J., Gao, C., & Jia, X. (2013). Wavelet Packet Analysis and Gray Model for Feature Extraction of Hyperspectral Data. IEEE Geoscience and Remote Sensing Letter, vol. 10, no. 4, pp. 682 - 686.

[32] Kuo, B. C., & Landgrebe, D. A. (2004). Nonparametric weighted feature extraction for classification. IEEE Transactions on Geoscience and Remote Sensing, vol. 42, no. 5, pp. 1096-1105.

[33] Yang, J.-M., Yu, P.-T., Kuo, B.-C., & Huang, H.-Y. (2007). A Novel Non Parametric Weighted Feature Extraction Method for Classification of Hyperspectral Image with Limited Training Samples. IEEE Symposium on Geoscience and Remote Sensing, Barcelona, 2007.

[34] Huang, H.-Y., & Kuo, B.-C. (2010). Double Nearest Proportion Feature Extraction for Hyperspectral-Image Classification. IEEE Transactions on Geoscience and Remote Sensing, vol. 48, no. 11, pp. 4034–4046.

[35] Wen, J., Tian, Z., Liu, X., & Lin, W. (2013), Neighborhood Preserving Orthogonal PNMF Feature Extraction for Hyperspectral Image Classification. IEEE Journal of Selected Topics in Applied Earth Observations and Remote Sensing, vol. 6, no. 2, pp. 759-768.

[36] Lee, C., & Landgrebe, D. A. (1993), Feature Extraction Based on Decision Boundaries. IEEE Transactions on Pattern Analysis and Machine Intelligence, vol. 15, no. 4, pp. 388-400.

[37] Mendenhall, M. J., & Merényi, E. (2008), Relevance-Based Feature Extraction for Hyperspectral Images. IEEE Transactions on Neural Network, vol. 19, no. 4, pp. 658–672.

[38] Cai, D., He, X., & Han, J. (2007). Semi-supervised discriminant analysis. IEEE 11th International Conference on Computer Vision, Rio de Janeiro. 2007.

[39] Camps-Valls, G., & Vila, J. (2006). Composite Kernels for Hyper Spectral Image Classification. IEEE Geoscience and Remote Sensing Letter, vol. 3, no. 1, pp. 93–97.

[40] Archibald, R., & Fann, G. (2007). Feature selection and classification of hyperspectral images with support vector machines. IEEE Geoscience and Remote Sensing Letter, vol. 4, no. 4, pp. 674–677.

[41] Camps-Valls, G., Bandos Marsheva, T. V., & Zhou, D. (2007). Semi-Supervised Graph-Based Hyperspectral Image Classification. IEEE Transactions on Geoscience and Remote Sensing, vol. 45, no. 10, pp. 3044–3054.

[42] Theodoridis, S., & Koutroumbas, K. (2009). Pattern Recognition, 4th Ed. Elsevier Academic Press.

[43] Chang, C., & Linin, C. (2008). LIBSVM—A Library for Support Vector Machines, Available: http://www.csie.ntu.edu.tw/~cjlin/libsvm.

[44] Foody, G. M. (2004). Thematic map comparison: Evaluating the statistical significance of differences in classification accuracy. Photogrammetric Engineering & Remote Sensing, vol. 70, no. 5, pp. 627–633.

[45] Liao, W., Pižurica, A., Scheunders, P., Philips, W., & Pi, Y. (2013). Semisupervised Local Discriminant Analysis for Feature Extraction in Hyperspectral Images. IEEE Transactions on Geoscience and Remote Sensing, vol. 51, no. 1, pp. 184-198.

[46] Xia, J., Chanussot, J., Du, P., & He, X. (2014). (Semi-) Supervised Probabilistic Principal Component Analysis for Hyperspectral Remote Sensing Image Classification. IEEE Journal of Selected Topics in Applied Earth Observations and Remote Sensing., vol. 7, no. 6, pp. 2225- 2237.

[47] Zhong, Y., Wu, Y., Xu, X., & Zhang, L. (2015). An Adaptive Subpixel Mapping Method Based on MAP Model and Class Determination Strategy for Hyperspectral Remote Sensing Imagery. IEEE Transactions on Geoscience and Remote Sensing, vol. 53, no. 3, pp. 1411- 1426.

[48] Zhong, Y., Zhang, L., Huang, B., & Li, P. (2006). An Unsupervised Artificial Immune Classifier for Multi/Hyperspectral Remote Sensing Imagery. IEEE Transactions on Geoscience and Remote Sensing, vol. 44, no. 2, pp. 420-431.

[49] Zhang, L., Zhong, Y., Huang, B., Gong, J., & Li, P. (2007). Dimensionality Reduction Based on Clonal Selection for Hyperspectral Imagery. IEEE Transactions on Geoscience and Remote Sensing, vol. 45, no. 12, pp. 4172- 4186.

[50] Imani, M. & Ghassemian, H. (2015). Feature reduction of hyperspectral images: Discriminant analysis and the first principal component. Journal of AI and Data Mining, vol. 3, no. 1, pp. 1-9.

[51] Hsu, P.-H. (2007). Feature extraction of hyperspectral images using wavelet and matching pursuit. ISPRS Journal of Photogrammetry & Remote Sensing, vol. 62, pp. 78–92.

[52] Li, F., Xu, L., Siva, P., Wong, A., & Clausi, D. A. (2015). Hyperspectral Image Classification With Limited Labeled Training Samples Using Enhanced Ensemble Learning and Conditional Random Fields. IEEE Journal of Selected Topics in Applied Earth Observations and Remote Sensing, vol. 8, no. 6, pp. 2427- 2438.

[53] Imani, M. & Ghassemian, H. (2015). Overlap-based feature weighting for feature extraction of hyperspectral remote sensing imagery. Journal of AI and Data Mining, vol. 3, no. 2, pp. 181-190.

8

Isolated Persian/Arabic handwriting characters: Derivative projection profile features, implemented on GPUs

M. Askari, M. Asadi, A. Asilian Bidgoli[*]and H. Ebrahimpour

Department of Computer Engineering, University of Kashan, Kashan, Iran.

*Corresponding author:asilian@gmail.com (A. AsilianBidgoli).

Abstract

For many years, researchers have studied high accuracy methods for recognizing the handwriting and achieved many significant improvements. However, an issue that has rarely been studied is the speed of these methods. Considering the computer hardware limitations, it is necessary for these methods to run in high speed. One of the methods to increase the processing speed is to use the computer parallel processing power. This paper introduces one of the best feature extraction methods for the handwritten recognition, called DPP (Derivative Projection Profile), which is employed for isolated Persian handwritten recognition. In addition to achieving good results, this (computationally) light feature can easily be processed. Moreover, Hamming Neural Network is used to classify this system. To increase the speed, some part of the recognition method is executed on GPU (graphic processing unit) cores implemented by CUDA platform. HADAF database (Biggest isolated Persian character database) is utilized to evaluate the system. The results show 94.5% accuracy. We also achieved about 5.5 times speed-up using GPU.

Keywords: *OCR, Persian Character, Projection Profile, Parallel Algorithms, GPU, CUDA.*

1. Introduction

There are many definitions for OCR (optical character recognition); however, the best definition is the procedure of converting visual texts by an electrical or mechanical machine into intelligible codes (like ASCII) for a computer [1]. OCR systems have many applications in sorting letters, reading, information checking, and converting manuscripts to digital texts. OCR is mainly divided into two categories: printed and manuscript recognition. Manuscript recognition is always more difficult due to the variety of handwritings. Another categorization is the division between online and offline types. In an offline system, a fixed image, usually a bitmap, is given for recognition, while in an online system, writing text and the recognition process occur simultaneously. Instances of such recognitions can be witnessed in mobile phones and tablets. Due to temporal criteria like pen movements, recognition is easier with an online system.

Recently, researchers have shown high interest in the manuscript recognition field; in the English language, such systems have achieved a high accuracy level up to 98% [2] and THEY ARE CURRENTLY BEING USED in practice. On the other hand, while more than half a billion people in the world use languages with the same form of writing as the Persian form (like Arabic), little research has been carried out on such languages and most research studies have worked on Chinese, Japanese, and English forms of writing [3]. This is due to the lack of financial support, tools like databases, dictionaries, and the complex nature of these writing forms [4]. The production of Persian/Arabic OCR can have other advantages like the recognition of historical scripts. Persian/Arabic forms of writing have not had a great deal of change in the literature. Therefore, such systems can also be used for the recognition of historical scripts [5].

The remainder of this paper is divided into several sections. The following section presents an introduction to Persian characters and reviews past works in OCR. Section 2 explains a procedure of character Recognition. The proposed method and its parts are presented in section 3.

Section 4 provides an explanation about CUDA and its utilization in this paper. Finally, the implementation of the proposed method and the conclusions are respectively provided in sections 5 and 6.

1.1. Persian Scrip

Unlike English, Persian scripts (also known as Farsi) are written from right to left, letters have no capital form, and are linked together in order to form a word.

The Persian alphabet has 32 letters and the Arabic alphabet has 28 letters. Each letter in a word can have one of the three positions: initial, central, or final. The letters in the final position can sometimes be isolated from their preceding letters as figure 1. Dots in Persian play an important role; many of the letters like 'پ' ,'ب' and 'ت' have the same main body and the only difference between them is the position and the number of dots.

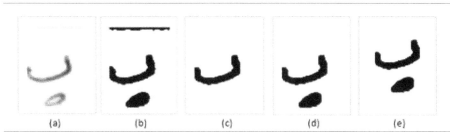

Figure 1. Preprocess stages. a)Main image. b) Binerized image. c) Biggest object of character. d)After applying morphology filter on b. e)Centralized action on d.

Lack of communication among Persian/Arabic OCR researchers is the cause of many repeated studies carried out in this field. Moreover, in the past, there was not any standard database to be used for comparison and each person used a different database for testing; therefore, it is not easy to compare different studies. For this reason, it is useful to set up competitions among researchers in this field. One of these competitions was ICDAR 2009 on the isolated Persian characters [6]. In this competition, the proposed systems were compared based on HODA, IFHCDB, and CENPARMI databases. The best result was obtained by a system based on a neural network.

1.2. Background

Persian OCR was first investigated in 1980s by Parhami, which could recognize some newspaper characters [7]. At the same time, another research was carried out by Badi on the Arabic alphabet. That system could recognize 12 printed letters with 90% accuracy.

In [8], Mozaffariet.al. proposed a new method for manuscript recognition. They used both structural and statistical features and the 1NN (nearest neighborhood) classifier. Their database consisted of 8 digits and they used 280 images for training and 200 images for testing. The accuracy was reported 94.4%.

In [9], a system is proposed for printed letters using chain code. In this system, the first image is thinned and then statistical features, such as the number of the dots, the position of the dots, the

number of the holes, and the statistical features extracted from the chain code, are sent to the 1NN classifier. This system was proposed for the recognition of different fonts, i.e. training is carried out with one font and testing with another. The average accuracy of this system was 97%.

In [10], [11], Haraty and Ghader use skeleton presentation for preprocessing. The structural and statistical features applied in these methods include the number and density of black pixels and the number of joint points, final points, loops, and sides. The classifiers of these systems were two neural networks. The recognition rate of these systems was 73% using a database of 2132 characters.

Safabakhsh and Adibi used continuous HMM (Hidden Markov Model) for the recognition of Nastaaligh manuscripts (a type of Persian calligraphy in which letters are slanted and some letters fall over the others to produce an aesthetic effect). In this type of writing, the recognition of base lines is difficult. Before recognition, this system removes slopes to prevent incorrect ordering of letters. This system uses a lexicon of 50 words, including all types of characters. The test data consisted of 100 words written by two people. Their method was recursive, i.e. at each stage, falsely recognized words were ignored, and the test was repeated. This system could reach 69% accuracy rate after 5 iterations and 91% accuracy rate after 20 iterations [12]. In [13], a system is proposed, which is a combination of MLP (Multi-Layer Perceptron) classifiers. The preprocessing stage in this system is smooth and binary. The feature vector includes structural features like the number of upper and lower dots and statistical features like densities of 57 regions in the image. They used 7 voting methods, such as MAX and SUM as classifiers, the best of which was Borda method with 96% precision rate. Their database consisted of 4800 images of words written by 100 people. About 50% of these images were used for training and the rest was used for verification and validation.

In 2003, a method was proposed for Arabic word recognition that contained 160 semi-continuous HMM [14]. This system thinned each word and used pixel rows of the thinned image as features. This system was used for 945 city names in Tunisia from IFN/ENIT database [15] and reached 89% accuracy.

Zahedi and Arjomandzadeh presented a system to correct space and half-space characters in Persian texts [16]. They used different statistical approach which uses a fertility-based IBM Model as word alignment by employing a parallel corpus which is created for the special purpose of Persian multi-part word edition.

In [17], a recognition system is introduced for recognizing printed Persian scripts. In this system, at first, lines are identified using a kind of projection and sub-words are separated with another projection. Subsequently, using an innovative algorithm, sub-words are divided into smaller parts and an MLP is used to detect these parts. If these parts are not recognized, they will return to the previous step to repeat the separation. These steps are repeated until no word is divided into smaller parts. If the system cannot recognize the words, the separation is performed again; however, this time, sub-word detection is performed from left to right.

The proposed method in this paper has 5% improvement compared with previous works [18] due to using DPP in four directions. In addition, parallel methods are employed to accelerate the algorithm 5.5 times. Since OCR is used in large contexts, such as Census, the running speed of the algorithm is an important factor in decreasing the cost.

2. Recognition procedure

The procedure of character recognition, like other forms of pattern recognition, consists of three steps: preprocessing, feature extraction, and classification.

In the preprocessing step, the image must be prepared for better recognition; in other words, preprocessing increases the accuracy using image features. In this step, some actions are performed,

such as noise reduction, slant correction, and normalization. Normalization consists of assimilating the image to our patterns such as the assimilation of the image size to the trained images. One part of the preprocessing that can exist in the systems is the segmentation of words into characters. Persian/Arabic word recognition systems can be divided into two types: 1. recognition by segmentation 2. Holistic methods in which the whole word is recognized at once. This method was previously used for speech recognition [4].

In the feature extraction step, some information is extracted from the raw image, which is called a feature. Particular features must be extracted according to the pattern and we are trying to recognize. These features can include unitary transformations, gradient, or zoning [19]. In character recognition, features are divided into structural and statistical. Structural features are based on the geometric shape of the letters and are related to the nature of the letters. Three examples of these geometrical patterns are loop, slant, and dots. Statistical features are the result of calculations on regions of the image like FFT and projection profile.

In the next step, the classification step, the system tries to determine to which class the pattern belongs; in other words, to which class the pattern is similar using the feature vector. The most common classification methods are ANN (artificial neural network), SVM (support vector machine), and HMM.

3. Proposed System

In this system, two stages of recognition are used in order to increase the accuracy. In the first stage, the letters are classified into 9 groups according to the similarity of their main bodies. Figure2 shows these 9 groups. In the preprocessing step of this stage, after binarization and centralization, the main part of a character remains and the others are eliminated.

1	2	3	4	5	6	7	8	9
ا	ـٮ	ج	د	س	ط	ک	ل	م
	ـپ	چ	ذ	ش	ظ	گ	ق	
	ـث	ح	ر	ص			ن	
	ـث	خ	ز	ض				
	ـٮ	ع	ژ	ی				
		غ	و					
			ه					

Figure 2. Persian character categories.

Other parts are removed so that only the main part of a character that is shared in the group is remained and additional parts are removed. After that, the DPP features are extracted as illustrated in section 4.2. These extracted features are given to the hamming network for classification. After this stage, characters are separated into 9 groups.

In the second stage, the character must be recognized in each group. In this stage, preprocessing consists of binarization, centralization, and morphology. In the first stage, the noise is removed using the main part; however, in the second stage, the noise must be eliminated by morphology. After that, similar to stage one, the DPP feature is extracted and a hamming classifier is used.

The next three sections describe the preprocessing, feature extraction, and classification of this system.

3.1. Preprocessing
We use the following operations for preprocessing the images in the database:

Binarization: This process is carried out for background elimination and noise reduction. Thus, by considering a threshold, the image is transformed into a zero and one image. This threshold is selected based on trial and error and the database using the classical method of Otsu. Subsequently, the image will be monochrome. Figure 1(a) presents the result of applying this method on the images.

Morphology: as shown in figure 1(b), a little noise remains after binarization. In this system, Erosion operator, which is one of the morphological operators, is applied to remove the noise [19]. Using this operation and a 4*4 mask, the noise with values smaller than this mask is removed (see Figure 1(d)).

Centralization: in this step, the character is moved to the center of the image using a linear function. This operation causes the features extracted from the images to be independent from the location of the character in the image. In the linear function, a rectangle surrounds the character and moves it to the center of the image. In figure 1(e), this operation is shown after applying it to figure 1(d).

Finding the main part: using this operation, the biggest part of the character (black pixels) remains and other parts are eliminated. This operation is good for noise removal; although, it may also remove the main information (see Figure 1(c)).

In this system, recognition has two stages. According to the stage at which preprocessing operations are carried out, only some of the

operations mentioned above are applied. This issue will be discussed in the "the proposed system" section.

3.2. Feature extraction
One of the biggest problems in handwritten character recognition is the variance of the character size in the database. For example, figure 3 presents a few examples of one character with different sizes in the dataset. Therefore, it is helpful to have features, which are not sensitive to size. Projection profile is a statistical feature that is sensitive to size. In this paper, we obtain a new feature using the derivative of Projection Profile that is scale invariant. This feature is called DPP and it is described in the following paragraph.

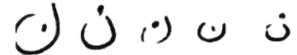

Figure 3. Some variety samples of character 'ن'.

First, projection profile is calculated in four directions. Assuming the image is I (x, y) with the size w*h pixels, projection profile in four directions (vertical, horizontal, 35° diagonal, and 135° diagonal) is calculated using the following equations.

$$\forall j = 1, 2, \ldots, h : D_1 = \sum_{i=1}^{w} I(i, j) \tag{1}$$

$$\forall j = 1, 2, \ldots, w : D_2 = \sum_{i=1}^{h} I(i, j) \tag{2}$$

$$\forall i = (2 - h), \ldots, w :$$
$$D_3(i + 3 - h) = \sum_{j=\max(1,i)}^{\min(w, i+h-1)} I(j - i + 1, j) \tag{3}$$

$$D_4(i + 3 - h) = \sum_{j=\max(1,i)}^{\min(w, i+h-1)} I(j - i + 1, w - j + 1) \tag{4}$$

In fact, D1, D2, D3, and D4 show the pixel density of each letter in rows, columns, and diameters. Figure 4 shows the results of using the Projection Profiles formulas. After that, the derivative of these values must be calculated so that the final features are obtained. The first order discrete derivative is calculated using the following relation [20].

$$\frac{df}{dx} = f(x+1) - f(x) \tag{5}$$

As shown in [19], calculating the derivative using the two neighbors of the corresponding pixel causes the derived value to become less sensitive to noise.

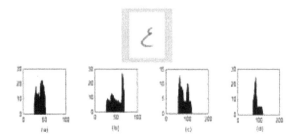

Figure 4. Projection Profile in 4 dimensions. a)Vertical b)Horizontal c)135° d) 35°.

Therefore, we use the following equation to calculate the derivative.

$$\frac{df}{dx} = f(x+1) - f(x-1) \tag{6}$$

Since we want to track the changes of the derivative, the sign of the derivative is important. Therefore, after calculating the derivative, the sign function is applied in order to obtain different scales for projection profiles.

$$S_i = \text{sign}\left(\frac{dD_i}{k}\right), i = 1,..4, k = 1,\ldots,\text{size}(D_i) \tag{7}$$

S_1, S_2, S_3, S_4 are signed vectors whose amounts are 0, -1 or 1 and we apply the following rules to normalize them and reduce class variance.

- For neighbors with the same value only one of them is considered.
- In order to remove noise, we consider only one threshold. If Si values change and return to previous values below the threshold, this change is ignored.

Figure 5 presents the derivative of projection profiles after applying the sign function. Now, the DPP feature is achieved and we can use it for recognition. By applying these rules to the database of character images (95 * 77 pixels), 20 values are obtained for each vector. Therefore, 80 elements are obtained as a feature vector for each image. As it is shown in figure 3, Persian characters in the dataset have different sizes, views, and places in the images. Thus, in the preprocessing step, all characters are aligned to the center of the image. Using DPP, the extracted features do not depend on the size of the character. Therefore, the shape and curvature of the character are important. In addition, the angle dependency can be reduced significantly by DPP in four directions.

3.3. Classification

In the proposed system, we used the Hamming network as a classifier. This network is a fully connected, competitive neural network, which is based on the hamming distance. After this network is trained with the training data, all the neurons compete until one of them wins and the test data is assigned to that class when a test data is given to the network [21]. This network calculates the similarity between the test and training data using the code in Algorithm 1.In this algorithm, 'x' is the test and 'y' is the trained data record with n dimensions. The term 'a' shows similar bits and 'd' shows different bits between the test and training samples. Finally, the negative value is the criterion for a winning neuron.

$$x^T.y = \sum_i x_i.y_i = a - d$$
$$d = n - a$$
$$x^T.y = 2a - n$$
$$a = 0.5(x^T.y + n)$$
$$-d = a - n = 0.5(x^T.y + n) - n$$
$$-d = 0.5(x^T.y) - 0.5n$$

Algorithm 1. Calculating hamming distance between two samples in Hamming Neural Network.

4. Using CUDA in parallel processing

Parallelism determines the future of computing science because on the one hand, when the number of transistors increases, increasing CPU speed will become very difficult. On the other hand, the need for simultaneous capabilities is ever increasing. Using multi-core processors is an endeavor to acquire parallelism, but these processors are expensive and the efficiency increases according to the maximum number of cores [22]. However, increasing the number of cores occurs very slowly. GPUs (Graphic Processing Units), which have recently gained importance, are appropriate tools to implement

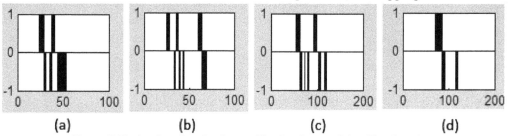

Figure 5. Derivative of projection profiles in after applying Sign function.

parallel algorithms.

The advantages of GPU over other parallelism methods are their high performance and availability. Figure 6 shows a comparison between different models of CPUs and GPUs [23].Each GPU contains many cores, which enable it to perform in parallel and carry out a number of operations at a speed many times more than the speed of a CPU. Figure 7 shows the inner structure of a GPU with 48 cores [25].

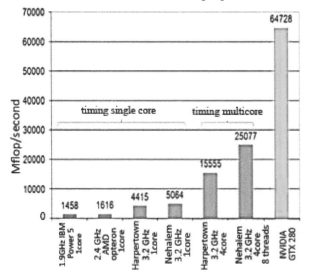

Figure 6. Performance of different CPUs and GPUs[24].

As we can see in this figure, the GPU has its own memory and there are not any intersections between GPU and CPU memories; thus, for executing a program, first, the data must be transferred to GPU memory and in the end, the outcomes must return to the main memory [23]-[26].In 2006, NVIDIA Company introduced CUDA platform for bulk parallel calculation with high efficiency on their GPUs. This platform was presented with a software environment that allows developers to write programs in C language and execute them on GPUs. Each CUDA program consists of two parts: a host and a device. Host is a program executed on the CPU and the device is executed in parallel on the GPU cores. In software application, each parallel program includes a number of threads, which are lightweight processes that are independent of the operations they perform. In CUDA, a set of threads form a block and a set of blocks form a Grid. There are different memory types in GPUs. Each thread has its own local memory and each Block has a shared memory that the inner threads have access to. There is also a global memory that all threads have access to. Moreover, there is another memory called the texture memory similar to the global memory, and all threads have access to, but its addressing mode is different and it is used for special data like images.

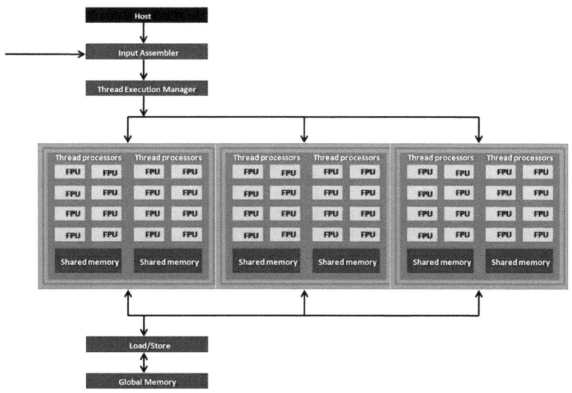

Figure 7. Nvidia Geforce 8800 architecture with 48 cores.

In the host part, the number of threads for the device part must be defined and the device part is executed using this number. Each thread can recognize its position using some CUDA functions and can work based on this position. Finally, the calculated results must return to the main memory.

GPUs are good tools to implement image-processing algorithms because many image operators are local and the operation must be performed on the pixels of each image. As a result, by considering one thread for each pixel (if the required number of threads can be defined), calculation time can be reduced to O(1). In [26], Yang implemented some of the best-known operators such as binarization and filtering by CUDA. Moreover, in [28], Gray uses CUDA for Motion Tracking.

The next section presents the implementation of the parallel algorithm using the hamming network in CUDA.

5. Hamming classifier implementation on GPUs using CUDA

The most time-consuming part of character recognition is searching for extracted features of the corresponding character in the hamming network. This time can be significantly reduced using CUDA and GPU configurations. First, the hamming distance should be calculated between the features of the corresponding character and each feature of the trained characters in the network. For this purpose, we use a two dimensional grid, whose configuration can be seen in figure 8. Up to 512 blocks can be defined in each block; however, for simplicity, we use 500 threads. If we have N training records, then the number of blocks, m, can be obtained by (8).

$$m = \sqrt{\frac{N}{500}} \qquad (8)$$

By considering such a configuration, each training data has one thread that must calculate the distance between that and the test data. The pseudo code of each thread is shown in algorithm 2. In this pseudo code, distance is a vector, which has N elements that keep the distance between each training data and test data and each distance is valued by one thread. Using this method, the computational cost of calculating the distance vector is reduced from O(N) to O(1).

Now, in order to find the final answer, we must only calculate the least value of the distance vector. The cost of the search algorithm is a sequence of O(N) order. Although, using the

SIMD architecture and tree Grid configuration, this cost can be reduced to O(log N) [29].

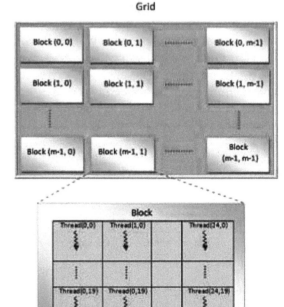

Figure 8. Grid configuration for calculating hamming distance with GPUs.

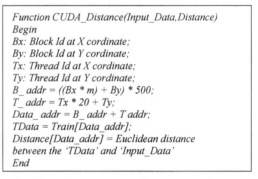

Algorithm 2.The pseudo code of calculating hamming distance between an input matrix and trained data using CUDA.

However, the grid must be reconfigured for each level of the tree in this way and this causes a decrease in speed and overloads. Thus, we only use two levels: There are $\sqrt{N}$ threads in the first level and $\sqrt{\sqrt{N}}$ threads in the second level. For the GPU configuration, a one dimension Grid is used and threads are in one dimension of blocks. The pseudo code related to the threads is shown in algorithm3. The output dimensions of this function, which is the result vector, are equal to the dimensions of the input vector. Therefore, the cost of finding the minimum is reduced from O(N) to O($\sqrt{\sqrt{N}}$). Finally, by giving the distance vector to this function and applying it two times, the least value of the function is obtained, which is considered the final answer. The architecture presented in this section is used to form hamming networks in the target system. The results section shows the increase in the speed obtained by this performance compared to the normal state.

6. Experimental results

A part of Hadaf database is used to test the system [30]. Hadaf is the biggest Persian isolated characters database that has over 10,000,000 samples. Thus, a subset with 47,695 samples is selected as the dataset. The dispersion of each letter is shown in table 2. The training dataset has 11,796 samples separated by minimum similarity. More specifically, 24% of whole dataset was selected as the training data and the rest was used as the test data. The size of the images is 77*95 pixels.

Table 1.The dispersion of characters in selected database.

ا	9192	ر	3562	ف	456
ب	1836	ز	1955	ق	238
پ	249	ژ	61	ك	315
ت	1233	س	3453	گ	695
ث	30	ش	369	ل	2369
ج	282	ص	218	م	4274
چ	53	ض	249	ن	3572
ح	1183	ط	173	و	1930
خ	493	ظ	49	ه	2305
د	2344	ع	1249	ي	3183
ذ	20	غ	105		

As it was mentioned, this system has two recognition stages, in the first stage, characters are clustered, and in the second stage, character class is recognized. The average recognition rate in stage one is 99.84%. The recognition rate of each cluster is shown in table 3.

Table 2. Recognition rate for each group presented in table 1.

Class	1	2	3	4	5	6	7
Detection Percent	99.95	99.90	99.94	99.95	99.70	100	99.61

Table 3. Recognition percent of each character within each group presented in table 3.

Char	Rec%	Char	Rec%	Char	Rec%
ا	100	ر	96.9	ف	93
ب	96.3	ز	94.3	ق	87
پ	97.4	ژ	100	ك	81.8
ت	94.7	س	89.5	گ	85.6
ث	100	ش	84.8	ل	93.4
ج	94.5	ص	95.3	م	100
چ	100	ض	87.3	ن	85.7
ح	95.1	ط	88.3	و	89.1
خ	97.1	ظ	85.7	ه	91.5
د	91.9	ع	84.2	ى	85.6
ذ	100	غ	95		

The recognition rate of characters within each group is calculated in the second stage. Some clusters have only one character like clusters 1 and 9; thus, for these clusters, stage two is not needed and recognition rate is the same as stage one. Finally, the recognition rate of 94.5% is

achieved. Table 4 shows the accuracy percentage of each character. The second aspect of this system is the usage of GPU parallel processing. For this purpose, the system is implemented by CUDA and it is executed using a 'GT 430' graphic card. This graphic card has 96 GPU cores. In table 5, the execution time in parallel mode is compared with the sequential mode on two different CPU models.

Table 4. Recognition execution time comparing between different processors.

Processor	Model	Execution Time(s)	GPU Speedup toward processor
GPU	GT 430	311.8	1
CPU	Core(TM) i7 CPU 3.2 GHz	1155.41	3.7
CPU	Core(TM)2 Duo 2.66 GHz	1705.69	5.4

7. Conclusion

In this research, two aspects of an OCR system are considered. From the first aspect, for the reliability and accuracy of the system, a new feature extraction method (DPP) is used. According to the experimental results, using this feature, the system can achieve a good recognition rate. Other proposed methods for Persian handwriting recognition did not use a similar database; thus, the exact comparison is not possible and the comparison of this method with others remains as a future work. However, this system has some advantages over other systems. In comparison to other methods, the recognition rate shows that this is one of the best methods.

Another advantage is the training dataset. In this system, the training dataset is a small part of the whole dataset (24%), whereas in some other studies, the majority of the dataset is used to train the data. Also in this system, the whole character set of Persian letters (32 classes) is considered, whereas only a part of the letters or digits is used in some previous studies. The second aspect of this system is its fast recognition. As mentioned before, some parts of this system are implemented on the CUDA platform and executed on GPU cores. As shown in the experimental results, this system was tested on some sequential and parallel configurations. In a common case, a normal CPU (Core(TM) 2 Duo 2.66 GHz) and a common GPU (GT430) were compared and speedup 5.4 was achieved. To our knowledge, in the previous works, there is no effort to use GPU parallel power for OCR systems.

References

[1] Rajavelu, A., Musavi, M. T., & Shirvaikar, M. V. (1989). A neural network approach to character

recognition. Neural Networks, vol. 2, no. 5, pp. 387-393.

[2] Holley, R. (2009). How good can it get? Analyzing and improving OCR accuracy in large scale historic newspaper digitization programs. D-Lib Magazine, vol. 15, no. 3/4.

[3] Mowlaei, A., & Faez, K. (2003). Recognition of isolated handwritten Persian/Arabic characters and numerals using support vector machines. 13th Workshop on Neural Networks for Signal Processing. NNSP'03, 2003.

[4] Amin, A. (1997). Off line Arabic character recognition: a survey. Proceedings of the Fourth International Conference on Document Analysis and Recognition, 1997.

[5] Khorsheed, M. S. (2003). Recognising handwritten Arabic manuscripts using a single hidden Markov model. Pattern Recognition Letters, vol. 24, no. 14, pp. 2235-2242.

[6] Mozaffari, S. & Soltanizadeh, H. (2009).Hndwritten Farsi/Arabic character recognition competition. 10th International Conference on Document Analysis and Recognition.

[7] Parhami, B., & Taraghi, M. (1981). Automatic recognition of printed Farsi texts. Pattern Recognition, vol. 14, no. 1, pp. 395-403.

[8] Mozaffari, S., Faez, K. & Ziaratban, M. (2005). Structural decomposition and statistical description of Farsi/Arabic handwritten numeric characters. Eighth International Conference on Document Analysis and Recognition.

[9] Zakian, H., Monadjemi, S., Ladani, B. T. & Zamanifar, K. (2008). Multi-font Farsi/Arabic isolated character recognition using chain codes. World Academy of Science, Engineering and Technology, vol. 43, pp. 67-70.

[10] Haraty, R. A. & Ghaddar, C. (2004). Arabic text recognition. Int. Arab J. Inf. Technol., vol. 1, no. 2, pp. 156-163.

[11] Haraty RA,C Ghaddar. (2003). Neuro-classification for handwritten arabic text. ACS/IEEE International Conference on Computer Systems and Applications, 2003.

[12] Safabakhsh, R., & Adibi, P. (2005). Nastaaligh handwritten word recognition using a continuous-density variable-duration HMM. Arabian Journal for Science and Engineering, vol. 30, no. 1, pp. 95-120.

[13] Nadir, F., Abdelatif, E., Tarek, K. & Mokhtar, S. (2005). Benefit of multiclassifier systems for Arabic handwritten words recognition. Eighth International Conference on Document Analysis and Recognition, 2005.

[14] Pechwitz, M. & Maergner, V. (2003). HMM based approach for handwritten Arabic word recognition

using the IFN/ENIT-database. 12th International Conference on Document Analysis and Recognition.

[15] Pechwitz, M., Maddouri, S., Märgner, V., Ellouze, N. & Amiri, H. (2002). IFN/ENIT-database of handwritten Arabic words. Proc. of CIFED, 2002.

[16] Zahedi, M. & Arjomandzadeh, A. (2015). A new model for persian multi-part words edition based on statistical machine translation. Journal of AI and Data Mining, vol. 4, no. 1, 27-34.

[17] Zand, M., Nilchi, A. & Monadjemi, SA. (2008). Recognition-based segmentation in Persian character recognition. Proceedings of World Academy of Science, Engineering and Technology.

[18] Arabfard, M., et al. (2011). Recognition of Isolated Handwritten Persian Characterizing Hamming Network. Innovative Computing Technology. Springer Berlin Heidelberg, pp. 293-304.

[19] Nixon, M. (2008). Feature extraction & image processing. Academic Press.

[20] Gonzalez, RC. & Woods, RE. (2002). Digital image processing. Prentice hall Upper Saddle River.

[21] Mehrotra, K., Mohan, CK. & Ranka, S. (1997). Elements of artificial neural networks. MIT press.

[22] Owens, J. D., Houston, M., Luebke, D., Green, S., Stone, J. E. & Phillips, J. C. (2008). GPU computing. Proceedings of the IEEE, vol. 96, no. 5, pp. 879-899.

[23] Nvidia, C. (2011). Nvidiacuda c programming guide. NVIDIA Corporation, vol. 120, no., pp. 18.

[24] Michalakes, J., & Vachharajani, M. (2008). GPU acceleration of numerical weather prediction. Parallel Processing Letters, vol. 18, no. 04, pp. 531-548.

[25] Anderson, RF., Kirtzic, JS. & Daescu, O. (2011). Applying parallel design techniques to template matching with GPUs. High Performance Computing for Computational Science–VECPAR 2010. Springer, pp. 456-468.

[26] ATI Stream Computing user guide (2009). rev1.4.0a.

[27] Yang, Z. Y. & Zhu, Y. Pu. (2008). Parallel image processing based on CUDA. International Conference on Computer Science and Software Engineering.

[28] GrauerGray, S., Kambhamettu, C. & Palaniappan, K. (2008). GPU implementation of belief propagation using CUDA for cloud tracking and reconstruction. IAPR Workshop on Pattern Recognition in Remote Sensing (PRRS 2008).

[29] Akl, S. G. (1989). The design and analysis of parallel algorithms. Prentice-Hall, Inc.

[30] Khosravi, S., et al.(2007). A comprehensive handwritten image corpus of isolated persian/arabic characters. 9th International Symposium on OCR development and evaluation, IEEE.

9

Estimating scour below inverted siphon structures using stochastic and soft computing approaches

M. Fatahi and B. Lashkar-Ara[*]

Civil Engineering Department, Jundi-Shapur University of Technology, Dezful, Iran.

*Corresponding author: Lashkarara@jsu.ac.ir (B. Lashkar-Ara).

Abstract

In this work, we use the non-linear regression, artificial neural network (ANN), and genetic programming (GP) approaches in order to predict an important tangible issue, i.e. the scour dimension downstream of inverted siphon structures. Dimensional analysis and non-linear regression-based equations are proposed for the estimation of the maximum scour depth, location of the scour hole, and location and height of the dune downstream of the structures. In addition, The GP-based formulation results are compared with the experimental results and other accurate equations. The analysis results show that the equations derived from the forward stepwise non-linear regression method have the correlation coefficients $R^2= 0.962, 0.971$, and 0.991, respectively. This correlates the relative parameter of the maximum scour depth (s/z) in comparison with the GP and ANN models. Furthermore, the slope of the fitted line extracted from computations and observations for dimensionless parameters generally presents a new achievement for sediment engineering and scientific community, indicating the superiority of the ANN model.

Keywords: *Scour, Inverted Siphon, Neural Network, Genetic Programming.*

1. Introduction

Scour is a worldwide natural phenomenon caused by the flowing stream on the sediment beds. The local scour downstream of a hydraulic structure poses an immense problem in designing the foundation and stability of the hydraulic structure of Sarkar and Dey [1]. If the scour depth becomes significant, the stability of the foundation of the structure may be endangered, with a consequent risk of damage and failure. Therefore, the prediction and control of scour is necessary. During the formative phase of the scour profile, the local sediment transport is rather active, while by approaching the equilibrium condition, the phenomenon tends to a ''purely hydraulic'' Ghetti and Zanovello [2] mechanism, in which the hole profile is the result of a mass balance between the removed and deposited particles inside the pool. The difference in height between the upstream and downstream bed levels of the river-

intersecting structures will form a vertical waterfall in the tail-water that plays an important role in grade-control structures. An example of these structures is the Balaroud inverted siphon structure in Dez irrigation and drainage network in the south of Andimeshk county, Khozestan province, Iran (Figure 1-a). The Balaroud inverted siphon is one of the largest national water structures that is situated in the irrigation and drainage network of Dez. Having a length of 990 m and a capacity of 156 m³/s, this structure transfers water of the Dez river through the beneath of the Balarod river. The Balaroud inverted siphon has an intensive general and local scour, as a consequence of the anomalous usage of the materials in the Balaroud River. Figure 1-b shows the conditions of the structure. A sketch of the scour downstream of Balaroud inverted siphon is shown in figure 2, having a weir width of b and a fall height of z.

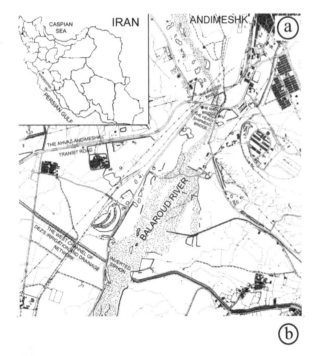

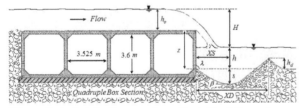

Figure 1. a) Location of studied area. b) Formation of grade-control structure in Balaroud river bed by protrusion of Balaroud inverted siphon structures located in Dez west irrigation system in SW of Iran.

Figure 2. A sketch of scour of an alluvial bed downstream of an inverted siphon structure.

It is worth mentioning that the erosive action of the flowing water causes a significant downstream local scour, and may cause problematic issues for these structures. Thus the structural design of the inverted siphon structures must include sufficient protective provisions against local scours.

An appropriate structural design of these structures requires full comprehension, and, somehow, prediction of the nature of the downstream scour, namely the location and extent of the scour.

Many experimental studies on scour downstream of hydraulic structures are available in the literature. Among these, we can refer to the studies carried out by Rouse [3], Doddiah et al. [4], Mason and Arumugam [5], D'Agostino [6], Robinson et al. [7], Bormann and Julien [8], and Bennett et al. [9].

Rouse [3] and Doddiah et al. [4] have shown that the scour depth s increases with time T, and its changes accord to the following relationship:

$$s/h = k_1 + k_2 \log\left(QT/bz^2\right) \quad (1)$$

where, k_1 and k_2 are constants; and h is the tail-water depth above the non-scoured bed level (Figure 2).

Bennett et Al. [9] have observed that a jet is separated from the over-fall, and diffuses downstream of the structure.

This jet is split into two wall-jets, forming two counter-rotating eddies (rollers), downstream and upstream of the diffuse jet, and eroding and forming the scour hole. The upstream roller is captive between the over-fall and the impinging jet. The circulation within the downstream roller causes a region of significant upwelling, and sediment deposition occurs as the flow directs toward the water surface. The D'Agostino [6] studies have neglected the influence of the bed grain-size, and he suggested equation (2) due to estimating XD; it is a distance between the downstream of the structure and the accumulated depositions crest.

$$XD/z = 3.55 \times \sqrt[3]{q^2/g}\Big/z + 0.34 \quad (2)$$

where, $q = Q/b$ is the discharged per unit weir width.

A large-scale model research work carried out by Bormann and Julien [8] has enabled the calibration of an equilibrium equation based on particle stability and its validation in a variety of conditions such as wall and vertical jets, free over-fall jets, submerged jets, and flow-over large-scale grade-control structures. According to the results obtained by Bormann and Julien [8], the relationship for estimating s is in the following form:

$$s = \left[\frac{0.611}{\left[\sin(0.436 + \beta')\right]^{0.8}} q^{0.6} \frac{U_0}{g^{0.8} d_{90}^{0.4}} \sin\beta'\right] - z \quad (3)$$

where, g is the acceleration due to gravity; z the difference in height between the crest of the grade-control structure and the bottom of the downstream undisturbed bed level; U_o is the mean flow velocity at the weir crest (equal to the jet entering velocity); and β' is the maximum side-angle of scour hole. The angle β' (Figure 2) is approximately equal to the jet angle, and has been experimentally inferred by Bormann and Julien [8]:

$$\beta' = 0.316 \sin \lambda + 0.15 \ln \left(\frac{z + y_0}{y_0} \right) + 0.13 \ln \left(\frac{h}{y_0} \right) - 0.05 \ln \left(\frac{U_0}{\sqrt{gy_0}} \right) \quad (4)$$

in which, λ is the downstream face angle of the grade-control structure (rad); and y_o is the water depth at the crest.

Mason and Arumugam [5] have tested some formulas for the scours under free-falling jets using model and prototype data. The authors obtained the best agreement between the selected equations and measurements for the model data using a representative diameter d_s equal to the mean particle size d_m. They have proposed a comprehensive model and prototype equation, which can be rewritten according to the suggestions made by Yen [10] in the following form:

$$\frac{s}{\sqrt[3]{q^2/g}} = \left(6.42 - 3.10 H^{0.1} \right) g^{-H/600} \times \left(\frac{gH^3}{q^2} \right)^{(20+H)/600} \left(\frac{H}{d_s} \right)^{0.1} \left(\frac{h}{H} \right)^{3/20} \quad (5)$$

where, H is the difference in height between upstream and tail-water level.

Azmathulla et al. [11] have predicted the relative scour depth downstream of ski-jump bucket spillway by genetic programming (GP) and artificial neural network (ANN). The GP-based estimations were found to be equally and more accurate than the ANN-based ones, especially when the underlying cause-effect relationship became more uncertain to model.

Lee et al. [12] have predicted the scour depth around bridge piers by the back-propagation neural network (BPNN) and non-linear relationships. They have shown that the scour depth around bridge piers can be efficiently predicted using BPNN.

The main objectives of this study were to investigate the scour process, estimating the maximum depth and location of the scour hole, and evaluating the maximum height and location of the sedimentary mound at the downstream of the grade-control structure. In this study, the experimental data obtained by the previous researchers was used, and the equations were reviewed and re-written using the D'Agostino and Ferro [13] studies in order to improve the accuracy of the existing relationships. In the next step, the hydroinformatic science and the soft computing technique were used to achieve more accuracy for the relationships of the hole's

characteristic and the sedimentary mound in alluvial ducts containing non-cohesive sediments. Zhang et al. [14] have provided a collection of high-quality research articles that address the broad challenges in bioinformatics and biomedicine of SCs and reflect the emerging trends in the state-of- the-art SC algorithms.

Asghari Esfandani and Nematzadeh [15] carried out research using the Genetic algorithm and Neural Network to make a hybrid method to predict air pollution in Tehran. The result show that the proposed method has a good agreement with field observations.

2. Research method

After evaluating the studies carried out by Veronese [16], Mossa [17], D'Agostino [18], Falciai and Giacomin [19], Lenzi et al. [20], and D'Agostino and Ferro [13], the study carried out by D'Agostino [18] was chosen for our study because it had a favorable situation for the experimental data analysis and processing. The data range used in the form of the revised effective relationships of the scour hole and sedimentary mound under grade-control structures with sharp-crested weir are shown in table 1.

Table 1. Changes in range of parameters used in this study

Parameter	Symbol	Unit	Range
Channel width	B	m	0.5
Weir width	B	m	0.15-0.3
Fall height	Z	m	0.41- 0.71
Total head above the weir crest	h_0	m	0.043-0.2006
Tail water depth	H	m	0.083-0.435
Water discharge	Q	L/s	8.35-83.35
Diameter of which 50-percent is finer	D_{50}	mm	4.1, 11.5
Diameter of which 90-percent is finer	D_{90}	mm	7, 17.6
Maximum scour depth	s	m	0.045-0.285
Location of the maximum scour depth to weir	XS	m	0.215-0. 705
Maximum height of the mound above the undisturbed bed level	h_d	m	0.0250.255
Location of the maximum height of stockpiling sediments	XD	m	0.24-1.705

According to the theory of dimensional analysis and also the characteristics shown in figure 2, all the affecting parameters in this research work are as what follow:

- Kinematic characteristics: Q is the discharge, and g is the acceleration due to gravity.
- Dynamic characteristics: ρ_s-ρ is the submerged weight of sediment particles; ρ is the mass density of fluid; and μ is the water viscosity.
- Geometric characteristics: z is the fall height; b is the weir width; B is the channel width; h is the tail water depth; H is the difference in height from the water level upstream of the weir to the tail-water level; D_{50} is the diameter for which 50% of particles are finer; and D_{90} is the diameter for which 90% of particles are finer.

Therefore, the following functional relationship can be expressed:

$$f\left(\varphi, z, b, B, h, H, Q, \rho_s - \rho, \rho, g, \mu, D_{50}, D_{90}\right) = 0 \quad (6)$$

in which φ is representative scour hole parameters containing as: s is the maximum scour depth; XS is the horizontal distance between the weir crest and the section of maximum scour depth; h_d is the maximum height of the mound above the undisturbed bed level and XD is the location of the maximum height of stockpiling sediments.

The dimensionless parameters were obtained according to (7) using the Buckingham π theorem, and the independent variables z and ρ, as the repeated variables, were selected.

$$f(\pi_1 = \frac{\varphi}{z}, \pi_2 = \frac{b}{z}, \pi_3 = \frac{B}{z}, \pi_4 = \frac{h}{2}, \pi_5 = \frac{H}{z}, \quad (7)$$

$$\pi_6 = \frac{D_{50}}{z}, \pi_7 = \frac{D_{90}}{z}, \pi_8 = \frac{\rho - \rho_S}{\rho}, \pi_9 = \frac{gz^5}{Qz^2}) = 0$$

The dimensionless parameters b/B, h/H, and D_{50}/D_{90} are the results of the combination of the dimensionless parameters π_2, π_3, π_4, π_5, π_6, and π_7. The dimensionless parameter $Q/\left(bz\sqrt{gD_{50}(\rho_s - \rho)/\rho}\right)$ is obtained through combination with the parameters π_2, π_6, π_8, and π_9.

$$f\left(\frac{\varphi}{z}, \frac{b}{z}, \frac{b}{B}, \frac{h}{H}, \frac{D_{90}}{D_{50}}, \frac{Q}{bz\sqrt{gD_{50}(\rho_s - \rho)/\rho}}, \frac{z\mu}{\rho Q}\right) = 0 \quad (8)$$

Parameter $z\mu/\rho Q$ is the Reynolds number that is neglected from its effect in the equations because of flow turbulence. As a result, (8) is summarized in the form of (9).

Parameter $Q/\left(bz\sqrt{gD_{50}(\rho_S - \rho)/\rho}\right)$ is emanated from the densimetric Froude number, and it is shown by $Fr_{D_{50}}$. Thus we can write:

$$\frac{\varphi}{z} = f\left(\frac{b}{B}, \frac{D_{90}}{D_{50}}, \frac{h}{H}, \frac{b}{z}, Fr_{D_{50}}\right) = 0 \quad (9)$$

In addition, the effect of the independent parameters b/z, h/H, Fr_{D50}, D_{90}/D_{50}, and b/B on the dependent parameters φ/z is introduced in the form of (10):

$$\frac{\varphi}{z} = a \times \left(\frac{b}{B}\right)^b \left(\frac{D_{90}}{D_{50}}\right)^c \left(\frac{h}{H}\right)^d \left(\frac{b}{z}\right)^e \left(Fr_{D_{50}}\right)^f \quad (10)$$

In this equation, the coefficients a, b, c, d, e, and f are constant numbers, and their effects are determined using the statistical analysis of the experimental observations made by the SPSS software using the non-linear regression technique by the forward stepwise regression method.

3. Results and discussion
3.1. Non-linear regression method
The SPSS software was used for determining the effective equations in this research work. The observed values for the independent dimensionless relative parameters b/z, h/H, Fr_{D50}, D_{90}/D_{50}, and b/B were evaluated versus the dependent parameters maximum scour relative depth s/z, maximum relative distance of maximum scour depth XS/z, relative height of sedimentary mound h_d/z, and maximum relative distance accumulation of sediments to weir toe XD/z in order to determine the mapping space between the independent and dependent parameters mentioned in (10). The mapping space between the independent and dependent parameters can be shown as (11)-(14):

$$\frac{s}{z} = 0.5292 \times \left(\frac{b}{B}\right)^{0.3104} \times \left(\frac{D_{90}}{D_{50}}\right)^{-0.0651} \times \left(\frac{h}{H}\right)^{0.0849} \times \left(\frac{b}{z}\right)^{0.5052} \times \left(Fr_{D_{50}}\right)^{0.5302} \quad (11)$$

$$\frac{XS}{z} = 1.8113 \times \left(\frac{b}{B}\right)^{0.0333} \times \left(\frac{D_{90}}{D_{50}}\right)^{-0.0839} \times \left(\frac{h}{H}\right)^{0.1161} \times \left(\frac{b}{z}\right)^{0.3583} \times \left(Fr_{D_{50}}\right)^{0.3601} \quad (12)$$

$$\frac{h_d}{z} = 1.369 \times \left(\frac{b}{B}\right)^{1.1387} \times \left(\frac{D_{90}}{D_{50}}\right)^{-1.5679} \times \left(\frac{h}{H}\right)^{-0.0573} \times \left(\frac{b}{z}\right)^{0.3413} \times \left(Fr_{D_{50}}\right)^{0.7772} \quad (13)$$

$$\frac{XD}{z} = 4.5856 \times \left(\frac{b}{B}\right)^{0.4987} \times \left(\frac{D_{90}}{D_{50}}\right)^{-0.6068} \times \left(\frac{h}{H}\right)^{0.05} \times \left(\frac{b}{z}\right)^{0.3136} \times \left(Fr_{D_{50}}\right)^{0.5035} \quad (14)$$

The fitting method of (11)-(14) extracted from the experimental results are shown in figures 3-6. The error analysis functions were used in order to evaluate the results obtained by the proposed equations.

A summary of the results is shown in table 2.

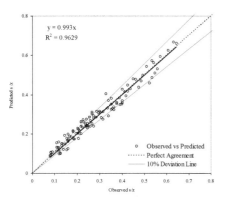

Figure 3. Comparison between observed and predicted equation (11) to estimate *s/z*.

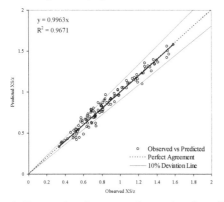

Figure 4. Comparison between observed and predicted equation (12) to estimate *XS/z*.

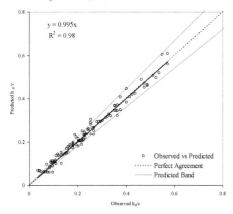

Figure 5. Comparison between observed and predicted equation (13) to estimate *h_d/z*.

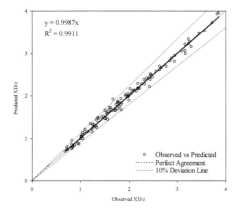

Figure 6. Comparison between observed and predicted equation (14) to estimate *XD/z*.

Table 2. Error functions from results suggested by equations (11)-(14) against experimental observations.

Parameter	RMSE	MPE	SEE	EF	m	R^2
s/z	0.0264	1.6378	0.026	0.9643	0.993	0.962
XS/z	0.0553	0.065	0.055	0.9674	0.9963	0.967
h_d/z	0.019	2.839	0.018	0.9804	0.995	0.98
XD/z	0.0743	0.028	0.074	0.9911	0.9987	0.991

The angular coefficient of the fitted line extracted from the results of (11)-(14) indicates that the non-linear regression estimates of the dimensionless parameter values s/z, XS/z, h_d/z, and XD/z are, respectively, 0.7%, 0.37%, 0.5%, and 0.13% lower than the observed values. The estimating bands of the above-mentioned four parameters used to determine the scour hole dimension are shown in figures 3-6. The skewness results obtained from the statistical prediction dimensionless parameters s/z, XS/z, h_d/z, and XD/z had desirable distributions.

3.2. Genetic programming

Genetic programming (GP) is used as one of the evolutionary algorithm techniques in order to flourish the presented relationship accuracy in the second part of this work. GP is an automatic programming technique used for evolving computer programs to solve problems. GP is frequently applied to the model structure identification problems in engineering applications. In such applications, GP is used to infer the underlying structure of either a natural or an experimental process in order to model the process numerically. GP is a member of the evolutionary algorithm (EA) family. EAs are based upon the Darwin's natural selection theory of evolution, where a population is progressively improved by selectively discarding the not-so-fit populations and breeding from the better populations. EAs work by defining a goal in the form of a quality criterion, and then using this goal to evaluate the solution candidates in a stepwise refinement of a dataset structures and return an optimal solution after a number of generations. GP can optimize both the structure of the model and its parameters. Since GP evolves an equation relating the output and input variables, it has the advantage of providing the inherent functional relationship explicitly over techniques like ANN [21].

After extracting the model by the GP method, the results obtained were analyzed using the error function, and compared with the experimental observations. All programmings were done in MATLAB (version 8.2.0.29).

The best input should be a considered pattern in order to determine the best response. Therefore, in the first step, various parameters that are effective in modeling such as the population members, number of generations, size of tree structures, and method of generation of initial population should be determined carefully with regards to the investigated data user.

The size of each tree structure has a significant role in the accuracy of the final model. determining the larger numbers than optimal value leads in reduction of the accuracy of the model the models are not presented mainly because the models made by GP in order to estimate the scour hole dimensions in the downstream grade-control structures were very long-scale.

The root mean square error (RMSE) is used to represent the fitness function. The $RMSE_i$ of an individual program i is evaluated using the following equation:

$$RMSE_i = \sqrt{\frac{1}{n}\sum_{j=1}^{n}(P_{ij} - T_j)^2} \qquad (15)$$

where, $P_{(ij)}$ is the value predicted by the individual program i for the fitness case j (out of n fitness cases), and T_j is the target value for the fitness case j.

For a perfect fit, $P_{(ij)} = T_j$ and $RMSE_i = 0$. Thus the RMSE index ranges from 0 to infinity, with 0 corresponding to the ideal. As it stands, $RMSE_i$ cannot be used directly as fitness since for the fitness proportionate selection, the fitness value must increase with efficiency. Thus to evaluate the fitness f_i of an individual program i, the following equation is used:

$$f_i = 1000\frac{1}{1 + RMSE_i} \qquad (16)$$

which obviously ranges from 0 to 1000, with 1000 corresponding to the ideal. In order to evolve a model with GP, the function set and the characteristic of the employed GP must be introduced. In this case, after setting composed functions of the operators ithave been used to achieve the best model evolved by GP.The final characteristics of the employed GP for all the scour parameters *(ds/z), (XS/z), (h_d/z),* and *(XD/z)* are shown in table 3.

GP against the experimental results for the parameters *s/z, XS/z, h_d/z,* and *XD/z* are shown in figures 7-10. The error analysis functions were used in order to evaluate the GP results, tabulating them in table 4.

Table 3. Characteristics of employed GP for *(ds/z),* *(XS/z), (h_d/z),* and *(XD/z)*.

Parameter	Definition	Value (ds/z), (XS/z)	Value (h_d/z), (XD/z)
P_1	Function set	+, −, *, √, ^2, cos, exp	+, −, *, √, ^2
P_2	Terminal set	b/B, D_{90}/D_{50}, h/H, b/Z, Fr d	b/B, D_{90}/D_{50}, h/H, b/Z, Fr d
P_3	Number of inputs	5	5
P_4	Fitness function	RMSE	RMSE
P_5	Error type	error function	error function
P_6	Crossover rate	0.85%	0.85%
P_7	Mutation rate	0.1%	0.1%
P_8	Gene reproduction rate	0.05%	0.05%
P_9	Population size	250	350
P_{10}	Number of generation	120	150
P_{11}	Tournament type	regular	regular
P_{12}	Tournament size	6	6
P_{13}	Max tree depth	4	4
P_{14}	Max node per tree	Inf	Inf
P_{15}	Constants range	[-10, +10]	[-10, +10]

The angular coefficient of the fitted line extracted from the results of the model made indicated that GP estimated the values for the dimensionless parameters s/z, XS/z, h_d/z, and XD/z to be, respectively, 0.78%, 0.9%, 1.2%, and 0.65% lower than the observed values. Figures 7-10 show the estimating bands for the above-mentioned four parameters to determine the scour hole dimensions by GP. The skewness results obtained from the predicted dimensionless parameters s/z, XS/z, h_d/z, and XD/z using the GP data mining system was satisfactory.

Table 4.. Error function of GP model against experimental observations.

Para meter	RMSE	MPE	SEE	EF	m	R^2
s/z	0.024	−2.06	0.024	0.969	0.992	0.97
XS/z	0.051	−0.79	0.051	0.972	0.991	0.97
h_d/z	0.020	−4.35	0.020	0.976	0.987	0.97
XD/z	0.105	−0.36	0.105	0.982	0.993	0.98

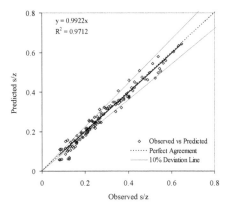

Figure 7. Comparison between observed and predicted GP to estimate *s/z*.

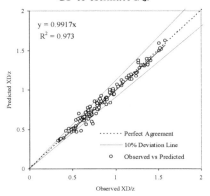

Figure 8. Comparison between observed and predicted GP to estimate *XS/z*.

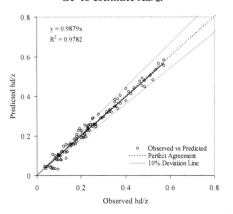

Figure 9. Comparison between observed and predicted GP to estimate h_d/z.

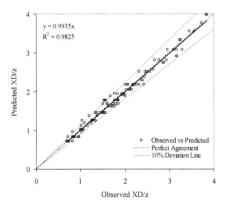

Figure. 10. Comparison between observed and predicted GP to estimate *XD/z*.

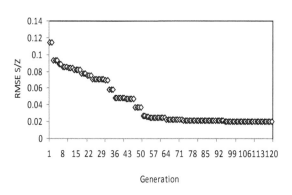

Figure 11. Root mean square error versus generation of *s/z*.

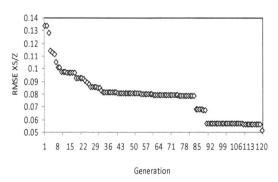

Figure 12. Root mean square error versus generation of *XS/z*.

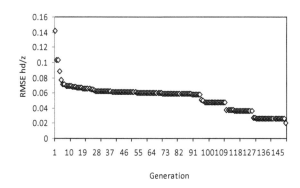

Figure 13. Root mean square error versus generation of h_d/z.

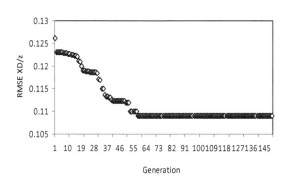

Figure 14. Root mean square error versus generation of *XD/z*.

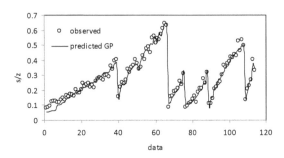

Figure 15. GP estimations of *s/z* versus measured ones

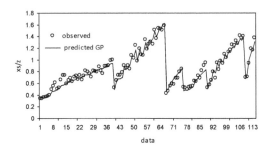

Figure 16. GP estimations of *XS/z* versus measured ones

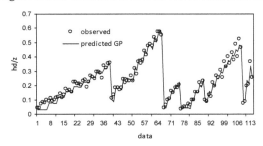

Figure 17. GP estimations of *h_d/z* versus measured ones

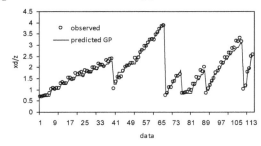

Figure 18. GP estimations of *XD/z* versus measured ones

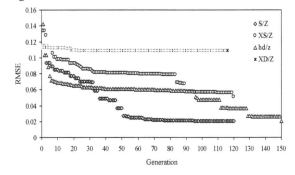

Figure 19. Root mean square error versus generation in GP.

3.3. Artificial neural network

The artificial neural network (ANN) is one of the most common network models, which generally presents a system of inter-connected neurons that can compute values from inputs. A neuron consists of multiple inputs and a single output. There is an input layer that acts as a distribution structure for the data being presented to the networks. This layer is not used for any type of processing. After this layer, one or more processing layers follow, called the hidden layers. The final processing layer is called the output layer in a network. This process is repeated until the error rate is minimized or reaches an acceptable level or until a specified number of iterations have been accomplished. In the ANN models, the sigmoid function is used. Here, in this work, we used the multi-layer perceptron (MLP) neural network model. An MLP is a feed-forward ANN model that maps sets of input data onto a set of appropriate outputs. An MLP consists of multiple layers of nodes in a directed graph, with each layer fully connected to the next one. The MLP-ANN models were used to estimate the dimensionless parameter values $(b/B, D_{90}/D_{50}, h/H, b/z, Fr_{D_{50}})$. For this purpose, 80% of the experimental data was used for network training, and the remaining 20% was used for testing the results obtained. This procedure was repeated for 1,000 times to achieve the best performance. The parameters *s/z*, *XS/z*, *h_d/z*, and *XD/z* were introduced as the input parameters to the model. The details of the MLP-ANN architecture is shown in table5.

Figures 20-23 show the performance of the MLP-ANN model to estimate the scour hole dimensions after training. Then 20% of the data that was not used in the training stage would be used to evaluate the performance of the model. The error function results of the neural network used for estimating the scour hole dimensions are summarized in table 6.

Table 5. Details of MLP-ANN architecture

parameter	Input layer	Hidden layer	Hidden layer	Output layer
s/z	5	6	4	1
XS/z	5	4	2	1
h_d/z	5	4	3	1
XD/z	5	3	1	1

Table 6. Statistical error functions of ANN for estimating scour hole dimensions for best network architecture

Parameter	Training				Testing			
	MPE	RMSE	EF	R^2	MPE	RMSE	EF	R^2
s/z	0.2514	0.0082	0.9811	0.9853	0.0345	0.0133	0.9908	0.9911
XS/z	1.6163	0.0326	0.9492	0.9737	−1.9160	0.0494	0.9793	0.9837
h_d/z	2.8802	0.0081	0.9756	0.9899	−2.1214	0.0186	0.9864	0.9885
XD/z	0.4463	0.0258	0.9937	0.9933	1.8970	0.0737	0.9935	0.9933

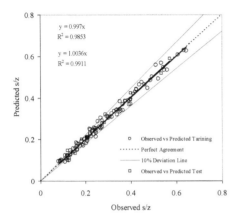

Figure 20. Comparison between observed and predicted s/z of ANN in training and testing stages.

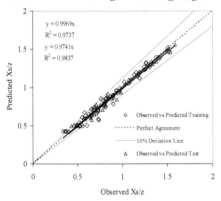

Figure 21. Comparison between observed and predicted XS/z of ANN in training and testing stages.

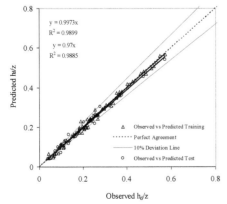

Figure 22. Comparison between observed and predicted h_d/z of ANN in training and testing stages

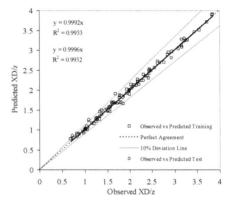

Figure 23. Comparison between observed and predicted XD/z of ANN in training and testing stages.

Comparing tables 2, 4, and 6 showed that the neural network model performed better in term of R^2, compared to the non-linear regression and GP methods. Also the estimated bands of the above-mentioned four parameters used to determine the scour hole dimension are shown in figures 20-23. The results of the statistical analysis conducted at various stages of training and testing is shown in figures 20-23. The skewness results obtained using the statistical prediction dimensionless parameters, i.e. s/z, XS/z, h_d/z, and XD/z, had desirable distributions. The angular coefficient of the fitted line extracted from the results of the model made indicated that ANN estimated the values for the dimensionless parameters, i.e. s/z, XS/z, h_d/z, and XD/z, to be 0.3%, 0.4%, 0.3%, and 0.08%, respectively, lower than the observed values in the training phase, the dimensionless parameter s/z, 0.2% more, and the dimensionless parameters XS/z, h_d/z, XD/z, 2.6%, 3%, and 0.04%, respectively, lower than the values observed in the testing phase. The skewness results obtained from the statistical prediction of the dimensionless parameters s/z, XS/z, h_d/z, and XD/z had desirable distributions.

3.4. Sensitivity analysis methods

Sensitivity analysis approaches can be classified in different ways. In this paper, they have been classified as mathematical, statistical or graphical. Other classifications focus on the capability, rather than the methodology, of a specific technique [22]. The classification approaches aim to understand the applicability of a specific method to a particular model and analysis objective.

3.4.1. Graphical methods for sensitivity analysis

Graphical methods give a representation of the sensitivity in the form of graphs, charts or surfaces. Generally, graphical methods are used to give a visual indication of how an output is affected by the variation in inputs [23]. Graphical methods can be used as a screening method before further analysis of a model or to represent complex dependencies between inputs and outputs [24, 25]. Graphical methods can be used to complement the results of mathematical and statistical methods for a better representation [26]. The sensitivity analysis was performed considering negligible h/H parameter impact, and thus we removed it from the equation, and (11)-(14) can be formed as follows:

$$\frac{s}{z} = 0.541 \times \left(\frac{b}{B}\right)^{0.294} \times \left(\frac{D_{90}}{D_{50}}\right)^{-0.008} \times \left(\frac{b}{z}\right)^{0.608} \times \left(Fr_{D_{50}}\right)^{0.561} \quad (17)$$

$$\frac{XS}{z} = 1.833 \times \left(\frac{b}{B}\right)^{-0.002} \times \left(\frac{D_{90}}{D_{50}}\right)^{-0.734} \times \left(\frac{b}{z}\right)^{0.500} \times \left(Fr_{D_{50}}\right)^{0.395} \quad (18)$$

$$\frac{h_d}{z} = 1.344 \times \left(\frac{b}{B}\right)^{1.141} \times \left(\frac{D_{90}}{D_{50}}\right)^{-1.601} \times \left(\frac{b}{z}\right)^{0.276} \times \left(Fr_{D_{50}}\right)^{0.753} \quad (19)$$

$$\frac{XD}{z} = 4.629 \times \left(\frac{b}{B}\right)^{0.489} \times \left(\frac{D_{90}}{D_{50}}\right)^{-0.567} \times \left(\frac{b}{z}\right)^{0.373} \times \left(Fr_{D_{50}}\right)^{0.522} \quad (20)$$

The fitting method for equations (17)-(20), extracted from the experimental results, are shown in figures 3-6. The error analysis functions were used in order to evaluate the results of the proposed equations. A summary of the results obtained are shown in table 7. The angular coefficient of the fitted line extracting the results of (17)-(20) indicates that the non-linear regression estimates the dimensionless parameter value s/z, XS/z, h_d/z, and XD/z to be, respectively, 0.85%, 0.74%, 0.9%, and 0.21% lower than the observed values. The estimating bands of the above-mentioned four parameters used to determine the scour hole dimension are shown in figures 15-18. The fitting method for equations (17)-(20), extracted from the experimental results, are shown in figures 24-27. The error analysis functions were used in order to evaluate the results of the proposed equations. A summary of the results obtained are shown in table 7.

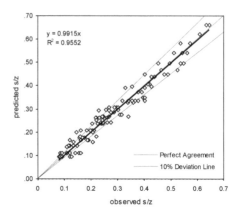

Figure 24. Comparison between observed and predicted equation (17) to estimate s/z.

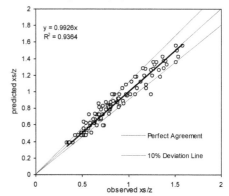

Figure 25. Comparison between observed and predicted equation (18) to estimate XS/z.

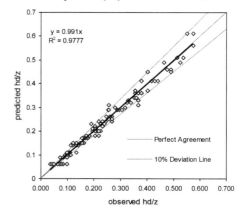

Figure 26. Comparison between observed and predicted equation (19) to estimate h_d/z.

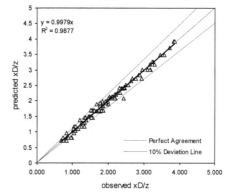

Figure 27. Comparison between observed and predicted equation (20) to estimate XD/z.

Table 5. Error functions from results suggested by equations (17)-(20) against experimental observations.

Parameter	RMSE	MPE	SEE	EF	m	R^2
s/z	0.028	1.843	0.028	0.957	0.991	0.955
XS/z	0.075	0.480	0.074	0.939	0.992	0.936
h_d/z	0.020	1.965	0.020	0.978	0.991	0.977
XD/z	0.087	0.066	0.087	0.987	0.997	0.987

4. Conclusion

By comparing the results tabulated in tables 2, 4, and6, it can be seen that the angular coefficient of the fitted line extracted from the results of the predicted parameters s/z, XS/z, h_d/z, and XD/z resulting from ANN is 45 degrees closer to the slope of the line of the non-linear regression and GP comparing to the predicted values. This indicates that the ANN model was more successful in estimating these parameters. The root mean square error had fewer values in predicting the parameter s/z, XS/z, h_d/z, and XD/z by ANN than non-linear regression and GP, and this indicates the advantage of this approach in estimation of these parameters. GP may serve as a robust approach, and it may open a new area for an accurate and effective explicit formulation of many water engineering problems. Generally, with regard to this point that since using the presented non-linear regression for estimating scour parameters does not require a computer, it can, therefore, be claimed that using the non-linear regression compared to GP and ANN in estimating the scour hole dimensions in the downstream grade-control structure is better and more tangible.

Acknowledgment

The authors would like to thanks Jundi-Shapur University of Technology, Dezul, Iran for the financial support of this work.

References

[1] Sarkar, A. & Dey, S. (2004). Review on local scour due to jets. International Journal of Sediment Research, vol. 19, no. 3, pp. 210-239.

[2] Ghetti, A. & Zanovello, A. (1954). Esame delle escavazioni d'alveo a valle di traverse mediante esperienze su modelli in piccola scala. Proc., 1st Convegno di Costruzioni Idrauliche, pp. 1-9

[3] Rouse, H. (1940). Criteria for similarity in the transportation of sediment, University of Iowa Studies in Engineering of Iowa, vol. 20, pp. 33-49.

[4] Doddiah, D., Albertson, M. L. & Thomas, R. (1953). Scour from jets. Proceedings: Minnesota International Hydraulic Convention, pp. 161-169.

[5] Mason, P. J. & Arumugam, K. (1985). Free jet scour below dams and flip buckets. Journal of Hydraulic Engineering, vol. 111, no. 2, pp. 220-235.

[6] D'Agostino, V. (1996). La progettazione delle controbriglie, Proc., 25th Convegno di Idraulica e Costruzioni Idrauliche,Torino, pp. 107-118 .(in Italian).

[7] Robinson, K. M., Hanson, G. J.& Cook, K. R. (1998). Velocity field measurements at an overfall. Pap. Am. Soc. Agric. Eng., 982063.

[8] Bormann, N. E. & Julien, P. Y. (1991). Scour downstream of grade-control structures. Journal of Hydraulic Engineering, vol. 117, no. 5, pp. 579-594.

[9] Bennett, S. J., Alonso, C. V., Prasad, S. N. & Ro¨mkens, M. J. M. (2000). Experiments on headcut growth migration in concentrated flows typical of upland areas, Water Resources Research, vol. 36, no. 7, pp. 1911–1922.

[10] Yen, C. L. (1987). Discussion on 'Free jet scour below dams and flip buckets, by Peter J. Mason and Kanapathypilly Arumugam. Journal of Hydraulic Engineering, vol. 113, no. 9, pp. 1200-1202.

[11] Azmathulla, H. MD., Ghani, A. AB., Zakaria, N. A., Lai, S. H., Chang, C. K., Leow, C. S. & Abuhasan, Z. (2008). Genetic programming to predict ski-jump bucket spillway scour. Journal of Hydrodynamics, Ser. B, vol. 20, no. 4, pp. 477-484.

[12] Lee, T. L., Jeng, D. S., Zhang, G. H. & Hong, J. H. (2007). Neural network modeling for estimation of scour depth around bridge piers. Journal of Hydrodynamics, Ser. B, vol. 19, no. 3, pp. 378-386.

[13] D'Agostino, V. & Ferro, V. (2004). Scour on alluvial bed downstream of grade-control structures. Journal of Hydraulic Engineering, vol. 130, no. 1, pp. 24-37.

[14] Zhang, Y., Balochian, S. & Bhatnagar, V. (2014). Emerging Trends in Soft Computing Models in Bioinformatics and Biomedicine . The Scientific World Journal, Article ID 683029, 3 pages.

[15] Asghari Esfandani, M. & Nematzadeh, H. (2016). Prediction of Air Pollution in Tehran: Genetic algorithm and back propagation neural network. Journal of AL and Data Mining. Vol. 4, no. 1, pp. 49-54.

[16] Veronese, A. (1937). Erosioni di fondo a valle di uno scarico. Annal. Lavori Pubbl, vol. 75, no. 9, pp. 717-726. (in Italian)

[17] Mossa, M. (1998). Experimental study on the scour downstream of grade-control structures, Proc. 26th Convegno di Idraulica e Costruzioni Idrauliche, Catania, September, vol. 3, pp. 581-594.

[18] D'Agostino, V. (1994). Indagine sullo scavo a valle di opere trasversali mediante modello fisico a fondo mobile. L'Energia elettrica, vol. 71, no. 2, pp. 37-51 (in Italian).

[19] Falciai, M. & Giacomin, A. (1978). Indagine sui gorghi che si formano a valle delle traverse torrentizie. Italia Forestale Montana, vol. 23, no. 3, pp. 111-123.

[20] Lenzi, M. A., Marion, A., Comiti, F. & Gaudio, R. (2000). Riduzione dello scavo a valle di soglie di fondo per effetto dell'interferenza tra le opera, Proc. 27th Convegno di Idraulica e Costruzioni Idrauliche, Genova, September, vol. 3, pp. 271–278 (in Italian).

[21] Jay awardena AW., Muttil N. & Fernando TMKG. (2005). Rainfall-Runoff Modelling using Genetic Programming. International Congress on Modelling and Simulation Society of Australia and New Zealand, pp. 1841-1847

[22] Saltelli, A., K. Chan. & E. M. Scott (Eds). (2000). Sensitivity Analysis. John Wiley and Sons, Ltd.: West Sussex, England.

[23] Geldermann, J. & Rentz, O. (2001). Integrated Technique Assessment with Imprecise Information as a Support for the Identification of Best Available Techniques. OR Spektrum, vol. 23, no. 1, pp. 137-157.

[24] Stiber, N. A., Pantazidou, M. & Small M. J. (1999). Expert System Methodology for Evaluating Reductive Dechlorination at TCE Sites. Environmental Science and Technology, vol. 33, no. 17, pp. 3012-3020.

[25] Critchfield, G. C. & Willard K. E.(1986). Probabilistic Analysis of Decision Trees Using Monte Carlo Simulation. Medical Decision Making, vol. 6, no. 1, pp. 85-92.

[26] McCamley, F. & R. K. Rudel. (1995). Graphical Sensitivity Analysis for Generalized Stochastic Dominance. Journal of Agricultural and Resource Economics, vol. 20, no. 2, pp. 403-403.

10

Evaluation of liquefaction potential based on CPT results using C4.5 decision tree

A. Ardakani[*] and V. R. Kohestani

Faculty of Engineering & Technology, Imam Khomeini International University, Qazvin, Iran.

*Corresponding author: a.ardakani@eng.ikiu.ac.ir (A.Ardakani)

Abstract

The prediction of liquefaction potential of soil due to an earthquake is an essential task in civil engineering. The decision tree has a structure consisting of internal and terminal nodes, which process the data to ultimately yield a classification. C4.5 is a known algorithm widely used to design decision trees. In this algorithm, a pruning process is carried out to solve the problem of the over-fitting. This article examines the capability of C4.5 decision tree for the prediction of seismic liquefaction potential of soil based on the Cone Penetration Test (CPT) data. The database contains the information about cone resistance (q_c), total vertical stress (σ_0), effective vertical stress (σ_0'), mean grain size (D_{50}), normalized peak horizontal acceleration at ground surface (a_{max}), cyclic stress ratio (τ/σ_0') and earthquake magnitude (M_w). The overall classification success rate for all the data set is 98%. The results of C4.5 decision tree have been compared with the available artificial neural network (ANN) and relevance vector machine (RVM) models. The developed C4.5 decision tree provides a viable tool for civil engineers to determine the liquefaction potential of soil.

Keywords: *Soil Liquefaction, Cone Penetration Test, Artificial Intelligence, C4.5 Decision Tree.*

1. Introduction

Seismically induced liquefaction in saturated soils is a phenomenon in which soil loses much of its strength or stiffness due to rising pore water pressure for a generally short period of time but nevertheless long enough for it to cause ground failure. Liquefaction of saturated sandy soils during the earthquakes causes building settlement or tipping, sand blows, lateral spreading, ground cracks, landslides, dam and high embankment failures and many other hazards. Liquefaction occurrence depends on the mechanical characteristics of the soil layers on the site, the depth of the water table, the intensity and duration of the ground shaking, the distance from the source of the earthquake and the seismic attenuation properties of in situ soil [1]. Determination of liquefaction potential of soil due to an earthquake is an important step for earthquake hazard mitigation. Because of the participation of a large number of factors that affect the occurrence of liquefaction during earthquake, the determination of liquefaction potential is a complex geotechnical engineering problem and has attracted considerable attention of geotechnical researchers in the past three decades. Several methods have been proposed to predict the occurrence of liquefaction. Many of these methods, are based on correlations between the in situ test measurements and observed field performance data, and are extensions of the "simplified procedure" pioneered by Seed and Idriss [2].

Amongst in situ tests, many researchers have adapted Cone Penetration Test (CPT) results as the basis for evaluation of liquefaction potential of the test method [3,4]. A primary advantage of the CPT is the nearly continuous information provided along the depth of the explored soil strata. The CPT is also considered more consistent and repeatable than other in situ test methods.

Artificial intelligence (AI) techniques such as artificial neural network (ANN) [4-6], support vector machine (SVM) [6-8] and relevance vector machine (RVM) [9,10] have been used to develop liquefaction prediction models based on in situ test database.

These models have the ability to operate on large quantities of data and learn complex model functions from examples, i.e., by training on sets of input and output data.

The greatest advantage of AI techniques over traditional modeling techniques is their ability to capture non-linear and complex interaction between variables of the system without having to assume the form of the relationship between input and output variables.

In the context of determination of liquefaction occurrence, this method can be trained to measure the relationship between the soil and earthquake characteristics with the liquefaction potential, requiring no prior knowledge of the form of the relationship.

Even though most of the introduced AI techniques have been successfully applied to CPT data, they do have shortcomings. For example, in the ANN approach, the optimum structure (e.g., number of inputs, hidden layers, and transfer functions) must be identified as a priori. This is usually done through a trial and error procedure.

The other major shortcoming is the black box nature of ANN model and the fact that the relationship between input and output parameters of the system is described in terms of a weight matrix and biases that are not accessible to the user [11].

Decision trees algorithms are quite transparent and also do not need optimization of model and internal parameters. Either a decision tree partitions or the input space of data set into mutually exclusive regions is assigned a label (classification tree) or a value to characterize its data points (regression tree). The decision tree has a structure consisting of internal and external nodes connected by branches. Each internal node is associated with a decision function to determine which node to visit next. Meanwhile, each external node, known as a terminal node or leaf node, indicates the output of a given input vector.

Figure 1 shows partitions of the input space into four non-overlapping rectangular regions, and each of which is assigned a labeled class 'Ci'.

C4.5 introduced by Quinlan [12] is a known algorithm widely used to design decision trees. This paper investigates the capability of C4.5 decision tree for the prediction of liquefaction potential of soil based on CPT data.

2. Materials and methods
2.1. Decision trees
Decision trees are fast and easy to use. The rules generated by decision trees are simple and accurate for most problems. Therefore, decision

trees are very popular and powerful tools in data mining [14].

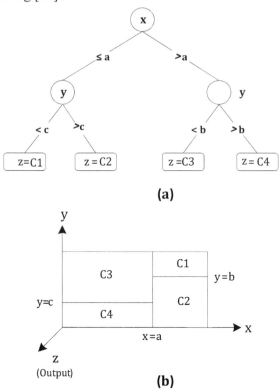

Figure 1. An example of a decision tree for classification (a) binary decision tree (b) feature space partitioning [13].

In general, a decision tree is a tree in which each branch node represents a choice between a number of alternatives and each leaf node represents a classification or decision [15]. An unknown (or test) instance is routed down the tree according to the values of the attributes in the successive nodes. When the instance reaches a leaf, it is classified according to the label assigned to the corresponded leaf.

In the first stage of model construction, a decision-tree induction algorithm is used to build the tree. Many algorithms for decision tree induction exist. Interactive Dichotomizer version 3 (ID3) and Commercial version 4.5 (C4.5) [13,16] are the most widely used with the classification and regression tree (CART) algorithm [17]. C4.5 algorithm is an extension of ID3 algorithm and the divide-and-conquer approach [12] whose main improvements included the pruning methodology and the processing of numeric attributes, missing values and noisy data.

The construction phase is begun at the root node where each attribute is evaluated using a statistical test to determine how well it can classify the training samples. The best attribute is chosen as the test at the root node of the tree. A descendant of the root node is then created for each either possible value of this attribute if it is a discrete-valued attribute or possible discretized interval of this attribute if it is a continuous-valued attribute. Next, the training samples are sorted to the appropriate descendant node.

The process is repeated using the training samples associated with each descendant node to select the best attribute for testing at that point in the tree. This forms a greedy search for a decision tree, in which the algorithm never backtracks to reconsider earlier node choices. Although it is possible to add a new node to the tree until all samples assigned to one node belong to the same class, the tree is not allowed to grow to its maximum depth. A node is only introduced to the tree only when there are a sufficient number of samples left from sorting. After the complete tree is constructed, a tree pruning is usually carried out to avoid data over-fitting.

A statistical test used in C4.5 for assigning an attribute to each node in the tree also employs an entropy-based measure. The assigned attribute is the one with the highest information gain ratio among attributes available at that tree construction point. The information gain ratio Gain Ratio(A, S) of an attribute $'A'$ relative to the sample set S is defined as

$$Gain\ Ratio(A, S) = \frac{Gain(A,S)}{Split\ Information(A,S)} \quad (1)$$

Where

$$Gain(A, S) = Ent(S) - \sum_{a \in A} \frac{|S_a|}{|S|} Ent(S_a) \quad (2)$$

and

$$Split\ Information(A, S) = -\sum_{a \in A} \frac{|S_a|}{|S|} log_2 \frac{|S_a|}{|S|} \quad (3)$$

S_a is the subset of S for which the attribute A has the value a. Obviously, the information gain ratio can be calculated straightaway for discrete-valued attributes. In contrast, continuous-valued attributes are needed to be discretised prior to the information gain ratio calculation.

2.2. Database

The database [5] used in this study consists of total 109 cases, 74 of them are liquefied cases and 35 of them are non-liquefied cases. The database contains: cone resistance (q_c), total vertical stress (σ_0), effective vertical stress (σ_0'), mean grain size (D_{50}), normalized peak horizontal acceleration at ground surface (a_{max}), cyclic stress ratio (τ/σ_0') and earthquake magnitude (M_w). The range of

values associated with each input variable is shown in table 1.

Generally in pattern recognition procedures (e.g., ANN, SVM or GP) it is common that the model construction is based on adaptive learning over a number of cases and the performance of the constructed model is then evaluated using an independent validation data set. Therefore, in the present study, a total of 74 datasets are considered for the training dataset, and other datasets are considered for the testing dataset. The training and testing datasets are the same as the ones used by Goh [5] and Samui [9].

Table 1. Range of values associated with the input variables used in liquefaction analysis.

Input variable	Range
Cone tip resistance, q_c (MPa)	1.0-31.4
Total vertical stress, σ_0 (kPa)	17-122
Effective vertical stress, σ_0' (kPa)	17-249
Mean grain size, D_{50} (mm)	0.06-0.67
Maximum horizontal ground surface acceleration, a_{max} (g)	0.1-0.8
Cyclic stress ratio, τ/σ_0'	0.06-0.72
Earthquake moment magnitude, M_w	6.6-7.8

3. Result and discussion

For building the model based on training data set, C4.5 algorithm implemented in WEKA software [18] was used. WEKA is written in Java and is freely available from Waikato University website [19].

The Decision tree generated by C4.5 algorithm is shown in figure 2, table 2 and table 3 illustrate the performance of C4.5 decision tree for training and testing dataset respectively. For the training patterns, three cases of liquefaction were wrongly classified. For the testing patterns, one case of liquefaction was wrongly classified.

Training and testing performance have been determined by using (4).

Training= Testing performance (%) =
$$\left(\frac{\text{No of data predicted accurately by C4.5}}{\text{Total data}}\right) \times 100 \quad (4)$$

As the results presented in table 2, the performances of C4.5 decision tree for training and testing data are comparable.

The successful prediction values are 95.9% for training and 97.1% for testing data whereas the overall success rate in predicting liquefaction in all cases is 96.3%. The overall classification success rate for the entire data set is slightly lower than the overal rate of ANN and RVM models reported by Goh   [5] and Samui [9], respectively (see Table 4).

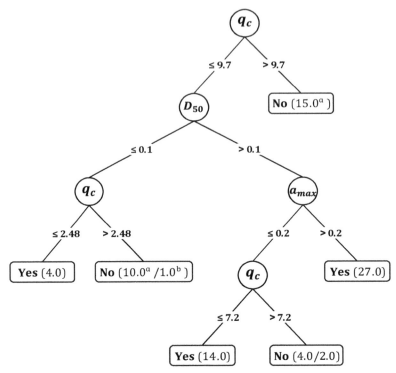

Figure 2. Decision tree generated by C4.5 algorithm.

[a] Number of cases in this partition.

[b] Number of cases misclassified.

Table 2. Performance of C4.5 for training dataset.

M_w	σ_0' (kPa)	σ_0 (kPa)	q_c (MPa)	a_{max} (g)	τ/σ_0'	D_{50} (mm)	Actual liquefied	Predicted liquefied?
7.5	53	36	3.20	0.16	0.15	0.331	Yes	Yes
7.5	87	52	1.60	0.16	0.16	0.331	Yes	Yes
7.5	99	58	7.20	0.16	0.17	0.331	Yes	Yes
7.5	152	83	5.60	0.16	0.17	0.331	Yes	Yes
7.5	91	63	5.45	0.16	0.14	0.331	Yes	Yes
7.5	127	80	8.84	0.16	0.15	0.331	Yes	No
7.5	211	120	9.70	0.16	0.15	0.331	Yes	No
7.5	86	46	8.00	0.16	0.19	0.30	No	No
7.5	95	50	14.55	0.16	0.18	0.30	No	No
7.7	58	48	10.00	0.23	0.18	0.32	No	No
7.7	73	54	16.00	0.23	0.20	0.32	No	No
7.7	96	65	15.38	0.23	0.21	0.32	No	No
7.7	54	46	1.79	0.23	0.17	0.32	Yes	Yes
7.7	64	52	4.10	0.23	0.19	0.32	Yes	Yes
7.7	96	67	7.96	0.23	0.21	0.32	Yes	Yes
7.7	114	75	8.97	0.23	0.22	0.32	Yes	Yes
7.8	57	42	1.70	0.40	0.35	0.06	Yes	Yes
7.8	114	69	9.40	0.40	0.41	0.25	Yes	Yes
7.8	148	85	5.70	0.40	0.42	0.25	Yes	Yes
7.8	162	92	7.60	0.40	0.42	0.30	Yes	Yes
7.8	17	17	1.50	0.40	0.27	0.17	Yes	Yes
7.8	25	21	1.00	0.40	0.32	0.17	Yes	Yes
7.8	34	25	5.00	0.40	0.36	0.17	Yes	Yes
7.8	38	34	2.50	0.40	0.29	0.14	Yes	Yes

M_w	σ'_0 (kPa)	σ_0 (kPa)	q_c (MPa)	a_{max} (g)	τ/σ'_0	D_{50} (mm)	Actual liquefied	Predicted liquefied?
7.8	57	43	2.60	0.40	0.34	0.14	Yes	Yes
7.8	76	52	3.20	0.40	0.37	0.16	Yes	Yes
7.8	89	58	5.80	0.40	0.39	0.16	Yes	Yes
7.8	122	74	3.50	0.40	0.40	0.16	Yes	Yes
7.8	181	102	8.40	0.40	0.41	0.16	Yes	Yes
7.8	38	29	1.70	0.40	0.35	0.12	Yes	Yes
7.8	40	29	3.50	0.40	0.36	0.12	Yes	Yes
7.8	51	35	4.10	0.40	0.38	0.12	Yes	Yes
7.8	29	27	5.50	0.40	0.29	0.17	Yes	Yes
7.8	57	40	9.00	0.40	0.37	0.32	Yes	Yes
7.8	23	21	7.00	0.40	0.29	0.48	Yes	Yes
7.8	34	26	1.18	0.40	0.35	0.48	Yes	Yes
7.8	48	33	4.24	0.40	0.38	0.48	Yes	Yes
7.8	76	71	11.47	0.40	0.27	0.16	No	No
7.8	160	111	15.76	0.40	0.34	0.20	No	No
7.8	59	56	11.39	0.20	0.14	0.21	No	No
7.8	78	65	12.12	0.20	0.15	0.21	No	No
7.8	99	75	17.76	0.20	0.17	0.14	No	No
7.8	74	49	2.65	0.20	0.19	0.14	Yes	Yes
7.8	53	35	4.40	0.20	0.20	0.16	Yes	Yes
7.8	61	39	3.00	0.20	0.20	0.16	Yes	Yes
7.8	156	81	9.00	0.20	0.23	0.08	Yes	No
7.8	99	55	2.00	0.10	0.11	0.14	Yes	Yes
7.8	95	52	1.10	0.20	0.23	0.07	Yes	Yes
7.8	209	106	15.50	0.10	0.11	0.08	No	No
7.8	217	110	6.50	0.10	0.11	0.08	No	No
7.8	91	53	9.00	0.10	0.11	0.10	No	No
7.8	101	58	2.50	0.10	0.11	0.10	No	No
7.8	112	63	16.50	0.10	0.11	0.10	No	No
7.8	91	68	13.65	0.10	0.06	0.25	No	No
7.8	114	58	8.47	0.20	0.24	0.062	No	No
7.8	228	112	4.55	0.20	0.23	0.067	No	No
7.8	249	122	5.79	0.20	0.22	0.067	No	No
7.8	121	55	2.48	0.20	0.25	0.062	Yes	Yes
7.8	114	56	1.57	0.20	0.25	0.062	Yes	Yes
7.8	213	103	1.45	0.20	0.23	0.67	Yes	Yes
7.8	220	106	2.15	0.20	0.23	0.67	Yes	Yes
7.8	230	111	2.60	0.20	0.23	0.67	Yes	Yes
7.8	213	103	2.73	0.20	0.23	0.67	Yes	Yes
7.8	219	106	1.78	0.20	0.23	0.67	Yes	Yes
7.8	211	108	7.64	0.20	0.22	0.67	No	No
6.6	29	29	25.60	0.80	0.44	0.11	No	No
6.6	48	36	24.70	0.80	0.57	0.11	No	No
6.6	64	42	31.40	0.80	0.64	0.11	No	No
6.6	29	29	1.43	0.80	0.44	0.11	Yes	Yes
6.6	64	42	2.48	0.80	0.64	0.11	Yes	Yes
6.6	96	54	4.03	0.80	0.72	0.11	Yes	Yes
6.6	29	29	3.30	0.80	0.44	0.06	No	No
6.6	48	36	8.80	0.80	0.57	0.06	No	No
6.6	64	42	6.70	0.80	0.64	0.06	No	No

Table 3. Performance of C4.5 for testing dataset.

M_w	σ_0' (kPa)	σ_0 (kPa)	q_c (MPa)	a_{max} (g)	τ/σ_0'	D_{50} (mm)	Actual liquefied	Predicted liquefied?
7.8	89	78	1.65	0.20	0.41	0.17	Yes	Yes
7.8	99	83	3.65	0.20	0.15	0.17	Yes	Yes
7.8	29	25	1.03	0.20	0.15	0.19	Yes	Yes
7.8	55	37	5.00	0.20	0.19	0.31	Yes	Yes
7.8	76	47	2.91	0.20	0.21	0.18	Yes	Yes
7.8	105	61	6.06	0.20	0.21	0.18	Yes	Yes
7.8	23	22	13.24	0.20	0.14	0.17	No	No
7.8	32	26	13.06	0.20	0.16	0.17	No	No
7.8	40	30	16.59	0.20	0.18	0.17	No	No
7.8	59	59	10.59	0.20	0.13	0.26	No	No
7.8	63	61	9.12	0.20	0.13	0.26	No	No
7.8	76	67	11.29	0.20	0.15	0.26	No	No
7.8	70	41	1.94	0.20	0.22	0.16	Yes	Yes
7.8	76	44	5.00	0.20	0.22	0.16	Yes	Yes
7.8	70	47	2.24	0.20	0.19	0.14	Yes	Yes
7.8	114	79	14.12	0.20	0.09	0.25	No	No
7.8	162	102	18.94	0.20	0.09	0.28	No	No
7.8	44	44	3.52	0.20	0.13	0.16	Yes	Yes
7.8	59	51	2.73	0.20	0.15	0.16	Yes	Yes
7.8	57	50	3.29	0.20	0.15	0.21	Yes	Yes
7.8	61	52	4.12	0.20	0.15	0.21	Yes	Yes
7.8	72	57	2.94	0.20	0.16	0.21	Yes	Yes
7.8	61	52	3.00	0.20	0.15	0.15	Yes	Yes
7.8	95	68	5.85	0.20	0.18	0.32	Yes	Yes
7.8	106	73	9.00	0.20	0.18	0.32	Yes	No
7.8	49	48	1.88	0.20	0.13	0.13	Yes	Yes
7.8	74	64	2.55	0.20	0.15	0.17	Yes	Yes
7.8	76	65	4.50	0.20	0.15	0.17	Yes	Yes
7.8	106	79	4.24	0.20	0.17	0.17	Yes	Yes
7.8	114	77	8.00	0.20	0.18	0.22	No	No
7.2	80	48	5.22	0.22	0.21	0.20	Yes	Yes
7.2	95	55	3.73	0.22	0.22	0.20	Yes	Yes
7.2	114	64	3.11	0.22	0.22	0.20	Yes	Yes
7.2	133	73	1.32	0.22	0.22	0.20	Yes	Yes
7.2	152	82	5.22	0.22	0.22	0.20	Yes	Yes

Table 4. Comparison of results of developed C4.5 decision tree with available ANN [5] and RVM models [9].

Method	Performance in terms of successful prediction (%)		
	Training	Testing	Overall
ANN [5]	98.6	94.3	97.2
RVM [9]	100	100	100
C4.5 decision tree	95.9	97.1	96.3

The ANN uses many parameters, such as the number of hidden layers, number of hidden nodes, learning rate, momentum term, number of training epochs, transfer functions, and weight initialization methods. Though the RVM has lower parameters compared with ANN, but RVM requires a selection of a suitable kernel function first and then setting of the specific parameters and these processes are time consuming. Moreover, these techniques will not produce an explicit relationship in the variables and thus, the developed model provides very little insight into the basic mechanism of the problem. Decision trees algorithms are quite transparent and also do not need optimization of model and internal parameters. The developed C4.5 decision tree, figure 2, can be used by geotechnical engineering professionals with the help of a spreadsheet to evaluate the liquefaction potential of soil for a future seismic event without going into complexities of model development whereas the available ANN and RVM models do not provide any explicit equations for professionals. Also in the C4.5 approach normalization or scaling of the data is not required, but is an advantage over ANN and RVM approach.

The limitations of the C4.5 decision trees need to be mentioned as well. Similar to other artificial intelligence techniques, decision trees have a limited domain of applicability and are mostly case dependent. Therefore, their generalization is limited and they are only applicable in the range of training data. However, the C4.5 model can always be updated to yield better results, as new data becomes available.

4. Conclusions

Liquefaction in soil is one of the major causes of concern in geotechnical engineering. The cone penetration test has proven to be an effective tool in characterization of subsurface conditions and analysis of different aspects of soil behavior, comprising estimating the potential for liquefaction on a specific site. In this paper, the C4.5 decision tree is used to predict the liquefaction potential of soil based on CPT data. The C4.5 model was trained and validated using a database of 109 liquefaction and non-liquefaction field case histories for sandy soils based on CPT results. The overall classification success rate for the entire data set is 96.3% and is comparable with those calculated using ANN and RVM models which were taken in the literature. Unlike available ANN and RVM models, the proposed model provide easily interpretable tree structure that can be used by geotechnical engineering professionals with the help of a spreadsheet to predict the liquefaction potential of soil for future seismic event without going into the complexities of model development using C4.5 decision tree. This model can be adopted for modeling different problems in geosciences.

References

[1] Rezania, M. Javadi, A. A. & Giustolisi, O. (2010). Evaluation of liquefaction potential based on CPT results using evolutionary polynomial regression. Computers and Geotechnics, vol. 37, no. 1, pp. 82-92.

[2] Seed, H. B. & Idriss, I. M. (1971). Simplified procedure for evaluating soil liquefaction potential. Journal of the Soil Mechanics and Foundations, vol. 97, no. 9, pp. 1249-1273.

[3] Youd, T. Idriss, I. Andrus, R. D. Arango, I. Castro, G. Christian, J. T. Dobry, R. Finn, W. L. Harder, L. F. & Hynes, M. E. (2001). Liquefaction resistance of soils: summary report from the 1996 NCEER and 1998 NCEER/NSF workshops on evaluation of liquefaction resistance of soils. Journal of Geotechnical and Geoenvironmental Engineering, vol. 127, no. 10, pp. 817-833.

[4] Juang, C. H. Yuan, H. Lee, D. H. & Lin, P. S. (2003). Simplified cone penetration test-based method for evaluating liquefaction resistance of soils. Journal of geotechnical and geoenvironmental engineering, vol. 129, no. 1, pp, 66-80.

[5] Goh, A. T. (1996). Neural-network modeling of CPT seismic liquefaction data. Journal of Geotechnical engineering, vol. 122, no. 1, pp. 70-73.

[6] Samui, P. & Sitharam, T. (2011). Machine learning modelling for predicting soil liquefaction susceptibility. Natural Hazards and Earth System Science, vol. 11, pp. 1-9.

[7] Goh, A. T. & Goh, S. (2007). Support vector machines: their use in geotechnical engineering as illustrated using seismic liquefaction data. Computers and Geotechnics, vol. 34, no. 5, pp. 410-421.

[8] Pal, M. (2006). Support vector machines based modelling of seismic liquefaction potential. International Journal for Numerical and Analytical Methods in Geomechanics, vol. 30, no. 10, pp. 983-996.

[9] Samui, P. (2007). Seismic liquefaction potential assessment by using relevance vector machine. Earthquake Engineering and Engineering Vibration, vol. 6, no. 4, pp. 331-336.

[10] Samui, P. & Karthikeyan, J. (2014). The Use of a Relevance Vector Machine in Predicting Liquefaction Potential. Indian Geotechnical Journal, vol. 44, no. 4, pp. 458-467.

[11] Javadi, A. A. Ahangar-Asr, A. Johari, A. Faramarzi, A. & Toll, D. (2012). Modelling stress–strain and volume change behaviour of unsaturated soils using an evolutionary based data mining technique, an incremental approach. Engineering Applications of Artificial Intelligence, vol. 25, no.5, pp. 926-933.

[12] Quinlan, J. R. (1993). C4.5: programs for machine learning. San Francisco: Morgan Kaufmann.

[13] Cho, J. H. & Kurup, P. U. (2011). Decision tree approach for classification and dimensionality reduction of electronic nose data. Sensors and Actuators B: Chemical, vol. 160, no. 1, pp. 542-548.

[13] Quinlan, J. R. (1993). C4.5: programs for machine learning. San Francisco: Morgan Kaufmann.

[14] Duch, W. Setiono, R. & Zurada, J. M. (2004). Computational intelligence methods for rule-based data understanding. Proceedings of the IEEE, vol. 92, no. 5, pp. 771-805.

[15] Hand, D. J. Mannila, H. & Smyth, P. (2001). Principles of data mining. London: MIT press.

[16] Quinlan, J. R. (1986). Induction of decision trees. Machine learning, vol. 1, no. 1, pp. 81-106.

[17] Breiman, L. Friedman, J. H. Olshen, R. A. & Stone, C. J. (1984). Classification and regression trees. Belmont: Wadsworth.

[18] Witten, I. H. & Frank, E. (2005). Data Mining: Practical machine learning tools and techniques. San Francisco: Morgan Kaufmann.

[19] Waikato University website (2015), Available: http://www.cs.waikato.ac.nz/~ml/.

11

Classification of emotional speech through spectral pattern features

A. Harimi[1*], A. Shahzadi[1], A.R. Ahmadyfard[2] and Kh.Yaghmaie[1]

1. Faculty of Electrical & Computer Engineering, Semnan University, Iran.
2. Department of Electrical Engineering and Robotics, Shahrood University of technology, Iran.

*Corresponding author: a.harimi@gmail.com (A. Harimi).

Abstract

Speech Emotion Recognition (SER) is a new and challenging research area with a wide range of applications in man-machine interactions. The aim of a SER system is to recognize human emotion by analyzing the acoustics of speech sound. In this study, Spectral Pattern features (SPs) and Harmonic Energy features (HEs) for emotion recognition are proposed. These features extracted from the spectrogram of speech signal using image processing techniques. For this purpose, details in the spectrogram image are firstly highlighted using histogram equalization technique. Then, directional filters are applied to decompose the image into 6 directional components. Finally, binary masking approach is employed to extract SPs from sub-banded images. The proposed HEs are also extracted by implementing the band pass filters on the spectrogram image. The extracted features are reduced in dimensions using a filtering feature selection algorithm based on fisher discriminant ratio. The classification accuracy of the proposed SER system has been evaluated using the 10-fold cross-validation technique on the Berlin database. The average recognition rate of 88.37% and 85.04% were achieved for females and males, respectively. By considering the total number of males and females samples, the overall recognition rate of 86.91% was obtained.

Keywords: *Speech emotion recognition, spectral pattern features, harmonic energy features, cross validation.*

1. Introduction

Speaking is the fastest and most natural method of communication among human beings [1]. This fact has motivated researchers to use speech as the primary mode in human computer interaction. In order to make a natural interaction, the machine should be intelligent enough to recognize speaker's emotion by analyzing the acoustics of his or her voice. This has introduced a relatively *new* and challenging research area with a wide range of applications in man-machine interaction, known as Speech Emotion Recognition (SER). SER can improve the performance of automatic speech recognition systems [1]. It is also useful in e-learning, computer games, medicine, psychology and in-car boards [2-4].

SER is commonly treated as a pattern recognition problem which includes three main stages: feature extraction, feature reduction and classification. Despite of widespread efforts, finding effective features is still one of the main challenges in SER [1]. Most acoustic features used in SER can be listed in two main categories: prosodic features and spectral features. Prosodic features, which are widely used in SER, have been shown to offer important emotional cues of the speaker [1, 5]. These features are usually derived from statistics of pitch and energy contours [5]. Spectral features, on the other hand, have received increased attention in recent years. These features which are generally obtained from the speech spectrum can improve the rate of recognition by providing complementary information for prosodic features [5].

Figures 1 (a) to (c) show the spectrograms of an utterance expressed by a woman in 3 different emotions; anger, neutral and boredom, respectively. In time-frequency representation of speech signal, when voicing is present, horizontal bands at the harmonics of the fundamental frequency of the vocal fold vibration will characterized the resulting spectrogram (pitch) [6].

As can be seen from Figure 1, harmonics, their position, stability and evolution are mostly related to the emotional state of the speaker. As it is reported by [1], in high arousal emotions such as anger, the resultant speech would be loud and fast with a higher pith average and wider pitch range. These conditions also induce the presence of strong high-frequency energy in the corresponding speech signal [1]. In low arousal emotions such as boredom, on the other hand, the resultant speech would be slow, low pitched and with little high-frequency energy [1]. These facts can be confirmed by Figures 1 (a) to (c).

The main contribution of this study is to propose Spectral Pattern features (SPs) and Harmonic Energy features (HEs) extracted from the speech spectrogram using image processing techniques. This scheme appears to be effective to fill the existing gap between time analysis methods and frequency analysis methods. The proposed SP and HE features are employed for classifying 7 emotions using a linear Support Vector Machine (SVM).

The reminder of this paper is organized as follows: Section 2 details the SPs and HEs proposed in this work, as well as prosodic and spectral features extracted for comparison purposes. Section 3 introduces the databases employed. Experimental results are presented and discussed in Section 4. The paper finally ends with conclusion remarks in section 5.

2. Feature extraction

In this section, we detail the proposed SPs and HEs extracted from the spectrogram of speech. Prosodic and spectral features considered in our experiments are also described. The prosodic and spectral features calculated in this study are by no means exhaustive, but serve as a representative sampling of the essential features. These features are used here as a benchmark, and also, to verify whether the SPs and HEs can serve useful additions to the widely used prosodic and spectral features.

2.1. Time-Frequency Representation Of Speech

Here, the silent part of speech signal is firstly discarded by a Voice Activity Detection (VAD) algorithm [7], and then the speech signal is passed through a pre-emphasize filter:

$$H(z) = 1 - \alpha z^{-1}, 0.9 \le \alpha \le 1 \qquad (1)$$

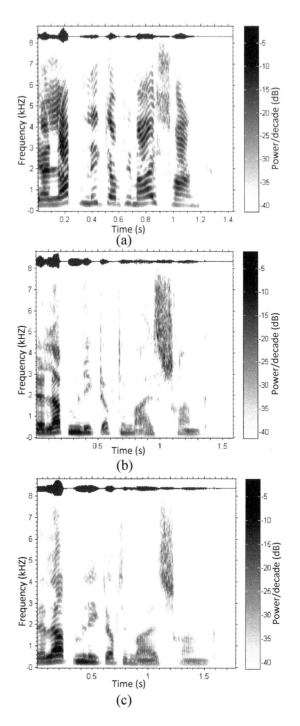

Figure 1. Spectrogram of an utterance expressed by a woman in 3 different emotions: (a) anger, (b) neutral, and (c) boredom.

As suggested by [8], α is set to 0.95 here. Although the speech signal is non-stationary in nature, it is assumed to remain stationary over a short duration of 20–30 ms. In this work, the pre-emphasized signal is segmented to frames of 320 samples length (20ms) with the shift of 160 samples (10ms) between two consecutive frames to retain a good quality of the signal and to avoid loss of information [8,9]. In order to reduce the edge effects at the two ends of the frames, Hamming window is multiplied with each frame. Then, N=512 length DFT of a windowed frame is computed to obtain the logarithmic power spectrum as [10]:

$$S_i(k) = \log_{10}((\text{Re}\{X_i(k)\})^2 + \tag{2}$$

$$(\text{Im}\{X_i(k)\})^2),$$

$$k = 0,1,...,N-1, i = 1,2,...,M$$

Where M is the total number of frames and $\tilde{X}_i(k)$ is the kth component of DFT of $\tilde{x}_i(n)$ (i^{th} windowed frame). Re{...} and Im{...} indicate real and imaginary parts, respectively. The spectrums of these frames, $S_i(k)$, are concatenated row-wise to construct the speech spectrogram, f(k,i), as [10]:

$$f(k,i) = \begin{bmatrix} S_1(0) & ... & S_M(0) \\ \cdot & \cdot & \cdot \\ \cdot & \cdot & \cdot \\ S_1(N-1) & ... & S_M(N-1) \end{bmatrix} \tag{3}$$

2.2. Spectral pattern features

In order to highlight the details of spectrogram image, the contrast of the image is firstly increased using histogram equalization [11]. Then, the image is decomposed to eight components by applying eight directional filters, H1 to H8, which have been shown in Figure 2 (a). The eight resultant images are binarized, and then the morphological operators "cleaning" and "removing" are applied to remove the isolated pixels and interior pixels, respectively. Finally, the desired patterns are detected using binary masking technique. The employed binary masks are shown in Figure 2 (b).

In order to unify the patterns that represent a same direction (H5 and H6 & also H7 and H8), the logical "OR" operator is used. Thus, we would have six different binary images representing six different directional patterns. In these images, the pixels with the value of one indicate the presence of the corresponding pattern, and in the contrary, the pixels with the value of zero indicate the absence of the corresponding pattern.

Since, the behavior of the energy bands vary over different frequency ranges, we decompose the *images in*to several sub bands. The simplest method is to simply divide the bandwidth equally. However, this does not seem appropriate, as it

does not correspond to the human ear [12]. The spectral resolution of the human ear varies logarithmically along the frequency, with better resolution at lower frequencies [13]. The Mel-scale and the Bark-scale which are empirically determined using human subjects are two potential choices. We decompose the images into 17 sub bands according to Bark-scale with non-overlapping filters. So, 102 sub-banded images will be obtained from the 6 binary images.

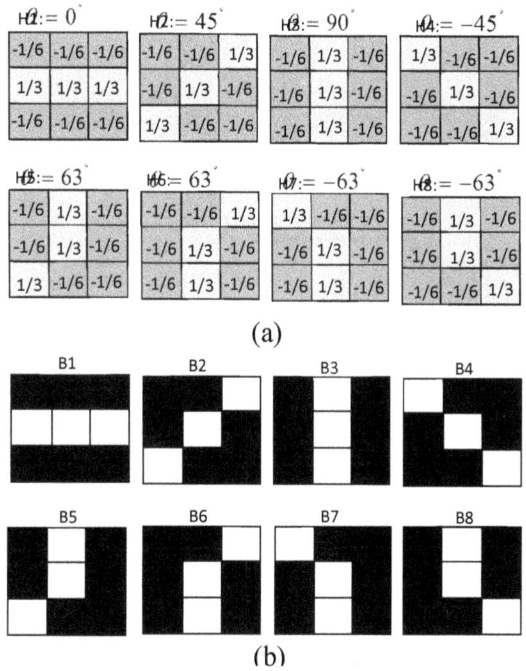

Figure 2. (a) Eight filters which are used to highlight eight directional patterns, (b) Eight binary masks which are used to detect eight directional patterns.

Two different types of features are extracted from each *sub-banded image:*

1) *The average number of patterns per frame in each sub band;* these features form the first 102 SP features of the SP Feature Vector, *SP_FV*. It could be formulated as follows:

$$SP\_FV(1:102) = \frac{1}{M}\sum_{r=1}^{R_q}\sum_{c=1}^{M}SI_{q,p}(r,c), \tag{4}$$

$$1 \le q \le 17, 1 \le p \le 6$$

Where $SI_{q,p}$ *is the* q^{th} *sub-band of the* p^{th} *image.* R_q is the number of rows in the $SI_{q,p}$ and M is the number of columns in the $SI_{q,p}$.

2) *The relative number of each pattern in each sub band;* these features form the second 102 features of the *SP_FV* and they could be determined as:

$$SP\_FV(103:204) = \frac{\sum_{r=1}^{R_q}\sum_{c=1}^{M} SI_{q,p}(r,c)}{\sum_{i=1}^{17}\sum_{r=1}^{R_i}\sum_{c=1}^{M} SI_{i,p}(r,c)}, \tag{5}$$

$$1 \le q \le 17, 1 \le p \le 6$$

The process of extracting SPs is schematically shown in Figure 3.

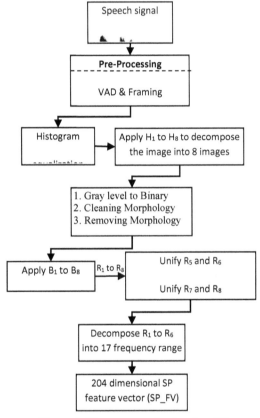

Figure 3. The process of extracting SPs.

2.3. Harmonic energy features

Harmonics of a speech signal are multiples of its fundamental frequency, F0, which is created by the vibration of the vocal folds. Since F0 varies over time, a filter bank consists of time varying band-pass filters is required to extract the harmonics of speech. In this filter bank, the central frequency of the hth band-pass filter at a certain time is the hth multiple of the fundamental frequency at that time, and the bandwidth is equal to the fundamental frequency [14].

In order to reduce the computational cost, we propose to implement the filter bank on the spectrogram image. In this method, the central frequency and cutoff frequencies of each of the sub-band filters on the image is determined as following. Firstly, the frequency range which is

covered by each pixel in the vertical direction determined as:

$$FR = f_s / 2R \tag{6}$$

Where fs and R are the sampling rate and the number of rows in the image, respectively. The position of central frequency for the hth filter in the ith column (i^{th} frame) could be determined as:

$$Fc_h(i) = h \times F0(i) / FR, 1 \le i \le M \tag{7}$$

Where $F0(i)$ is the fundamental frequency of the ith frame which is computed using the autocorrelation-based pitch tracking algorithm [15]. The locations of the first and second cutoff frequencies on the image could be determined as follows:

$$Fs_{h,1}(i) = Fc_h(i) - F0(i) / 2FR \tag{8}$$
and
$$Fs_{h,2}(i) = Fc_h(i) + F0(i) / 2FR \tag{9}$$

Where $Fs_{h,1}(i)$ and $Fs_{h,2}(i)$ are the lower and upper cutoff frequencies of the hth sub-band filter in the ith column of image, respectively. The obtained values should be rounded to be used for digital images.

The energy of the hth harmonic in the ith frame could be determined as:

$$E_h(i) = \sum_{k=Fs_{h,1}(i)}^{Fs_{h,2}(i)} f(k,i), 1 \le i \le M \tag{10}$$

Where $f(k,i)$ is the gray level of the pixel located in the kth row and i^{th} column of the spectrogram image determined by equation (3). Figure 4 shows the 1th, 5th, 9th and 13th sub-band filters on the spectrogram image.

In this figure, the $F0$ contour and its 5th, 9th and 13th harmonics are indicated with black dashed lines. Each of these curves could be considered as the center frequency of the corresponding sub-band filter. The cutoff frequencies of each filter are also depicted around the center frequencies by solid lines.

In summary, the log energy contour of each harmonic could be computed by adding the gray level of the pixels within the corresponding pass band.

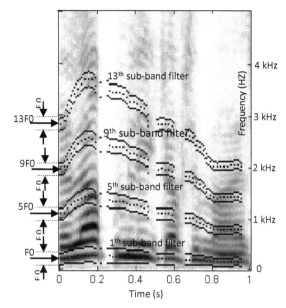

Figure 4. Implementation of the band pass filters on spectrogram image to determine harmonic energy contours.

In this work, we determine the energy contours of the 13 first harmonics. Then, we apply 20 statistical functions to these contours to extract HEs. The statistical functions are also applied to their first and second derivatives (velocity and acceleration) to capture the dynamical information of the curves. These functions include: min, max, range, mean, median, trimmed mean 10%, trimmed mean 25%, 1st, 5th, 10th, 25th, 75th, 90th, 95th, and 99th percentile, interquartile range, mean average deviation, standard deviation, skewness and kurtosis [16,17]. So, in total, $3 \times 20 \times 13 = 780$ HE features have been extracted here.

2.4. Prosodic features

Prosodic features form the most widely used features in SER [1,5]. In order to extract these types of features, statistical properties of pitch and energy tracking contours are commonly used. Here, 20 time domain functions are applied to capture the statistical information of pitch and energy tracking contours. These functions include: min, max, range, mean, median, trimmed mean 10%, trimmed mean 25%, 1st, 5th, 10th, 25th, 75th, 90th, 95th, and 99th percentile, interquartile range, average deviation, standard deviation, skewness and kurtosis [16,17]. These functions are also applied to the first and second derivatives of the contours as a common practice [5]. So, we have in total 60 pitch-based features and 60 energy-based features.

The widely used Zero-Crossing Rate (ZCR) and the Teager Energy Operator (TEO) [18] of the speech signal are also examined here. These features do not directly relate to prosody but in this work we evaluate their performance along with prosodic features. TEO conveys information about the nonlinear airflow structure of speech production [19]. The TEO for a discrete-time signal x_n is defined as:

$$TEO(x_n) = x_n^2 - x_{n-1}x_{n+1} \tag{8}$$

In order to extract ZCR and TEO related features, we apply the 20 statistical functions to ZCR and TEO curves and their deltas and double deltas. Finally, we have 240 prosodic features.

2.5. Spectral features

We employ two types of spectral features: The Mel-Frequency Cepstral Coefficients (MFCCs) and formants are reported as effective spectral features for emotion recognition [20-23]. Here, the first 12 MFCCs and 4 formants are extracted from 20 ms Hamming-windowed speech frames every 10 ms, and so their contours are formed. Finally, the 20 functions described in section 2.3, are applied to extract spectral features from the extracted contours and their first and second derivatives. In total, 960 spectral features are extracted here.

3. Emotional speech data

The Berlin database of German emotional speech [24] is a well-known public database. The performance of many SER systems has been evaluated using this database [5,25-28]. This database includes 535 utterances with 10 different contexts expressed by ten professional actors (5 males and 5 females) in 7 emotions. Table 1 lists the numbers of samples for the emotion categories.

Table 1. Number of samples in the Berlin database.

Emotion	Female	Male
Anger	67	60
Joy	44	27
Boredom	46	35
Neutral	40	39
Disgust	35	11
Fear	32	37
Sadness	37	25
All	301	234

4. Experimental results and discussion

In this study, it is assumed that a gender classifier with perfect classification accuracy, which is proposed by [29], is employed in the first stage, so the system is implemented completely separate for males and females. Features from training data are linearly scaled to [-1, 1] before applying linear Support Vector Machine (SVM). Features from test data are also scaled using the trained linear mapping function [5]. In order to avoid the curse of dimensionality [30], a filter-based feature selection scheme based on the Fisher Discriminant Ratio (FDR) is employed to remove irrelevant features. In this method, the FDR evaluates individual features by means of measuring the inter-classes distance against the intra-class similarity as [5]:

$$FDR(u) = \frac{2}{C(C-1)} \sum_{c_1} \sum_{c_2} \frac{(\mu_{c_1,u} - \mu_{c_2,u})^2}{\sigma_{c_1,u}^2 + \sigma_{c_2,u}^2} \quad (8)$$

$$,1 \le c_1 < c_2 \le C$$

where $\mu_{c_i,u}$ and $\sigma_{c_i,u}^2$ represent the mean and variance of the uth feature of the ith class, respectively. $i = 1, 2, \ldots, C$, and C is the total number of classes. Features with little discrimination ratio can then be removed by a thresholding process.

The features proposed here are first compared to prosodic and spectral features, using FDR criterion before applied to the classifier. To this end, the features are ranked by their FDR values using all samples in the Berlin database and then, FDR values averaged over the top N_{fdr} FDR-ranked features. Figures 5 and 6 show the average FDR curves of prosodic, spectral and proposed SP and HE features as a function of N_{fdr} for females and males, respectively. Since there are only 240 prosodic features, all the curves are depicted for 240 features. These curves roughly illustrate discrimination power of features regardless of the utilized classifier.

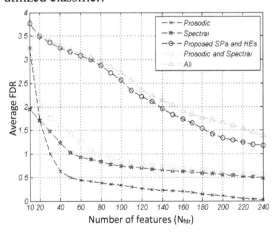

Figure 5. average FDR curves different types of features (females).

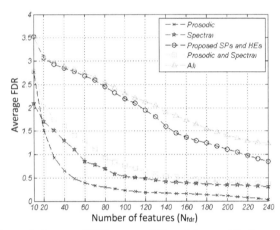

Figure 6. Average FDR curves different types of features (males).

As can be seen from Figures 5 and 6, the proposed SPs and HEs consistently exhibit considerably better discrimination power than the conventional prosodic and spectral features and their combination. However, combining the prosodic and spectral features to the SPs and HEs can slightly upgrade the discrimination power of features. Interestingly, for all types of features, the average FDR of females are higher than males. This shows that the extracted features are more discriminative for females' emotions than males' emotions.

As mentioned earlier FDR can only evaluate discriminative power of each feature individually. So, in order to evaluate power of a feature set in classification, we use directly classification accuracy as a criterion. The classification accuracy represents the performance of the employed classifier as a function of N_{top} features, which are chosen by the FDR-based feature selection algorithm. The classification accuracy is determined as the number of samples correctly recognized divided by the total number of samples. As a common practice for small sample size problems [31], results are produced using 10-fold cross-validation here. In this technique, in each class, samples have been randomly divided into 10 non-overlapping subsets approximately equal in size. In each validation trial, nine subsets from each class are taken for training, and the remaining one kept unseen until the testing phase. The overall recognition rate is achievable by averaging over the results of the 10 validation trials. In this work, we determine the accuracy curves for different types of features using a linear multi-class SVM. The computed curves are depicted in Figures 7 and 8 for females and males, respectively.

According to Figures 7 and 8, for both females and males, spectral features are superior to prosodic and proposed SP and HE features. However, by combining the proposed features with the prosodic and spectral features, the maximum recognition rates of 88.37% and 85.04% are achievable using 700 and 250 top FDR features, for females and males, respectively. Interestingly, all accuracy curves suggest that females' emotions can be classified more accurately than males' emotions. This may be due to the fact that females are more emotionally perceptive and emotional stimuli than males are [32].

Moreover, Figures 7 and 8 show that the classification accuracy is initially improved by increasing the number of features, but after a critical value further increase of the number of features result in degrading the performance. This can be explained as the curse of dimensionality, overfitting or peaking phenomenon [33], wherein the optimal number of features could be represented as a function of the number of samples and correlation of the features [34].

Tables 2 and 3 represent the confusion matrices of applying the proposed classifier for classifying 7 emotions using the combination of all types of features. In Tables 2 and 3, the left-most column is the true classes and the top row indicates the recognized classes. Furthermore, the rate column shows the average recognition rate for each class, which is determined as the number of samples correctly recognized and divided by the total number of samples in the class. The precision of each class is calculated as the number of samples correctly is classified and divided by the total number of samples assigned to the class.

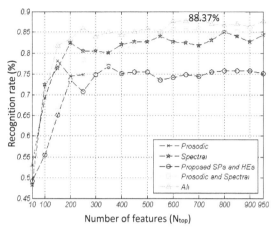

Figure 7. Accuracy curves for different types of features (females).

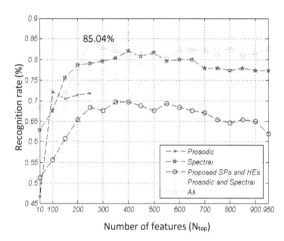

Figure 8. Accuracy curves for different types of features (males).

Table 2. Confusion matrix for classification of 7 emotions using proposed classifier (females).

Emotion	Anger	Boredom	Disgust	Fear	Joy	Neutral	Sadness	Rate (%)
Anger	56	0	0	1	10	0	0	83.58
Boredom	0	42	0	0	0	4	0	91.30
Disgust	0	0	34	1	0	0	0	97.14
Fear	1	0	1	28	1	0	1	87.50
Joy	9	0	1	0	34	0	0	77.27
Neutral	0	3	0	0	0	37	0	92.50
Sadness	0	2	0	0	0	0	35	94.56
Precision (%)	84.85	89.36	94.44	93.33	75.56	90.24	97.22	
Overall accuracy: 88.37%								

Table 3. Confusion matrix for classification of 7 emotions using proposed classifier (males).

Emotion	Anger	Boredom	Disgust	Fear	Joy	Neutral	Sadness	Rate (%)
Anger	56	0	0	1	3	0	0	93.33
Boredom	0	30	0	0	0	4	1	85.71
Disgust	0	0	8	1	1	0	1	72.733
Fear	3	0	0	32	1	1	0	86.49
Joy	6	0	0	0	21	0	0	77.78
Neutral	1	6	1	0	0	30	1	76.92
Sadness	0	2	0	1	0	0	22	88.00
Precision (%)	84.85	78.95	88.89	91.43	80.77	85.71	88.00	
Overall accuracy: 85.04%								

As can be seen from Tables 2 and 3, the ambiguity in classification of anger vs. joy and also boredom vs. neutral are responsible for major part of error in the proposed classifier. This may be due to the fact that most of the acoustic features employed for SER are related to arousal [35], and so are they not discriminative for valence related emotions such as anger and joy [5,35].

By considering the total number of 301 female and 234 male samples, the overall recognition rate of 86.91% is obtained for the proposed SER system.

It can be also useful to review performance Figures reported on the Berlin database by other works. Although the numbers cannot be fairly compared due to different conditions of experiments such as different data partitioning, they can be useful for general benchmarking. The recognition rate of 86.90% is achieved under 10-fold cross-validation in [25]. The recognition rate of 88.8% is reported by employing a three-stage classification scheme for recognizing six emotions only [26]. In [5], 85.6% accuracy is obtained under 10-fold cross-validation for classifying 7 emotions. In [36], the best average recognition rate of 85.5% is reported using a multi-class SVM classifier.

5. Conclusion

The aim of this study was to evaluate the proposed SPs and HEs for the recognition of human emotions from speech. These features have also been compared to conventional prosodic and spectral features in terms of FDR score and classification accuracy. This paper has demonstrated the potential and promise of the SPs and HEs for emotion recognition. The following conclusions can be drawn from the present study.

First, harmonics, their position, stability and evolution are mostly related to the emotional state of the speaker. This affects the behavior of energy bands and spectral patterns on the spectrogram image.

Second, although the SPs and HEs are superior to conventional prosodic and spectral features in term of FDR score, they are not the best in classification performance. However, these features boost the classification accuracy when used to augment the conventional prosodic and spectral features.

Also, our experiments reveal that females' emotions can be recognized more accurate than males' emotions. Moreover, most acoustic features employed for SER are discriminative for classifying emotions based on arousal level while they are ineffective for classification of valence related emotions [5,35]. This fact results in the ambiguity in classification of anger vs. joy and also boredom vs. neutral which is responsible for major part of error in most SER systems.

In order to improve the performance of current speech emotion recognition systems, the structure of the classifier can be optimized. To this end, tandem classifiers can be employed for classification of valence related emotions. Also, finding effective features for classifying valence related emotions can be a beneficial research focus. Moreover, as ultimate aim of a speech emotion recognition system is to recognize emotions for real work data, evaluating the proposed system under different conditions such as the presence of noise and chatter is useful.

References

[1] M. El Ayadi, M.S. Kamel, F. Karray, "Survey on speech emotion recognition: Features, classification schemes, and databases," Pattern Recognition 44, 572–587, 2011.

[2] B. Schuller, G. Rigoll, M. Lang, "Speech emotion recognition combining acoustic features and linguistic information in a hybrid support vector machine-belief network architecture", in: Proceedings of the ICASSP, (1), 577–580, 2004.

[3] D. J. France, R.G. Shiavi, S. Silverman, M. Silverman, M. Wilkes, "Acoustical properties of speech as indicators of depression and suicidal risk", IEEE Trans. Biomedical Eng. 47 (7), 829–837, 2007.

[4] J. Hansen, D.C. Icarus, "source generator based real-time recognition of speech in noisy stressful and Lombard effect environments", Speech Commun. 16 (4), 391–422, 1995.

[5] S. Wu, T.H. Falk, W.Y. Chan, "Automatic speech emotion recognition using modulation spectral features", Speech Communication 53, 768‑785, 2011.

[6] P. Gomez Vilda, J.M. Ferrandez Vicente, V. Rodellar Biarge, R. Fernandez Baillo, "Time-frequecy representations in speech perception", Neurocomputing, 72, 820–830, 2009.

[7] J. Sohn, N. S. Kim, and W. Sung. "A statistical model-based voice activity detection", IEEE Signal Processing Lett., 6 (1), 1–3, 1999.

[8] L. Rabiner, B.H. Juang, "Fundamentals of Speech Recognition", Prentice Hall, Englewood Cliffs, NJ, 1993.

[9] T. Kinnunen, H. Li, "An overview of text-independent speaker recognition: from features to

supervectors", Speech Communication, 52 (1), 12–40, 2010.

[10] P. K. Ajmera, D.V. Jadhav, R.S. Holambe, "Text-independent speaker identification using Radon and discrete cosine transforms based features from speech spectrogram", Pattern Recognition, 44, 2749–2759, 2011.

[11] R. C. Gonzalez, R.E. Woods, "Digital image processing", Pearson Prentice Hall, 2008.

[12] K. M. Indrebo, R. J. Povinelli, M. T. Johnson, "Sub-banded reconstructed phase space for speech recognition", Speech Communication, 48, 750-774, 2006.

[13] B. Gold, N. Morgan, "Speech and Audio Signal Processing". John Wiley and Sons, 2000.

[14] Z. Xiao, E. Dellandrea, W. Dou, L. Chen, "Automatic Hierarchical Classification of Emotional Speech". Ninth IEEE International Symposium on Multimedia Workshops, ISMW '07, 56, 2007.

[15] S, Gonzalez, M. Brookes, "A pitch estimation filter robust to high levels of noise (PEFAC)", Proc EUSIPCO, 2011.

[16] J. Krajewski, S. Schnieder, D. Sommer, A. Batliner, B. Schuller, "Applying multiple classifiers and non-linear dynamics features for detecting sleepiness from speech". Neurocomputing, 84, 65–75, 2012.

[17] B. Schuller, M. Wimmer, L.M. osenlechner, C. Kern, G. Rigoll, "Brute-forcing hierarchical functional for paralinguistics: A waste of feature space?", Proceedings International Conference on Acoustics, Speech, and Signal Processing, 33, 4501–4504, 2008.

[18] J, Kaiser, "On a simple algorithm to calculate the 'energy' of a signal". Internat. Conf. on Acoustics, Speech and Signal Processing, 1, 381–384, 1990.

[19] G. Zhou, J. Hansen, J. Kaiser, "Nonlinear feature based classification of speech under stress". IEEE Trans. Audio Speech Language Process, 9, 201–216, 2001.

[20] T, Polzehl, A, Schmitt, F, Metze, M, Wagner, "Anger recognition in speech using acoustic and linguistic cues". Speech Communication, 53, 1198–1209, 2011.

[21] C.C. Lee, E. Mower, C. Busso, S. Lee, S. Narayanan, "Emotion recognition using a hierarchical binary decision tree approach". Speech Communication, 53, 1162–1171, 2011.

[22] L, He, M. Lech, N.C. Maddage, N.B. Allen, "Study of empirical mode decomposition and spectral analysis for stress and emotion classification in natural speech. Biomedical Signal Processing and Control", 6, 139–146, 2011.

[23] P. Laukka, D. Neiberg, M. Forsell, I. Karlsson, K. Elenius, "Expression of affect in spontaneous speech: Acoustic correlates and automatic detection of irritation and resignation. Computer Speech and Language", 25, 84–104, 2011.

[24] F. Burkhardt, A. Paeschke, M. Rolfes, W. Sendlmeier, B. Weiss, "A database of German emotional speech". Interspeech, 1517‑1520, 2005.

[25] B. Schuller, D. Seppi, A. Batliner, A. Maier, S. Steidl, "Emotion recognition in the noise applying large acoustic feature sets". In: Proc.Speech Prosody, 2006.

[26] M. Lugger, B. Yang, "Cascaded emotion classification via psychological emotion dimensions using a large set of voice quality parameters". In: Proc. Internat. Conf. on Acoustics, peech and Signal Processing, (4), 4945–4948, 2008.

[27] E.M. Albornoz, D.H. Milone, H.L. Rufiner, "Spoken emotion recognition using hierarchical classifiers". Computer Speech and Language 25, 556–570, 2011.

[28] N. Kamaruddin, A. Wahab, C. Quek, "Cultural dependency analysis for understanding speech emotion". Expert Systems with Applications, 11, 028, 2011.

[29] M. Kotti, C. Kotropoulos, "Gender classification in two Emotional Speech databases", ICPR, 2008.

[30] C. Bishop, "Pattern Recognition and Machine Learning". New York: Springer, 2006.

[31] J. R. Raudays, A.K. Jain, "Small Sample Size Effects in Statistical Pattern Recognition: Recommendations for Practitioners". IEEE T PATTERN ANAL, 13, 252–264, 1991.

[32] S. Whittle, M. Yücel, M.B.H. Yap, N.B. Allen, "Sex differences in the neural correlates of emotion: Evidence from neuroimaging". Biological Psychology. 87, 319– 333, 2011.

[33] S. Theodoridis, K. Koutroumbas, "Pattern recognition". Academic Press, 2008.

[34] C. Sima, E.R. Dougherty, "The peaking phenomenon in the presence of feature-selection", Pattern Recognition Letters, 29, 1667–1674, 2008.

[35] E. Kim, K. Hyun, S. Kim, Y. Kwak, "Speech emotion recognition using eigen-fft in clean and noisy environments", in: The 16th IEEE International Symposium on Robot and HumanInteractive Communication, RO-MAN, 689–694, 2007.

[36] H. Altun, G. Polat, "Boosting selection of speech related features to improve performance of multi-class SVMs in emotion detection", Expert systems with Applications, 36, 8197–8203, 2009.

12

Development of a framework to evaluate service-oriented architecture governance using COBIT approach

M. Dehghani[1] and S. Emadi[2]*

1. Department of Computer College of Engineering, Yazd Science and Research Branch, Islamic Azad University, Yazd, Iran.
2. Department of Computer College of Engineering, Yazd Branch, Islamic Azad University, Yazd, Iran.

Corresponding author: emadi@iauyazd.ac.ir (S.Emadi).

Abstract

Nowadays organizations require an effective governance framework for their service-oriented architecture (SOA) in order to enable them to use a framework to evaluate their current state governance and determine the governance requirements, and then to offer a suitable model for their governance. Various frameworks have been developed to evaluate the SOA governance. In this paper, a brief introduction to the internal control framework COBIT is described, and it is used to show how to develop a framework to evaluate the SOA governance within an organization. The SOA and information technology expert surveys are carried out to evaluate the proposed framework. The results of this survey verify the proposed framework.

Keywords: *Service-oriented Architecture; Service-oriented Architecture Maturity; Service-oriented Architecture Governance; Service-oriented Architecture Adoption; Service-oriented Architecture Governance Evaluation, COBIT.*

1. Introduction

A service-oriented architecture (SOA) has created a framework to integrate business processes [1,2] and support information technology (IT) infrastructure as secure standardized services that can be reused and combined to address changing the business priorities [3]. SOA has created opportunities to provide loosely-coupled and interoperable services to service the providers at different Quality of Service (QoS) and cost levels in a number of service domains. This provides a unique opportunity for businesses to dynamically select services that better meet their business and QoS needs in a cost-effective manner [4]. SOA can be a basis for the components and the constant changing of software programs [1]. SOA focuses mainly on service governance [5], and can reduce the interoperability problems within the IT structure that can evolve in more flexibility for the business, decrease the IT cost, and improve business IT alignment [6]. Among the different potential causes of SOA project failures, lack of IT governance, which should be supplied from the beginning, is one of them. Without governance, an organization is not capable of fully understanding the SOA value [7]. SOA processes provide benefits for all stakeholders. SOA is a kind of strategic investment that supports enterprise and its functions in projects [8]. An organization can provide high quality and reliable services, while SOA governance is successful. These services have led to the efficiency and effectiveness of an organization [9]. Appropriate design and implementation of SOA governance can help organizations to achieve high levels of agility, and respond to customers in the market. In order to evaluate the current status of SOA governance, all organizations require an evaluation framework. The framework could be useful in determining the SOA governance requirements and providing a suitable SOA governance model.

This framework ensures the alignment of SOA governance with business, IT with SOA strategy. It is useful in identifying the competencies and current processes of an organization. It can be used to determine what an organization should do and what it should not.

The SOA governance maturity models are one of the main tools used to evaluate the SOA governance. A SOA governance maturity model specifies the actions to be taken in transition to a SOA based on a gradual approach and the organization service oriented maturity, and this helps organizations to move toward service-orientation [10].

To date, many models have been proposed for governance maturity such that each one of the models for a particular landscape that looked to governance on certain aspects of governance are concentrated. Table 1 shows an overview of some models of governance maturity that are in the field of SOA.

Table 1. Review of SOA governance maturity models.

Model	Features	Governance maturity levels	SOA adoption domains	SOA maturity levels	Processes maturity level
(Software AG, 2005) [8]	-In this model, as soon as it was completed, the initial phase of planning for the systematic development of SOA can be started. From this point onward, SOA governance as a comprehensive tool support is important. In this model, the move towards higher IT and SOA governance is needed. -SOA adoption domain is not considered.	✓		✓	
(Bieberstein et al., 2005) [11]	-In this model, maturity level and the adoption of service-oriented architecture are completely and clearly not covered, and only the maturity levels of governance are considered.		✓	✓	
(Afshar et al., 2007) [12]	-In this model, service-oriented architecture adoption domain is not completely covered but the maturity level of service-oriented architecture and governance maturity levels is considered.	✓			
(MARKS, 2008) [10]	-Related features of each level of governance are separated and comprehensive. -The governance issues including roles and responsibilities for each level governance and alignment governance are considered. - This model only focuses on SOA governance maturity levels and lowers the considered SOA maturity levels and SOA adoption domains.	✓			
(Scheper and kratz, 2009) [13]	-This model does not specify SOA governance maturity levels and SOA adoption domains clearly, and only presents SOA maturity levels for business process, and on this basis, proposes some actions for governance.			✓	
(Hassanzadeh and Namdarian, 2010) [2]	- In this model of SOA governance, which considers the maturity of the proposed SOA and service-oriented, the better picture of the status in terms of the type of governance.	✓		✓	

By analyzing the proposed governance maturity model in order to evaluate the SOA governance, it was found out that the available models did not have the essential ability to assess the maturity of the organization processes. Therefore, a governance maturity model is required to evaluate the maturity level of processes in addition to assessing the governance maturity levels of SOA. COBIT governance maturity model can play an important role in evaluating the SOA governance based on the trajectory of process-oriented organizations, which has been used in the recent years. Thus far, various models of COBIT framework have been proposed [14].

COBIT4.1 is a manageable and control-based process framework that covers the entire business process of an organization, and exposes it in a logical structure that can be managed and controlled effectively. This framework helps government agencies in conducting self-assessment and in determining to what extent the implementation of IT governance has been done. The primary purpose of this model is to monitor the organization IT to see that it is not designed to evaluate the architecture governance independently. There is no precise survey on SOA from the aspect of governance evaluation. According to the relationship between the COBIT4.1 model goals and SOA (i.e. business and IT alignment), it can be found out that the processes of this model have the highest correlation and value with respect to SOA. This model can be used as a suitable factor to evaluate the governance on SOA [14, 15]. Nevertheless, one of the challenges of using this framework is the lack of a method to evaluate the governance on SOA. Therefore, this study was conducted to provide a framework to show the status of the governance on SOA using the COBIT governance maturity model and the main aspects of a comprehensive SOA governance maturity.

This paper has been organized as follows: Section 2 introduces and surveys the main aspects of the SOA governance maturity model. Section 3 provides a brief review about the COBIT 4.1 framework and the governance maturity model. The proposed framework is described in section 4. In section 5, the proposed framework is evaluated, and finally, in section 6, conclusion of the discussions is presented.

2. Main aspects of SOA governance maturity model

Implementation and formalization of SOA governance is an essential phase for organizational maturity in SOA. The maturity model can be used as a measurement tool to assess the level of quality of some activities.

Marks (2008) has presented a comprehensive model for the SOA governance maturity model. Evaluation of the maturity level by implementing a SOA maturity model reflects the organizational governance implications on the organizational governance [10, 16]. However, the presented framework seeks to identify the measurement tools, and integrate them into a unified model for the COBIT framework.

2.1. General SOA maturity model

SOA maturity model is a framework that is used to prepare an organization for a successful adoption of SOA. It defines a standard path to progress toward SOA; it is like an airport control tower. As an airport control tower navigates an airplane in its way for a successful landing, the SOA maturity model guides an organization to adopt SOA and achieve higher levels of SOA maturity. In this way, the organization can evaluate the level of maturity in the field of SOA. In fact, a SOA maturity model provides an image of SOA maturity model in the organization based on major requirements, and shows the main gaps that the organization should consider [2]. A brief description of the SOA maturity model that has been proposed so far is described.

The Service Integration Maturity Model (SIMM) was provided by IBM in 2005. It consists of seven levels of maturity such as silo, integrated, componentized, simple services, composite services, and virtualized services, and allows movement towards a SOA by accepting different states of an institution [17]. The model identifies the target in certain circumstances, and provides guidelines to show how to reach the desired situation [17]. The IT Service Capability Maturity Model (ITSCMM) was provided in 2005. It concentrates on determining the maturity level of services, and involves all the necessary actions required for setting up SOA. The service capability maturity model increases the organization capability in identifying and running the IT services with five levels including initial, repeatable, defined, managed, and optimizing. The Enterprise SOA Maturity Model (ESOAMM) divides the SOA maturity model into four levels including traditional development and integration, developing web applications, developing composite applications, and automate business processes [18]. Another maturity model is the SOA Maturity Model (SOAMM), which was provided in 2005. This model focuses on service-oriented maturity, and its goal is to support the gradual process adoption of SOA and suggest methods for it. Designers have designed this model with the received feedbacks of 2000 architects. This model divides SOA maturity into five levels including Initial Services, Architected Services, Business/Collaborative Services, Measured Services, and Optimized Services [17].

2.2. SOA adoption maturity model

The most important benefit of the SOA maturity model is that it can help to guide SOA adaption. However, the model helps to coordinate the different paths to SOA inside a company. SOA adoption is a gradual process. In many cases, SOA adoption begins from the initial level of maturity. Some organizations may apply SOA in an organization unit level, and others may apply it in the business level .The issue of SOA adoption was created to help the organizations to recognize their level of SOA maturity. The SOA maturity model adoption helps to understand, accept, and determine the goals and strategic level of an organization [3]. One of the adoption maturity models is a model that was provided by Marks in 2008. Various phases of this maturity model are the initial phase of SOA, strategy and planning phase of SOA, SOA governance model development phase, platform phase of SOA and SOA governance platform, SOA reference implementation, SOA program, SOA similarity and acceleration, and stable model of SOA. Another adoption of the maturity model is the model presented by Inganti (2007), which includes four levels involving the intra-department level, inter-department/business unit level, inter-business level, and enterprise level [18].

3. COBIT 4.1

The control objectives for information and its related technologies (i.e. COBIT) are a set of the best IT practices provided by Audit Association and Information Systems Control (2007) with a process-control approach. COBIT 4.1 has 4 domains involving Plan and Organize (PO), Acquire and Implement (AI), Deliver and Support (DS), and Monitor and Evaluate (ME), and 34 processes and a 318 control objective in the IT evaluating domain. This framework provides measures and indices to help managers, auditors, and IT users to have maximum benefits of developing the observance and appropriate IT control in an organization [19]. Each one of these domains and its related processes are shown in table 2.

Table 2. IT processes identified by COBIT 4.1 [20].

Plan and Organize (PO)	Deliver and Support (DS)
PO1 Define a strategic IT plan	DS1 Define and manage service levels
PO2 Define the information architecture	DS2 Manage third-party services
PO3 Determine technological direction	DS3 Manage performance and capacity
PO4 Define IT process, organization, and relationships	DS4 Ensure continuous service
PO5 Manage the IT investment	DS5 Ensure system security
PO6 Communication management aims and direction	DS6 Identify and allocate costs
PO7 Manage IT human resources	DS7 Educate and train users
PO8 Manage quality	DS8 Manage service desk and incidents
PO9 Asses and manage IT risks	DS9 Manage the configuration
PO10 Manage projects	DS10 Manage problems
	DS11 Manage data
	DS12 Manage the physical environment
	DS13 Manage operation
Acquire and Implement (AI)	**Monitor and Evaluate (ME)**
AI1 Identify automated solutions	ME1 Monitor and evaluate IT performance
AI2 Acquire and maintain application software	ME2 Monitor and evaluate internal control
AI3 Acquire and maintain technology infrastructure	ME3 Ensure regulatory compliance
AI4 Enable operation and use	ME4 Provide IT governance
AI5 Procure IT resources	
AI6 Manage changes	
AI7 Install and accredit solutions and changes	

3.1. Governance maturity model from COBIT 4.1 viewpoint

The present COBIT4.1 framework contains 34 processes, which provide an IT maturity model driven from the Software Engineering Institute Capability Maturity Model. This framework evaluates the maturity level of an organization. Then the organization evaluation is ranked between the absence level (0) and the optimized level (5) [19]. One of the most important applications of this maturity model is to determine the maturity level by an organization itself, and to specify the existing gaps to achieve the maximum level of maturity. Consequently, in order to fill the existing gaps, the organization programs the practical improvements in internal control system

of IT. Indeed, this model specifies the IT organization ability to address the business needs and its alignment with the business and strategic demands [21]. Different levels of maturity in the aforementioned model can be classified as shown in figure 1.

4. Proposed framework

As mentioned earlier, moving toward process-oriented in an organization has been improved significantly, so the process efficiency shows the organization efficiency. When the organization processes are recognized and managed correctly, a desired output will be gained. Thus the use of a reference framework seems imperative. What should be considered to choose a framework is a

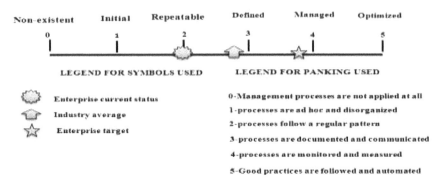

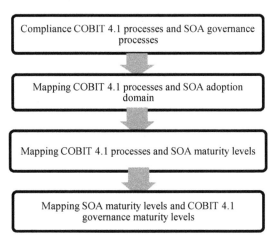

Figure 1. Graphic representations of COBIT 4.1 governance maturity model [19].

reference model that covers all activities of the organization, and that can be used as a road map. Since the COBIT governance process maturity model is an international comprehensive and adopted model, it can be confirmed. This framework provides comprehensive results to the IT managers to plan, develop, and upgrade the maturity level [20]. It may be considered as an evaluation model but the lack of a suitable SOA governance maturity model avoids to be used as an evaluation model.

In this context, this study intended to use the main aspects of the governance maturity model of SOA in order to provide a desirable framework for the COBIT 4.1 governance maturity model. Since this model is based on SOA, the framework can be used to evaluate the SOA governance. In this study, four main areas of the COBIT 4.1 model, which has a total of 34 processes, were addressed as the evaluation indices of the proposed framework. Accordingly, the proposed framework was done in 4 steps. Figure 2 shows the main steps of the proposed framework.

Step 1: Compliance COBIT 4.1 processes and SOA governance processes

COBIT 4.1 processes play a significant role in the governance maturity evaluation. The compliance between the COBIT 4.1 processes and the main processes in SOA governance was considered as the first step to present the proposed framework. It is the main role in the SOA governance maturity evaluation. In this compliance, all the main processes of SOA governance for developing the proposed framework in COBIT 4.1 are positioned. this work reviews all the 34 COBIT 4.1 processes, and finds possible relationships or connections with the main process SOA governance done. Table 3 shows how the compliance COBIT 4.1 processes with the main processes of SOA governance could be divided into 4 areas according to the COBIT 4.1 process indicated.

Figure 2. Main steps of proposed framework.

Step 2: Mapping COBIT 4.1 processes and SOA adoption domain

The SOA adaption domain and its relation to the maturity of SOA, i.e. one of the aspects of the proposed framework, was extracted from the model proposed by Inganti and Arvamudan (2007). They used a multi-aspect viewpoint in their SOA maturity model, and proposed the aspects that were important to implement SOA. They included the reception domain of SOA, the maturity level of SOA, and the SOA development steps. Considering these aspects makes the complete picture of the current level of SOA maturity [3]. To determine the maturity level of SOA in this model, SOAMM which has five levels including Initial Services, Architected Services, Business/Collaborative Services, Measured Services, and Optimized Services was used, and the four domain intra-department, inter-departments/business unit level, inter-business units and within the enterprise level were taken into consideration for adoption [18].

Table 3. Relationship between COBIT 4.1 process and main processes of SOA governance.

• PO1: Define a strategic plan	
SOA Governance processes	• **Service Portfolio Planning** • **(Business) Application Portfolio Planning** In SOA, the strategic planning is taking place in the business and service portfolio planning, in which a long-term planning is determined to decide which services and applications to develop and maintain to maximize business-IT alignment.
• **PO2: Determine technological direction**	
SOA Governance processes	• **Service Developing Policies** In SOA, the technical direction is set in the service developing policies, in which the technology and standards used for realizing the services should be determined. This also includes policies related to the use of technologies and Standards for the development of services, naming policies, and agreements on metadata. Another important aspect is the determination of service granularity.
• **AI6: Manage change**	
SOA Governance processes	• **Version (release) Management** In SOA, special attention is required for managing the changes outlined in version (release) management. Since the services have an enterprise wide reach, the impact of changes and new release will increase. To stay in control of the services, it is important to properly manage the number of service versions in use, to have clear rules on migration to new versions and the support of older versions.
• **DS1: Define and manage service levels**	
SOA Governance processes	• **Service Level Agreements** In SOA, where services can be consumed through the whole organization (or even outside the organization), service levels should be managed as well. This requires a formalized relation between service consumer and service provider. This ongoing process should ensure (and improve) the quality by meeting the agreed service levels and also includes monitoring and timely reporting to stakeholders on the accomplishment of service levels.
• **DS3: Manage performance and capacity**	
SOA Governance processes	• **Runtime Qualities** For SOA, this is described as runtime qualities. The call for a service will increase due to its enterprise wide reach. Therefore, the capacity has to raise to be able to handle all requests. This together with the message oriented character of SOA (this will affect the performance of IT) calls for special attention to Performance and Capacity Management.
• **DS6: Ensure system security**	
SOA Governance processes	• **Security Policies** SOA requires more complex security solutions to permit access to multiple applications, when executing a service. Another security issue within SOA is the need for encryption in confidential messages. Therefore, SOA requires a special attention to this objective.
• **DS9: manage the configuration**	
SOA Governance processes	• **Service Repository** The service repository is also a kind of configuration repository, in which business consumers can see which services are available, and under which conditions. • **Service Life Cycle Management** The service life cycle management can be grouped within managing the configuration, as well. In this aspect, configuration of the services is managed mainly in the pre and con production phase.
• **DS10: manage problems**	
SOA Governance processes	• **Error Tracking and resolution (exception handling)** This is also valid for SOA because of the execution of chains of services which require attention for error tracking and resolution. An effective problem management process maximizes system availability, improves service levels, reduces costs, and improves customer convenience and satisfaction.
• **DS13: Manage operation**	
SOA Governance processes	• **Transaction management** The execution of chains of services requires operation management. Operations which are operated on a long-term period need to be able to be tracked on their progress. Therefore, this objective is important for SOA.
• **ME1: Monitor and evaluate IT performance**	
SOA Governance processes	• **System (service) Monitoring** Since the introduction of SOA can be expensive, it is important to show the value of IT to the business. Monitoring the usage of service can be an appropriate way to make the reuse of services visible. Monitoring is needed to make sure that the right things are done and are in line with the set directions and policies. Therefore, this objective needs special attention for SOA.
• **ME2: Ensure compliance with external requirements**	
SOA Governance processes	• **Methods for dealing with regulatory requirements** For SOA, with its (inter) organizational reach, compliance is an important aspect because small deviations can result in serious problems.

Step 3: Mapping COBIT 4.1 processes and SOA maturity levels

Since SOA maturity is one of the framework aspects of the COBIT governance maturity, SOAMM has its most attention and focus on SOA maturity between the proposed maturity models of SOA, and follows the gradual process of SOA adoption [18], and thus it has been used in the integrated framework of this maturity model.

Step 4: Mapping SOA maturity levels and COBIT 4.1 governance maturity levels

To provide a framework, mapping occurs between the maturity levels of SOA and the COBIT 4.1 governance maturity in the last step. When maturity level maximizes, governance needs to be modified, i.e. once SOA was implemented and it reached a new maturity level, using the previous governance would not be simple [2].

Figure 3 shows the proposed framework to evaluate governance on a SOA. The framework consists of four aspects including process domain, SOA adoption domain, SOA maturity levels, and COBIT 4.1 governance maturity level. Using this framework, the level of SOA adoption domain and action level of COBIT 4.1 governance maturity can be determined according to the SOA maturity level of the organization.

Table 4 demonstrates the measures of each one of the four dimensions of the proposed framework in detail.

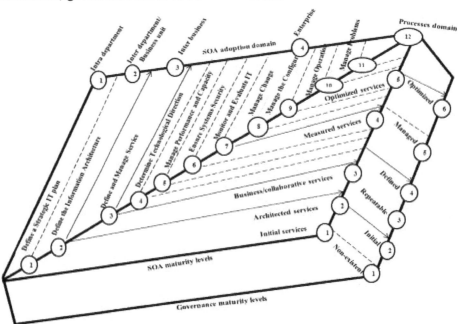

Figure 3. Conceptual framework to evaluate SOA governance.

4.1. Mapping proposed framework, COBIT5

Among the different models, the COBIT framework proposed in the recent years, COBIT5 with respect to the features that this framework is having [22]. In the existing processes along the main aspects of this framework, a comprehensive IT governance maturity model for SOA assess the maturity level of governance on the SOA used. Section 4.1 and table 5 summarize that the changes in the proposed framework are based on COBIT5 described.

5. Evaluation of proposed framework

In this study, the data type was quantitative, and the paradigm was positivism. The data collection tool questionnaire is based on the 5-point Likert's scale. In order to test the proposed framework, a sample of 18 experts in the field of SOA was included [24].

In this study, to determine the goal and achieve the correct result, 4 main hypotheses were defined involving the aspects and relations between the governance processes and the main aspects of a comprehensive SOA governance maturity model. The main hypotheses of this study are:

A: The hypotheses related to the 4-fold dimensions of the proposed framework.

B: The hypotheses related to the communication between the organization process domains and the SOA adoption domain.

C: The hypotheses concerning the relation of the existing organization process domains and the SOA maturity model.

D: The hypotheses related to the communication between the maturity levels of SOA and the maturity levels of COBIT governance.

Table 4: Measure of process domain [21], SOA maturity levels, SOA adoption domain [3], and COBIT governance maturity levels [18].

Measure	SOA governance maturity level	Measure	SOA maturity levels	Measure	SOA adoption domain	Measure	process domain
-The lack of any process; the organization still did not understand that we must consider the context of such establishment.	Non-existent governance level	- Initial learning phase - Pilot projects - Legacy integration - Apply SOA technology to immediate organizational - Define initial budget for SOA project - ESB -Service and policy repository -Governance using policies and service definition	Initial service level	- Individual departments slowly beginning to engineer their systems to be service-oriented. - Proof of concept projects, smaller SOA rollouts, and integration projects are undertaken at this stage. - There is little or no cross business interaction. - The governance charter has not yet been instituted, and there are only the beginnings of an organization wide sponsorship and visibility for the SOA effort.		-Updating the long run process	Define a Strategic IT plan
-There are no standardized procedures but there are certain approaches that individually do.	Initial governance level	-Exception Management Service -Translate service for types of message -Security and performance management -Applying SOA formally -Specify technology standards for SOA -Training SOA in the organization	Architected service level	- This is the second stage of SOA adoption, where various departments within a business units are SOA-enabled and interact with each other using architected services. -The beginnings of SOA reuse are found at this stage along with the evolution of a Rudimentary governance charter.	Inter-department business unit SOA adoption domain	-Create a data dictionary of the rules for writing data -Data classification scheme and security levels	Define the Information Architecture
-The level processes have been developed to some extent. Similar procedures are performed by the same. -There is no formal training in this domain; there is no communication with standard procedures and individual responsibility.	Repeatable governance level	-The relationship between business and technology -Business Responsiveness -Full support of the same process of business -Policy to create and change business processes -Business Process Management	Collaborative service level	-A firm step in the direction of enterprise SOA enablement is the interaction of services across business units. -Service reuse is maximized at this point. -A firmly established governance module institutes policies, processes and standards to be followed, while creating new services. -A service repository ensures maximum service reuse -Regular Business Activity Monitoring ensures the optimal functioning of services	Inter business SOA adoption domain	- Monitoring and reporting of complementary services stakeholders	Define and Manage Service Levels
-The level of standard procedures, but these procedures are documented and have been associated with the training of high level, but are only a formality.	Defined governance level	-Connect internal services with external service -Extend business processes to external organizations -Implement cross enterprise security -External services enablement, translation of protocols - Long running transactions					

(Continued) Table 4: Measure of process domain [21], SOA maturity levels, SOA adoption domain [3], and COBIT governance maturity level [18].

Measure	SOA governance maturity level	Measure	SOA maturity levels	Measure	SOA adoption domain	Measure	Process domain
-The assessment of compatibility between Procedures governance -Continually improve processes. -Governance processes to a level of corporate governance of the institution and to improve the quality and effectiveness of the method used.	Managed governance level	-Business Activity Monitoring (BAM) -Define and meet business oriented performance metrics. -Performance measurement in real-time. -Separate services from programs. - Virtual infrastructure - Dynamic infrastructure -Separate services for managing, monitoring and responding to events	Measured service level	-This is a highly evolved stage of SOA adoption where the whole enterprise makes use of Optimized services that can be dynamically configured based on real-time data.		-identifying, analyzing and developing a databank of new technologies -Continuous monitoring of the market -Registering and maintaining the security rules, responsibilities, standards and IT policies -Maintain the integrity of information and information technology assets -Definition of performance indicators -Systematic reporting and monitoring performance time periods specified in	Determine Technological Direction Manage Performance and Capacity Ensure Systems Security
- Governance processes for the governance of the institution in a manner consistent level of performance and to improve the quality and Effectiveness is used.	Optimized governance level	-Provides automation in business processes -Implement self-correcting business processes -Reacting to actions according to rules to optimize business goals -Combination services and program in the runtime -Architecture with the automatically configurable -Event-driven automation for optimization -Self-organized enterprise -Provide enterprise-wide leadership for business and SOA governance -SOA governance in the enterprise level	Optimized service level		Enterprise SOA adoption domain	- Monitoring and planning of actions related to changes in application infrastructure -Primary data collection configuration -Update the configuration repository -Determine the baseline assessment and validation of configuration data Storage and archive -Modification levels of service - Improve customer satisfaction -Maintaining data integrity -Business interruption loss -Control operational costs of IT -Identification requirements compliance with laws and regulations -Evaluation results are reviewed and extended compliance with other laws and regulations, information technology and business	Monitor and Evaluate IT Performance Manage Change Manage the Configuration Manage Problems Manage Operation Ensure Regulatory Compliance

Table 5: Mapping proposed framework, COBIT5.

Aspect	COBIT4.1	COBIT5	Description
Process	**1. Plan and Organize(PO)**	**1. Align, Plan and Organise (APO)**	The COBIT 5 process reference model divides the governance and management processes of enterprise IT into two main process domains: • Governance—Contains five governance processes; within each process, evaluate, direct and monitor (EDM)5 practices are defined. • Management—Contains four domains, in line with the responsibility areas of plan, build, run and monitor (PBRM), and provides end-to-end coverage of IT. These domains are an evolution of the COBIT 4.1 domain and process structure. The names of the domains are chosen in line with these main area designations, but contain more verbs to describe them: – Align, Plan and Organise (APO) – Build, Acquire and Implement (BAI) – Deliver, Service and Support (DSS) – Monitor, Evaluate and Assess (MEA) More information on this site: www.isaca.org/cobit is visible.
	PO1: Define a strategic IT plan	APO01 Manage Strategy	
	PO2 Define the information architecture	APO03. Manage Enterprise Architecture	
	2. Acquire and Implement(AI)	**2. Build, Acquire and Implement (BAI)**	
	AI6: Manage changes	BAI06. Manage Changes	
	3. Deliver and Support(DS)	**3. Deliver, Service and Support (DSS)**	
	DS1 Define and manage service levels	APO09. Manage Service Agreements	
	DS3 Manage performance and capacity	BAI04. Manage Availability and Capacity	
	DS6: Ensure system security	BAI06:Manage Security Services	
	DS9 Manage the configuration	BAI10. Manage Configuration Framework	
	DS10 Manage problems	DSS03. Manage Problems	
	DS13:Manage operation	DSS01. Manage Operations	
	4. Monitor and Evaluate(ME)	**4. Monitor, Evaluate and Assess (MEA)**	
	ME1:Monitor and evaluate it performance	MEA01. Monitor, Evaluate and Assess Performance and Conformance	
	ME2:Ensure compliance with external requirements	MEA03. Monitor, Evaluate and Assess Compliance With External Requirements	
Maturity model	**Cobit4.1 Maturity levels**	**COBIT5 ISO/IEC 15504 based Capability levels**	The COBIT 5 product set includes a process capability model, based on the internationally recognised ISO/IEC 15504Software Engineering—Process Assessment standard. This model will achieve the same overall objectives of process assessment and process improvement support, i.e., it will provide a means to measure the performance of any of the governance (EDM-based) processes or management (PBRM-based) processes, and will allow areas for improvement to be identified
	5-Optimized	5-Optimized	
	4- Managed and Measured	4-Predictable	
	3- Defined	3-Established	
	N/A	2- Managed	
	N/A	1-Performed	
	2- Repeatable 1-ad hoc 0-Non existence	0-Incomplete	
SOA adoption domain	1-Inter-department business unit SOA adoption domain	1-Inter-department business unit SOA adoption domain	All SOA adoption domain proposed framework, are mapped to cobit5.
	2-Inter business SOA adoption domain	2-Inter business SOA adoption domain	
	3-Enterprise SOA adoption domain	3-Enterprise SOA adoption domain	
SOA maturity levels	1-Initial service level	1-Initial service level	All SOA maturity levels proposed framework, are mapped to cobit5.
	2-Architected service level	2-Architected service level	
	3-Business service level	3-Business service level	
	4-Collaborative service level	4-Collaborative service level	
	5-Measured service level	5-Measured service level	
	6-Optimized service level	6-Optimized service level	

5.1. Validity and reliability of questionnaire

To conduct the questionnaire's justifiability test, pilot questionnaires were randomly handed out to

5 of the managers and reporters at first; of course, the results obtained confirmed the questionnaire's justifiability. The durability option is another technical characteristic of the measurement tool, which points to the accuracy, confidentiality, integrity or repeatability of the test results. Durability refers to how much the acquired points scored by each user can show their actual point. Cronbach's alpha technique was chosen to evaluate the durability [24, 25]. This technique is calculated via the internal correlations' mean among the content evaluator elements, and it shows a good durability when it is close to the number. Using the Statistical Package for the Social Sciences (SPSS), the durability was studied, and the Cronbach's alpha was calculated to be 0.94, which showed a good durability among the questions [24].

5.2. Population and sample
The population included some experts in the field of SOA. Considering the limited number of experts in the field of SOA, the snowball sampling method was used. According to Hakim (1987), small samples can be used to develop and test explanations, particularly in the early stages of the work. Previous studies have used small samples to gain expert feedback to evaluate and support the model development [26]. Therefore, 30 questionnaires were distributed. Finally, 18 completed questionnaires were returned and used.

5.3. Data analysis
In this study, the inferential statistical techniques were used in analyzing the calculated performance, and confirming the hypothesis was performed by the binomial test in (0.05 significance level and cut point = 3) SPSS software. Tables 6-9 show the results of the research hypotheses. The results of the hypothesis test A are shown in table 6. According to this table, the value for the significant level column is lower than 0.05, and the frequency of observation for the category (>3) is more than other categories. Thus the hypothesis was approved, and it could be concluded with 95% confidence.
The results of the hypothesis test B are shown in table 7. According to this table, the value for the significant level column is lower than 0.05, and the frequency of observation for the category (>3) is more than the other categories. Thus the hypothesis was approved, and it could be concluded with 95% confidence.

The results of the hypothesis test C are shown in table 8. According to this table, the value for the significance level column is lower than 0.05, and the frequency of observation for the category (>3) is more than the other categories. Thus the hypothesis was approved, and could be concluded with 95% confidence.
The results of the hypothesis test D are shown in table 9. According to this table, the value for significance level column is lower than 0.05, and the frequency of observation for the category (>3) is more than other categories. Thus the hypothesis was approved, and it could be concluded with 95% confidence.

6. Conclusions and recommendations
Organizations need to evaluate the progress rate in implementing the SOA process and establishment of a SOA governance system to understand their level of progress and identify the required processes, mechanisms, and procedures to be successful. Thus a desired framework to evaluate SOA governance was proposed based on the COBIT 4.1 framework that is one of the important frameworks in the IT domain. It was used for evaluating governance maturity in IT domain and for using the main aspects of a comprehensive SOA governance maturity model. A questionnaire was prepared, and experts gave feedback to confirm the framework aspects that the studied results confirm framework aspects. In this work, it is recommended that the proposed framework should be validated for the application of service-oriented framework to assess the maturity of an organization. They are needed for a successful recovery. This framework has features and a process covering one of the important parts. In the proposed framework of the current study, the SOA governance status is considered with the existing organization processes from SOA organization status in the field of service-orientation and the necessary organization governance. An organization can better recognize its current status using this roadmap, and can specify its next status. to follow this work, it is recommended that this framework should be used to measure the SOA maturity of an organization or a specific case in order to validate the application of the proposed framework. Furthermore, because of the wide range of SOA governance processes and limitations, it was not possible to evaluate the maturity levels of all governance processes, and so it is recommended that the next research works should evaluate the maturity levels of other processes.

Table 6: Result of testing hypothesis of A section (sig. level 0.05)

Dimensions	Group	Category	N	Observed prop.	Exact sig. (2-tailed)	Reject/Confirm the hypothesis
SOA maturity levels	1	≤3	0	0/00		
	2	>3	18	1/00	0/000	confirm
	Total		18	1/00		
SOA governance maturity levels	1	≤3	0	0/00		
	2	>3	18	1/00	0/000	confirm
	Total		18	1/00		
SOA adoption domain	1	≤3	0	0/00		
	2	>3	18	1/00	0/000	confirm
	Total		18	1/00		
Processes domain	1	≤3	2	0/11		
	2	>3	16	0/89	0/001	confirm
	Total		18	1/00		

Table 7: Result of testing hypothesis of A section (sig. level 0.05)

Measures	Group	Category	N	Observed prop.	Exact sig. (2-tailed)	Reject/Confirm the hypothesis
Measured related to define a strategic IT plan process, used for inter-department/business unit SOA adoption	1	≤3	2	0/11		
	2	>3	16	0/89	0/001	confirm
	Total		18	1/00		
Measured related to define the information process, used for inter-department/business unit SOA adoption	1	≤3	2	0/11		
	2	>3	16	0/89	0/001	confirm
	Total		18	1/00		
Measured related to define and manage service levels process, used for inter-business unit SOA adoption domain	1	≤3	0	0/00		
	2	>3	18	1/00	0/000	confirm
	Total		18	1/00		
Measured related to determine technological direction process, used for Enterprise SOA adoption domain	1	≤3	4	0/22		
	2	>3	14	0/78	0/031	confirm
	Total		18	1/00		
Measured related to manage performance and capacity process, for used Enterprise SOA adoption domain	1	≤3	4	0/22		
	2	>3	14	0/78	0/031	confirm
	Total		18	1/00		
Measured related to ensure system security process, used for Enterprise SOA adoption domain	1	≤3	2	0/11		
	2	>3	16	0/89	0/001	confirm
	Total		18	1/00		
Measured related to monitor and evaluate IT performance process, used for Enterprise SOA adoption domain	1	≤3	2	0/11		
	2	>3	16	0/89	0/001	confirm
	Total		18	1/00		
Measured related to manage changes process, used for Enterprise SOA adoption domain	1	≤3	4	0/22		
	2	>3	14	0/78	0/031	confirm
	Total		18	1/00		
Measured related to manage configuration process, used for Enterprise SOA adoption domain	1	≤3	4	0/22		
	2	>3	14	0/78	0/031	confirm
	Total		18	1/00		
Measured related to manage problem process, used for Enterprise SOA adoption domain	1	≤3	4	0/22		
	2	>3	14	0/78	0/031	confirm
	Total		18	1/00		
Measured related to manage operation process, used for Enterprise SOA adoption domain	1	≤3	4	0/22		
	2	>3	14	0/78	0/031	confirm
	Total		18	1/00		
Measured related to ensure regulatory compliance process, used for Enterprise SOA adoption domain	1	≤3	4	0/22		
	2	>3	14	0/78	0/031	confirm
	Total		18	1/00		

Table 8: Result of testing hypothesis of C section (sig. level 0.05)

Measures	Group	Category	N	Observed prop.	Exact sig. (2-tailed)	Reject/Confirm the hypothesis
Measured related to define a strategic it plan process, used for architected service level of SOA maturity	1 2 Total	≤3 >3	4 14 18	0/22 0/78 1/00	0/031	confirm
Measured related to define the information process, used for architected service level of SOA maturity	1 2 Total	≤3 >3	0 18 18	0/00 1/00 1/00	0/000	confirm
Measured related to define and manage service levels process, used for business/collaborative service level of SOA maturity	1 2 Total	≤3 >3	2 16 18	0/11 0/89 1/00	0/001	confirm
Measured related to determine technological direction process, used for measured service level of SOA maturity	1 2 Total	≤3 >3	0 18 18	0/00 1/00 1/00	0/000	confirm
Measured related to manage performance and capacity process, for measured service level of SOA maturity	1 2 Total	≤3 >3	4 14 18	0/22 0/78 1/00	0/031	confirm
Measured related to ensure systems security process, used for measured service level of SOA maturity	1 2 Total	≤3 >3	0 18 18	0/00 1/00 1/00	0/000	confirm
Measured related to monitor and evaluate it performance process, used for measured service level of SOA maturity	1 2 Total	≤3 >3	2 16 18	0/11 0/89 1/00	0/001	confirm
Measured related to manage changes process, used for optimized service level of SOA maturity	1 2 Total	≤3 >3	4 14 18	0/22 0/78 1/00	0/031	confirm
Measured related to manage configuration process, used for optimized service level of SOA maturity	1 2 Total	≤3 >3	4 14 18	0/22 0/78 1/00	0/031	confirm
Measured related to manage problem process, used for optimized service level of SOA maturity	1 2 Total	≤3 >3	4 14 18	0/78 0/22 1/00	0/031	confirm
Measured related to manage operation process, used for optimized service level of SOA maturity	1 2 Total	≤3 >3	4 14 18	0/22 0/78 1/00	0/031	confirm
Measured related to ensure regulatory compliance process, used for optimized service level of SOA maturity	1 2 Total	≤3 >3	4 14 18	0/22 0/78 1/00	0/031	confirm

Table 9: Result of testing hypothesis of D section (sig. level 0.05)

Measures	Group	Category	N	Observed prop.	Exact sig. (2-tailed)	Reject/Confirm the hypothesis
Measured related to non-existent governance level, used for architected service level of SOA maturity	1	≤3	4	0/22		
	2	>3	14	0/78	0/031	confirm
	Total		18	1/00		
Measured related to initial/ad hoc governance level, used for architected service level of SOA maturity	1	≤3	4	0/22		
	2	>3	14	0/78	0/031	confirm
	Total		18	1/00		
Measured related to repeatable but intuitive governance level, used for business/collaborative service SOA maturity	1	≤3	2	0/11		
	2	>3	16	0/89	0/001	confirm
	Total		18	1/00		
Measured related to defined process governance level, used for business/collaborative service level SOA maturity	1	≤3	2	0/11		
	2	>3	16	0/89	0/001	confirm
	Total		18	1/00		
Measured related to managed and measurable governance level, used for measured service level SOA maturity	1	≤3	0	0/00		
	2	>3	18	1/00	0/000	confirm
	Total		18	1/00		
Measured related to optimized governance level, used for optimized service level SOA maturity	1	≤3	0	0/00		
	2	>3	18	1/00	0/000	confirm
	Total		18	1/00		

References

[1] Hassanzadeh, A. & Namdarian, L. (2011). Developing a Framework for evaluating service oriented Architecture Governance (SOAG), Knowledge Based systems, vol. 24, no. 5, pp. 716-730.

[2] Hassanzadeh, A. & Namdarian, L. (2010). Developing a framework for service oriented Architecture Governance Maturity (SOAGM), in Telecommunications (IST), 5th International Symposium, pp.513-520.

[3] Meier, F. (2006). Service oriented architecture maturity models: A guide to SOA adoption? M.Sc. Thesis, School of Humanities and Informatics, University of Skövde.

[4] Menasc'e, D.A., et al. (2010). On optimal service selection in service oriented architectures, Performance Evaluation, pp.659–675.

[5] Yashar, F. (2009). SOA governance – how best to embrace it? Part 3: Governance Maturity, Tooling, Vitality and Success patterns. Available: http://www.ibm.com/developerworks/webservices/library/ws-SOAGovernancepart3/index.html.

[6] Keen, M. & Adamski, D. (2007). Implementing Technology to Support SOA Governance and Management, IBM, International Technical Support Organization.

[7] Pingfeng L., & Raahemi, B. (2011). Knowledge sharing in dynamic virtual enterprises: a socio-technological perspective, Knowledge-Based Systems vol. 24, pp.427-443.

[8] Software AG, (2005). SOA Governance Rule Your SOA, BPTrends, pp.1-12.

[9] Hurwitz, J., et al. (2007). Service oriented Architecture for Dummies, Wiley publishing, Inc.

[10] Marks, E. A. (2008). Service-oriented architecture (SOA) governance for the services driven enterprise: John Wiley & Sons.

[11] Bieberstein, N., et al. (2005). Impact of service-oriented architecture on enterprise systems, organizational structures, and individuals. IBM Systems Journal, vol. 44, no. 4, pp.691–708.

[12] Afshar, M., et al. (2007). SOA Governance: Framework and Best Practices. Available: http://www.oracle.com/us/technologies/soa/oracle-soa-governance-best-practice-066427.pdf

[13] Scheper, T. & Kratz, B. (2009). SOA Governance Maturity – An Architect's View, IBM Corporation, vol.4, Issue 11.

[14] IT Governance Institute, (2007). COBIT 4.1 Excerpt, Available: https://www.isaca.org/Knowledge-Center/cobit.

[15] Stantchev, V. & Stantcheva, L. (2013). Applying IT-Governance Frameworks for SOA and Cloud Governance, in Information Systems, E-learning, and Knowledge Management Research. vol. 278, M Lytras, D. Ruan, R. Tennyson, P. Ordonez De Pablos, F. García Peñalvo, and L.Rusu, Eds., ed: Springer Berlin Heidelberg, pp.398-407.

[16] Joukhadar, G. & Rabhi, F. (2015). SOA governance – road into maturity, Australasian Conference on Information Systems, pp. 1-9.

[17] Arsanjani, A. & Holley, K. (2006). The Service Integration Maturity Model: achieving flexibility in the transformation to SOA, in Proceedings of the IEEE International Conference on Services Computing, pp.515.

[18] Inganti, S. and Aravamudan, S. (2007). SOA maturity model, BP Trends, pp.1-23.

[19] Tambotoh, J. J., & Latuperissa,. R. (2014). The Application for Measuring the Maturity Level of Information Technology Governance on Indonesian Government Agencies Using COBIT 4.1 Frameworks, Intelligent Information Management, vol.6, pp. 12-19.

[20] De Haes, S., & Van Grembergen, W. (2015). COBIT as a Framework for Enterprise Governance of IT Enterprise Governance of Information Technology (pp. 103-128): Springer.

[21] Falahah. (2010). Implementation of modified maturity level measurement model for AI1 COBIT Framework (Case study: IT Management audit of PT.POS Indonesia), in Information and Communication Technology for the Muslim World (ICT4M), International Conference on, pp.B-8-B-13.

[22] IT Governance Institute (ITGI). (2012). COBIT 5: A Business Framework for the Governance and Management of Enterprise IT. Available: www.isaca.org/cobit/pages/default.aspx.

[23] BAG, V .(2008). Service-Oriented Architecture in Banking: A Governance Framework, M.Sc. Thesis, Industrial Engineering &Management Science, University of Eindhoven.

[24] Bernardi, R. A. (1994). Validating research results when Cronbach's alpha is below. 70: A Methodological procedure. Educational and Psychological Measurement, vol. 54, no.3, pp.766-775.

[25] Salehi, J. A. (2007). The advanced statistical analysis, Hastan publication, 2nd edition.

[26] Beecham, S, et al. (2005). Using an expert panel to validate a requirements process improvement model, The Journal of Systems and Software, vol. 76, pp. 251-275.

13

Direct adaptive fuzzy control of flexible-joint robots including actuator dynamics using particle swarm optimization

M. Moradi Zirkohi[*] and S. Izadpanah

Department of Electrical Engineering, Behbahan Khatam Alanbia University of Technology, Behbahan, Iran.

*Corresponding author: moradi@bkatu.ac.ir (M. Moradi).

Abstract

In this paper, a novel direct adaptive fuzzy system is proposed to control flexible-joint robots including actuator dynamics. This design includes two interior loops. The inner loop controls the motor position using the proposed approach, while the outer one controls the joint angle of robots using a proportional-integral-derivative (PID) control law. One novelty of this paper is the use of a particle swarm optimization (PSO) algorithm for optimizing the control design parameters in order to achieve the desired performance. It is worthy of note that to form the control law by considering practical considerations, just the available feedbacks are used. It is beneficial for industrial applications, where the real-time computation is costly. The proposed control approach has a fast response with a good tracking performance under the well-behaved control efforts. The stability is guaranteed in the presence of both the structured and unstructured uncertainties. As a result, all the system states remain bounded. The results of the simulation conducted on a two-link flexible-joint robot show the efficiency of the proposed scheme.

Keywords: *Fuzzy System, Particle Swarm Optimization, Flexible-Joint Robot, Actuator Dynamics.*

1. Introduction

Due to the non-linearities and coupling effects, the trajectory tracking control of robot manipulators with joint flexibilities is a challenging problem. Compared with the rigid robots, the number of degrees of freedom becomes twice the number of control actions due to flexibility in the joints, and the matching property between the non-linearities and inputs is lost [1]. As a result, to improve the performance and to avoid the unwanted oscillations for practical applications, joint flexibility must be taken into account in both modeling and control. However, to simplify the complexity of the controller design, most controllers for industrial robots are designed based on the rigid-robot assumption [2]. As a result of considering the actuator dynamics and joint flexibility, the controller design would become extremely complex. Therefore, the modeling and control of the flexible-joint robots are more difficult than those of the rigid robots [3]. The torques are the inputs to the system equations. However, in many papers, such as the feedback linearization method [4], the adaptive sliding

mode technique [5], and the proportional-derivative control approach [6] dynamics of the actuators for providing the desired torques are excluded [7]. It has been shown that actuator dynamics form an important part of the complete robot dynamics, especially in the cases of high-velocity movement and highly-varying loads [8]. One of the drawbacks of these previously-published results is that they require velocity measurements. Moreover, in practical robotic systems, the velocity measurements obtained through tachometers are contaminated by noise [9-11].

More specifically, the major limitation associated with the mentioned control schemes is that these schemes assume that torques can be directly applied to the robot links, i.e. the actuator dynamics is ignored and the control is designed at a dynamic level with the torque as input. Researchers often refer to this method as the torque-control strategy.

To solve the aforementioned problems, the voltage-control strategy was proposed [12]. In this strategy, the actuator dynamics is also taken into account, and the voltages of motors are considered as the inputs of the robotic system including the actuators and robot manipulators. Recently, robust control [13] and non-linear adaptive control [14] of flexible-joint robots have been developed using the voltage-control strategy. On the other hand, including the electrical sub-system of the actuator dynamics causes several challenging problems. Some of these reasons are as follow [15]: 1) The electrical sub-system increases the complexity of the system model such that a 5th order non-linear differential equation should be employed for describing a single link flexible joint robot [16]. 2) Any practical control system is subject to some upper and lower bounds that limit the actuator input command. In addition, there are unwanted non-linearities, which come from dynamical effects such as deadzone, backlash, and hysteresis. These constraints make the control design problem extremely difficult.

Alternatively, fuzzy control, as a model-free approach, can be easily designed to control non-linear uncertain systems [17]. So far, fuzzy control of robot manipulators has received considerable attention for overcoming uncertainty, non-linearity, and coupling [17-19]. The fuzzy adaptive control approaches are classified into two categories, direct adaptive fuzzy control and indirect adaptive fuzzy control algorithms [17]. In the direct adaptive fuzzy control, the fuzzy controller is a single fuzzy system constructed (initially) from the control knowledge. On the other hand, in the indirect adaptive fuzzy control, the fuzzy controller comprises a number of fuzzy systems constructed (initially) from the plant knowledge.

This paper discusses the problem of designing a novel direct adaptive fuzzy control for a class of flexible-joint robotic manipulators including actuator dynamics in the presence of uncertainties associated with both the robot and motor dynamics. An advantage is that it uses the voltage-control strategy instead of the torque-control strategy, which is simpler, less computational, and more effective than the torque-control strategy. An electrically-driven manipulator is then controlled via its motors as individual single-input/single-output systems. The design includes two interior loops: the inner loop controls the motor position using the proposed approach, while the outer loop controls the joint angle of the robot using a proportional-integral-derivative (PID) control law. In addition, performance of the control system is improved by optimizing the PID gains.

Another novelty of this paper is the use of a particle swarm optimization (PSO) algorithm for optimizing the control design parameters in order to achieve the desired performance. It is worthy of note that one of the advantages of the proposed method is that there is no need for a velocity measurement. Based on the Lyapunov stability theorem, the stability analysis was presented. Finally, simulations were conducted on two-link robotic manipulators to show the effectiveness of the proposed control scheme. As a result, the advocated design methodology not only assures a closed-loop stability but also a desired tracking performance can be achieved for the overall system.

The rest of the paper is organized as follows: Section 2 presents modeling of the flexible-joint robots. Section 3 introduces PSO. Section 4 develops the proposed method. Section 5 presents the simulation results, and finally, Section 6 concludes the paper.

2. Electrically-driven fexible-joint robot dynamics

Consider a flexible-joint robot, which is driven by geared permanent magnet dc motors. If the joint flexibility is modeled by a linear torsional spring, the dynamic equations of motion can be expressed as follow [13, 14]:

$$D(\theta)\ddot{\theta} + C(\theta,\dot{\theta})\dot{\theta} + g(\theta) + \tau_d = \\ K(r\theta_m - \theta) \tag{1}$$

$$J\ddot{\theta}_m + B\dot{\theta}_m + rK(r\theta_m - \theta) = \tau \tag{2}$$

where, $\theta \in R^n$ is a vector of joint angles, $\theta_m \in R^n$ is a vector of rotor angles, and $\tau_d \in R^n$ denotes unknown disturbances including unstructured dynamics and unknown payload dynamics. Thus this system possesses $2n$ coordinates as $[\theta \ \theta_m]$. The matrix $D(\theta)$ is an $n \times n$ matrix of manipulator inertia, $C(\theta,\dot{\theta})\dot{\theta} \in R^n$ is the vector of centrifugal and Coriolis forces, $g(\theta) \in R^n$ is a vector of gravitational forces, and $\tau \in R$ is a torque vector of motors. The diagonal matrices J, B and r represent the coefficients of the motor inertia, motor damping, and reduction gear, respectively. The diagonal matrix K represents the lumped flexibility provided by the joint and reduction gear. To simplify the model, both the joint stiffness and gear coefficients are assumed constant. The vector of gravitational forces $g(\theta)$ is assumed a function of only the joint positions as used in the simplified model [20]. Note that the vector and matrix are represented in the bold form for clarity.

System (1-2) is highly non-linear, extensively computational, heavily coupled, and a multi-input/multi-output system with $2n$ coordinates. Complexity of the model has been a serious challenge in robot modeling and control in the literature. It is expected to face a higher complexity if the proposed model includes the actuator dynamics. In order to obtain the motor voltages as inputs, consider the electrical equation of the geared permanent magnet DC motors in the following matrix form:

$$u = RI_a + L\dot{I}_a + K_b\dot{\theta}_m \qquad (3)$$

where $u \in R^n$ is a vector of motor voltages, $I_a \in R^n$ is a vector of motor currents, and $\dot{\theta}_m$ is a vector of rotor velocities. The diagonal matrices R, L and K_b represent the coefficients of armature resistance, armature inductance, and back-emf constant, respectively. The motor torque τ as an input for dynamic equation (2), is produced by the motor currents as:

$$K_m I_a = \tau \qquad (4)$$

where, K_m is a diagonal matrix of the torque constants. Equations (1-4) form the robotic system such that the voltage vector u is the input vector, and the joint angle vector θ is the output vector.

The dynamics of the electrical robot (1)-(4) in the state space is formed as:

$$\dot{X} = f(X) + bu + \vartheta \qquad (5)$$

where:

$$f(X) = \begin{bmatrix} X_2 \\ D^{-1}(X_1)(-g(X_1) - KX_1 - C(X_1, X_2)X_2 \\ +Krx_3) \\ J^{-1}(rKX_1 - r^2KX_3 - BX_4 + K_mX_5) \\ -L^{-1}(K_bX_4 + RX_5) \end{bmatrix}$$

$$b = \begin{bmatrix} 0 \\ 0 \\ 0 \\ 0 \\ L^{-1} \end{bmatrix}, X = \begin{bmatrix} \theta \\ \dot{\theta} \\ \theta_m \\ \dot{\theta}_m \\ I_a \end{bmatrix}, \vartheta = \begin{bmatrix} 0 \\ -D^{-1}(X_1)\tau_d \\ 0 \\ 0 \\ 0 \end{bmatrix}$$

where, $X_1 = \theta, X_2 = \dot{\theta}, X_3 = \theta_m, X_4 = \dot{\theta}_m$ and $X_5 = I_a$.

Equation (5) shows a highly-coupled non-linear large system, where the state vector X includes vectors of position and velocity to the motor and the joint and the motor current.

3. Particle swarm optimization

The particle swarm optimization (PSO) algorithm is a population-based search algorithm based on the simulation of the social behavior of birds within a flock [21]. This algorithm optimizes a problem by having a population of candidate solutions and moving these particles around in the search-space according to simple mathematical formulae over the particle position and velocity. The position of each particle is changed based on the experiences of the particle itself and those of its neighbors [22,23]. Consequently, the particles tend to fly towards the better searching areas over the searching space [24,25].

The velocity of the ith particle (v_i) is calculated as follows [23,26]:

$$v_i(t+1) = w\,v_i(t) + c_1r_1(pbest_i(t) - x_i(t)) + c_2r_2(gbest(t) - x_i(t)) \qquad (6)$$

where, in the ith iteration, x_i is the particle position, $pbest_i$ is the previous best particle position, $gbest$ is the previous global best position of particles, w is the inertia weight, c_1 and c_2 are the acceleration coefficients namely the cognitive and social scaling parameters, respectively, and r_1 and r_2 are two random numbers in the range of [0 1].

The new position of the th particle is then calculated as [26]:

$$x_i(t+1) = x_i(t) + v_i(t+1) \qquad (7)$$

The PSO algorithm is performed repeatedly until the goal is achieved. The number of iterations can be set to a specific value as a goal of optimization. In addition, to enhance the performance of PSO based on the experimental results, the inertia weight was proposed to control the velocity, as [27]:

$$w = (w_1 - w_2)(\frac{iter_{max} - iter}{iter_{max}})^n + w_2 \qquad (8)$$

where, n is the non-linear modulation index, w decreases from a higher value w_1 to a lower value w_2 and $iter_{max}$ is the maximum iteration number. Moreover, proper fine-tuning of the parameters c_1 and c_2 in (6) may result in faster convergence of the algorithm and alleviation of the local minima [28]. Hence, c_1 and c_2 are given as:

$$c_1 = (c_{1i} - c_{1f})(\frac{iter_{max} - iter}{iter_{max}}) + c_{1f}$$

$$c_2 = (c_{2i} - c_{2f})(\frac{iter_{max} - iter}{iter_{max}}) + c_{2f} \qquad (9)$$

where, c_{1i} and c_{2i} are the initial values for the acceleration coefficient c_1 and c_2 and c_{1f} and c_{2f} are the final values for the acceleration coefficients c_1 and c_2, respectively [28, 29].

Simulations were carried out with various constraint optimization problems to find out the best ranges of values for c_1 and c_2. From the results, it was observed that the best solutions were determined when changing c_1 from 2.5 to 0.5 and changing c_2 from 0.5 to 2.5 over the full range of search [29].

4. Proposed control law

To control such a complicated system, a novel simple controller was proposed using a voltage-control strategy. The design includes two interior loops: the inner loop controls the motor position, while the outer loop controls the joint angle of the robot manipulator. The outer loop provides the desired trajectory for the inner loop.

4.1. Designing inner loop

In order to design the inner loop to control the motor position, the electrical equation for a permanent magnet dc motor is written as:

$$u = RI_a + L\dot{I}_a + k_b\dot{\theta}_m + \vartheta \qquad (10)$$

Where R, L and k_b denote the armature resistance, inductance, and back emf constant, respectively, u is the motor voltage, I_a is the motor current, θ_m is the rotor position, and ϑ represents the external disturbance (assumed to be bounded).

The motor angle θ_m, as an output, can be controlled via the voltage u, as an input. From (10) we have:

$$\dot{\theta}_m = \frac{1}{k_b}u - \frac{RI_a + L\dot{I}_a}{k_b} - \frac{\vartheta}{k_b} \qquad (11)$$

Using feedback linearization by assuming $\vartheta = 0$, a perfect control law can be obtained as:

$$u_{eq} = k_b(\frac{RI_a + L\dot{I}_a}{k_b} + \dot{\theta}_{md} + \alpha(\theta_{md} - \theta_m)) \qquad (12)$$

where, α is a positive gain, and θ_{md} is a desired motor angle.
Substituting (12) into (11), and after some manipulation, yields:

$$\dot{e} + \alpha e = 0 \qquad (13)$$

where, e is the tracking error, expressed by $e = \theta_{md} - \theta_m$. It can be concluded that the error approaches zero using the control law (12).

Feedback linearization is one of the popular techniques used in the non-linear control approaches. Feedback linearization can convert a multi-input/multi-output non-linear system to single-input/single-output linear decoupled systems. However, feedback linearization suffers from some problems such as model uncertainty and additional computations in control efforts. In fact, a perfect model is required to apply feedback linearization, while a perfect model is not available. Therefore, performances of control strategies are dependent on the model used in the feedback linearization [30].

From (12), one can note that the feedback linearization controller requires an exact cancellation of non-linearities to achieve the desired performance. In the presence of uncertainties, the non-linearities may not get canceled exactly, which may result in a poor performance, and thus, it is necessary to compensate for the effects of the uncertainties. To overcome this drawback, the following control law is proposed:

$$u = u_D + k_b u_s \qquad (14)$$

where, u_D is the output of an adaptive fuzzy system, and u_s can be considered as an extra term to overcome uncertainties. Substituting (14) into (11) gives:

$$\dot{\theta}_m = \frac{1}{k_b}u_D + u_s - \frac{RI_a + L\dot{I}_a}{k_b} - \frac{\vartheta}{k_b} + \frac{1}{k_b}u_{eq} - \frac{1}{k_b}u_{eq} \qquad (15)$$

By substituting (12) into (15), one can obtain:

$$\dot{\theta}_m = \frac{1}{k_b}u_D + u_s - \frac{RI_a + L\dot{I}_a}{k_b} - \frac{\vartheta}{k_b} + \frac{RI_a + L\dot{I}_a}{k_b} + \dot{\theta}_{md} + \alpha(\theta_{md} - \theta_m) - \frac{1}{k_b}u_{eq} \qquad (16)$$

After some simple manipulations, we have:

$$\dot{\theta}_m = \dot{\theta}_{md} + \alpha(\theta_{md} - \theta_m) + \frac{1}{k_b}(u_D - u_{eq}) + u_s - \varphi \qquad (17)$$

where, $\varphi = \frac{\vartheta}{k_b}$. The role of u_s is presented by (17). It is quite obvious from (17) that u_s is employed to attenuate the external disturbance. Further simplification gives:

$$\dot{e} = -\alpha e + \frac{1}{k_b}(u_{eq} - u_D) + \varphi - u_s \qquad (18)$$

where, e is $\theta_{md} - \theta_m$.

We design a fuzzy controller using two variables as the inputs to the fuzzy controller namely the tracking error e and its derivative $\dot{e}$. If three membership functions are given to each fuzzy input, the whole control space is covered by nine fuzzy rules. The linguistic fuzzy rules are proposed in the form of:

$$R^l : if \ e \ is \ A^l \ and \ \dot{e} \ is \ B^l \ then \ y = y^l \qquad (19)$$

where, R^l denotes the lth fuzzy rule for $l = 1,...,9$ In the lth rule, y^l is a crisp output, and A^l and B^l are the fuzzy membership functions belonging to the fuzzy variables e and $\dot{e}$, respectively. Three Gaussian membership functions, namely Positive (P), Zero (Z), and Negative (N) are defined for input e in the operating range of the manipulator. They are expressed as:

$$\mu_N(e) = \begin{cases} 1 & e \leq -1 \\ 1 - 2(e-1)^2 & -1 \leq e \leq -.5 \\ 2e^2 & -.5 \leq e \leq 0 \\ 0 & e \geq 0 \end{cases}$$

$$\mu_P(\dot{e}) = \begin{cases} 0 & \dot{e} \leq 0 \\ 2\dot{e}^2 & 0 \leq \dot{e} \leq .5 \\ 1 - 2(\dot{e}+1)^2 & .5 \leq \dot{e} \leq 1 \\ 1 & \dot{e} \geq 1 \end{cases} \qquad (20)$$

$$\mu_z(e) = \exp(-\frac{e^2}{2\sigma^2}), \ \sigma = .5$$

The membership functions of $\dot{e}$ are given the same as e. If we use the singleton fuzzifier and the center average defuzzifier, u_D is calculated by:

$$u(e|\Theta) = \sum_{l=1}^{9} y^l \xi_l(e,\dot{e}) = \Theta^T \xi \qquad (21)$$

where

$\Theta^T = [y^1 \ y^2 \ ... \ y^9], \xi = [\xi_1 \ \xi_2 \ ... \ \xi_9]$ and $e = [e \ \dot{e}]$. In the meantime, ξ_l is expressed as

$$\xi_l(e,\dot{e}) = \frac{\mu_{A^l(e)}\mu_{B^l(\dot{e})}}{\sum\limits_{l=1}^{l=9} \mu_{A^l(e)}\mu_{B^L(\dot{e})}} \qquad (22)$$

where, $\mu_{A^l(e)}, \mu_{B^l(\dot{e})} \in [0 \ 1]$. The parameter Θ in (21) is determined by the adaptive rule afterward.

According to the universal approximation theorem, there exists an optimal fuzzy system $u_D^*(\mathbf{x}|\Theta)$ in the form of (21) such that:

$$u_D^*(e,\dot{e}) = \Theta^{*T} \zeta + \varepsilon \qquad (23)$$

where, ε is the approximation error, assumed to be bounded by $|\varepsilon| \leq \rho$, where ρ is a positive scalar. Employing a fuzzy system to approximate u_D yields:

$$u_D(e|\Theta) = \Theta^T \zeta \qquad (24)$$

where, $\hat{\Theta}$ is the estimated vector of Θ. One can obtain:

$$u_D^*(e|\Theta) - u_D(e|\Theta) = \tilde{\Theta}^T \zeta + \varepsilon \qquad (25)$$

where, $\tilde{\Theta} = \Theta^* - \hat{\Theta}$.

Using (18), and by adding and subtracting $u_D^*(e|\Theta)$, one can obtain:

$$\dot{e} = -\alpha e + \frac{1}{k_b}(u_D^*(e|\Theta) - u_D(e|\Theta)) - \frac{1}{k_b}w + \varphi - u_s \qquad (26)$$

where, $w = u_D^*(e|\Theta) - u_D$. Substituting (25) into (26) yields:

$$\dot{e} = -\alpha e + \frac{1}{k_b}(\tilde{\Theta}^T \zeta) - \frac{1}{k_b}w + \varphi + \in -u_s \qquad (27)$$

where, $\in = \frac{\varepsilon}{k_b}$. To establish convergence of the error, a lyapunove function is defined as:

$$V = 0.5e^2 + \frac{1}{2\gamma_1}\tilde{\Theta}^T \tilde{\Theta} \qquad (28)$$

where, γ_1 is a positive constant. Taking the time derivative of the above equation yields:

$$\dot{V} = e\dot{e} + \frac{1}{\gamma_1}\tilde{\Theta}^T \dot{\tilde{\Theta}} \qquad (29)$$

Substituting (27) into (29) yields:

$$\dot{V} = e(-\alpha e + \frac{1}{k_b}(\tilde{\Theta}^T \zeta) - \frac{1}{k_b}w + \varphi + \in - u_s) + \frac{1}{\gamma_1}\tilde{\Theta}^T \dot{\tilde{\Theta}} \qquad (30)$$

After some simple manipulations, one can obtain:

$$\dot{V} = -\alpha e^2 + \tilde{\Theta}^T(\frac{e}{k_b}\zeta + \frac{1}{\gamma_1}\dot{\tilde{\Theta}}) - \frac{e}{k_b}w + e(\varphi + \in - u_s) \qquad (31)$$

Suppose that $u_s = e$. Thus:

$$\dot{V} = -e^2(\alpha + 1) + \tilde{\Theta}^T(\frac{e}{k_b}\zeta + \frac{1}{\gamma_1}\dot{\tilde{\Theta}}) - \frac{e}{k_b}w + e(\varphi + \in) \qquad (32)$$

To establish the convergence, the following adaptive law is given:

$$\dot{\Theta} = \gamma_1 e \zeta / k_b \tag{33}$$

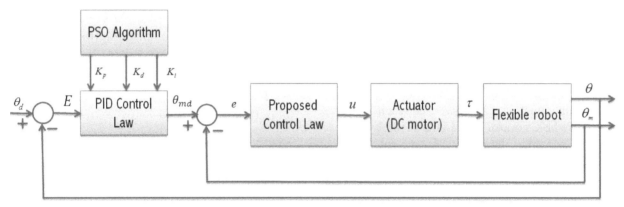

Figure 1. Block diagram of control system.

In order to evaluate the adaptive law (33), we substitute it into (32) to obtain:

$$\dot{V} = -e^2(\alpha+1) - \frac{e}{k_b}w + e(\varphi + \epsilon) \tag{34}$$

For achieving $\dot{V} \leq 0$, (34) can be recast as:

$$\dot{V} \leq -e^2(\alpha+1) - \frac{e}{k_b}w + |e||(\varphi + \epsilon)| \tag{35}$$

For achieving $\dot{V} \leq 0$, it is required that:

$$e(\varphi + \epsilon) - \frac{e}{k_b}w \leq 0 \tag{36}$$

From the universal approximation theorem, it can be expected that the terms ϵ and w should be very small, if not equal to zero, in the adaptive fuzzy system. Hence, using the Cauchy–Schwartz inequality, and by assuming that $|(\varphi + \epsilon)| \leq \rho_1$, where ρ_1 is a positive scalar, we can obtain:

$$e(\varphi + \epsilon) \leq |e|\rho_1 \tag{37}$$

Thus in order to satisfy (36), we suggest:

$$|e|\rho_1 = \frac{e}{k_b}w \tag{38}$$

Substituting for $\rho_1 = \frac{e}{|e|k_b}w$ in (35) gives:

$$\dot{V} \leq -e^2(\alpha+1) \tag{39}$$

Therefore, $e \in L_\infty$, and $\int_0^\infty e^2 \leq -(\alpha+1)^{-1}\int_0^\infty \dot{V} < \infty$

implies $e \in L_2$. In addition, we have already assumed that $\varphi \in L_\infty$. As a result, (27) implies $\dot{e} \in L_\infty$. Hence, asymptotic convergence of error can be concluded using the Barbalat's lemma. Namely, $\lim_{t \to \infty}|e(t)| = 0$.

4.2. Designing outer loop

The outer loop is designed to control the joint angle and providing the desired θ_{md} to the inner loop using a PID ordinary control law as:

$$\theta_{md} = k_d\dot{E} + k_pE + k_i\int E\,dt \tag{40}$$

where, k_p, k_d, and k_i are positive constant gains. $E = \theta_d - \theta$ denotes the joint tracking error, θ is the actual joint angle, and θ_d is the desired joint angle. To enhance the control system performance, the gains of PID control law are optimized using PSO. In addition, according to the proof given by [14], the robotic system is stable as well. As a conclusion, based on the stability analysis, all the signals required to form (14) are bounded.

To clarify the proposed control algorithm, a block diagram of the control system is depicted in figure 1.

In addition, to summarize the above analysis, a design procedure for the proposed approach is proposed as follows:

Step 1: Construct membership function for e and $\dot{e}$.

Step 2: Designing inner loop: Specify the desired coefficients γ_1 and α.

Step 3: Designing outer loop: Apply PSO algorithm, and find optimal specify coefficients k_p, k_d and k_i.

Step 4: Obtain the control law in (14), and apply it to the electrically-driven flexible-joint robot.

5. Simulation results

In this section, the proposed approach is applied to control a two-link flexible-joint robotic manipulator, as shown in figure 2, as described by [11,31]:

Table 1. Motor parameters.

Motors	R	k_b	L	J	B	r	K
1,2	1.26	0.26	0.001	0.0002	0.001	0.01	500

$$D(\theta) = \begin{bmatrix} m_1 l_1^2 + m_2(l_1^2 + l_2^2 + 2l_1 l_2 c_2) & m_2 l_2^2 + m_2 l_1 l_2 c_2 \\ m_2 l_2^2 + m_2 l_1 l_2 c_2 & m_2 l_2^2 \end{bmatrix} \quad (41)$$

$$C(\theta, \dot\theta) = \begin{bmatrix} -2m_2 l_1 l_2 s_2 \dot\theta_2 & m_2 l_1 l_2 s_2 \dot\theta_2 \\ m_2 l_1 l_2 s_2 \dot\theta_2 & 0 \end{bmatrix} \quad (42)$$

$$g(\theta) = \begin{bmatrix} m_2 l_2 g c_{12} + (m_1 + m_2) l_1 g c_1 \\ m_2 l_2 g c_{12} \end{bmatrix} \quad (43)$$

where, m_1 and m_2 are the masses of links 1 and 2, respectively; l_1 and l_2 are the lengths of links 1 and 2, respectively; s_i denotes $\sin(\theta_i)$, c_i denotes $\cos(\theta_i)$, c_{ij} denotes $\cos(\theta_i + \theta_j)$ for $i = 1,2$ and $j = 1,2$, and g is the acceleration of gravity. The parameters of the robot used for simulation are $l_1 = l_2 = 1m, m_1 = 10kg, m_2 = 8kg$ and $g = 9.8m/s^2$. The parameters of motors are given in table 1. Note that the inductances of motors are taken into account to consider a more complicated model in simulations.

The desired joint trajectory for the joints is smooth, expressed as $\theta_d = 1 - \cos(\pi t/20)$, shown in figure 3.

The maximum voltage of each motor is set to $u_{max} = 40v$. We set the adaptation law with $\hat\Theta(0) = 0$ and $\gamma_1 = 200$ for both motors.

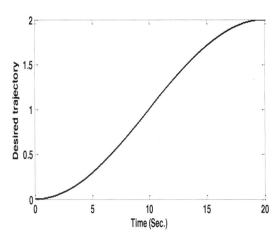

Figure 3. Desired trajectory for joints 1 and 2.

The PSO algorithm searches by 20 particles, and the maximum iteration $iter_{max}$ is set to 100. The maximum inertia weight w_1 and the minimum inertia weight w_2 are given by 0.9 and 0.4, respectively. The coefficients c_{1i} and c_{2i} are set to 2.5 and 0.5, respectively. In addition, the coefficients c_{1f} and c_{2f} are set to 0.5 and 2.5, respectively. For the purpose of comparison, simulation studies in three cases are carried out.

Case 1: In this simulation, no uncertainty is considered. The PID gains are set to $k_p = 20, k_i = 10$ and $k_d = 2$. The performance of the control system is shown in figure 4. It is evident that the control system is performed well. The maximum value of tracking error is 0.135. The motor voltages behave well under the maximum permitted value of 40 V, as shown in figure 5. It is interesting to note that the control input is free of chattering. The adaptation of parameters in the adaptive law (33) is shown in figure 6. The simulation results confirm the effectiveness of the proposed method.

Case 2: In this simulation, to have a better comparison, and to enhance the control performance, the GA and PSO algorithms are used to optimize the PID control law gains in the outer loop. The search spaces of PID gains are defined as

$$0 < k_p < 600, 0 < k_d < 600, 0 < k_i < 20.$$

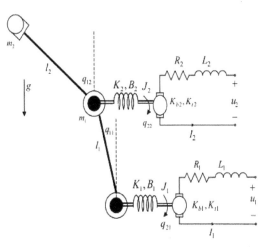

Figure 2. Flexible-joint two-link robot actuated by brushed DC motors [2].

Before proceeding by the optimization operations, a performance criterion must be defined.

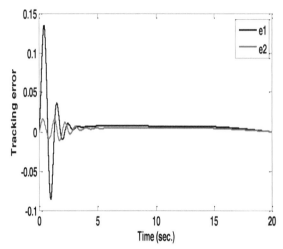

Figure 4. Tracking performance of proposed approach.

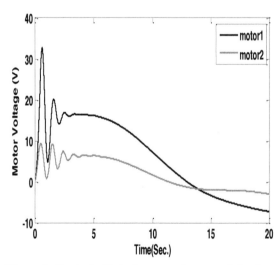

Figure 5. Control effort of proposed approach (motor voltages).

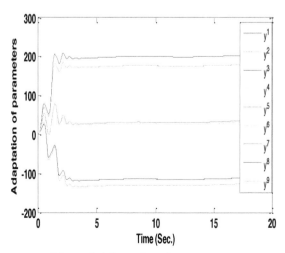

Figure 6. Adaptation of parameters.

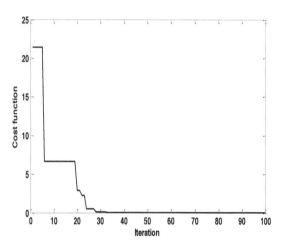

Figure 7. Desired Convergence of cost function.

In this paper, the cost function (CF) is defined as:

$$CF = \frac{1}{20} \int_0^{20} (e_1^2 + e_2^2) dt \qquad (44)$$

Owing to the randomness of the mentioned algorithms, their performance cannot be judged by the result of a single run. Many trials with different initializations should be made to acquire a useful conclusion about the performance of algorithms. An algorithm is robust if it gives consistent results during all the trials.

In order to run the PSO and GA algorithms, a population with a size of 20 for 100 iterations is used. Regarding (44), comparison of the results for 20 independent trials is shown in table 2.

Table 2. Comparison of optimized PID parameters.

Method	Best	Mean	Worst
GA	0.4316	0.6376	0.9376
PSO	0.1594	0.1604	0.1622

This comparison shows that PSO is superior to GA because the best and the mean values obtained by PSO are very close to the worst value. Hence, to save space afterward, just the PSO results are presented. In addition, the optimization process for PSO is depicted by figure 7 by calculating the cost function in the global best value at each run.

It is seen that the cost function is well converged. The trajectory of the PID gains is shown in figure 8. It confirms the success of the optimization process by using the PSO algorithm. As seen, the final values for the PID gains are found as $k_p = 408.89, k_d = 246.98, k_i = 13.87$. Figure 9 illustrates the tracking errors. The maximum value for the tracking error for joint 1 is about 0.083, i.e. about 61% of its value in case 1. It can be concluded that the PSO algorithm has worked well to enhance the control performance.

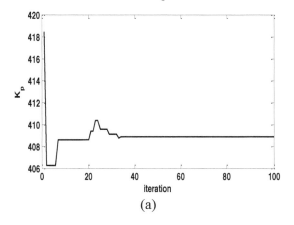

(a)

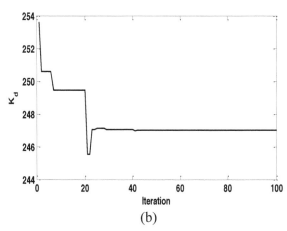

(b)

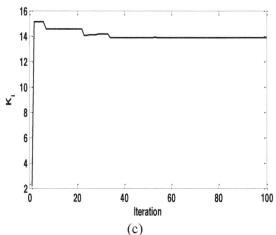

(c)

Figure 8. Finding PID gains: (a) trajectory of k_p, (b) trajectory of k_d, (c) trajectory of k_i.

Case 3: In this simulation, performance of the proposed approach in the presence of the uncertainties associated with both robot and motor is investigated. In this regard, for the robustness evaluation of the controllers, external disturbances are added to the robot system. The disturbance is inserted into the input of each motor as a periodic pulse function with a period of 2 S, amplitude 4 V, time delay of 0.7 S, and pulse width 30% of

period. This form of disturbance is an example of any form that can be applied but it includes jumps to cover the complex cases.

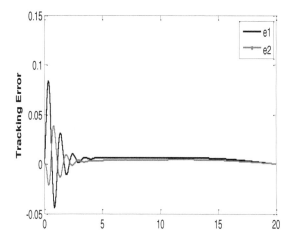

Figure 9. Tracking performance of proposed approach in optimal case.

We also choose the exogenous disturbances as: $\tau_d = [-3\cos(5t) \quad 3\sin(5t)]^T$. Moreover, the motors and robots' link parameters are considered to be 80% of their real values defined as before. The optimal values of PID gains that have been achieved using the PSO algorithm in Case 1 are used. The performance of the control system is shown in figures 10 and 11.

It is evident that the effects of disturbances are represented as small jumps on the curves of tracking errors. In addition, the tracking error in the presence of time-variant disturbance is, to some extent, more than the previous case. These figures show that not only there is no sign of chattering in the control inputs in the presence of the time-variant disturbance, but also they are smooth and in the permitted interval.

The simulation results thus demonstrate that the proposed approach can effectively control the flexible-joint robotic system with model uncertainties and disturbances.

Case 4: To have a better comparison, the proposed method is compared with a non-linear, approach proposed in [14]. The tracking performance of the mentioned approach in [14] is illustrated in figure 12. The maximum value for tracking error is 0.235, i.e. significantly larger than its value in case 2. Generally, it is evident that both methods have performed well. However, to some extent, the proposed approach has perform better.

6. Conclusion

This paper presents a direct adaptive fuzzy controller for flexible-joint electrically-driven robots, considering uncertainties in both the actuator and manipulator dynamics. The design includes two interior loops: the inner loop controls the motor position using the proposed approach, while the outer loop controls the joint angle of the robot using a PID control law. The proposed approach is based upon the voltage-control strategy, which is superior to the well-known torque-control strategy.

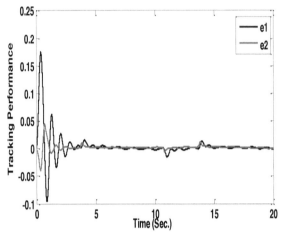

Figure 10. Tracking performance under disturbance.

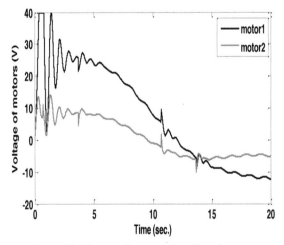

Figure 11. Motor voltages under disturbance.

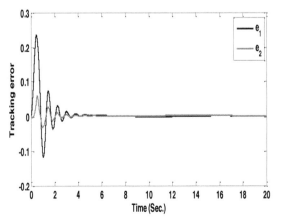

Figure 12. Tracking performance of proposed approach presented in [14].

The main advantage of our proposed methodology is that it uses available feedbacks as an important advantage from a practical viewpoint, the actuator dynamics is considered, and the control performance is also enhanced using the PSO algorithm. The stability analysis has verified the control method, and the simulation results have confirmed its effectiveness.

It is noted that the extension of the proposed method to the controller design for AC motors deserve further investigations. Practical implication of the proposed theoretical results is also part of our future works. It is worthy of note that from the simulation results, it can be concluded that the theoretic results obtained have potentials in applications.

References

[1] Brogliato, B., Ortega, R., & Lozano, R. (1995). Global tracking controllers for flexible-joint manipulators: a comparative study. Automatica, vol. 31, no. 7, pp. 941-956.

[2] Yen, H.-M., Li, T.-H. S., & Chang, Y.-C. (2012). Adaptive neural network based tracking control for electrically driven flexible-joint robots without velocity measurements. Computers & Mathematics with Applications, vol. 64, no. 5, pp. 1022-1032.

[3] Lewis, F. L., Abdallah, C. T., & Dawson, D. M. (1993). Control of robot manipulators, Macmillan New York.

[4] Spong, M. W., & Vidyasagar, M. (2008). Robot dynamics and control, John Wiley & Sons.

[5] Huang, A.-C., & Chen, Y.-C. (2004). Adaptive sliding control for single-link flexible-joint robot with mismatched uncertainties. Control Systems Technology, IEEE Transactions on, vol. 12, no. 5, pp. 770-775.

[6] De Luca, A., Siciliano, B., & Zollo, L. (2005). PD control with on-line gravity compensation for robots with elastic joints: Theory and experiments. Automatica, vol. 41, no. 10, pp. 1809-1819.

[7] Ozgoli, S., & Taghirad, H. (2006). A survey on the control of flexible joint robots. Asian Journal of Control, vol. 8, no. 4, pp. 332-344.

[8] Tarn, T., et al. (1991). Effect of motor dynamics on nonlinear feedback robot arm control. Robotics and Automation, IEEE Transactions on, vol. 7, no. 1, pp. 114-122.

[9] Li, Y., Tong, S., & Li, T. (2013). Adaptive fuzzy output feedback control for a single-link flexible robot manipulator driven DC motor via backstepping. Nonlinear Analysis: Real World Applications, vol. 14, no. 1, pp. 483-494.

[10] Nicosia, S., & Tomei, P. (1990). Robot control by using only joint position measurements. Automatic

Control, IEEE Transactions on, vol. 35, no. 9, pp. 1058-1061.

[11] Peng, J., Liu, Y., & Wang, J. (2014). Fuzzy adaptive output feedback control for robotic systems based on fuzzy adaptive observer. Nonlinear Dynamics, vol. 78, no. 2, pp. 789-801.

[12] Fateh, M. M. (2008). On the voltage-based control of robot manipulators. International Journal of Control, Automation, and Systems, vol. 6, no. 5, pp. 702-712.

[13] Fateh, M. M. (2012). Robust control of flexible-joint robots using voltage control strategy. Nonlinear Dynamics, vol. 67, no. 2, pp. 1525-1537.

[14] Fateh, M. M. (2012). Nonlinear control of electrical flexible-joint robots. Nonlinear Dynamics, vol. 67, no. 4, pp. 2549-2559.

[15] Izadbakhsh, A., & Fateh, M. (2014). Robust Lyapunov-Based Control of Flexible-Joint Robots Using Voltage Control Strategy. Arabian Journal for Science and Engineering, vol. 39, no. 4, pp. 3111-3121.

[16] Huang, A.-C., & Chien, M.-C. Design of a regressor-free adaptive impedance controller for flexible-joint electrically-driven robots, Proc. Industrial Electronics and Applications, 2009. ICIEA 2009. 4th IEEE Conference on, IEEE.

[17] Wang, L.-X. (1999). A course in fuzzy systems, Prentice-Hall press, USA.

[18] Vahedi, M., Hadad Zarif, M., & Akbarzadeh Kalat, A. (2016). An indirect adaptive neuro-fuzzy speed control of induction motors. Journal of AI and Data Mining, vol. 4, no. 2, pp. 243-251.

[19] Abdelhameed, M. M. (2005). Enhancement of sliding mode controller by fuzzy logic with application to robotic manipulators. Mechatronics, vol. 15, no. 4, pp. 439-458.

[20] Kim, E. (2004). Output feedback tracking control of robot manipulators with model uncertainty via adaptive fuzzy logic. Fuzzy Systems, IEEE Transactions on, vol. 12, no. 3, pp. 368-378.

[21] Spong, M. W. (1987). Modeling and control of elastic joint robots. Journal of dynamic systems, measurement, and control, vol. 109, no. 4, pp. 310-318.

[22] Engelbrecht, A. P. (2007). Computational intelligence: an introduction, John Wiley & Sons.

[23] Nickabadi, A., Ebadzadeh, M. M., & Safabakhsh, R. (2011). A novel particle swarm optimization algorithm with adaptive inertia weight. Applied Soft Computing, vol. 11, no. 4, pp. 3658-3670.

[24] Tungadio, D., et al. (2015). Particle swarm optimization for power system state estimation. Neurocomputing, vol. 148, pp. 175-180.

[25] Md Rozali, S., Fua'ad Rahmat, M., & Husain, A. R. (2014). Performance Comparison of Particle Swarm Optimization and Gravitational Search Algorithm to the Designed of Controller for Nonlinear System. Journal of Applied Mathematics, vol. 2014.

[26] Poli, R., Kennedy, J., &Blackwell, T. (2007). Particle swarm optimization. Swarm intelligence, vol. 1, no. 1, pp. 33-57.

[27] Shi, Y., & Eberhart, R. A modified particle swarm optimizer, Proc. Evolutionary Computation Proceedings, 1998. IEEE World Congress on Computational Intelligence., The 1998 IEEE International Conference on, IEEE.

[28] Chatterjee, A., & Siarry, P. (2006). Nonlinear inertia weight variation for dynamic adaptation in particle swarm optimization. Computers & Operations Research, vol. 33, no. 3, pp. 859-871.

[29] Arumugam, M. S., Rao, M., & Chandramohan, A. (2008). A new and improved version of particle swarm optimization algorithm with global–local best parameters. Knowledge and Information systems, vol. 16, no. 3, pp. 331-357.

[30] Ratnaweera, A., Halgamuge, S. K., & Watson, H. C. (2004). Self-organizing hierarchical particle swarm optimizer with time-varying acceleration coefficients. Evolutionary Computation, IEEE Transactions on, vol. 8, no. 3, pp. 240-255.

[31] Slotine, J.-J. E., & Li, W. (1991). Applied nonlinear control, Prentice-Hall Englewood Cliffs, NJ.

[32] Ho, H., Wong, Y.-K., & Rad, A. B. (2007). Robust fuzzy tracking control for robotic manipulators. Simulation Modelling Practice and Theory, vol. 15, no. 7, pp. 801-816.

14

Feature extraction in opinion mining through Persian reviews

E. Golpar-Rabooki[1], S. Zarghamifar[2*] and J. Rezaeenour[3]

1. Department of Mathematics, University of Qom, Qom, Iran
2. Department of Computer Engineering, University of Qom, Qom, Iran
3. Department of Industrial Engineering, University of Qom, Qom, Iran

Corresponding author: saghi_zarghami@yahoo.com (S. Zarghamifar).

Abstract

Opinion mining deals with an analysis of user reviews for extracting their opinions, sentiments and demands in a specific area, which plays an important role in making major decisions in such areas. In general, opinion mining extracts user reviews at three levels of document, sentence and feature. Opinion mining at the feature level is taken into consideration more than the other two levels due to orientation analysis of different aspects of an area. In this paper, two methods are introduced for a feature extraction. The recommended methods consist of four main stages. First, opinion-mining lexicon for Persian is created. This lexicon is used to determine the orientation of users' reviews. Second, the preprocessing stage includes unification of writing, tokenization, creating parts-of-speech tagging and syntactic dependency parsing for documents. Third, the extraction of features uses two methods including frequency-based feature extraction and dependency grammar based feature extraction. Fourth, the features and polarities of the word reviews extracted in the previous stage are modified and the final features' polarity is determined. To assess the suggested techniques, a set of user reviews in both scopes of university and cell phone areas were collected and the results of the two methods were compared.

Keywords: *Opinion Mining, Feature Extraction, Opinion-mining Lexicon, Corpus, Parts-of-speech Tagging, Syntactic Dependency Parsing.*

1. Introduction

As the Web 2.0 and the social networks evolve, many data were published on the Internet. Such data have newly potential applications, different groups of which are sporadically detected. Generally, data contained text documents published on the web can be classified in two groups: Objective (realistic) and Subjective. Realities are real and observable commands about independent identities and the events happened around the world. However, subjective commands reflect on human emotions and observations and the people have about the outside world and its events [1].Search engines can retrieve data from realistic documents based on keywords referring to realities. Yet, to retrieve and analyze subjective documents, it seems inefficient to use them [2].

Opinion mining and sentiment analysis have drawn much attention since the last decade, while they extract users' reviews and detect their polarity inside subjective texts. Among the applications of opinion mining, we suggest to the followings:

- *Analysis of Online Customers' reviews*
Increasing number of websites, which attempt to collect visitors' reviews about a particular product or service, reveals the significance of opinion mining. It can be utilized as an offer to buy or not to buy a particular product or use special services, as well as a consultant for manufacturers, to extract customers' desirable features and provide high quality products and services [3].

- *Representation of Proper Advertisement*
Investigating the issues and reviews discussed in a blog or a forum, we can display an advertisement with higher probability to be seen. For example, if the reviews brought up in a forum about a specific product is positive, advertisements of that product would be very likely to be seen by users of the related forum. However, were the reviews negative, it might be better to display competing products in advertisements [4].

● *Investigation Of Public Opinions*

To investigate public reviews on a particular issue several sources on the Internet (including specific forums, Twitter, etc.) can be examined and collect and evaluate users' reviews about the issue in question.

As it is defined in [5], opinion mining is only to identify positive, negative and/or neutral reviews; however, any opinion word is given a weight based on the subject of text and its polarity, in sentiment analysis. The weight means the probability or number considered for positivity or negativity of a word. As an example in [6], a weight of 0.01 is assigned to word "dirty" provided the subject is hotel and the polarity is negative; while the same word with the same subject and positive polarity gains a weight of 0.00001.

The opinion words are used to express positive and/or negative sentiments. For example, the words such as "good", "beautiful" and "wonderful" induce positive feelings in human and the words like "bad", "ugly" and "terrible" are some words with negative polarity. Polarity of any means feelings and estimation brought into the mind by such a word. It should be noted that most of the opinion words are adjectives and adverbs; however, some nouns including "junk" and "hell" and verbs such as "hate" and "love" also carry sentiment information and thus need to be considered.

In opinion mining lexicon, any opinion word is mentioned along with its polarity. It might be weighted or non-weighted.

Though a variety of methods have been introduced to establish opinion mining lexicon and several opinion mining lexicons have been created which are available to the public, it seems very unlikely to develop an opinion mining lexicon that contain all opinion words and include all areas and languages. A word can have a positive polarity in an area and a negative or neutral polarity in another area. For example, the word "unpredictable" has a negative polarity in the field of electronic instruments, but it has a positive polarity in the field of movie.

In this paper, two methods are introduced for extracting the features. The first one extracts nouns with the highest frequency as features only by using parts-of-speech tagging. Then, it will extract all other features, making use of the extracted features and the opinion words that described them. The second method deals with extracting the features and expanding opinion mining lexicon, using parts-of-speech tagging,

syntactic dependency parsing and a number of Persian grammar rules.

The proposed method consists of four main steps. First, two lexicons are established for two suggested methods in order to extract the features. Second, the preprocessing stage includes unification of writing, tokenization, creating parts-of-speech tagging and syntactic dependency parsing. Third, extracted features use two proposed methods and fourth, the features and opinion words gained in the previous step are modified. Finally, the polarity of the features are determines.

2. Review of literature

The first opinion mining lexicon was established in 1997, using syntactic structure [7].

In 2002, Pang and Lee classified the texts into two neutral and polarized groups, making use of machine learning algorithms. They used three algorithms including Support Vector Machines (SVM), Naïve Bayes and Maximum Entropy Model [2].

In 2003, an opinion mining lexicon was established based on dependency criteria, which include two main stages. At the first stage, syntactic phrases including adjectives or adverbs are extracted from different sentences according to syntactic category label of phrases. At the second stage, the polarity of each extracted phrase is determined [8].

In the same year, Riloff et al devised a method to extract subjective sentences using Bootstrapping method in which the sentences are firstly categorized into two classes (sentences related to user's opinion and all other sentences) from a lexicon and an unlabeled set of data by using two classifiers. Then, some patterns are extracted from such sentences that will be returned to the classifier in the form of an iterative algorithm [9].

Yi et al extracted the features of users' reviews, using hybrid model presented in [10-11]. Their method was based on parts-of-speech and feature tagging using training set. They merely considered accuracy evaluation criteria.

Liu and Hu (2004) extracted the features by identifying and frequency nouns in the collection of documents [12]. They used parts-of-speech tagging to identify nouns.

In 2005, OPINE method was introduced including four steps of features identification, identifying the reviews related to each feature, determination of reviews' polarity and the final ranking [13]. In this method, Pointwise Mutual Information (PMI) calculation was used to identify the words.

Mei et al (2007) proceeded to extract features by creating a pattern in a specific area using Hidden Markov Model (HMM) [14].

Many other methods were presented based on pattern creation in order to extract the features in a specific area [15-16-17].

In 2008, Titove and McDonald extracted the features using Dirichlet Allocation Method and finally ranked each feature considering the user's opinion on the feature in question [18]. In this study, features are divided into two groups including fine-grained and coarse-grained.

Liu et al extracted the features and extended the lexicon by making use of syntactic dependency parsing and Persian rules. Their method was using only a basic lexicon containing a limited number of opinion words [19].

In 2012, Shams introduced an unsupervised method to determine polarity of Persian documents in which each word is weighted using two PLSASA and LDASA algorithms based on the subject in which it lays [6].

The review of literature shows that many methods suggested to extract features on a specific area require training data specific to such an area. Since there are now no training sets for this purpose in different areas of Persian, we apply two methods not dependent on a specific area, which use merely parts-of-speech tagging and syntactic dependency parsing to extract features [12-19].

3. The Proposed method

The method suggested in this study is at the feature level and includes four main stages including creation of lexicon, pre-processing, feature extraction and post-processing. Each of these stages will be explained in details later in this paper.

Overview of the proposed method is shown in the figure 1 below:

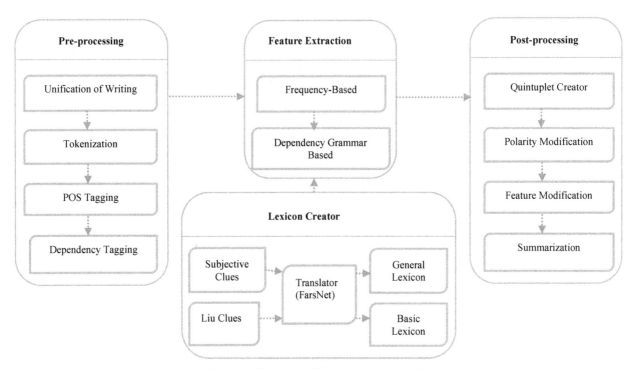

Figure 1. Overview of the suggested method.

3.1. Creation of opinion mining lexicon

The first step in opinion mining is creation of lexicon. Considering the works done on all languages (other than English) indicate that the method used in most languages for creation of lexicon is to translate an existing lexicon into the target language and then make any modification to it. The same method is used in this investigation to create two lexicons. The first lexicon is a comprehensive one for using in

frequency-based feature extraction. The other one including much smaller number of positive and negative words than the first lexicon is created for using in a dependency grammar based feature extraction. The words contained in this lexicon such as "good", "beautiful", "bad" and "ugly" could be approximately seen in all areas to express emotions. The presented algorithm develops this lexicon. Subjective Clues [20] lexicon as one of the best-known and the most important opinion-mining lexicons in English were translated into Persian. For this translation, FarsNet tools as a free lexicon was used [21-22]. In this method, Persian equivalent of the word in question is found and then is added to Persian lexicons along with its synonyms. To determine the polarity of the words translated in the lexicon, all words inherit their polarity from their English equivalents. It means that if a word has a positive label in English, all its equivalents will also gain positive label after translation. Inheritance of polarity is made, because concepts are usually independent from languages [6] and a word suggesting a positive concept in a language has almost its positive concept after translation into another language. The lexicon created in [12-23] was used to create a basic lexicon. We have used FarsNet for translation at this stage. To create a basic lexicon, Persian equivalents of the word are used and synonyms are ignored. This is because we aimed to create a primary lexicon which will be expanded in later stages by analyzing the documents. Due to the lack of polarity in English lexicon, polarity of the words after translation is determined manually. Furthermore, a group of words, which are not seemingly common in Persian texts were deleted manually.

Simple translation of a lexicon has some problems. In order to modify the Persian lexicon, all the words were checked and the ones labeled incorrectly were modified manually.

Finally, 6746 words were created in the comprehensively generated lexicon where 3866 words had negative polarity, 273 words had neutral polarity and the remaining with positive polarity.

In the basic lexicon production, the total number of words is 575 in which 288 ones had negative polarity, 36 ones had neutral words, and the remaining were with positive polarity.

3.2. Pre-processing
This stage includes several steps to create data required by feature extraction algorithm at the next stage. These steps consist of unification of writing, tokenization, parts-of speech tagging and syntactic dependency parsing.

3.2.1. Unification of writing
There are some letters in Persian, which are written by different methods in a variety of character encoding standards. As an example, each of the letters "ى" and "ک" are found in different forms in Persian texts. In the unification of writing stage, such letters are uniformed.

3.2.2. Tokenization
Each document is segmented into its constituent words. In order to determine the words, each review is firstly segmented based on punctuation marks («!» «.» «؟»«،».«؛»«؛»), and then, the resulting sentences are divided into their constituent words.

3.2.3. Parts-of speech tagging
A Part-Of-Speech Tagging (POS) assigns parts of speech to each word (and other token), such as noun, verb, adjective, etc. There are two main steps to create parts-of-speech system based on data. At the first step, labeling pattern is resulted by making use of a training set. At the next step, an appropriate label would be provided for any input word based on the pattern resulted in the previous step.

Parts-of-speech tagging on the reviews segmented into words in the previous step is labeled by TNT tagger software and Bijankhan corpus at this stage [24].

3.2.4. Syntactic dependency parsing
A syntactic dependency will be semantically defined as a binary operation that takes as arguments the denotations of the two related words (both the head and the dependent), and gives as a result for a more elaborate arrangement of their denotations [25]. Generally, for any input sentence in dependency parsing, one graph is constructed and there are two general approaches including data and grammar.

In supervised learning method, there are two main steps for constructing a dependency parsing system. At the first step, dependency grammar is gained by using a training set. As the dependency grammar is achieved, parsing pattern will be gained. At the next step, a dependency graph will be constructed for each input sentence based on the pattern resulted in the previous step.

In this step, syntactic dependency tagging is done on the reviews using MST Parser software and Dadegan Persian dependency framework [25-26].

3.3. Feature extraction
Creating lexicon and preparing documents, we will introduce the third stage. Positive polarity of any document does not mean user's positive opinion about all features of such a document. This status is also true about the negative documents. The comments expressed by the users are a collection of positive and negative reviews on different aspects of an issue. At this stage as the most important suggested method, features (aspects) of an object commented by the users are

extracted. Two methods are suggested to extract such features including frequency-based feature extraction and dependency grammar based feature extraction, which will be introduced later in the next section.

3.3.1. Frequency-based feature extraction

In this method, a set of nouns and noun phrases is gained per document. For this purpose, the words with part-of-speech tag of "N" are known as noun and the set of nouns with part-of-speech tag of "N N" are considered as noun phrases and will be added to set of nouns in such a document. As an example, in the sentence "university environment was extremely good", the phrase, "university environment" as a noun phrase and "environment" and "university" each as a noun are selected and added to set-of-words. At the next step, we determine the number of each of the nouns (bag-of-word) gained at the previous step among total current lists. To do this, a new set including all words extracted at the previous stage is constructed and then, the frequency of each word is specified. At the next step, nouns with a frequency higher than a threshold are extracted as important features. Frequency threshold can be any number, which is usually determined by experience.

At the final step, we will use the following idea to extract features with a frequency lower than defined frequency threshold. The opinion words can be utilized to describe different features. For example, noun phrase "university environment" in the previous example is selected as a feature and tagged in the documents; considering the sentence in the previous example, a commenter has used the word "good" to describe this feature. Now, we can search the word "good" in entire documents and then extract the noun found before it as a feature. As a result, in a sentence like "university staff were very good". "University staff" is extracted as a feature. Opinion words are found using the general lexicon constructed at the first stage.

3.3.2. Dependency grammar based feature extraction

This is a bootstrapping method which starts to work merely by a basic lexicon. However, the extracted features are used in the next round to extract other features and expend the lexicon.

This method is based on rules naturally existing in language dependency relationships. As an example, in sentence "this phone has a good appearance", if we know the word "good" as an opinion word, we could extract the word "appearance" as a feature through dependency grammar.

In table 1, the rules applied in this method for extracting features and expanding opinion words are shown:

Table 1. Rules of dependency grammar.

Rule	Relations and constraint	Output
1	$(OW$ Dep $POS(ADJ))$ or $(OW$ Dep $POS(ADV)POS(ADJ))$ Dep∈ $\{CONJ\}$	ADJ is new *Opinion word* $If(CONJ \in Contrary$ words$)$ Polarity$(ADJ) = -$ Polarity(OW) *Else* Polarity$(ADJ) = $ Polarity(OW)
2	$(SBJ(POS(N))$ Dep $OW)$	$SBJ(N)$ is new *Feature*
3	$(F$ Dep $MOS(POS(ADJ))$ $)$	$MOS(ADJ)$ is new *Opinion word*
4	$(F$ Dep $POS(N))$ or $(F\ MOZ(POS(N)))$ Dep∈ $\{CONJ\}$	N is new Feature
5	$(F\ NPOSTMOD(POS(ADJ))$ Dep $MOS(POS(ADJ)))$	$F+ NPOSTMOD$ is new Feature

Description:
OW = opinion word   *F= Feature*   *MOS =Mosnad*   *SJB=Subject*
ADJ =Adjective   *CONJ= Conjunction*   *NPOSTMOD=Subsequent Adjective*   *MOZ= Mozaf*

Rule1: if a word is an opinion word and is followed by a conjunction and an adjective and/ or the conjunction is followed by an adverb and an adjective, respectively, the word tagged as an adjective will be selected as an opinion word. This rule is considered as the inverse. It means that if a word contains an opinion word with a conjunction and an adjective before it, the word tagged as an adjective will be an opinion word. To identify the polarity of a new word, if conjunction is in contrary word group, polarity of the new word is opposite to that by which we extracted the new word. If the conjunction is not in this group, both words have the same polarity.

For example, suppose that the word "beautiful" is tagged as OW with positive polarity. In this case, taking this rule into consideration, we can extract the word "attractive" in a sentence like "it has a beautiful and attractive appearance" as a new opinion word with the positive polarity. Furthermore, the word "fragile" in the sentence "it has a beautiful, but fragile frame" is an opinion word with negative polarity.

3.3.3. Contrary word

The contrary words include former and anterior sentences/words with different polarities. For example, the polarity of the sentence after "but" is opposite to the polarity of the sentence followed by "but". We translated and modified a list of contrary words shown in [19] and used it to identify such words in an opinion-mining system.

Rule 2: If a word is an opinion word (OW) with a POS tag of MOS (Mosnad is a property of a noun, an adjective or a pronoun ascribed to the subject of a sentence whose main verb is a linking verb. The relation between the verb and Mosnad is MOS), we will consider a word tagged subject (SJB) in the sentence as a new feature. As an example, in the sentence "my university is very beautiful", the word "university" is a new feature.

Rule 3: this rule is exactly the opposite of the previous rule; that is if a word in the sentence is a feature, then the word with MOS role in the sentence which is also an adjective, will be extracted as an opinion word.

Rule 4: if a word is a feature (F) followed by a conjunction and a noun and/or a noun with a MOZ (Ezafe dependents in Persian are nouns or pronouns which follow a head noun and signify a possessed-possessor, first name-last name, etc. relation with the head noun. The relation between a noun and its Ezafe dependent is MOZ) role, the noun is selected as the feature. This rule is considered as the inverse. It means that if a word is a feature with a conjunction and a noun before it, the related noun will be a new feature. For example, in the sentence "it has a library and a small buffet". If the word "library" is tagged as a feature, the word "buffet" is also extracted as a new feature.

Rule5: according to observations, if the feature and opinion word are specified in a sentence and the feature is followed by a word with adjective

(POS tagging) and NPOSTMOD (Adjectives in their positive and comparative forms together with post-noun numerals are considered post-modifiers of noun.

The relation between a noun and its post-modifiers is NPOSTMOD) roles which have not been separated from an opinion word through conjunction, the feature and the adjective after it can be considered as a noun phrase and a new feature. The structure of the noun phrase is shown in [27]. According to studies, most of noun phrases used in comments include only noun and a subsequent adjective. As an instant, in the sentence "امکانات رفاهی آنجا افتضاح بود", the words "امکانات رفاهی" can be considered as a new feature, provided that "امکانات" is a feature, and "افتضاح" is an opinion word.

The algorithm suggested is shown in figure 2. Inputs of this algorithm are the basic lexicon and a set of users' reviews. At the first step, words of lexicon will be searched in all documents and any words found in any document are tagged newly as an opinion word.

At the next step, the rules are applied sequentially and the words extracted in the document are tagged as a feature and/or opinion word, considering the type of such words and are also added to the related set-of-words. In the next round, we will search the newly extracted words (features and opinion words) until the time when no new word is found.

3.4. Post-processing

At this stage, we proceed to modify the features and the polarity of opinion words extracted at the previous stage. The step of opinion words' polarity correction is used only for dependency grammar based feature extraction, which has also expanded the lexicon while implementing the algorithm.

3.4.1. Establishment of quintuples and set of opinion words

In this section, a record is created per any feature in each review, which includes five characteristics including feature, polarity, date, writer and type. Furthermore, a set of opinion words describing the feature is created for each record. To clarify this issue, the record created for the sentence "speaker on the camera is too weak and unqualified to play video sounds" is shown in figure 3.

The polarity of the feature is determined by adding the polarities of opinion words describing the feature and considering the negative-makers' roles in the sentence.

```
Input: Opinion word Dictionary {O}, Review Data R
Output: All possible Features {F}, The Expanded Opinion Lexicon {O-Expanded}
Function:
1. {O-Expanded} = {O}
2. {F} =∅, {O} =∅, {TempF} =∅
3. for each {O}
4.         For each parsed sentence in R
5.                 Label Opinion words based on Opinion words in {O}
6.         Endfor
7.         Remove {O}
8. Endfor
9. for each {TempF}
10.        For each parsed sentence in R
11.                Label Features based on Features in {TempF}
12.        Endfor
13.        Remove {TempF}
14. Endfor
15. For each parsed sentence in R
16.        Extract Opinion word {O'} using rule1 and add to {O} and {O-Expanded}
17. Endfor
18. For each parsed sentence in R
19.        Extract Feature {F'} using rule2 and add to {F} and {TempF}
20. Endfor
21. For each parsed sentence in R
22.        Extract Opinion word {O'} using rule3 and add to add to {O} and {O-Expanded}
23. Endfor
24. For each parsed sentence in R
25.        Extract Feature {F'} using rule4 and add to {F} and {TempF}
26. Endfor
27. For each parsed sentence in R
28.        Extract Feature {F'} using rule5 and add to {F} and {TempF}
29. Endfor
30. Repeat 3 till size ({TempF}) =0, size ({O}) =0
```

Figure 2. Dependency grammar based feature extraction.

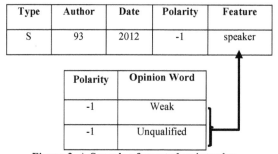

Type	Author	Date	Polarity	Feature
S	93	2012	-1	speaker

Polarity	Opinion Word
-1	Weak
-1	Unqualified

Figure 3. A Sample of created quintuples.

Negative-makers in Persian. The negative-maker means a word or words, which reverse the polarity of a sentence. Since the opinion mining aims to determine positivity or negativity of an opinion, it will be highly important to study negative-makers' roles in this field. In Persian, most negative-makers appeared in the verb of a sentence. To identify negative-makers of Persian verbs, we will follow the method explained in [6]. In this method, we used Bijankhan corpus to identify verbs. In this method, all negative verbs were first tagged manually. Then, for further expansion and coverage, all verbs with negative-maker suffixes such as "ن", "نمی" and all forms of "نخواه" were expanded. Some of the resulted words will be definitely meaningless and inapplicable. For example, a word like "ناست" (ن+است) created

by this method is not a correct word, but no problem will arise because such words are not included in data sets. Negative verbs are used to reverse polarity and examine the role of negative-makers.

3.4.2. Modification of extracted opinion words' polarity

Some opinion words extracted by the second method do not assigned any polarity. The reason is that such words were extracted using the features. The features have themselves no polarity and the opinion words describe them and determine their polarity. To solve this problem, we will work according to the following method:
We will firstly determine quintuplet of opinion word. Then, we observe polarity of features before and after such a record. If the polarity of

both records is positive and/or negative, we will allocate it to an opinion word and modify also the polarity of features in quintuplet. Observation shows that if two sentences in comments are positive, the sentence between them is often positive and vice versa. For example, in the following text: "Scientific knowledge of the university was so low. Class times were organized carelessly. Also, class features were so low" if we do not set the polarity for the second sentence, because of the polarity similarity between first and third sentence, second sentence polarity will be set to negative; equal to the first and third sentence. If this rule is not applied, we will determine polarity of the entire opinion in the review and will regard the polarity of the intended word as a document and accordingly, we will modify its feature polarity.

3.4.3. Modification of feature
In [28], a list of common unintelligible words in Persian documents is provided. For example, the word "viewpoint"("لحاظ") is tagged as noun and subsequently as a feature in many reviews. To resolve this problem, prepared list is used to modify the feature. However, a group of these words do not have noun roles and are not applicable in this section. Then, using [29], synonym features are specified and the features with the highest frequency in documents are considered as the main feature and the main feature replaced their synonyms. Also, we provided a list of names of universities, models and cell phone manufacturers and used them to modify the extracted features, because such names are tagged as features according to observations. For this purpose, each feature containing one of these words is corrected and the related word is deleted from this feature.

3.4.4. Feature-based summarization
After constructing quintuplets and correcting them, a summarization of reviews can be provided and represented for each feature as resulted by opining mining. In [23], visual tools like a bar graph are used to show summarizations. This study has such a capability and is possible to prepare reports using quintuplets.

4. Analysis of results
In this section, we will evaluate the method proposed for the opinion mining. Then, we compare the results of the dependency grammar based method with the results published in Liu's article [19] using the above method in English

sentences. The first step in evaluation of each system is to select a data set on which the system's performance is evaluated. This is the reason we start this section by introducing the established data set and will explain the results obtained. To evaluate this method, we will make use of the most important basic approaches in the opinion mining.

4.1. Opinion mining data set
Lack of adequate data in natural language processing areas and its subset is one of the current problems in this group of activities. For this reason, two data sets were prepared from users' reviews in the fields of university and cell phone. Users' reviews on the cell phone collected and classified form the site http://www.digikala.com. The reviews about the university were obtained by a group of academic people filling in the form designed for this purpose. In the field of university, 90 reviews were totally selected, 45 ones out of which were negative and the other 45 reviews were positive. In the field of cell phone, 250 reviews were selected from the mentioned site including 125 positive reviews and 125 negative ones. All collected documents were reviewed and spell-checked by Virastyar software. The most important reason why we used this software was to delete the spaces and putting virtual space between the words. In any document, features of each document, opinion words with their polarity, sentence polarity and document polarity were tagged manually for final evaluation of the suggested methods.

Table 2 shows the information related to data sets.

Table 2. Data sets.

Data Set	Number of reviews	Number of sentences
University area	90	598
Cellphone area	250	1409

4.2. Evaluation of the proposed method
To evaluate the proposed method for extraction of features and opinion words in this study, three measures including Precision, Recall and F-measure were used. Accuracy measures were used to evaluate the polarity assigned to dependency grammar based feature extraction method in this study.

4.2.1. Evaluation of extracted features
The results show that though the frequency-based extraction algorithm has a higher precision, but recall and f-measure evaluation in the dependency

grammar-based extraction method has been considerably improved.

Table 3. Precision for extracted features.

Data set	Precision	
	Frequency based	dependency grammar
University area	0.92	0.88
Cellphone area	0.94	0.92

Table 4. Recall for extracted features.

Data set	Recall	
	Frequency based	dependency grammar
University area	0.64	0.83
Cellphone area	0.72	0.86

Table 5. F-measure for extracted features.

Data set	F-Measure	
	Frequency based	dependency grammar
University area	0.75	0.85
Cellphone area	0.81	0.89

4.2.2. Evaluation of extracted opinion words

The results of opinion words extraction evaluation using dependency grammar based feature extraction in two areas including university and cell phone is shown below. Due to the use of general lexicon in frequency-based extraction algorithm which was not expended in this method, we are going to evaluate merely the dependency grammar based feature extraction.

Table 6. Evaluation for extracted opinion words.

Data set	dependency grammar		
	Precision	Recall	F-Measure
University area	0.83	0.79	0.81
Cellphone area	0.88	0.82	0.85

4.2.3. Evaluation of extracted opinion words' polarity

As mentioned earlier, the polarity of a word is sometimes dependent on the area where it is used. The Accuracy related to the opinion words' polarity extracted by dependency grammar based feature extraction is evaluated in accordance with the table 7.

Table 7. Accuracy for extracted opinion words' polarity.

Data Set	Accuracy
	dependency grammar
University area	0.73
Cellphone area	0.66

4.3. Comparison of dependency grammar based method in Persian and English data set

To evaluate the dependency grammar based method in English text, Liu [19] has used five different data sets.

Table 8. Liu data set.

Data Set	Number of reviews	Number of sentences
D1	45	597
D2	34	346
D3	41	546
D4	95	1716
D5	99	740

Results of "D1" dataset are compared with the results of the university dataset and the results of the "D4" dataset are compared with the result of cell phone dataset, since there is the same number of sentences in each dataset.

Table 9. Comparison D1 and university data set.

Data Set	Precision	Recall	F-Measure
D1	0.87	0.81	0.84
University area	0.88	0.83	0.85

Table 10. Comparison D4 and cellphone data set.

Data Set	Precision	Recall	F-Measure
D4	0.81	0.84	0.82
Cellphone area	0.92	0.86	0.89

5. Conclusions and future work

In this investigation, two methods were applied to extract features in Persian reviews which are not limited to a specific area and do not require training data set for such an extraction. In frequency-based feature extraction method, the parts-of-speech tagging and noun frequency were only used in entire documents for feature extraction. In the dependency grammar based feature extraction method, syntactic dependency parsing was merely used to extract features and expand the opinion words.

The results indicate that the dependency-grammar -based method has a better performance compared to frequency-based in extracting features. Furthermore, using this method, there will be no problem in creating a comprehensive lexicon which will cover all areas, because this method starts its performance by making use of a basic lexicon with limited number of words and will expand it later using users' reviews.

The results suggest that the dependency grammar based method does not work properly in determining polarity of newly extracted opinion words.

As the last discussion in this paper, the works which could be conducted in the future to improve and expand the proposed method are suggested as follows:

- Identification of co-reference resolution in Persian texts
- Not ignoring the sentences which contain opinion words implicitly
- Identification of a feature indicator: many opinion words can be used for any features. For example, the words "good", "bad", etc., but, some of these words are indicators of specific features. As an example, the word "large" in the sentence "this phone is very large" is an indicator of size feature. Identifying such words in the system, further and more precise features can be extracted.

- Considering the subject in an opinion mining
- Conversion of colloquial writing to formal writing
- Analysis of sentiments expressed using weighting algorithms

References

[1] Stavrianou, A. & Chauchat, H. (2008). Opinion Mining Issues and Agreement identification in Forum Texts. Atelier FOuille des Données d'OPinions (FODOP 08), France, 2008.

[2] Pang, B., Lee, L. & Vaithyanathan, S. (2002). Thumbs up? Sentiment classification using machine learning techniques. The ACL-02 conference on Empirical methods in natural language processing, vol. 10, pp. 79–86.

[3] Sepehri, M. (2009). Chi-Square for features selection in Opinion mining in Persian text. 2nd National Conference on Computer/Electrical and IT Engineering (CEIC'09), Hamedan, Iran, 2009.

[4] Nicholls, C. & Song, F. (2010). Comparison of Feature Selection Methods for Sentiment Analysis. Advances in Artificial Intelligence, vol. 6085, pp. 286-289.

[5] Liu, B. (2012). Sentiment Analysis and Opinion Mining. Morgan and Claypool. Atlanta, USA.

[6] Shams, M. (2012). Opinion mining and Sentiment Analysis in Persian Documents. University of Tehran, Iran.

[7] Hatzivassiloglou, V. & McKeown, K. R. (1997). Predicting the semantic orientation of adjectives. The eighth conference on European chapter of the Association for Computational Linguistics, Madrid, Spain, pp. 174-181.

[8] Turney, P. D. & Littman, M. L. (2003). Measuring praise and criticism: Inference of semantic orientation from associaCon. ACM TransacCons on InformaCon Systems (TOIS), vol. 21, no. 4, pp. 315-346.

[9] Riloff, E., Wiebe, J. & Wilson, T. (2003). Learning subjective nouns using extraction pattern bootstrapping. The seventh conference on Natural language (CONLL), Edmonton, Canada, vol. 4, pp. 25–32.

[10] Zhai, C. & Lafferty, J. (2001). Model-based Feedback in the Language Modeling Approach to Information Retrieval. The tenth International Conference on Information and Knowledge Management. Berlin, Heidelberg, Springer-Verlag. pp. 403-410.

[11] Yi, J., Nasukawa, T., Bunescu, R. & Niblack, W. (2003). Sentiment Analyzer: Extracting Sentiments about a Given Topic using Natural Language Processing Techniques. The Third IEEE International Conference on data mining, pp. 427 – 434.

[12] Hu, M. & Liu, B. (2004). Mining and Summarizing Customer Reviews. Proceedings of the tenth ACM SIGKDD international conference on Knowledge discovery and data mining. Seattle, WA, USA, pp. 168-177.

[13] Popescu, A. & Etzioni, O. (2005). Extracting Product Features and Opinions from Reviews. The conference on Human Language Technology and Empirical Methods in Natural Language Processing. Vancouver, British Columbia, Canada, pp. 339-346.

[14] Mei, Q., Ling, X., Wondra, M., Su, H. & Zhai, C. (2007). Topic Sentiment Mixture: Modeling Facets and Opinions in Weblogs. The 16th international conference on World Wide Web, pp. 171-180.

[15] Liu, Y., Huang, X., An, A. & Yu, X. (2007). ARSA: A Sentiment-Aware Model for Predicting Sales Performance Using Blogs. The 30th annual international ACM SIGIR conference on Research and development in information retrieval, pp. 607-614.

[16] McDonald, R., Hannan, K., Neylon, T., Wells, M. & Reynar, J. (2007). Structured Models for Fine-to-Coarse Sentiment Analysis. The 45th Annual Meeting of the Association of Computational Linguistics. Prague, Czech Republic. pp. 432–439.

[17] Su, Q., et al. (2008). Hidden Sentiment Association in Chinese Web Opinion Mining. The 17th international conference on World Wide Web. Beijing, China. pp. 959-968.

[18] Titov, I. & McDonald, R. (2008). A Joint Model of Text and Aspect Ratings for Sentiment Summarization. The Association for Computational Linguistics, pp. 308-316.

[19] Qiu, G., Liu, B., Bu, J. & Chen, C. (2011). Opinion Word Expansion and Target Extraction through Double Propagation. Computational Linguistics. vol.37, no.1, pp. 9-27.

[20] Wiebe, J. M. (2000). Learning subjective adjectives from corpora. The Seventeenth National Conference on Artificial Intelligence and Twelfth Conference on InnovaCve ApplicaCons of ArCficial Intelligence, 2000, pp. 735–740.

[21] Shamsfard, M., et al. (2010). Semi-Automatic Development of FarsNet; the Persian WordNet. 5th Global WordNet Conference, Mumbai.

[22] The FarsNet website (2013), Available: http://nlp.sbu.ac.ir/site/farsnet/.

[23] Liu, B., Hu, M. & Cheng, J. (2005). Opinion Observer: Analyzing and Comparing Opinions on the Web. The 14th International World Wide Web conference. Chiba, Japan. pp. 342-351.

[24] Raja, F., et al. (2007). Evaluation of part of speech tagging on Persian text. The Second Workshop on Computational approaches to Arabic Script-based Languages, Linguistic Institute Stanford University, Stanford, California, USA, pp. 120-127.

[25] Dadegan Research Group. (2012). Persian Dependency Treebank Version 1.0, Annotation Manual and User Guide. Supreme Council of Information and Communication Technology (SCICT).

[26] Rasooli, M., Kouhestani, M. & Moloodi, M. (2013). Development of a Persian Syntactic Dependency Treebank. The 2013 Conference of the North American Chapter of the Association for Computational Linguistics: Human Language Technologies (NAACL HLT). Atlanta, USA.

[27] Kavoosi Nejad, S. (2000). Delete the noun group in Persian language. Academy of Letters. vol.16, pp. 109-127.

[28] Sanji, M. & Davar-Panah, M. R. (2010). Identification of non-sense words (common) Automatic indexing of documents in Persian. Journal of Library and Information Science, vol.12, no.48, pp. 23-35.

[29] Khoda-Parasti, F. (1997). Comprehensive dictionary of synonyms and antonyms in Farsi. Fars Encyclopedia.

[30] Tasharofi, S., Raja, F. & Oroumchian, F. (2007). Evaluation of Statistical Part of Speech Tagging of Persian Text. International Symposium on Signal Processing and its Applications. Sharjah, United Arab Emirates.

[31] Elahi-Manesh, M. H. & Minaee, B. (2011). The hidden Markov model part of speech labeling in Persian texts. Journal of information science, computer science education and Islamic Studies, vol.34, pp.102-106.

15

Adaptive RBF network control for robot manipulators

M. M. Fateh[1*], S. M. Ahmadi[2] and S. Khorashadizadeh[1]

1. Department of Electrical Engineering, University of Shahrood, Shahrood, Iran.
2. Department of Mechanical Engineering, University of Shahrood, Shahrood, Iran.

*Corresponding author: mmfateh@shahroodut.ac.ir (M. M. Fateh).

Abstract

The uncertainty estimation and compensation are challenging problems for the robust control of robot manipulators which are complex systems. This paper presents a novel decentralized model-free robust controller for electrically driven robot manipulators. As a novelty, the proposed controller employs a simple Gaussian Radial-Basis-Function network (RBF network) as an uncertainty estimator. The proposed network includes a hidden layer with one node, two inputs and a single output. In comparison with other model-free estimators such as multilayer neural networks and fuzzy systems, the proposed estimator is simpler, less computational and more effective. The weights of the RBF network are tuned online using an adaptation law derived by stability analysis. Despite the majority of previous control approaches which are the torque-based control, the proposed control design is the voltage-based control. Simulations and comparisons with a robust neural network control approach show the efficiency of the proposed control approach applied on the articulated robot manipulator driven by permanent magnet DC motors.

Keywords: *Adaptive Uncertainty Estimator, RBF Network Control, Robust Control, Electrically Driven Robot Manipulators.*

1. Introduction

Torque Control Strategy (TCS) has attracted many research efforts in the field of robot control [1-3]. The robust torque-based control tries to overcome problems such as nonlinearity, coupling between inputs and outputs and uncertainty raised from manipulator dynamics. It is also assumed that the actuators can perfectly generate the proposed torque control laws for the joints. This assumption may not be satisfied due to the dynamics, saturation and some practical limitations associated with actuators. The problems associated with manipulator dynamics will be removed if a robust control approach can be free from manipulator model. Considering this fact, Voltage Control Strategy (VCS) [4-5] was presented for electrically driven robot manipulators. This control strategy is free from manipulator model but is dependent on actuator model. Nevertheless, the uncertainty estimation and compensation can be effective in VCS to improve the control performance [6]. Using the

estimation of uncertainty, this paper presents a voltage-based robust neural-network control for electrically driven robot manipulators which is model-free from both manipulator and actuators. The proposed design has a simpler design compared with alternative valuable voltage-based robust control approaches such as fuzzy estimation-based control [7], observer-based control [8], adaptive fuzzy control [9], neural-network control [10], fuzzy-neural-network control [11] and intelligent control [12] were presented for electrically driven robot manipulators. The simplicity and efficiency of the proposed control approach is shown through a comparison with the robust neural network control approach given by [10].

In most conventional robust approaches such as sliding mode control, the uncertainty bound parameter should be known in advance or estimated. The tracking error and smoothness of the control input are significantly affected by this parameter. The switching control laws resulted from these robust control methods may cause the chattering problem which will excite the un-modeled dynamics and degrade the system performance. As a result, too high estimation of the bounds may cause saturation of input, higher frequency of chattering in the switching control laws, and thus a bad behavior of the whole system, while too low estimation of the bounds may cause a higher tracking error [13].

Generally, uncertainty estimation and compensation are essential in robust tracking control of robots and the control performance is entirely enhanced by these crucial tasks. Function approximation methods play an important role in this stage and various tools such as fuzzy logic, neural networks, optimization algorithms, trigonometric function and orthogonal functions series have been used. In the two past decades, fuzzy logic [14-17] and neural networks [18-20] and neuro-fuzzy control [21] have been frequently employed in control systems and different control objectives have been successfully fulfilled due to their powerful capability in function approximation [22]. As important criteria, the simplicity and efficiency of the estimator should be paid attention since complex estimators require excessive memory, computational burden and many parameters. Tuning or online adaptation of these parameters significantly influences the estimator performance and increases the computations, as well.

One of the effective tools to approximate a function is the Radial-Basis-Function (RBF) networks. Applications of RBF networks in the robust control of nonlinear systems can be classified into direct and indirect adaptive control [23-26]. In direct adaptive control, RBF networks are employed as controllers. The network parameters are tuned online using adaptation laws derived from stability analysis.

Indirect application of RBF networks consists of two stages. In the first stage, the system dynamics are estimated using RBF networks and in the second stage, the estimated functions are used to design the control laws.

The novelty of this paper is to propose a robust model-free control for electrically driven robot manipulators using a simple RBF network as an uncertainty estimator in the decentralized controller. The simplicity of estimator is for using RBF network which consists of a hidden layer with one node, two inputs and a single output. Compared with the conventional robust control, the proposed robust control requires neither the uncertainty bound parameter nor the bounding

functions. In addition, it is free from the chattering problem.

The robust RBF network control is compared with a robust Neural Network control (robust NN control) given by [10]. The robust NN control has two interior loops. The inner loop is a voltage controller for motor using two-layer neural networks whereas the outer loop is a current controller using two-layer neural networks for providing the desired current. The robust RBF network control has a simpler design by using only one control loop and a RBF network.

The structure and design of the proposed Gaussian RBF network used as an adaptive uncertainty estimator in this paper is simpler than the fuzzy system used in [27] as an adaptive fuzzy controller [27]. These two designs have different structures. An interesting result is that fuzzy systems and neural networks can be designed somehow to perform the same behavior.

This paper is organized as follows. Section 2 explains modeling of the robotic system including the robot manipulator and motors. Section 3 develops the robust RBF network control approach. Section 4 describes the RBF network for estimation of the uncertainty. Section 5 presents the stability analysis. Section 6 illustrates the simulation results. Finally, section 7 concludes the paper.

2. Modeling

The robot manipulator consists of n links interconnected at n joints into an open kinematic chain. The mechanical system is assumed to be perfectly rigid. Each link is driven by a permanent magnet DC motor through the gears. The dynamics is described [28] as

$$\mathbf{D}(\mathbf{q})\ddot{\mathbf{q}} + \mathbf{C}(\mathbf{q},\dot{\mathbf{q}})\dot{\mathbf{q}} + \mathbf{g}(\mathbf{q}) = \boldsymbol{\tau}_r - \boldsymbol{\tau}_f(\dot{\mathbf{q}}) \qquad (1)$$

Where $\mathbf{q} \in R^n$ is the vector of joint positions, $\mathbf{D}(\mathbf{q})$ the $n \times n$ matrix of manipulator inertia, $\mathbf{C}(\mathbf{q},\dot{\mathbf{q}})\dot{\mathbf{q}} \in R^n$ the vector of centrifugal and Coriolis torques, $\mathbf{g}(\mathbf{q}) \in R^n$ the vector of gravitational torques, $\boldsymbol{\tau}_f(\dot{\mathbf{q}}) \in R^n$ the vector of friction torques and $\boldsymbol{\tau}_r \in R^n$ the joint torque vector of robot.

Note that vectors and matrices are represented in bold form for clarity. The electric motors provide the joint torque vector as follows [28]

$$\mathbf{J}\mathbf{r}^{-1}\ddot{\mathbf{q}} + \mathbf{B}\mathbf{r}^{-1}\dot{\mathbf{q}} + \mathbf{r}\boldsymbol{\tau}_r = \boldsymbol{\tau}_m \qquad (2)$$

Where $\boldsymbol{\tau}_m \in R^n$ is the torque vector of motors, $\mathbf{J}$, $\mathbf{B}$ and $\mathbf{r}$ are the $n \times n$ diagonal matrices for motor coefficients namely the inertia, damping, and reduction gear, respectively. The joint velocity vector $\dot{\mathbf{q}}$ and the motor velocity vector $\dot{\mathbf{q}}_m \in R^n$ are related through the gears to yield

$$r\dot{\mathbf{q}}_m = \dot{\mathbf{q}} \tag{3}$$

In order to obtain the motor voltages as the inputs of system, we consider the electrical equation of geared permanent magnet DC motors in the matrix form,

$$\mathbf{R}\mathbf{I}_a + \mathbf{L}\dot{\mathbf{I}}_a + \mathbf{K}_b r^{-1}\dot{\mathbf{q}} + \varphi = \mathbf{v} \tag{4}$$

Where $\mathbf{v} \in R^n$ is the vector of motor voltages, $\mathbf{I}_a \in R^n$ is the vector of motor currents and $\varphi \in R^n$ is a vector of external disturbances. $\mathbf{R}$, $\mathbf{L}$ and $\mathbf{K}_b$ represent the $n \times n$ diagonal matrices for the coefficients of armature resistance, inductance, and back-emf constant, respectively.

The motor torque vector τ_m as the input for dynamic (2) is produced by the motor current vector,

$$\mathbf{K}_m \mathbf{I}_a = \tau_m \tag{5}$$

Where $\mathbf{K}_m$ is a diagonal matrix of the torque constants. Using (1-5), obtains the state-space model

$$\dot{\mathbf{x}} = \mathbf{f}(\mathbf{x}) + \mathbf{b}\mathbf{v} - \mathbf{b}\varphi \tag{6}$$

Where $\mathbf{v}$ is considered as the inputs, $\mathbf{x}$ is the state vector and $\mathbf{f}(\mathbf{x})$ is of the form of

$$\mathbf{f}(\mathbf{x}) = \begin{bmatrix} \mathbf{x}_2 \\ \left(\mathbf{J}r^{-1} + r\mathbf{D}(\mathbf{x}_1)\right)^{-1} \cdot \\ \left(-\left(\mathbf{B}r^{-1} + r\mathbf{C}(\mathbf{x}_1, \mathbf{x}_2)\right)\mathbf{x}_2 - rg(\mathbf{x}_1) + \mathbf{K}_m\mathbf{x}_3 - r\tau_r(\mathbf{x}_2)\right) \\ -\mathbf{L}^{-1}\left(\mathbf{K}_b r^{-1}\mathbf{x}_2 + \mathbf{R}\mathbf{x}_3\right) \end{bmatrix}$$

$$\mathbf{b} = \begin{bmatrix} \mathbf{0} \\ \mathbf{0} \\ \mathbf{L}^{-1} \end{bmatrix}, \quad \mathbf{x} = \begin{bmatrix} \mathbf{q} \\ \dot{\mathbf{q}} \\ \mathbf{I}_a \end{bmatrix} \tag{7}$$

The state-space (6) shows a highly coupled nonlinear system in a non-companion form. The complexity of model is a serious challenge for the control of the robot.

To avoid much more complexity, many works have ignored the motors' dynamics. However, considering the motors' dynamics is required in high-speed and high-accuracy applications.

3. Robust control design

By substituting (2), (3) and (5) into (4), the voltage equation of the i th motor in the scalar form can be expressed by

$$RK_m^{-1}Jr^{-1}\ddot{q} + (RK_m^{-1}Br^{-1} + K_b r^{-1})\,\dot{q} \tag{8}$$
$$+RK_m^{-1}r\tau_r + L\dot{I}_a + \varphi = v$$

Where $\ddot{q}$, $\dot{q}$, τ_r, $\dot{I}_a$ and φ are the ith element of the vectors $\ddot{\mathbf{q}}$, $\dot{\mathbf{q}}$, τ_r, $\dot{\mathbf{I}}_a$ and φ, respectively.

Equation (8) can be rewritten as

$$\ddot{q} + F = v \tag{9}$$

Where F is referred to as the lumped uncertainty expressed by

$$F = (RK_m^{-1}Jr^{-1} - 1)\ddot{q} + L\dot{I}_a + \varphi + \tag{10}$$
$$(RK_m^{-1}Br^{-1} + K_b r^{-1})\,\dot{q} + RK_m^{-1}r\tau_r$$

Let us define

$$u = \ddot{q}_d + k_d(\dot{q}_d - \dot{q}) + k_p(q_d - q) + \hat{F} \tag{11}$$

Where $\hat{F}$ is the estimate of F, q_d is the desired joint position, k_p and k_d are the control design parameters. In order to estimate F, this paper designs a simple RBF network as an uncertainty estimator. In order to protect the motor from over voltage, the motor voltage must be under a permitted value v_{max}.

Therefore, a voltage limiter is used for each motor to hold the voltage under the value v_{max}. Then, a robust control law is proposed as

$$v(t) = v_{max}\,sat(u/v_{max}) \tag{12}$$

Where

$$sat(u/v_{max}) = \begin{cases} 1 & if \quad u > v_{max} \\ u/v_{max} & if \quad |u| \le v_{max} \\ -1 & if \quad u < -v_{max} \end{cases} \tag{13}$$

The control scheme is presented in figure 1.

4. Adaptive uncertainty estimator

Applying control law (12) to the system (9) obtains the closed loop system

$$\ddot{q} + F = v_{max}\,sat(u/v_{max}) \tag{14}$$

In the case of $u > v_{max}$, according to (13) we have

$$\ddot{q} + F = v_{max} \tag{15}$$

Therefore, the estimator $\hat{F}$ is not effective in the closed loop system.

In the case of $u < -v_{max}$, according to (13) we have

$$\ddot{q} + F = -v_{max} \tag{16}$$

Therefore, the estimator $\hat{F}$ is not effective in the closed loop system.

In the case of $|u| \le v_{max}$, according to (9), (11) and (13) we have

$$\ddot{q} + F = (\ddot{q}_d + k_d(\dot{q}_d - \dot{q}) + k_p(q_d - q)) \tag{17}$$
$$+ \hat{F}$$

Therefore, the closed loop system can be written as

$$\ddot{e} + k_d\dot{e} + k_p e = F - \hat{F} \tag{18}$$

Where e is the tracking error expressed by

$$e = q_d - q \qquad (19)$$

This paper suggests a simple RBF estimator for every joint as

$$\hat{F} = \hat{p}\exp(-(e^2 + \dot{e}^2)) \qquad (20)$$

Where $\hat{p}$ is an adaptive gain. One can easily represent (20) as

$$\hat{F} = \hat{p}\zeta \qquad (21)$$

Where ζ is expressed as

$$\zeta = \exp(-(e^2 + \dot{e}^2)) \qquad (22)$$

The estimator $\hat{F}$ defined by (21) can approximate F adaptively based on the universal approximation of RBF networks [22]. Thus,

$$|F - \hat{F}| \leq \rho \qquad (23)$$

Where ρ is a positive scalar. Suppose that F can be modeled as

$$F = p\zeta + \varepsilon$$

Where ε is the approximation error and vector p is constant. Assume that

$$|F - p\zeta| \leq \beta \qquad (25)$$

Considering (24) and (25) shows that $|\varepsilon| \leq \beta$ in which β is the upper bound of approximation error. The dynamics of tracking error can be expressed by substituting (24) and (21) into (18) to have

$$\ddot{e} + k_d\dot{e} + k_p e = (p - \hat{p})\zeta + \varepsilon \qquad (26)$$

The state space equation in the tracking space is obtained using (26) as

$$\dot{E} = AE + B\omega \qquad (27)$$

Where

$$A = \begin{bmatrix} 0 & 1 \\ -k_p & -k_d \end{bmatrix}, \; B = \begin{bmatrix} 0 \\ 1 \end{bmatrix}, \; E = \begin{bmatrix} e \\ \dot{e} \end{bmatrix}$$

$$\omega = (p - \hat{p})\zeta + \varepsilon \qquad (28)$$

Consider the following positive definite function [27]

$$V = 0.5 E^T SE + \frac{1}{2\gamma}(p - \hat{p})^2 \qquad (29)$$

Where γ is a positive scalar, S and Q are the unique symmetric positive definite matrices satisfying the matrix Lyapunov equation as

$$A^T S + SA = -Q \qquad (30)$$

Taking the time derivative of V gives that

$$\dot{V} = 0.5\dot{E}^T SE + 0.5 E^T S\dot{E} - (p - \hat{p})\dot{\hat{p}}/\gamma \qquad (31)$$

Substituting (27), (28) and (30) into (31) yields to

$$\dot{V} = (p - \hat{p})\left(E^T S_2 \zeta - \frac{1}{\gamma}\dot{\hat{p}}\right) \qquad (32)$$

$$+ E^T S_2 \varepsilon - 0.5 E^T QE$$

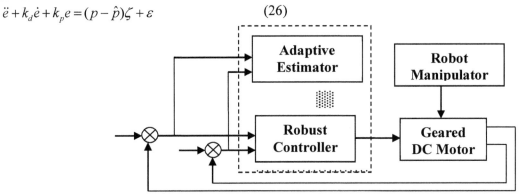

Figure 1. Proposed robust RBF network control.

Where S_2 is the second column of S. Since $-0.5 E^T QE < 0$ for $E \neq 0$, if the adaptation law is given by

$$\dot{\hat{p}} = \gamma E^T S_2 \zeta \qquad (33)$$

Then

$$\dot{V} = -0.5 E^T QE + E^T S_2 \varepsilon \qquad (34)$$

The tracking error is reduced if $\dot{V} < 0$. Therefore, the convergence of E is guaranteed if

$$E^T S_2 \varepsilon < 0.5 E^T QE$$

Using the Cauchy–Schwartz inequality and $|\varepsilon| \leq \beta$, we can obtain,

$$E^T S_2 \varepsilon \leq \| E \| . \| S_2 \| . |\varepsilon| < \beta \| E \| . \| S_2 \| \qquad (36)$$

Since $\lambda_{min}(Q)\| E \|^2 \leq E^T QE \leq \lambda_{max}(Q)\| E \|^2$, in order to satisfy (35), it is sufficient that

$$\beta \| S_2 \| < 0.5\lambda_{min}(Q)\| E \| \quad \text{or} \qquad (37)$$

$$2\beta \| S_2 \| / \lambda_{min}(Q) \square \; \delta_0 < \| E \|$$

Where δ_0 is a positive constant, $\lambda_{min}(Q)$ and $\lambda_{max}(Q)$ are the minimum and maximum eigenvalues of Q, respectively. Thus, we have $\dot{V} < 0$ as long as $\delta_0 < \| E \|$. This means that the tracking error becomes smaller out of the ball with the radius of δ_0. As a result, the tracking error ultimately enters into the ball. On the other hand $\dot{V} > 0$ if $\delta_0 > \|E\|$. This means that the tracking error does not converge to zero.

According to (33), the parameter of the RBF network estimator is calculated by

$$\hat{p}(t) = \hat{p}(0) + \int_0^t \gamma E^T S_2 \zeta d\tau \tag{38}$$

Where $\hat{p}(0)$ is the initial value.

Result 1: The tracking error e and its time derivatives $\dot{e}$ are bounded and ultimately enters into a ball with a radius of δ_0.

To evaluate the final size of error, it is worthy to note that it depends on the upper bound of approximation error, β, and the control design parameters k_p and k_d. Selecting large values for k_p and k_d, will provide a small size of tracking error. To evaluate the size of estimation error ρ in (23), one can substitute (24) into (23) to have

$$|p\zeta + \varepsilon - \hat{p}\zeta| \le |(p - \hat{p})\zeta| + |\varepsilon| \tag{39}$$

Thus, to satisfy (23), ρ can be given by

$$\rho = |(p - \hat{p})\zeta| + \beta \tag{40}$$

5. Stability analysis

A proof for the boundedness of the state variables θ, $\dot{\theta}$ and I_a is given by stability analysis. In order to analyze the stability, the following assumptions are made:

Assumption 1 The desired trajectory q_d must be smooth in the sense that q_d and its derivatives up to a necessary order are available and all uniformly bounded [28].

As a necessary condition to design a robust control, the external disturbance must be bounded. Thus, the following assumption is made:

Assumption 2 The external disturbance φ is bounded as $|\varphi(t)| \le \varphi_{max}$.

Control law (12) makes the following assumption.

Assumption 3 The motor voltage is bounded as $|v| \le v_{max}$.

The motor should be sufficiently strong to drive the robot for tracking the desired joint velocity under the maximum permitted voltages. According to result1, $E = [q_d - q \quad \dot{q}_d - \dot{q}]^T$ is bounded. Since q_d and $\dot{q}_d$ are bounded in assumption 1,

Result 2: The joint position q and joint velocity $\dot{q}$ are bounded.

From (4), we can write for every motor

$$RI_a + L\dot{I}_a + K_b r^{-1}\dot{q} + \varphi = v \tag{41}$$

Substituting control law (12) into (41) yields

$$RI_a + L\dot{I}_a + K_b r^{-1}\dot{q} + \varphi = v_{max} sat(\frac{u}{v_{max}}) \tag{42}$$

That is

$$RI_a + L\dot{I}_a = w \tag{43}$$

$$w = v_{max} sat(u / v_{max}) - k_b r^{-1}\dot{q} - \phi \tag{44}$$

The variables $\dot{q}$ and ϕ are bounded according to result 2 and assumption 2, respectively. Additionally, $|v_{max} sat(u / v_{max})| \le v_{max}$.

Consequently, the input w in (43) is bounded. The linear differential (43) is a stable linear system based on the Routh-Hurwitz criterion. Since the input w is bounded, the output I_a is bounded.

Result 3: The current I_a is bounded.

As a result of this reasoning, for every joint, the joint position q, the joint velocity $\dot{q}$ and the motor current I_a are bounded. Therefore, the system states $\mathbf{q}$, $\dot{\mathbf{q}}$ and $\mathbf{I_a}$ are bounded and the stability of system is guaranteed.

6. Simulation results

The robust RBF network control is simulated using an articulated robot driven by permanent magnet DC motors.

The details of robot is given by [6]. The maximum voltage of each motor is set to $u_{max} = 40\ V$. The parameters of motors are given in table 1. The desired joint trajectory for all joints is shown in figure 1. The desired position for every joint is given by

$$\theta_d = 1 - \cos(\pi t / 5) \quad \text{for} \quad 0 \le t < 10 \tag{45}$$

Table 1. Specifications of DC motors.

u_{max} (V)	R (Ω)	K_b ($\frac{V.s}{rad}$)	L (H)	J_m ($\frac{Nm.s^2}{rad}$)	B_m ($\frac{Nm.s}{rad}$)	r
40	1.26	0.26	0.001	0.0002	0.001	0.01

The external disturbance φ in (8) for every joint is given by

$$\varphi = \begin{cases} 0 & 0 \le t \le 2 \text{ and } 4 \le t \le 6 \text{ and } 8 \le t \le 10 \\ 1 & 2 \le t \le 4 \text{ and } 6 \le t \le 8 \end{cases} \tag{46}$$

Tracking performance: The robust RBF network control in (12) is simulated with adaptive law (38) and the following parameters

$$A = \begin{bmatrix} 0 & 1 \\ -100 & -20 \end{bmatrix}, S_2 = \begin{bmatrix} 50 \\ 6 \end{bmatrix},$$

$$\gamma = 5000, \hat{p}(0) = 0 \tag{47}$$

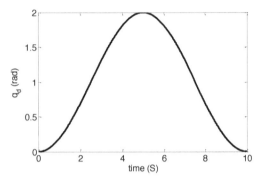

Figure 2. The desired joint trajectory.

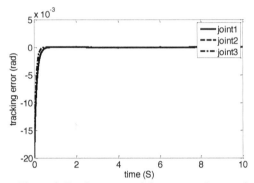

Figure 3. Performance of the proposed control.

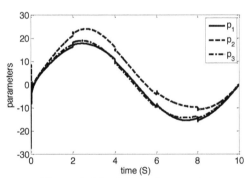

Figure 4. Adaptation of parameters.

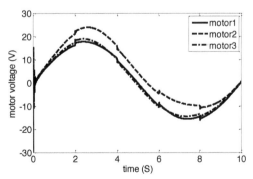

Figure 5. Control efforts of the proposed control.

The initial errors for all joints are given $0.02 rad$. The tacking performance is very good as shown in figure 3. All joint errors finally go under $4.2 \times 10^{-5} rad$ without overshoot.

The adaptation of parameters for all joints is shown in figure 4. All parameters are varied to cover all effects of higher order terms in RBF

network estimators. Motors behave well under the permitted voltages as shown in figure 5.

The control efforts are increased when starting because of the initial tracking error. Simulation results confirm the effectiveness of the robust RBF network control.

A comparison: The robust RBF network control is compared with a robust Neural Network control (robust NN control) given by [10]. The control structure has two interior loops. The inner loop is a voltage controller for motor using two-layer neural networks whereas the outer loop is a current controller using two-layer neural networks for providing the desired current.

The control design is based on the stability analysis using Lyapunov theory. As a comparison it is noted that the robust RBF network control is much simpler since it has only one control loop using a RBF network.

The parameters of the robust NN control are set to $\Lambda = 100$, $k_\tau = 30$, $k_v = 1$, $k_1 = 0.1$, $k_\omega = 1$, $\Gamma = 1000$, $\hat{W}_1(0) = 0$ and $\hat{W}_2(0) = 0$. The initial errors and external disturbances for all joints are the same as ones used in Simulation 1.

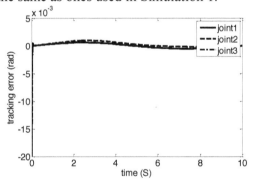

Figure 6. Performance of the robust NN control.

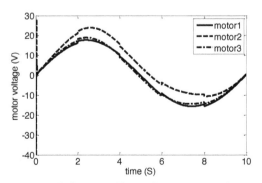

Figure 7. Control efforts of the robust NN control.

The control performance of [10] is shown in figure 6. Both control approaches are robust with a good tracking performance. Figure 8 shows voltages applied to the motors.

The control efforts in figure 7 are smooth and permitted. The robust RBF network control is much simpler, less computational, less number of design parameters and has better control performance. On the other hand, the tracking error of the robust NN control will be decreased by increasing the gains however the chattering phenomenon will be increased.

7. Conclusion

This paper has presented a novel robust model-free control approach for electrically driven robot manipulators. It has been found that the complex dynamics of the robotic system can be estimated by using a RBF network in a decentralized structure as an estimator of uncertainty. The robust controller has become model-free by using this estimator to compensate the uncertainty. The proposed adaptive mechanism has guaranteed the stability and provided a good tracking performance. The performance of the proposed estimator in the robust control system has been very good as shown by simulations. In order to have a simple design with easy implementation yet good performance it has been confirmed that using only the tracking error and its time derivatives is sufficient to form the estimator. A comparison with a robust NN control has shown that the proposed control approach is simpler in design, less computational and better control performance.

References

[1] Abdallah, C., Dawson, D., Dorato, P. & Jamshidi, M. (1991). Survey of robust control for rigid robots. IEEE Control System Magazine, vol. 11, no. 2, pp. 24-30.

[2] Qu, Z. & Dawson, D. (1996). Robust tracking control of robot manipulators. IEEE Press, Inc., New York.

[3] Sage, H. G., De Mathelin, M. F. & Ostertag, E. (1999). Robust control of robot manipulators: A survey. International Journal of Control, vol. 72, no. 16, pp. 1498-1522.

[4] Fateh, M. M. (2008). On the voltage-based control of robot manipulators. International Journal of Control and Automation System, vol. 6, no. 5, pp. 702-712.

[5] Fateh, M. M. (2010). Robust voltage control of electrical manipulators in task-space. International Journal of Innovative Computing Information and Control, vol. 6, no. 6, pp. 2691-2700.

[6] Fateh, M. M. & Khorashadizadeh, S. (2012). Robust control of electrically driven robots by adaptive fuzzy estimation of uncertainty. Nonlinear Dynamics, vol. 69, pp. 1465-1477.

[7] Chang, Y. C. & Yen, H. M. (2009). Robust tracking control for a class of uncertain electrically driven robots. Control Theory & Applications, IET, vol. 3, pp. 519-532.

[8] Oya, M., Chun-Yi, S. & Kobayashi, T. (2004). State observer-based robust control scheme for electrically driven robot manipulators. IEEE Transactions on Robotics, vol. 20, pp. 796-804.

[9] Jae Pil, H. and Euntai, K. (2006). Robust tracking control of an electrically driven robot: adaptive fuzzy logic approach. IEEE Transactions on Fuzzy systems, vol. 14, pp. 232-247.

[10] Kwan, C., Lewis, F. L. & Dawson, D. (1998). Robust neural-network control of rigid-link electrically driven robots. IEEE Transactions on Neural Networks, vol. 9, no. 4, pp. 581-588.

[11] Rong-Jong, W. & Muthusamy, R. (2013). Fuzzy-Neural-Network Inherited Sliding-Mode Control for Robot Manipulator Including Actuator Dynamics. IEEE Transactions on Neural Networks and Learning Systems, vol. 24, pp. 274-287.

[12] Chang, Y. C., Yen, H. M. & Wu, M. F. (2008). An intelligent robust tracking control for electrically-driven robot systems. International Journal of Systems Science, vol. 39, pp. 497-511.

[13] Fateh, M. M. (2010). Proper uncertainty bound parameter to robust control of electrical manipulators using nominal model. Nonlinear Dynamics, vol. 61, no. 4, pp. 655-666.

[14] Kim, E. (2004). Output feedback tracking control of robot manipulator with model uncertainty via adaptive fuzzy logic. IEEE Transactions on Fuzzy Systems, vol. 12, no. 3, pp. 368-376.

[15] Hwang, J. P. & Kim, E. (2006). Robust tracking control of an electrically driven robot: adaptive fuzzy logic approach. IEEE Transactions on Fuzzy Systems, vol. 14, no. 2, pp. 232-247.

[16] Ho, H. F., Wong Y. K. & Rad, A. B. (2008). Adaptive fuzzy approach for a class of uncertain nonlinear systems in strict-feedback form. ISA Transactions, vol. 47, pp. 286-299.

[17] Senthilkumar, D. & Mahanta, C. (2010). Identification of uncertain nonlinear systems for robust fuzzy control. ISA Transactions, vol. 49, pp. 27-38.

[18] Peng, J. & Dubay, R. (2011). Identification and adaptive neural network control of a DC motor system with dead-zone characteristics. ISA Transactions, vol. 50, no. 4, pp. 588-598.

[19] Huang, S. N., Tan, K. K. & Lee, T. H. (2008). Adaptive neural network algorithm for control design of rigid-link electrically driven robots. Neurocomputing, vol. 71, pp. 885-894.

[20] Sun, T., Pei, H., Yan, Y., Zhou, H. & Zhang, C. (2011). Neural network-based sliding mode adaptive control for robot manipulators. Neurocomputing, vol. 74, pp. 2377-2384.

[21] Alavandar, S. & Nigam, M. J. (2009). New hybrid adaptive neuro-fuzzy algorithms for manipulator

control with uncertainties–comparative study. ISA Transactions, vol. 48, no. 4, pp. 497-502.

[22] Park, J. & Sandberg, J. W. (1991). Universal approximation using radial-basis-function Network. Neural Computation, vol. 3, pp. 246-257.

[23] Sanner, R. M. & Slotine, J. E. (1992). Gaussian networks for direct adaptive control. IEEE Transactions on Neural Networks, vol. 3, pp. 837-863.

[24] Ge, S. S. & Wang, C. (2002). Direct Adaptive NN Control of a Class of Nonlinear Systems. IEEE Transactions on Neural Networks, vol. 13, no. 1, pp. 214-221.

[25] Sridhar, S. & Hassan, K. K. (2000). Output feedback control of nonlinear systems using RBF neural networks. IEEE Transactions on Neural Networks, vol. 11, no. 1, pp. 69-79.

[26] Yang, Y. & Wang, X. (2007). Adaptive H∞ tracking control for a class of uncertain nonlinear systems using radial-basis-function neural networks. Neurocomputing, vol. 70, pp. 932-941.

[27] Fateh, M. M. & Fateh, S. (2012). Decentralized direct adaptive fuzzy control of robots using voltage control strategy. Nonlinear Dynamics, vol. 70, pp. 919-1930.

[28] Spong, M. W., Hutchinson, S. & Vidyasagar, M. (2006). Robot Modelling and Control: Wiley. Hoboken.

16

Extraction of Drug-Drug Interaction from Literature through Detecting Linguistic-based Negation and Clause Dependency

B. Bokharaeian[*] and A. Diaz

Facultad de Informática, Universidad Complutense de Madrid, Calle del Prof. José G! Santesmases, Madrid, Spain.

Corresponding author: behrou.bo@ucm.es (B. Bokharaeian).

Abstract

Extracting biomedical relations such as drug-drug interaction (DDI) from text is an important task in biomedical natural language processing. Due to the large number of complex sentences in biomedical literature, researchers have employed some sentence simplification techniques to improve the performance of the relation extraction methods. However, no significant improvement has been reported in literature, since the task is difficult. This paper aims to explore clause dependency related features alongside to linguistic-based negation scope and cues to overcome complexity of the sentences. The results show through employing the proposed features combined with a bag of words kernel, the performance of the used kernel methods improves. Moreover, experiments show that the enhanced local context kernel outperforms other methods. The proposed method can be used as an alternative approach for sentence simplification techniques in biomedical area which is an error-prone task.

Keywords: *Drug-Drug Interaction, Relation Extraction, Negation Detection, Clause Dependency.*

1. Introduction

Although being relatively new, biomedical relation extraction from text is a fast-growing topic in Natural Language Processing (**NLP**) research field. Considering the ever increasing number of biomedical researches with the huge number of unstructured biomedical text resources being involved, it seems to be highly demanding to extract biomedical relations out of scientific texts and reports. Biomedical Natural Language processing or briefly BioNLP refers to the text mining applied to literature of the biomedical and molecular biology domain.

With **Drug-Drug interaction** being a serious event in medicine, automatic extraction of these interactions from text is an important task to be carried out in BioNLP. A drug-drug interaction (DDI) usually occurs when the activity level of one drug is changed by another drug. According to the reports by U.S. Food and Drug Administration (FDA) and other acknowledged studies, annual life-threatening DDI's occurring in the United States exceed two million cases [1]. With the purpose of recording DDIs, many academic researchers and pharmaceutical companies have tried to develop either relational or structural databases such as [2,3]. However, most valuable researches and information are still found only within unstructured text documents such as scientific publications and technical reports.

Moreover, since biomedical relations, such as *protein-protein* and *drug-drug interactions*, significantly contribute to identification of biological and medical processes, biomedical relation extraction is believed to be a very important research topic within the field. Many of the existing works on biomedical relation extraction task in the literature (including the DDI detection) are approached via supervised binary relation extraction [4]. As such, other types of algorithms including complex relation extraction algorithms and semi-supervised ones are expected to be incorporated into this kind of the relation extraction task [5].

Role identification of clauses incorporated in complex sentences in the course of DDI detection is another linguistic- driven task which is carried out in this research. According to linguistics, an

independent clause, or main clause, is the one that can be seen as a complete sentence, by itself, expressing a complete thought. Moreover, a **dependent clause** refers to a group of words, including a subject and a verb, which does not express a complete thought and cannot stand alone. It usually extends the meaning of the main clause [6]. Consequently, a **complex sentence** consists of one independent clause along with one or more dependent clauses. Moreover, the term clause connects or refers to a word used to join or to connect clauses to compose complex sentences. **Coordinators**, **conjunctive adverbs**, and **subordinators** are three types of connectors. As an example, in the following sentence:

- *Although* (specific drug or food interactions with mifepristone has not been studied), (it is possible) *that* < ketoconazole, itraconazole, erythromycin, and grapefruit juice may inhibit its metabolism.>

In this sample, "Although" and "that" are two subordinator connectors separating three different clauses identified in "(" and "<". The main clause has been enclosed with "<". Two other clauses are dependent clauses which complement the main clause.

One of the few researches on relation extraction task with clauses which had been taken into account, was the one carried out by [7]. They tried to select the best clauses to develop a sentence simplification algorithm and reported some improvements regarding different types of rules they used for the sake of simplification and clause selection procedures.

This research is an attempt to extend identified text or subtree features in three kernel-based methods, namely **global context kernel** (GCK) method, **local context kernel** (LCK) [8] method, and **subtree** [9] kernel. The extension has been carried out in two steps. First, several clause connectors are detected whether components of the kernel methods - token or subtree – exist in a dependent or independent clause and second, type of the clause was identified.

On the other hand, detecting negative assertions is essential in most BioMedical text mining tasks, where in general, the aim is to derive factual knowledge from textual data. According to linguistics [10], **negation** is a morphosyntactic operation in which a lexical item denies or inverts the meaning of another lexical item or construction. Likewise, a **negator** is a lexical item that expresses negation. Negation is commonly used in clinical and biomedical text documents and

is an important origin of low precision in automated information retrieval systems [11]. Exploring efficiency of linguistic-based negation related features is another purpose of this research. In the next section, some of the previous related works and resources will be reviewed.

2. Related works

The first Drug-Drug interaction corpus initially developed by [12] had a pile of 579 xml files describing DDIs randomly collected from the *DrugBank* database [13]. In 2011, the first DDI Extraction competition was held with the aim of encouraging researchers to explore new methods for extracting drug-drug interactions. The best results obtained in the course of detecting and classifying DDIs were a F-measure of 65.74%, a precision of 65.04% and a recall of 71.92% [14]. As a part of SemEval-2013 (International Workshop on Semantic Evaluation), the second competition was held in 2013. A novel corpus was developed which included not only the one used in 2011 [12] but some *Medline* abstracts. The participant teams developed solutions on the basis of either supervised or sentence-level relation extraction methods; the best F-measure achieved was 75%[15]. It is worth mentioning that the authors have participated in this challenge and the details of the developed system can be found at [16].

Additionally, several machine learning approaches have already been developed to extract relations from text including Sequence kernels [8], Tree kernels (parse tree based) [9], and Graph kernels (graph parsing-based) [17]. Two more recent approaches undertaken by [18] and [14] ranked first and second in DrugDDI challenge 2013, respectively. Chowdhury and his colleagues [18] have used linear combination of a feature based kernel, a Shallow Linguistic (SL) kernel and Path-enclosed Tree (PET) kernel to proposed a hybrid kernel. Defining a multiplicative constant they went for assigning a higher (or lower) weight to the information obtained by tree structures. In another work, Thomas and his colleagues [14] proposed a two-step approach starting with extraction of candidates using ensembles comprised of up to five different classifiers and then relabeling to one of the four categories. Moreover, other types of machine learning approaches such as maximal frequent sequence have been employed effectively in DDI extraction [19]. A survey about different machine learning tools in DDI related tasks can be found here [20]. Additionally, considering negation when addressing relation extraction task, Faisal

Chowdhury and colleagues [21] developed a list of such features as the nearest verb to the candidate entities in the parse tree and few negation cues, by which the SVM classifier was fed. Although, some improvement was observed but there was nothing providing how much the negation identification's performance has improved.

It is worth mentioning that two negation detection methods have been developed and employed for annotating the used corpora: a **linguistic-based** approach and an **event-oriented** approach. Two of the known negation annotated corpora are the linguistically-focused, scope-based **BioScope** and the event-oriented **Genia**. In BioScope, scopes aim to recognize the position of the key negated event in the sentence. Furthermore, all arguments of these key events are also under the scope [22]. In the Genia event, biological concepts (relations and events) have been annotated for negation, but no linguistic cues have been annotated for them [23]. In fact, the main objective of the BioScope corpus is to investigate this language phenomenon in a general, task-independent and linguistically-oriented manner.

As another subtask utilized to perform relation extraction task, sentence and clause simplification goes for modification, enhancement, classification or otherwise processing an existing piece text in such a way that the prose's grammar and structure is greatly simplified with the original meaning and information remained unchanged [24]. Moreover, being a text simplifying system, ISIMP [25] attempts to improve text mining tools including relation extraction tasks. Another research [26] performed on the same line, went for some simplification techniques to simplify complex sentences by splitting the clauses. They split the clauses before implementing some simplification rules to generate new simple sentences.

Throughout the rest of this paper, first the proposed method and its components are explained. It explains the process of employing the extracted features in combination with other kernel methods. Then, in the fourth section, the results are exhibited, and in the last section, the results are discussed and concluded, and some suggestions are given for future works.

3. Method

In this section, we begin our discussion by extending the DrugDDI corpus through negation scopes and cues [27]. Then feature extraction, general framework and other components of the implemented system are explained (Figure 2).

In order to use the negation effects in the course of relation extraction task, an extension of the two mentioned DrugDDI corpora, especially the Drug Bank section in the 2013 version, annotated with negation scope and negation cue was prepared (Figure 1).

All the sentences of the DrugDDI 2011, which consists of 5806 different sentence and 579 files, were used and automatically annotated and then due to possible mistakes that may have happened in the automatic process, a manual checking was carried out. Obviously, because every combination of drug names can be a DDI candidate in the corpus, each sentence may explain more than a DDI candidate. Therefore, as can be understood from table 1, DrugDDI and the produced NegDDI-DrugBank corpus have 31,270 DDI candidates. It is worth mentioning that, in this paper, "["is used to indicate the start point of the negation scope, and "]"to indicate the ending point; also "{"and "}"are used for identifying negation cue. One example is illustrated in the sentence below:

- [Concomitant use of bromocriptine mesylate with other ergot alkaloids is {not} recommended].

In passive sentences with the following structure "It (this or that) + finite format of to be + not + past participate"; scope opens at the beginning of the sentence.

The NegDDI-DrugBank corpus was prepared by adding new XML "negationtag" at the end of each sentence XML tag within which "negation cues" and "negation scopes" are used. The extended NegDDI-DrugBank corpus is available for public use[1].

3.1 Feature extraction

Researchers have proposed complicated kernel based methods to use different shallow or deep features to capture different types of complex sentences. However, most of the previous literatures [28] suggest that, rather than simple sentences of single clause, more errors are to be produced by complex compound sentences which are, by the way, very common in the biomedical literature.

Describing global context kernel, local context kernel, and subtree kernel, respectively, the three tables represent complex and compound sentences which are very commonly used in biomedical literature to produce higher error rates than those of simple sentences with just one clause. As it can

---

[1]http://nil.fdi.ucm.es/sites/default/files//NegDDI_DrugBank.zip

be seen in the tables where error analysis results are reported, these mistakes are more frequently undertaken when approaching via solely shallow linguistic processes [8]. Such approaches include

tokenization, sentence splitting, Part-of-Speech (PoS) tagging and lemmatization.

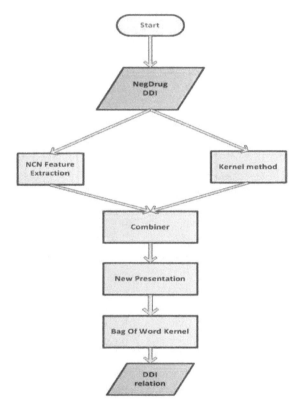

```
<sentence id="DDI-DrugBank.d297.s4" text="Concurrent therapy with ORENCIA and TNF antagonists is not recommended.">
    <entity charOffset="24-30" id="DDI-DrugBank.d297.s4.e0" text="ORENCIA" type="brand"/>
    <entity charOffset="36-50" id="DDI-DrugBank.d297.s4.e1" text="TNF antagonists" type="group"/>
    <pair ddi="true" e1="DDI-DrugBank.d297.s4.e0" e2="DDI-DrugBank.d297.s4.e1" id="DDI-DrugBank.d297.s4.p0" type="advise"/>
    <negationtags><xcope> Concurrent therapy with ORENCIA and TNF antagonists is <cue>not</cue>
    recommended</xcope>.</negationtags>
</sentence>
```

Figure 1. The extended unified XML format of a sentence with negation cue in NegDDI-DrugBank corpus.

Figure 2. The Basic components of the implemented and proposed method.

In the rest of this section, the implemented algorithms for extracting clause related features along with the negation scope and cues are introduced.

3.1.1 Clause related features
As mentioned earlier, the position of independent or the dependent clauses, and also the type of dependent clause (e.g. Adverbial, adjective or noun) are known to be among major factors contributing into relation extraction process. This makes it of critical importance to distinguish independent clauses from the dependent ones.

As presented in table 1, more than 27% of the DDI candidates in the testing part of NegDDI-DrugBank corpus and 19% of those in the training part contain, at least, one dependent clause. Table I show that the frequency of subordinating clauses in sentences with negation cues is higher than that in other types of sentences. Therefore, due to the large number of sentences with more than one clause, the complex structure of these sentences, and their higher associated rate of error together with the important role they play when using negation concept, it will be very important to take clause dependency features into account.

Different types of dependent clauses can alter the sentence's overall meaning in distinct ways. For instance, a **concessive clause** is the one beginning with "although" or "even though", expressing an idea opposite to the main part of the sentence; as an example see the following sentence:

- *Although* there may be decreased *zalcitabine* activity because of lessened active metabolite formation, <the clinical relevance of these in vitro results is not known>.

Here the main clause (enclosed with "<") has opposite meaning to that of the dependent clause which indicates some changes in the *zalcitabine* activity. Another type of clause frequently seen within the NegDDI-DrugBank corpus is the **adverbial** clause. One of the connectors used within these adverbial clauses is while. See the following sentence as an example:

- The amount of metformin absorbed (**while** taking Acarbose) was bioequivalent to the amount absorbed (**when** taking placebo), (as indicated by the plasma AUC values.)

Table 1. Statistics of the ddi candidates with more than one clause in negddi-drugbank.

Category	Number of candidates with more than one clause	Total candidates	*Rate*
Test part	1401	5265	27%
Train part	5015	26005	19%
Have negation in test part	396	1409	28%
without negation in test part	1005	3898	26%

Analyzing different types of dependent clauses, two feature categories were extracted. The first category encompassed 28 Boolean features corresponding to 28 clause connectors. Consequently 28 Boolean features were extracted corresponding to the 28 clause connectors. A selected list of the most used connecters and their frequencies in the corpus can be found in table 2.

The other feature category was based on substructures (tokens or subtrees) used in the applied method; it identified whether substructure was inside the main clause or not. For instance, similar to features used in the Global context kernel, three new text features were extracted with "IDC" prefix for tokens inside the independent clause and "DC" for those inside the dependent clause. Similarly, in order to improve the subtree kernel, other new subtrees were defined corresponding to the usual subtrees. In short, when it is inside the dependent clause, this subtree comes

with DC prefix added before its root name, while the IDC prefix was used for subtrees inside the independent clause.

Table 2. Statistics of the most frequent clause connectors in negddi-drugbank corpus.

Clause connector	Frequency.
Although	651
While	3358
When	511
Anywhere	29
Until	186
Till	710
Because	58
Even though	625
Since	1307
But	123
Unless	347
Total	7905

Constituent parse trees have been analyzed to detect whether a substructure is inside the main clause or within the dependent one. The proposed algorithm gives a "DC" prefix to the substructure provided that shortest path between the token, or the subtrees root, and the main root contains a subordinate clause node (SBAR) (Fig. 3); otherwise, it gives the substructure an "IDC" prefix. For example, for the sentence with its constituent parse tree shown in Fig. 3, "DC-clinical" is a new token made by the program due to existence of a "SBAR" along the path which connects the token to the main root.

Such a new token which can be placed on the left, right or between the two drug names within the original sentence beside other newly produced tokens, is the result of the proposed improved version of Global and Local context kernel. Via such an approach, one may create three new corresponding text features.

The improved version of the subtree kernel produced a new subtree with "IDC-IN" as its root based on the subtree on the upper left of figure 3 containing the leaf "although" and the root IN.

3.1.2. Negation related features

In addition to previous features, we conducted some experiments on negation related features. Regarding the position of drug names (inside or outside the negation scope), there are 6 different possibilities to be used as 6 features:

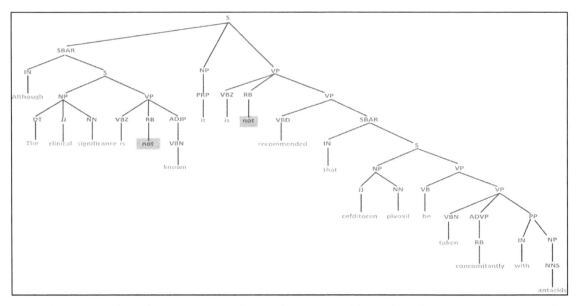

Figure 3. A sample of constituent parse tree of a complex sentence with two dependent clauses and two negation cues.

- BothinsideNegSc: A Boolean feature set to "true" when both drugs are inside the negation scope with other situations being false.

- BothLeftSNegSc: A Boolean feature set to "true" when both drugs are on the left side of the negation scope with other situations being false.

- BothRightNegSc: A Boolean feature set to "true" when both drugs are on the right side of the negation scope, while other situations are false.

- OneLeftOneInsideNegSc: A Boolean feature set to "true" when one drug is on the left side of the negation scope and the other is inside, with other situations being false.

- OneRightOneInsideNegSc: A Boolean feature set to "true" when one drug is on the right side of the negation scope and the other is inside, with other situations being false.

- OneLeftOneRightSc: A Boolean feature set to "true" when one drug is on the right side of the negation scope and the other one on the left, with other situations being false.

The features were used alongside with clause related features to enhance the performance of the used kernel methods. The next section will describe the proposed method based on the extracted features.

3.2 DDI extraction using bag of words kernel

The newly created presentation obtained from mentioned features was classified using a **bag-of-words** based kernel method which tries to find a polynomial combination of the features commonly known as the kernel function (Figure 2) support vector machine with *SMO* [**29**] implemented was used which outperformed other implementations of SVM, according to the performed experiments in the study, , e.g. *libSVM*, in terms of convergence rate and quality of results. *Weka* API was used as the implementation platform. Executed without a stemming step, the term minimum frequency of bag-of-words based kernel method was set to one. For all the mentioned methods, every feature was considered blind, so as to replace all drug names within the generated features with two general terms, i.e. "DrugName" was used for the two drugs with their interaction being investigated while "OtherDrugNames" was the term used for the other drugs. In order to be aligned with pharmaceutical texts, the tokenization process was carried out using Stanford *BioNLPTokenizer* [30]; however, Stanford parser was used to parse constituents. Moreover, as the method via which the winning team of DDI extraction challenges 2011 was approached, *TreeTagger* was employed for the sake of **Lematization** and **Pos tagging**. Additionally, some guidelines which has been suggested in [31] has been employed for improving the performance.

4. Results

In this section, comparative results of the augmented methods are presented in terms of F-measure along with those of the original methods. In this section, the results of two different types of validation experiments are presented. Firstly, similar to SemEval DDI challenges, the training set of the Drug Bank corpus was used to train the system while the test set was utilized for testing the system. Secondly, the NegDDI-DrugBank corpus 2013 was 10-fold cross validated with the results being displayed. Subsequently, a statistical sign test is presented to show the significance of the improvements caused by the proposed method compared to other three methods used. The section is closed by presenting the error analyses performed on the results of the system.

Table 3 demonstrates associated results with the improved Global context kernel method (with **CLA** postfix for clause related and **NEG** for negation related features) undertaken along with the original ones. The first row in the table displays the results for those sentences with negation cue but no clause connectors, in the testing dataset. The second row shows the results for candidates with negation cue and clause connectors. The third and the fourth rows show the results for sentences without negation cue, but with and without clause connectors, respectively. The last row contains the results for entire testing dataset.

10-fold cross validation of NegDDI-DrugBank 2013 (both testing and training sets) led to the results reported in table 4. In addition to previous features, the negation related features are denoted by NEG postfix. As the table shows, F-measure was increased in the course of 10-fold cross validation experiments with the best F-measure for the proposed methods being the one obtained by the proposed local context kernel-(CLA) method (81.8%).

According to the reported results in tables 3, 4 and 5, the proposed method is proved to successfully improve the F-measure across all tested categories. In global context kernel method, sentences with no negation cues and with clause connectors exhibited the best improvements with an average increase of +4% in the value of F-measure. Similarly, in local context kernel, the best improvement was 3.9%.

On the other hand, similar experiments to those conducted by global context kernel were carried out by the modified local context kernel with the best performance exhibited by the dataset containing the sentences without negation cues and clause connectors, just like what was observed for the global context kernel (Table 4).

However, the system succeeded to realize satisfyingly enough improvement in the performance of the other three datasets in terms of detecting DDIs, satisfactorily.

Also, similar to global context kernel, by considering tokens in the original LCK, some duplicated features were generated by negation scope and cue, and clause dependency features;

such feature generation is associated with system performance degradation.

In addition to the two mentioned sequence kernel methods, several experiments were carried out with subtree kernel which can be seen in table 5. With an average increase of +9.8% in the value of F-measure, sentences without negation cues but with clause connectors in the subtree kernel demonstrated the best improvements (Table 5). And an average of 3% was the best improvement which was obtained through employing both categories of features.

Last but not the least, the results of experiments undertaken on the improved subtree kernel with clause related features (Table 5) indicated the best performance and the highest improvement rate (2.1%) was obtained for clause related features which are the ones associated with the dataset containing sentences with clause connectors but no negation cues. Similarly, the highest improvement rate for both categories of features (9.8%) is the one associated with this dataset of sentences.

The results showed that, compared to other methods, the subtree kernel was relatively more effective in detecting DDIs within complex sentences; this seems to be because, rather than the other two used sequence kernels, it generally extracts a larger deal of structural and componential information from the sentences.

However, no significant improvement was observed for those sentences with negation cues, scopes and connectors. As explained before, this is possibly because of very good performance of the original subtree kernel when applied on this type of sentences, so that invented features are not so effective.

It is also worth mentioning that simple **cause-effect** and **time** connectors are considered to be the most frequent clause connectors. As shown in table 2, as the first and second most frequently used clause connectors in the NegDDI-DrugBank corpus, "when" and "but" are an adverbial clause connector and a coordinating conjunction, respectively.

Additionally, a set of additional experiments grounded on basic simplification methods were conducted in order to reduce complexity of the sentences. However, no better result was obtained through the additional experiments. For instance, substituting the dependent clause with an independent clause feature caused no improvements in the system performance.

With an F-measure of (comparable with 65.7% corresponding to the first system in DDI extraction challenge 2011 implemented by "Humboldt University of Berlin"), improved Local context kernel method (LCK-CLA) which produced the best obtained results for the testing set.

Table 3. Obtained results for global context kernel method with combination of negation and clause related feature sets in terms of f-measure.

Test Category	M (%)	M+ CLA (%)	Dif. (%)	M+ NEG+ CLA	Dif. (%)
With negation No connector	56.6	59.6	+3.0	57.8	+1.2
With negation With connector	51.7	53.9	+2.2	52.3	+0.6
No negation With connector	62.3	66.3	+4.0	63.7	+1.5
No negation No connector	64.7	65.8	+1.1	64.8	+0.1
Total	61.7	63.9	+2.2	62.4	+0.7

Table 4. Obtained results for subtree kernel method with combination of negation and clause related used feature sets in terms of f-measure.

Test Category	M (%)	M+ CLA (%)	Dif. (%)	M+ NEG+ CLA (%)	Dif. (%)
With negation No connector	60.9	60.9	+0.9	59.9	-1.0
With negation With connector	63.2	63.6	+0.4	63.2	0
No negation With connector	58.6	60.7	+2.1	68.4	+9.8
No negation No connector	36.3	37.3	+1	38.6	+2.3
Total	47.1	48.1	+1	50.1	+3.0

Table 5. Obtained results for local context kernel method with combination of negation and clause related used feature sets in terms of f-measure.

Test Category	M (%)	M+ CLA (%)	Dif. (%)	M+ NEG+ CLA (%)	Dif. (%)
With negation No connector	62.6	63.8	+1.2	61.5	-1.3
With negation With connector	58.0	61.9	+3.9	50.9	-7.2
No negation With connector	64.8	65.9	+1.1	65.7	+1.0
No negation No connector	63.9	64.9	+1	64.2	+0.2
Total	63.4	64.7	+1.3	63.0	-0.4

Table 6. Obtained results for 10-fold cross validation for three original kernel methods with combination of negation and clause related feature sets in terms of f-measure.

Method (M) name	M (%)	M+ NEG	Dif. (%)	M+ CLA	Dif. (%)	M+ NEG+ CLA	Dif. (%)
Global context Kernel	77.4	77.3	-0.1	78.9	+1.5	77.9	+0.2
Local context kernel	80.7	81.1	+0.4	81.8	+1.1	81.7	+1
Subtree kernel	71.9	72.1	+0.2	73.8	+1.9	74.9	+3

Error analysis

Some error identification analyses are presented in this section. The identified sources of error can be categorized as follows:

- Although most of the clause connectors can simply be identified by a superficial analysis (as in the experiments), there are, challenging clause connectors with possible alternative speech parts within a sentence. Such sorts of connectors are most problematic as there may be different speech parts (such as demonstrative pronouns) within the sentence. Thus, for the sake of simplicity, it was not used as a clause connector feature. Other similar clause connectors were either considered or ignored by whether they took common speech roles in scientific medical articles. For instance, "when" was considered as a connector only being a common speech role within the mentioned articles; it was, however, ignored as an information question word. In both cases, more precise in-depth procedures and experiments are required to achieve correct detections.

- As previously-mentioned, overlapping of the proposed features with those used in the original relation extraction method was another source of error. For instance, the studied clause connectors were associated with equivalent tokens within both original sequence kernels. Such situations downgrade the final performance of the system. Several experiments carried out on this problem revealed improvements once a manual **feature selection** method was undertaken. Therefore, undertaking an effective automatic feature selection method for each of the proposed methods can improve the system.

- All extraction systems (including the proposed system herein) suffer from **parentheses** as another source of inaccuracy. For instance, some parentheses contain a clause or explanation in which a drug name is used, see the sentence below:

– Although specific drug or food interactions with mifepristone have not been studied, on the basis of this drugs metabolism by CYP 3A4, it is possible that *ketoconazole*, itraconazole, erythromycin, and grapefruit juice may inhibit its metabolism (increasing serum levels of *mifepristone*).

Here, *ketoconazole* and *mifepristone* are two drug names interacting in the corpus. However, parentheses may prevent their interaction from being detected by the system. A simplification algorithm could be implemented to get rid of the parentheses issue.

5. Discussion and conclusion

Being an important task in the course of Biomedical Natural Language Processing, supervised biomedical relation extraction tries to extract relations between biomedical entities. Among other critical biomedical relations, this paper investigated Drug- Drug interactions. Many methods have been developed to extract DDI relations. However, substantial studies on the effects of clause dependency on the relation extraction task are yet to be reported, so as to propose adequate methods in this regard. Besides, sentences with negation cue(s) have more clause connectors compared to those with no negation cue; therefore it is very important to take clause connectors and dependent clauses in to consideration when trying to resolve a negation action.

In addition, the results confirmed that it is of great importance to take clause connectors and different types of clauses into account when performing relation extraction task.

This research undertook some experiments to use a few basic simplification methods (such as taking the main clause as a separate feature) to overcome issues associated with complex sentences; however, no significant improvement was achieved. It is believed that a combination of a simplification technique with a pronoun resolution method specifically-prepared-for-drug can improve the performance. To be used either in terms of a pre-processing step or along with other methods, such an algorithm may give better results. Moreover, the proposed method can be employed as an alternative approach to the sentence simplification error-prone task in the biomedical area.

Although the current results are promising, one of the challenging discussions is whether all kernel methods benefit from such features. As results of the subtree kernel for sentences with negation cues and clause connectors demonstrated, the authors believe that more advanced kernels deriving more informative features from different presentations of the sentence, may fail to benefit from the proposed features.

References

[1] Lazarou, J., Pomeranz, B. H. & Corey, P. N. (1998). Incidence of adverse drug reactions in hospitalized patients: A meta-analysis of prospective studies. JAMA, vol. 279, no. 15, pp. 1200-1205.

[2] Gaulton, A. et al. (2012). ChEMBL: a large-scale bioactivity database for drug discovery. Nucleic acids research, vol. 40, no. D1, pp. D1100--D1107.

[3] Ylva, B. et al. (2009). SFINX—a drug-drug interaction database designed for clinical decision support systems. European journal of clinical pharmacology, vol. 65, no. 6, pp. 627-633.

[4] Kadir, R. A. & Bokharaeian, B. (2013). Overview of biomedical relations extraction using hybrid rule-based approaches. Journal of Industrial and Intelligent Information Vol, vol. 1, no. 3.

[5] McDonald, R. et al. (2005). Simple Algorithms for Complex Relation Extraction with Applications to Biomedical IE. In Proceedings of the 43rd Annual Meeting on Association for Computational Linguistics, Stroudsburg, PA, USA, 2005, pp. 491-498.

[6] Rowan, M. & Harris, K. (1989). Explaining grammatical concepts. Journal of Basic Writing, pp. 21-41.

[7] Miwa, M., Saetre, R., Miyao, Y. & Tsujii, J. (2010). Entity-focused sentence simplification for relation extraction. In Proceedings of the 23rd international conference on computational linguistics, 2010, pp. 788-796.

[8] Giuliano, C., Lavellim ,A. & Romano, L. (2006). Exploiting Shallow Linguistic Information for Relation Extraction from Biomedical Literature. In 11th Conference of the European Chapter of the Association for Computational Linguistics (EACL '06), Trento, Italy, 2006, pp. 401-408.

[9] Vishwanathan, S. V. N. & Smola, A. (2003). Fast Kernels for String and Tree Matching. In Advances In Neural Information Processing Systems 15, 2003, pp. 569-576.

[10] Eugene, E. L., Anderson, S., Jr. Dwight D., & Douglas Wingate, J. (2004). Glossary of linguistic terms. Camp Wisdom Road Dallas: SIL International , 2004.

[11] Chapman, W., Bridewell, W., Hanbury, P., Cooper, G. F., & Buchanan, B. G. (2002). Evaluation of Negation Phrases in Narrative Clinical Reports, 2002.

[12] Segura-Bedmar, I., Mart, P. (2011). The 1st DDIExtraction-2011 Challenge Task: Extraction of Drug-Drug Interactions from Biomedical Texts. CEUR-WS, vol. 761, pp. 1-9.

[13] Wishart, D. S. et al. (2007). DrugBank: a knowledgebase for drugs, drug actions and drug targets," Nucleic acids research, 2007.

[14] Thomas, P., Neves, M. , Solt, I. , Tikk, D. & Leser, U. (2011). Relation Extraction for Drug-Drug Interactions using Ensemble Learning. In Proceedings of the First Challenge task on Drug-Drug Interaction Extraction (DDIExtraction 2011), 2011, pp. 11-18.

[15] Segura-Bedmar, I. , Martinez, P. & Herrero-Zazo, M. (2013). SemEval-2013 Task 9 : Extraction of Drug-Drug Interactions from Biomedical Texts (DDIExtraction 2013). In Second Joint Conference on Lexical and Computational Semantics (*SEM), Volume 2: Seventh International Workshop on Semantic Evaluation (SemEval 2013), Atlanta, USA, 2013, pp. 341-350.

[16] Bokharaeian, B. & Diaz, A. (2013). NIL UCM: Extracting Drug-Drug interactions from text through combination of sequence and tree kernels. In Second Joint Conference on Lexical and Computational Semantics (*SEM), Atlanta, Georgia, USA, 2013, pp. 644.

[17] Airola A. et al. (2008). All-paths graph kernel for protein-protein interaction extraction with evaluation of cross-corpus learning. BMC bioinformatics, vol. 9 Suppl 11, 2008.

[18] Chowdhury, Md., Faisal, M. & Lavelli, A. (2013). Exploiting the Scope of Negations and Heterogeneous Features for Relation Extraction: A Case Study for Drug-Drug Interaction Extraction. In Proceedings of the 2013 Conference of the North American Chapter of the Association for Computational Linguistics: Human Language Technologies, Atlanta, Georgia, June 2013, pp. 765-771.

[19] Blasco, G., Santiago S. M Mola-Velasco, Danger, R. & Rosso, P. (2011). Automatic drug-drug interaction detection: A machine learning approach with maximal frequent sequence extraction. Interactions, vol. 2397, no. 755, p. 3152.

[20] Danger, R., Segura-Bedmar, I., Martinez, P., & Rosso, P. (2010). A comparison of machine learning techniques for detection of drug target articles. Journal of biomedical informatics, vol. 43, no. 6, pp. 902-913.

[21] Chowdhury, F., Lavelli, A. & Kessler, F. (2013). Exploiting the Scope of Negations and Heterogeneous Features for Relation Extraction: A Case Study for

Drug-Drug Interaction Extraction. In HLT-NAACL13, 2013, pp. 765-771.

[22] Szarvas, G., Vincze, V., Farkas, R. & Csirik, J. (2008). The BioScope corpus: annotation for negation, uncertainty and their scope in biomedical texts. In Proceedings of the Workshop on Current Trends in Biomedical Natural Language Processing, 2008, pp. 38-45.

[23] Vincze, V., Szarvas, G., Mora, G., Ohta, T., & Farkas, R. (2011). Linguistic scope-based and biological event-based speculation and negation annotations in the BioScope and Genia Event corpora. Journal of Biomedical Semantics, vol. 2, no. Suppl 5, p. S8, 2011.

[24] Siddharthan, A. (2014). A survey of research on text simplification. The International Journal of Applied Linguistics, pp. 259-98.

[25] Peng, Y., Tudor, C. O., Torii, M., Wu, C. H. & Vijay-Shanker, K. (2012). iSimp: A sentence simplification system for biomedicail text. In Bioinformatics and Biomedicine (BIBM), 2012 IEEE International Conference on, Oct 2012, pp. 1-6.

[26] Segura-Bedmar, I., Martinez, P. & Pablo-Sanchez, C. (2011). A linguistic rule-based approach to extract drug-drug interactions from pharmacological documents. BMC Bioinformatics, vol. 12, no. Suppl 2, p. S1.

[27] Bokharaeian, B., Diaz, A., Neves, M., & Francisco,V. (2014). Exploring Negation Annotations in the DrugDDI Corpus. In Proceedings of the Fourth Workshop on Building and Evaluating Resources for Health and Biomedical Text Processing, 2014, pp. 84-91.

[28] Segura-Bedmar, I., Martinez, P. & de Pablo-S, C. (2011). Using a Shallow Linguistic Kernel for Drug-Drug Interaction Extraction. Journal of Biomedical Informatics, vol. In Press, Corrected Proof, 2011.

[29] Joachims, T. (1999). Making large scale SVM learning practical. Universitat Dortmund, Tech. rep. 1999.

[30] McClosky, D., Surdeanu, M., & Manning, C. (2011). Event Extraction As Dependency Parsing for BioNLP 2011. In Proceedings of the BioNLP Shared Task 2011 Workshop, Stroudsburg, PA, USA, 2011, pp. 41-45.

[31] Pakzad, A. & Minaei Bidgoli, B. (2016). An improved joint model: POS tagging and dependency parsing. Journal of Artificial Intelligence & Data Mining, vol. 4, no. 1, pp. 1-8.

17

Feature reduction of hyperspectral images: Discriminant analysis and the first principal component

M. Imani and H. Ghassemian[*]

Faculty of Electrical & Computer Engineering, Tarbiat Modares University, Tehran, Iran

*Corresponding author: ghassemi@modares.ac.ir (H. Ghassemian).

Abstract

When the number of training samples is limited, feature reduction plays an important role in classification of hyperspectral images. In this paper, we propose a supervised feature extraction method based on discriminant analysis (DA) which uses the first principal component (PC1) to weight the scatter matrices. The proposed method, called DA-PC1, copes with the small sample size problem and has not the limitation of linear discriminant analysis (LDA) in the number of extracted features. In DA-PC1, the dominant structure of distribution is preserved by PC1 and the class separability is increased by DA. The experimental results show the good performance of DA-PC1 compared to some state-of-the-art feature extraction methods.

Keywords: *Discriminant Analysis, Principal Component, Feature Reduction, Hyperspectral, Classification.*

1. Introduction

Due to the recent advances of remote sensing instruments, hyperspectral imaging has become a fast growing technique in the field of remote sensing [1]. Hyperspectral imaging sensors with acquiring a large number of spectral bands allows us to better distinguish many subtle objects and materials [2]. An important application of hyperspectral imaging is image classification [3-6]. However, as the inputs of hyperspectral datasets are high-dimensional vectors whose coordinates are highly correlated, the direct use of classical models for hyperspectral image classification faces several difficulties particularly when the number of available training samples is limited. With a fixed number of training samples, hyperspectral image classification accuracy can first increase as the dimensionality of data increases, but decays with the dimensionality higher than some optimum value. In other words, Hughes phenomenon occurs [7]. One of the main approaches to mitigate this problem is dimensionality reduction [8-11].

Feature reduction can be done with feature selection or feature extraction. In feature selection approaches, just an appropriate subset of original features is selected usually using a discrimination criterion and a search algorithm [12-18]. Thus, the physical meaning of data is preserved using the feature selection. However, in the feature extraction method, a linear or nonlinear transformation is applied to the original features to extract some new features [19-26]. Depending on the use of labeled samples for training feature extraction, theses techniques are divided into supervised ones, which use the class label information, and unsupervised ones, which do not use the class label information for training.

Principal component analysis (PCA) and linear discriminant analysis (LDA) are the most widely used unsupervised and supervised linear feature extraction methods, respectively [27]. PCA finds the principal components in accordance with the maximum variance of a data matrix. Thus, after such a transformation, the dominant structure of the distribution can be well preserved in the reduced subspace. The generated principal components are linear combination of the original features and are uncorrelated. PCA searches directions with a large variance in the data and subsequently projects data onto it. The position of data in the reduced feature space may be inappropriate to distinguish between classes to have a good classification. LDA utilizes the label information to infer class separability. LDA seeks projection directions on which the ratio of the between-class scatter to within-class scatter is maximized. Some difficulties with LDA method are as follows. When the number of training samples is limited, the accurate estimate of scatter matrices may not be obtained and the within-class scatter matrix becomes singular. Thus LDA has no reasonable performance in small sample size situation. Moreover, LDA can extract maximum $c - 1$ features (c is the number of classes) which is not always sufficient for representing the original data.

As the generalized discriminant analysis (GDA) provides a mapping of input vectors into a high dimensional feature space, it can deal with nonlinear discriminant analysis using kernel function operator [28]. Using a different kernel, one can cover a wide class of nonlinearities. GDA, which is the kernelized version of LDA, can extract maximum $c - 1$ features. Nonparametric weighted feature extraction (NWFE) has been proposed for improving LDA [29]. To put different weights on samples to compute the weighted means, defining new nonparametric between-class and within-class scatter matrices to obtain more than $c - 1$ features is the main idea of NWFE. In order to alleviate the negative influence of outliers in class-mean based methods, authors in [30] have proposed a novel linear dimensionality reduction technique called median–mean line based discriminant analysis (MMLDA) method. They rectify to some extent the position of the class-mean caused by outliers by introducing the median–mean line as an adaptive class-prototype.

In this paper, we propose a supervised feature extraction method based on discriminant analysis (DA). The proposed method uses the first principal component (PC1) to weight scatter matrices. So, in addition to class discrimination information contained in the Fisher criterion (maximizing the between-class scatter and minimizing the within-class scatter), the proposed method can use the data representation and reconstruction information to preserve the main structure of original data in the reduced subspace. Moreover, the non-parametric form of scatter matrices and the use of regularization method help to extraction of more than $c - 1$ features and also to solve the singularity problem.

We introduce the proposed method in section 2, called DA-PC1, with more details. Then, in section 3, the extensive experiments show that the proposed method outperforms popular feature extraction methods in terms of classification accuracy. Finally, the conclusions are discussed in section 4.

2. DA-PC1

The proposed feature extraction method, DA-PC1, uses the discriminant analysis to increase the separability between classes. DA-PC1 maximizes the between-class scatter matrix and minimizes the within-class scatter matrix. It defines the weighted non-parametric scatter matrices to provide three main advantages: 1- DA-PC1 copes with the singularity problem of within-class scatter matrix in the small sample size situation. 2- It can extract more than $c - 1$ features where c is the number of classes. 3- In addition to class discrimination information, it uses the reconstruction information contained in the first principal component for weighting the scatter matrices. In the first step, we compute the first principal component (PC1) of data. For reaching this purpose, we estimate the covariance matrix of data as follows:

$$\Sigma_x = \frac{1}{N-1}\sum_{i=1}^{N}(x_i - \overline{x})(x_i - \overline{x})^T \qquad (1)$$

where, $x_i \in \mathcal{R}^d$ ($i = 1, 2, ..., N$) is the ith pixel of hyperspectral image, d is the number of spectral bands, N is the total number of samples (pixels) and $\overline{x}$ is the total mean of data that is given by:

$$\overline{x} = \frac{1}{N}\sum_{i=1}^{N} x_i \qquad (2)$$

The PC1 is obtained by using the eigenvector v_1 correspondence with the largest eigenvalue of Σ_x. Then, we have:

$$PC1(x_i) = v_1^T x_i \; ; \; (i = 1, 2, ..., N) \qquad (3)$$

The between-class scatter matrix (S_b) and the within-class scatter matrix (S_w) are calculated as follows:

$$S_w = \sum_{j=1}^{n}\sum_{\substack{i=1 \\ l_i = l_j}}^{n} w_{ij}(x_{ti} - x_{tj})(x_{ti} - x_{tj})^T \qquad (4)$$

$$S_b = \sum_{j=1}^{n}\sum_{\substack{i=1 \\ l_i \neq l_j}}^{n} w_{ij}(x_{ti} - x_{tj})(x_{ti} - x_{tj})^T \qquad (5)$$

where, x_{ti} ($i = 1, 2, ..., n$) is the i th training sample, n is the total number of training samples and $l_i \in \{1, 2, ..., c\}$ is the class label of sample x_{ti}, and c is the number of classes.

The closer the principal components of two samples x_{ti} and x_{tj} are, the larger weight w_{ij} will be. Thus, the weight w_{ij} ($i = 1, ..., n; j = 1, ..., n$) is calculated as follows:

$$w_{ij} = \frac{1}{\left|PC1(x_{ti})-PC1(x_{tj})\right|^2+1} \qquad (6)$$

The number one is added to the denominator because w_{ij} should not be infinite. In above equation, we have:

$$PC1(x_{ti}) = v_1^T x_{ti} \; ; \; (i = 1, 2, ..., n) \qquad (7)$$

To degrade the singularity problem and thus, to increase the classification accuracy, we regularize the matrix S_w as follows:

$$S_w = 0.5S_w + 0.5 diag(S_w) \qquad (8)$$

Because of non-parametric form of S_w and also with the regularization of it, DA-PC1 copes with the singularity problem in small sample size situation. Because of non-parametric form of S_b, DA-PC1 can extract more than $c - 1$ features. DA-PC1 uses both the information contained in the DA and PC1. DA-PC1 increases the class separability using DA. Moreover, the PC1, which is in accordance with the maximum variance of data matrix, can preserve the dominant structure of distribution in the reduced subspace after transformation.

3. Experiments and results

The performance of DA-PC1 is compared with LDA, NWFE, GDA, MMLDA, and PCA. To assess the performance of classification, we use the accuracy and reliability of classes, the average accuracy, the average reliability, kappa coefficient [31] and also the McNemar test results [32]. The definitions of these measures are represented below.

The accuracy (Acc.) and reliability (Rel.) for each class are defined as $Acc = \gamma/\alpha$ and $Rel = \gamma/\beta$ respectively where γ is the number of testing samples that are correctly classified, α denotes the total testing samples of class and β is the total samples which are labeled as this class. The kappa coefficient is defined as follows:

$$Kappa = \frac{N\sum_{k=1}^{c} t_{kk} - \sum_{k=1}^{c} t_{k+}t_{+k}}{N^2 - \sum_{k=1}^{c} t_{k+}t_{+k}} \qquad (9)$$

where, N and c denote the number of testing samples and the number of classes, respectively. t_{kk} is the number of samples correctly classified in class k, t_{k+} is the number of testing samples labeled as class k, and t_{+k} is the number of samples predicted as belonging to class k. The McNemar test is used to assess the statistical significance of differences in classification results. The parameter Z_{12} in McNemar test is defined as follows:

$$Z_{12} = \frac{f_{12}-f_{21}}{\sqrt{f_{12}+f_{21}}} \qquad (10)$$

where, f_{12} is the number of samples which are labeled correctly by classifier 1 and incorrectly by classifier 2. The difference in the accuracy between two classifiers is said to be statistically significant if $|Z_{12}| > 1.96$. If classifier 1 is more accurate than classifier 2, we have $Z_{12} > 0$ and otherwise $Z_{12} < 0$.

Kennedy Space Center (KSC) was acquired by the NASA Airborne Visible/Infrared Imaging Spectrometer (AVIRIS) instrument over the KSC, Florida, on March 23, 1996. It contains 13 ground-truth classes and 512×614 pixels. This hyperspectral image has 224 spectral channels which after discarding water absorption and noisy bands, 176 bands are retained. Indian Pines dataset was acquired by the AVIRIS sensor in 1992. This image scene contains 145×145 pixels and 16 classes which 10 classes of it are chosen for our experiments. The Indian dataset has 220 spectral bands, where 20 bands were discarded because of the atmospheric affection. The Pavia University dataset was provided by the Reflective Optics System Imaging Spectrometer (ROSIS) with a spatial resolution of $1.3\,m$ per pixel. The number of spectral channels in the original recorded image is 115 (with a spectral range from 0.43 to $0.86\,\mu m$) which after the removal of the noisy bands, 103 spectral bands are selected. This urban image contains nine classes and 610×340 pixels.

We used three different classifiers for classification of reduced datasets: support vector machine (SVM), maximum likelihood (ML), and nearest neighbor (NN). The Gaussian distribution is assumed for datasets in ML classifier. We use the Radial basis function (RBF) kernel and the one-against-one multiclass classification algorithm for SVM classification. We test the penalty parameter C of SVM between [10– 1000] with a step size increment of 20 and the γ parameter of the RBF kernel between [0.1– 2] with a step size increment of 0.1. The best values of free parameters are obtained using a 5-fold cross validation approach.

The training samples are chosen randomly from entire datasets and the remaining samples are used for testing. Each experiment is repeated 10 times, with different random training samples in each time, and the average results are reported.

The average classification accuracies versus the number of extracted features are shown in figure 1 for Indian dataset with a) SVM classifier, 10 training samples, b) ML classifier, 10 training samples, c) NN classifier, 10 training samples, d)

SVM classifier, 15 training samples, e) ML classifier, 15 training samples, f) NN classifier, 15 training samples, g) SVM classifier, 30 training samples, h) ML classifier, 30 training samples, i) NN classifier, 30 training samples, j) SVM classifier, 60 training samples, k) ML classifier, 60 training samples, l) NN classifier, 60 training samples. In most cases, the better performance of DA-PC1 compared to other feature extraction methods can be seen.

Figure 1 shows that the efficiency of LDA using just 10 and 15 training samples is very weak because of singularity of within-class scatter matrix. Moreover, LDA and GDA can extract maximum $c - 1 = 9$ features which are insufficient in some cases for accurate classification of data.

The classification accuracies of reduced data in different number of extracted features with using 15 training samples per class for KSC dataset obtained by a) SVM classifier, b) ML classifier, and c) NN classifier are shown in figure 2. The accuracy and reliability of classes obtained by 15 training samples and SVM classifier are represented for Indian (with 6 extracted features) and KSC (with 8 extracted features) datasets in table 1 and table 2, respectively.

The McNemar test results and the ground truth map (GTM) and the classification maps of theses cases are shown in table 3, figures 3, and 4, respectively.

In table 3, Z_{rc} denotes each case of table where r is the row and c is the column. The highest classification accuracies are represented in table 4. The numbers in the parentheses are the number of features which achieve the highest average classification accuracy in each method. In most cases, DA-PC1 obtains the maximum classification accuracy compared to other methods.

Just in the following cases, other feature extraction methods obtain more classification accuracy compared to the proposed method. In Pavia University dataset, with using ML classifier, the best classification accuracy is obtained by GDA, MMLDA, and PCA methods and with using NN classifier, MMLDA obtains the best result for this dataset.

Moreover, in KSC dataset, with using ML classifier, the maximum classification accuracy is obtained by GDA. In figure 5, we compare the performance of DA-PC1 with PCA and LDA in a fixed number of extracted features with varying the number of training samples from 5 to 130

samples per class, for Indian dataset with a) SVM classifier and 6 extracted features, b) ML classifier and 5 extracted features, c) NN classifier and 9 extracted features. The following points can be concluded from the results of this experiment:

1) When the training set is small, PCA works better than LDA and when the training set is large, LDA works better than PCA.

2) When the number of training samples is limited, DA-PC1 is superior to both the PCA and LDA and when the high number of training samples is available, with using SVM and NN classifiers, LDA outperforms DA-PC1. However, in this case, DA-PC1 has yet reasonable performance.

3) With using ML classifier, the performance of DA-PC1 is better than PCA and LDA in both cases of small and large training set.

In general, when we use the parametric classifiers such as ML, which need to calculate the mean vectors and covariance matrices of classes and have more sensitivity to the training set, the use of DA-PC1 is preferable compared to PCA and LDA whether the training set size is small or large. But, when we use the non-parametric classifiers such as SVM and NN, which have the less sensitivity to the number of training samples, DA-PC1 is preferable using small training set and LDA is preferable with large training set.

4. Conclusion

In this paper, the DA-PC1 method is proposed for feature extraction of hyperspectral images. In DA-PC1, the first principal components of training samples are used for weighting of scatter matrices in the DA. Thus, in addition to increasing the class separability, the signal representation in the reduced subspace may be improved.

The experimental results show that with using parametric classifiers such as ML, the use of DA-PC1 is superior to PCA and LDA whether the training set size is small or large. Also, with using non-parametric classifiers such as SVM and NN, the use of DA-PC1 is superior to PCA and LDA with a small training sample size. Moreover, the comparison of DA-PC1 with the state-of-the-art feature extraction methods such as NWFE, GDA, and MMLDA shows the better performance of DA-PC1 for feature reduction and classification of hyperspectral images particularly in small sample size situation.

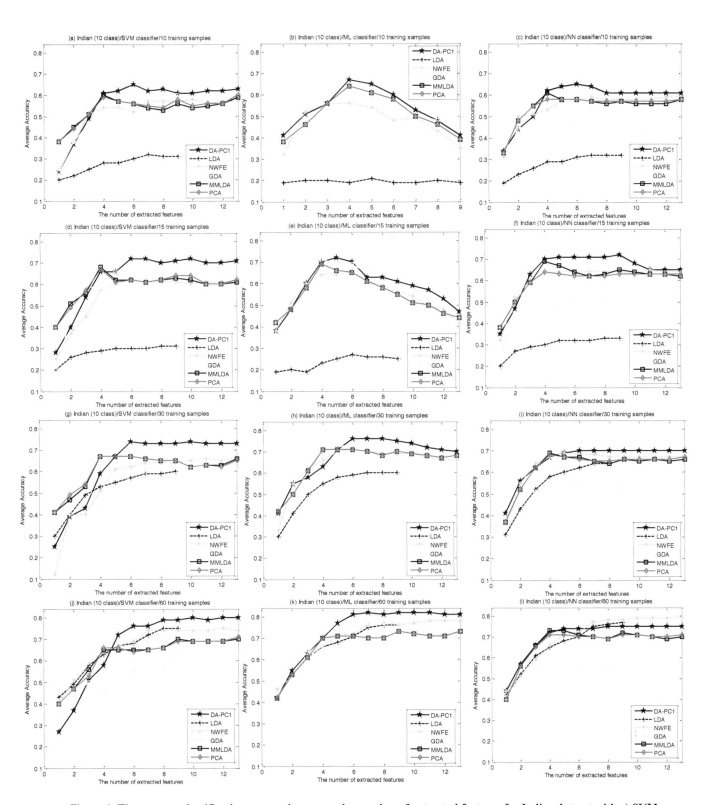

Figure 1. The average classification accuracies versus the number of extracted features for Indian dataset with a) SVM classifier, 10 training samples, b) ML classifier, 10 training samples, c) NN classifier, 10 training samples, d) SVM classifier, 15 training samples, e) ML classifier, 15 training samples, f) NN classifier, 15 training samples, g) SVM classifier, 30 training samples, h) ML classifier, 30 training samples, i) NN classifier, 30 training samples, j) SVM classifier, 60 training samples, k) ML classifier, 60 training samples, l) NN classifier, 60 training samples.

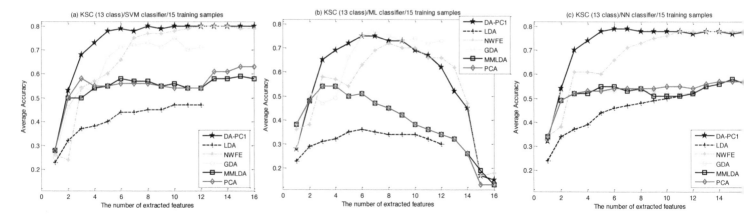

Figure 2. The average classification accuracies versus the number of extracted features for KSC dataset using 15 training samples obtained by a) SVM classifier, b) ML classifier, and c) NN classifier.

Table 1. The accuracy and reliability of classes of Indian dataset obtained by SVM classifier, 15 training samples and 6 extracted features.

No	Name of class	# samples	DA-PC1 Acc.	DA-PC1 Rel.	LDA Acc.	LDA Rel.	NWFE Acc.	NWFE Rel.	GDA Acc.	GDA Rel.	MMLDA Acc.	MMLDA Rel.	PCA Acc.	PCA Rel.
1	Corn-no till	1434	0.94	0.36	0.81	0.32	0.91	0.29	0.91	0.30	0.91	0.30	0.93	0.30
2	Corn-min till	834	0.77	0.53	0.21	0.37	0.43	0.41	0.60	0.46	0.46	0.39	0.45	0.41
3	Grass/pasture	497	0.68	0.44	0.10	0.25	0.57	0.35	0.53	0.34	0.35	0.22	0.39	0.26
4	Grass/trees	747	0.76	0.41	0.42	0.05	0.53	0.47	0.53	0.40	0.61	0.49	0.60	0.53
5	Hay-windrowed	489	0.79	0.62	0.42	0.47	0.74	0.57	0.45	0.65	0.79	0.45	0.78	0.45
6	Soybeans-no till	968	0.66	0.87	0.34	0.49	0.79	0.83	0.83	0.79	0.58	0.79	0.60	0.78
7	Soybeans-min till	2468	1.00	0.54	0.92	0.13	1.00	0.51	0.35	0.12	1.00	0.32	1.00	0.42
8	Soybeans-clean till	614	0.78	1.00	0.45	0.99	0.78	0.99	0.73	0.95	0.72	0.99	0.73	1.00
9	Woods	1294	0.95	0.20	1.00	0.02	0.95	0.13	0.95	0.50	0.95	0.36	1.00	0.42
10	Bldg-Grass-Tree-Drives	380	0.53	0.59	0.33	0.20	0.58	0.39	0.63	0.47	0.55	0.51	0.55	0.50
	Average Acc. and Average Rel.		0.72	0.68	0.30	0.31	0.62	0.59	0.64	0.62	0.62	0.60	0.62	0.60
	Kappa coefficient		0.60		0.19		0.51		0.56		0.54		0.54	

Table 2. The accuracy and reliability of classes of KSC dataset obtained by SVM classifier, 15 training samples and 8 extracted features.

No	Name of class	# samples	DA-PC1 Acc.	DA-PC1 Rel.	LDA Acc.	LDA Rel.	NWFE Acc.	NWFE Rel.	GDA Acc.	GDA Rel.	MMLDA Acc.	MMLDA Rel.	PCA Acc.	PCA Rel.
1	Scrub	761	0.80	0.95	0.50	0.59	0.67	0.96	0.77	0.91	0.72	0.93	0.68	0.92
2	Willow swamp	243	0.87	0.86	0.42	0.54	0.88	0.91	0.84	0.84	0.68	0.46	0.67	0.48
3	Cabbage palm hammock	256	0.88	0.80	0.29	0.26	0.82	0.81	0.87	0.76	0.72	0.74	0.59	0.75
4	Cabbage palm/oak hammock	252	0.56	0.52	0.11	0.23	0.70	0.44	0.50	0.32	0.25	0.30	0.30	0.31
5	Slash pine	161	0.63	0.43	0.24	0.25	0.42	0.42	0.30	0.30	0.40	0.30	0.43	0.26
6	Oak/broadleaf hammock	229	0.59	0.52	0.54	0.19	0.45	0.32	0.20	0.26	0.38	0.29	0.35	0.28
7	Hardwood swamp	105	0.93	0.64	0.51	0.27	0.90	0.75	0.85	0.76	0.48	0.41	0.49	0.46
8	Graminoid marsh	431	0.67	0.79	0.55	0.47	0.83	0.69	0.82	0.75	0.41	0.35	0.28	0.30
9	Spartina marsh	520	0.93	0.73	0.20	0.43	0.82	0.82	0.91	0.77	0.79	0.69	0.85	0.62
10	Cattail marsh	404	0.82	0.97	0.73	0.88	0.74	0.96	0.72	0.87	0.39	0.42	0.42	0.42
11	Salt marsh	419	0.98	0.95	0.47	0.31	0.99	0.85	0.93	0.95	0.94	0.92	0.93	0.87
12	Mud flats	503	0.80	0.96	0.33	0.45	0.79	0.91	0.75	0.89	0.27	0.44	0.29	0.46
13	Water	927	0.98	1.00	0.93	0.97	0.98	0.99	0.98	0.98	0.94	0.92	0.96	0.98
	Average Acc. and Average Rel.		0.80	0.78	0.45	0.45	0.77	0.76	0.73	0.72	0.57	0.55	0.56	0.55
	Kappa coefficient		0.81		0.46		0.78		0.77		0.59		0.59	

Table 3. The values of parameter Z obtained by McNemar test.

Indian/ SVM classifier/15 training samples/ 6 features							KSC/ SVM classifier/15 training samples/ 8 features					
	DA-PC1	LDA	NWFE	GDA	MMLDA	PCA		DA-PC1	LDA	NWFE	GDA	MMLDA	PCA
DA-PC1	0	48.92	15.65	6.15	9.63	9.27	DA-PC1	0	35.74	5.93	7.75	27.62	28.83
LDA	-48.92	0	-38.58	-44.26	-42.58	-42.77	LDA	-35.74	0	-32.18	-30.94	-13.80	-12.92
NWFE	-15.65	38.58	0	-8.40	-5.95	-6.33	NWFE	-5.93	32.18	0	2.00	22.44	23.59
GDA	-6.15	44.26	8.40	0	3.00	2.66	GDA	-7.75	30.94	-2.00	0	21.73	22.80
MMLDA	-9.63	42.58	5.95	-3.00	0	-1.23	MMLDA	-27.62	13.80	-22.44	-21.73	0	1.53
PCA	-9.27	42.77	6.33	-2.66	1.23	0	PCA	-28.83	12.92	-23.59	-22.80	-1.53	0

GTM   DA-PC1   LDA   NWFE   GDA   MMLDA   PCA

Figure 3. GTM and the classification maps of Indian dataset obtained by SVM classifier, 15 training samples and 6 extracted features.

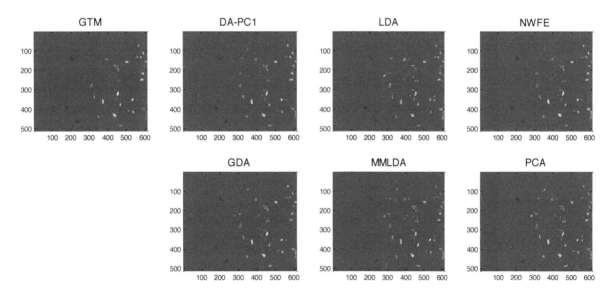

Figure 4. GTM and the classification maps of KSC dataset obtained by SVM classifier, 15 training samples and 8 extracted features.

Table 4. The highest classification accuracies achieved by 15 training samples.

Dataset	Classifier	DA-PC1	LDA	NWFE	GDA	MMLDA	PCA
Indian	SVM	**0.72 (6)**	0.31 (8)	0.62 (6)	0.66 (5)	0.68 (4)	0.67 (4)
	ML	**0.72 (5)**	0.27 (6)	0.65 (6)	0.71 (4)	0.69 (4)	0.69 (4)
	NN	**0.72 (9)**	0.33 (8)	0.65 (11)	0.49 (6)	0.69 (4)	0.64 (4)
Pavia University	SVM	**0.79 (6)**	0.53 (6)	0.74 (12)	0.74 (6)	**0.79 (11)**	0.77 (11)
	ML	0.80 (6)	0.49 (5)	0.79 (3)	**0.81 (4)**	**0.81 (4)**	**0.81 (4)**
	NN	0.78 (6)	0.57 (5)	0.76 (10)	0.73 (8)	**0.80 (11)**	0.77 (5)
KSC	SVM	**0.80 (8)**	0.47 (10)	**0.80 (12)**	0.75 (10)	0.59 (15)	0.63 (15)
	ML	0.75 (6)	0.36 (6)	0.72 (8)	**0.77 (7)**	0.54 (3)	0.54 (3)
	NN	**0.79 (6)**	0.52 (12)	0.78 (11)	0.54 (7)	0.58 (15)	0.57 (14)

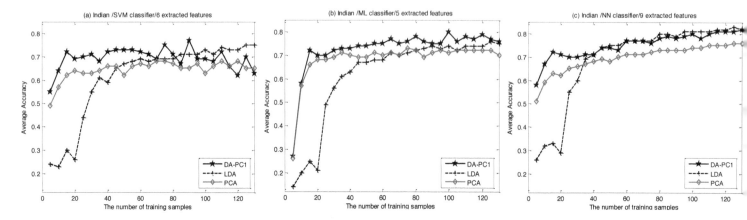

Figure 5. The comparison of performance of DA-PC1 with PCA and LDA in a fixed number of extracted features with varying the number of training samples for Indian dataset with a) SVM classifier and 6 extracted features, b) ML classifier and 5 extracted features, c) NN classifier and 9 extracted features.

References

[1] Richards, J. A. & Jia, X. (2006). Remote sensing digital image analysis, 4th Ed. New York: Springer Verlagl.

[2] Antonio, P., Jon, A. B., Joseph, W. B., Jason, B., Lorenzo, B., Gustavo, C., Jocelyn, C., Mathieu, F., Paolo, G., Anthony, G., Mattia, M., James, C. T. & Giovanna, T. (2009). Recent Advances in Techniques for Hyperspectral Image Processing. Remote Sensing of Environment, vol. 113, no.1, pp. S110-S122.

[3] Benediktsson, J. A., Pesaresi, M. & Amason, K. (2003). Classification and Feature Extraction for Remote Sensing Images From Urban Areas Based on Morphological Transformations. IEEE Transactions on Geoscience and Remote Sensing, vol. 41, no. 9, pp. 1940–1949.

[4] Yanfei, Z. & Liangpei, Z. (2012). An Adaptive Artificial Immune Network for Supervised Classification Of Multi-/Hyperspectral Remote Sensing Imagery. IEEE Transactions on Geoscience and Remote Sensing, vol. 50, no. 3, pp. 894–909.

[5] Moser, G. & Serpico, S. B. (2013). Combining Support Vector Machines and Markov Random Fields in an Integrated Framework for Contextual Image Classification. IEEE Transactions on Geoscience and Remote Sensing, vol. 51, no. 5, pp. 2734–2752.

[6] Demir, B. & Ertürk, S. (2009). Clustering-Based Extraction of Border Training Patterns for Accurate SVM Classification of Hyperspectral Images. IEEE Geoscience and Remote Sensing Letters, vol. 6, no. 4, pp. 840 - 844.

[7] Hughes, G. F. (1968). On The Mean Accuracy of Statistical Pattern Recognition. IEEE Transactions on Information Theory, vol. IT-14, no. 1, pp. 55–63.

[8] Korycinski, D. , Crawford, M. , Barnes, J. W. & Ghosh, J. (2003). Adaptive Feature Selection for Hyperspectral Data Analysis Using A Binary Hierarchical Classifier and Tabu Search. IEEE Symposium on Geoscience and Remote Sensing, Toulouse, France, 2003.

[9] Li, S., Wu, H., Wan, D. & Zhu, J. (2011). An Effective Feature Selection Method for Hyperspectral Image Classification Based on Genetic Algorithm and Support Vector Machine. Knowledge-Based Systems, vol. 24, no. 1, pp. 40-48.

[10] Yin, J., Wang, Y. & Hu, J. (2012). A New Dimensionality Reduction Algorithm for Hyperspectral Image Data Using Evolutionary Strategy. IEEE Transactions on Industrial Informatics, vol. 8, no. 4, pp. 935–943.

[11] Jia, X., Kuo, B. C. & Crawford, M. (2013). Feature Mining for Hyperspectral Image Classification. Proceedings of the IEEE, vol. 101, no. 3, pp. 676-697.

[12] Zhang, Q., Tian, Y., Yang, Y. & Pan, C. (2015). Automatic Spatial–Spectral Feature Selection for Hyperspectral Image via Discriminative Sparse Multimodal Learning. IEEE Transactions on Geoscience and Remote Sensing, vol. 53, no. 1, pp. 261-279.

[13] Li, S. & Wei, D. (2014). Extremely High Dimensional Feature Selection via Feature Generating Samplings. IEEE Transactions on Cybernetics, vol. 44, no. 6, pp. 737-747.

[14] Ladha, L. & Deepa, T. (2011). Feature Selection Methods and Algorithms. International Journal on Computer Science and Engineering, vol. 3, no. 5, pp. 1787–1797.

[15] Serpico, S. B. & Bruzzone, L. (2001). A New Search Algorithm for Feature Selection in Hyperspectral Remote Sensing Images. IEEE Transactions on Geoscience and Remote Sensing, vol. 39, no. 7, pp. 1360–1367.

[16] Peng, H., Long, F. & Ding, C. (2005). Feature Selection Based on Mutual Information: Criteria of Max Dependency, Max-Relevance, and Min-Redundancy. IEEE Transactions on Pattern Analysis and Machine Intelligence, vol. 27, no. 8, pp. 1226-1238.

[17] Liu, X., Wang, L., Zhang, J., Yin, J. & Liu, H. (2014). Global and Local Structure Preservation for Feature Selection. IEEE Transactions on Neural Networks and Learning Systems, vol. 25, no. 6, pp. 1083–1095.

[18] Yuan, Y., Zhu, G. & Wang, Q. (2015). Hyperspectral Band Selection by Multitask Sparsity Pursuit. IEEE Transactions on Geoscience and Remote Sensing, vol. 53, no. 2, pp. 631–644.

[19] Imani, M. & Ghassemian, H. (2014). Band Clustering-Based Feature Extraction for Classification of Hyperspectral Images Using Limited Training Samples. IEEE Geoscience and Remote Sensing Letters, vol. 11, no. 8, 1325 – 1329.

[20] Jia, Y.-f., Li, Y.-j., Fu, P.-b. & Tian, Y. (2015). Nearest Feature Line and Point Embedding for Hyperspectral Image Classification. IEEE Geoscience and Remote Sensing Letters, vol. 12, no. 3, pp. 651-655.

[21] Kang, X., Li, S., Fang, L. & Benediktsson, J. A. (2015). Intrinsic Image Decomposition for Feature Extraction of Hyperspectral Images. IEEE Transactions on Geoscience and Remote Sensing, vol. 53, no. 4, pp. 2241-2253.

[22] Imani, M. & Ghassemian, H. (2014). Feature Extraction Using Attraction Points for Classification of Hyperspectral Images in a Small Sample Size Situation. IEEE Geoscience and Remote Sensing Letters, vol. 11, no. 11, pp. 1986 - 1990.

[23] Dhanjal, C., Gunn, S. R. & Shawe-Taylor, J. (2009). Efficient Sparse Kernel Feature Extraction Based on Partial Least Squares. IEEE Transactions on Pattern Analysis and Machine Intelligence, vol. 31, no. 8, pp. 1347-1361.

[24] Kamandar, M. & Ghassemian, H. (2013). Linear Feature Extraction for Hyperspectral Images Based on Information Theoretic Learning. IEEE Geoscience and Remote Sensing Letters, vol. 10, no. 4, pp. 702 - 706.

[25] Xia, J., Chanussot, J., Du, P. & He, X. (2015). Spectral–Spatial Classification for Hyperspectral Data Using Rotation Forests with Local Feature Extraction and Markov Random Fields. IEEE Transactions on Geoscience and Remote Sensing, vol. 53, no. 5, pp. 2532–2546.

[26] Imani, M. & Ghassemian, H. (2015). Feature Space Discriminant Analysis for Hyperspectral Data Feature Reduction. ISPRS Journal of Photogrammetry and Remote Sensing, vol. 102, pp. 1 – 13.

[27] Fukunaga, K. (1990). Introduction to statistical pattern recognition. San Diego, CA. USA: Academic.

[28] Baudat, G. & Anouar, F. (2000). Generalized Discriminant Analysis Using a Kernel Approach. Neural Computation, vol. 12, pp. 2385–2404.

[29] Kuo, B. C. & Landgrebe, D. A. (2004). Nonparametric Weighted Feature Extraction for Classification. IEEE Transactions on Geoscience and Remote Sensing, vol. 42, no. 5, pp. 1096-1105.

[30] Xu, J., Yang, J., Gu, Z. & Zhang, N. (2014). Median–mean Line Based Discriminant Analysis. Neurocomputing, vol. 123, pp. 233–246.

[31] Cohen, J. (1960). A Coefficient of Agreement From Nominal Scales. Educational and Psychological Measurements, vol. 20, no. 1, pp. 37–46.

[32] Foody, G. M. (2004). Thematic Map Comparison: Evaluating the Statistical Significance of Differences in Classification Accuracy. Photogrammetric Engineering and Remote Sensing, vol. 70, no. 5, pp. 627–633.

18

Face Recognition using an Affine Sparse Coding approach

M. Nikpour[1], M.- R Karami[1*] and R. Ghaderi[2]

1. Electrical and Computer Engineering Department, Babol Noushirvani University of Technology, Babol, Iran.
2. Nuclear Engineering Department, Shahid Beheshti University of Tehran, Tehran, Iran.

*Corresponding author: Mkarami@nit.ac.ir (M.Karami).

Abstract
Sparse coding is an unsupervised method that learns a set of over-complete bases to represent the data such as image and video. Sparse coding has had an increasing attraction for image classification applications in the recent years. However in the cases where there are some similar images from different classes, such as face recognition applications, different images may be classified into the same class, and hence the classification performance may be decreased. In this paper, we propose an Affine Graph Regularized Sparse Coding approach for the face recognition problem. Experiments performed on several well-known face datasets show that the proposed method can significantly improve the face classification accuracy. In addition, some experiments are performed to illustrate the robustness of the proposed method to noise. The results obtained show the superiority of the proposed method in comparison to some other methods in face classification.

Keywords: *Sparse Coding, Manifold Learning, Face Recognition, Graph Regularization.*

1. Introduction

Face recognition is a significant task in image processing and computer vision studies. It is a challenging problem due to two reasons. Firstly, the face images of individual persons are mostly like each other and secondly, the face images are captured under challenging conditions like different poses, different conditions, and different illuminations [1].

Many methods have been introduced for face recognition in the recent years [2-5]. One of the appropriate methods used in this field is the sparse coding-based approach [6]. Sparse coding can represent images using a few active coefficients [7]. Accordingly, the interpretation and application of the sparse representations are easy, and simplify many image processing operations such as image classifications [8].

One of the most important targets in sparse coding applications is preserving the quality of sparse representation. In order to achieve this target, many works have been done to modify the sparsity constraint. In [9], the authors have added a nonnegative constraint to the objective function of the basis sparse coding method for improving

the sparse coding method. In [3], the authors have analyzed the working mechanism for sparse representation-based classification, and have indicated that the collaborative representation sparsity makes this method powerful for face classification.

In [10], the authors have proposed a face recognition method based on the discriminative locality preserving vectors. In [11], the authors have improved the sparse coding method by adding a Laplacian term. In [12], the authors have proposed a sparse and dense hybrid representation (SDR) framework to alleviate the problems of sparse representation-based classification (SRC).

When the images are similar, the dictionary learned from the images cannot effectively encode the manifold structure of the images, and the similar images from different classes may be classified in the same class accordingly. Many research work have been done on dictionary learning. In [13], the authors have used the Fisher discrimination dictionary learning for sparse representation. In [14], the authors obtained a robust and reliable dictionary to improve the performance of dictionary learning algorithms for face recognition. At first, the virtual face images are produced, and then an elaborate objective function is designed, and based on this objective function, they obtain an efficient algorithm to generate a robust dictionary.

Similar images lie on a manifold structure, and the images from different classes lie on different manifold structures [15]. It has been shown that if the geometrical structure is used and the local invariance is considered, the learning performance can be significantly improved. Recently, many literatures have focused on manifold learning problems, which represent the samples from different manifold structures. To preserve the geometrical information of the data, the authors in [16] have proposed to extract a good feature representation through which the manifold structure of data is spotted. The other methods such as graph regularization [11] and using weighted ℓ2-norm constraint are also introduced for improving the sparse representation. In [17], the authors have proposed a graph-based algorithm, called Graph regularized Sparse Coding (GraphSC), to give sparse representations that well-consider the local manifold structure of the data. Using Graph Laplacian as a smooth operator, the sparse representations obtained vary smoothly along the geodesics of the data manifold.

For solving the sparse coding problems, the authors in [15] have proposed a feature sign search method. This method reduces the non-differentiable problem to an unconstrained quadratic programming (QP). This problem can be solved rapidly by the optimization process. Our work also uses the feature sign search method to solve the proposed AGRSC optimization problem. For adapting the dictionary to achieve sparse representation, the authors in [18] have proposed a K-SVD method to learn the dictionary using orthogonal matching pursuit or basis pursuit.

Regarding the recent improvements in sparse coding and manifold learning, the two main problems of face recognition can still be investigated. We propose an Affine Graph Regularized Sparse Coding (AGRSC) algorithm to construct robust sparse representations for classifying similar images accurately. Specifically, the objective function of sparse coding has incorporated the Affinity term to make similar faces far from each other. Moreover, to improve the objective function with more discriminating power in data representation, we also incorporated the graph Laplacian term of coefficients in our objective function. This term

can consider the geometrical structure of the data space by taking into account the local manifold structure of the data [17]. The experimental results verify the effectiveness of our AGRSC approach.

This paper is continued as follows: In section 2, the sparse coding and graph regularized sparse coding are described. In section 3 the proposed method is introduced. The experimental setup and results are indicated in section 4 and consequently, conclusions are drawn in section 5.

2. Preliminaries

This section introduces sparse coding and affine graph regularized sparse coding which are employed in this paper.

2.1. Sparse coding

Assume a data matrix $Y = [y_1, \ldots, y_n] \in R_{m \times n}$ where n is the number of samples in the m-dimensional feature space. Let $\Phi = [\varphi_1, \ldots, \varphi_k] \in R_{m \times k}$ be the dictionary matrix where each column φ_i represents a basis vector in the dictionary, and $X = [x_1, \ldots, x_n] \in R_{k \times n}$ be the coding matrix where each column x_i is a sparse representation for a data point y_i. Assuming the reconstruction error for a data point follows a zero-mean Gaussian distribution with isotropic covariance, while taking a Laplace prior to the coding coefficients and a uniform prior to the basis vectors, the maximum posterior estimate of Φ and X given Y is reduced to:

$$(1)$$

$$\min_{\Phi, X} \|Y - \Phi X\|_F^2 + \alpha \sum_{i=1}^{n} |x_i| \quad st. \|\varphi_j\|^2 \leq c, \forall i = 1, 2, \ldots, k$$

In the above equation α is a parameter for regularizing the level of sparsity of the codes obtained and the approximation of initial data. The objective function in (1) is not convex in Φ and X, and therefore, solving the above equation is not easy in this case. However, it is convex in either Φ or X. Therefore, solving this problem is done by alternatively optimizing Φ while fixing X and vice versa. As a result, the above-mentioned problem can be split into two reduced least squares problems: an ℓ1-regularized and an ℓ2-constrained, both of which can be solved efficiently by the existing optimization software [15].

2.2. Graph regularized sparse coding

In [17], the authors have proposed a method called the Graph Regularized Sparse Coding (GraphSC) method, which considers the manifold assumption to make the basis vectors with respect to the intrinsic geometric structure underlying the input data. This method assumes that if two data points y_i and y_j are close in the intrinsic geometry of data distribution, then their codes φ_i and φ_j are also close. Consider a set of n-dimensional data points $y_1, ..., y_n$;.GraphSC constructs a p-nearest neighbor graph G with n vertices each representing a data point. Let W be the weight matrix of G, if y_i is among the p-nearest neighbor of y_j, $W_{i,j} = 1$; otherwise,

$$W_{i,j} = 0. \quad D = diag(d_1, ..., d_n), \quad d_i = \sum_{j=1}^{n} W_{ij} \quad \text{and}$$

graph Laplacian $L = D - W$. A reasonable criterion for preserving the geometric structure in graph G is to minimize:

$$\frac{1}{2}\sum_{i,j=1}^{n}\left\|x_i - x_j\right\|^2 W_{i,j} = Tr(XLX^T). \quad (2)$$

By replacing the result into (1), GraphSC [1] is obtained:

$$\min_{\Phi, X}\left(\left\|Y - \Phi X\right\|_F^2 + \gamma Tr(XLX^T) + \alpha \sum_{i=1}^{n}\left|x_i\right|\right).$$

$$st. \quad \left\|\varphi_i\right\|^2 \leq c, \forall i = 1, 2, ..., k \quad (3)$$

In (3), γ is a parameter for regularizing the weight between sparsity of the codes obtained and preserving the geometrical structure.

3. Proposed method

In this section, we present the AGRSC algorithm for robust face recognition, which extends GraphSC by taking into account the affinity constraints on the samples. In the proposed method, at first, the Histogram of Gaussian (HOG) descriptor is extracted from face images. This descriptor is used in computer vision and image processing for the purpose of object detection. The technique counts the occurrences of gradient orientation in localized portions of an image. Due to the high dimensions of the descriptors, Principle Component Analysis (PCA) is applied to reduce dimensions of the descriptors. Then the sparse codes are extracted with the proposed method and at last these codes are classified with the Support Vector Machine (SVM) classifier. In figure 1, one can see the steps involved in the proposed method.

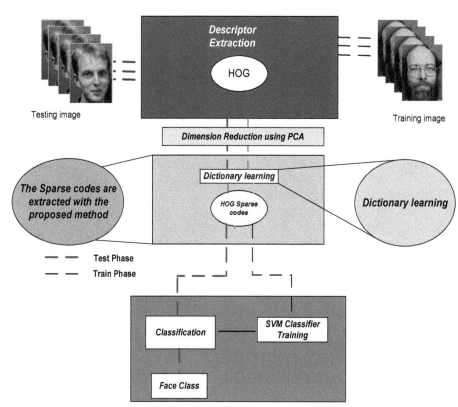

Figure 1. Diagram of proposed method for face recognition.

In the next section, before the AGRSC descriptions, we give some explanations for the HOG feature extraction.

3.2. Feature extraction

As mentioned earlier, the HOG feature is extracted for the sparse coding step. The HOG [19] characterizes the local object appearance and shape of faces by the local intensity gradients or edge direction distribution.

Assume that P is a facial image and $P(x,y)$ is the intensity of pixel at the (x,y) coordinate.

The process of HOG extraction is shown in figure 2. At first, the HOG descriptor of the facial image is divided into some blocks and each block is subdivided into smaller squares called cells.

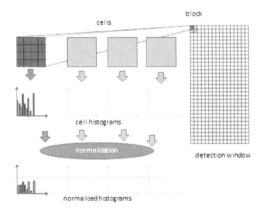

Figure 2. Extraction procedure of HOG feature

The histogram for each cell is computed using (4).

$$C_k = \sum_{k=1}^{9} V(x,y)$$

$$V(x,y) = \begin{cases} G(x,y) & \theta(x,y)\,in\ \ bin_k \\ 0 & \theta(x,y)\,not\ \ in\ \ bin_k, \end{cases} \quad (4)$$

where, $G(x,y)$ and $\theta(x,y)$ are the amplitude and directions of gradients at each pixel, respectively, and calculated using (12), and the gradient direction in the interval $[0, \pi]$ is divided into 9 bins.

$$G(x,y) = \sqrt{G_x^2(x,y) + G_y^2(x,y)}$$

$$(5)$$

$$\theta(x,y) = \tan^{-1}(\frac{G_y(x,y)}{G_x(x,y)}).$$

where, $G_x(x,y)$ and $G_y(x,y)$ are the horizontal and vertical gradients respectively, computed using (6).

$$G_x(x,y) = P(x+1,y) - P(x-1,y)$$

$$G_y(x,y) = P(x,y+1) - P(x,y-1). \quad (6)$$

After the histogram extraction for each block, the histograms are normalized as follows:

$$N = \sqrt{\frac{C}{(\|C\|_1 + e)^2}}, \quad (7)$$

where, e is a small positive value in the case of an empty cell. At last, the histograms are combined to obtain the HOG feature representing the facial image.

3.3. Sparse code extraction

In linear sparse coding, a collection of k atoms $\varphi_1, \varphi_2, ..., \varphi_k$ is given that forms the columns of the over-complete dictionary matrix Φ. For extracting the sparse codes from the descriptors, we should have dictionary atoms for sparse code extraction, and this, in turn, needs a dictionary learning step.

The dictionary learning was done using the method proposed in [13]. We used a Fisher discrimination-based (FDDL) method. A structured dictionary $\Phi = [\varphi_1, \varphi_2, ..., \varphi_c]$ is learned instead of learning a shared dictionary to all classes, where φ_i is the class-specified sub-dictionary associated with class i, and c is the total number of classes. Assume that Y= $[y_1, y_2, ..., y_c]$ is the set of training samples, where y_i is the sub-set of the training samples from class I, X= $[x_1, x_2, ..., x_c]$ represents the coding coefficient matrix of Y over Φ, and x_i is the coding coefficients of y_i over Φ. The learning process uses the Fisher discrimination criterion [13]. Based on this criterion, the dictionary atoms are imposed on the coding coefficients so that they have small within-class scatter but big between-class scatter. This property could improve the facial image classification accuracy significantly.

The sparse codes of a feature vector $y \in R^m$; with a $l0$-minimization problem can be determined:

$$\min_{W \in R^m} \|W\|_0, s.t. \quad x = G_\Phi(W), \quad (8)$$

where, the function G_Φ is defined as $G_\Phi(w) = \Phi w$. In the proposed AGRSC method, the main technical difficulty is the proper interpretation of the function $G_\Phi(w)$ in the manifold setting, where the atoms $\varphi_1, \varphi_2, ..., \varphi_k$ are points in M, and Φ denotes the set of atoms, and due to the non-linearity property in this case, it is no longer possible to create a matrix with atoms. Moving to the more general manifold setting, we have forsaken the vector space structure in R^m.

In the linear sparse coding, each point is considered as a vector whose definition requires a reference point. However, in the AGRSC setting, each point cannot be considered as a vector and therefore, must be considered as a point. This particular viewpoint is the main source of differences between the linear and AGRSC sparse codings.

Mathematically, we can view an image as a point in a high dimensional vector space whose dimensionality is equal to the number of pixels in the image [20]. Therefore, the descriptors extracted from facial images are on a high dimension manifold. When two facial images are similar to each other, these manifolds are overlapped in some sections. In order to solve this problem, in this paper, a new method is proposed to modify the usual notion of sparsity by adding an affine constraint to reduce the feature vector dimension on a manifold. A vector y is defined as an affine sparse vector if it can be written as follows [21]:

$$y = w_1\varphi_1 + w_1\varphi_1 + ... + w_n\varphi_n$$
$$w_1 + w_2 + ... + w_n = 1. \tag{9}$$

According to the definition, if the vector is constructed with combination of the affine samples, it can be mapped on the space with the lower dimension. The extracted sparse code vectors are in the space with high dimension manifold. Representing these vectors in places where the manifolds have interferences is very challenging. However if the facial images in a data set are effectively parameterized by a small number of continuous variables, then they will lie on or near a low-dimensional manifold in this high-dimensional space [22]. For representing a vector, if the sample selections are done based on only the nearest neighbors and the sparsity term, some of the samples may be selected from the irrelevant manifold; however, if the selected samples have the affinity constraint in addition, since the samples can be considered on the manifold with locally low dimension, only the samples on the relevant manifold could be selected. For a better perception of the proposed method, see figure 3.

Two overlapped manifolds are shown in the figure. Figure 3a indicates a representation of the samples a,b, and c regarding only the sparsity term, and figure 3b indicates the representation of the same points regarding the manifold constraints in addition to the sparsity constraint. The samples A and B in both figures 3a and 3b are represented by the atoms from the corresponding manifolds correctly. These two samples haven't any conflict with the other manifold.

Sample c is under different conditions. As indicated earlier, this sample is located on the green manifold. If you represent this sample with its adjacent atoms, and only consider the sparsity term, we should consider the other manifold samples for representation the same as figure 3.a. However, if we consider the GraphSc ($Tr(XLX^T)$) and Affinity terms for its representation in addition, we will reach a better conclusion. As previously pointed out, the term $Tr(XLX^T)$ emphasizes on the problem that if the samples of a manifold are close to each other, their codes will be close to each other as well. Also the Affinity constraint forces a collection of the closest neighbors of the concerned dictionary atoms for representing every sample. Therefore, a collection of weights for every sample are chosen in a way that every point is represented by a linear combination of its neighbors. The former samples are located on a manifold with high dimensions and the objective of the Affinity term is to reduce its dimensions. The characteristic of this new term causes sample c to be represented with utilization of the concerned manifold data (Figure 3b).

According to the above-mentioned descriptions, we can add an affinity term to (1):

$$\min_{\Phi, X} \left(\|Y - \Phi X\|_F^2 + \gamma Tr(XLX^T) + \alpha \sum_{i=1}^{n} |x_i| \right) \tag{10}$$

$$st. \quad \sum_{i=1}^{n} x_i = 1.$$

The constraint term $\sum_{i=1}^{n} x_i = 1$ is added to the main criterion as a lagrangian coefficient, which leads to:

$$\min_{\Phi, X} \|Y - \Phi X\|_F^2 + \gamma Tr(XLX^T) + \alpha \sum_{i=1}^{n} |x_i| + \beta (1 - \sum_{i=1}^{n} x_i)^2, \tag{11}$$

where, β is a parameter for tuning the affinity constraint. To tune parameters $\alpha, \beta,$ and γ, some experiments were done, which are described in the next section.

3.4. Solution of AGRSC

We applied the feature-sign search algorithm [15] to solve the optimization problem (11).

To solve non-differentiable problems in non-smooth optimization methods, a necessary condition for a parameter vector to be a local minimum is that the zero-vector should be a member of the sub-differential set containing all the sub-gradients in the parameter vector [23].

Following [17, 23], the optimization of AGRSC was divided into two steps: 1) ℓ1-regularized least squares problem; the affine graph regularized sparse codes X were learned with dictionary Φ fixed, and 2) ℓ2-constrained least squares problem; the dictionary Φ was learned with affine graph regularized sparse codes X fixed. The above two steps were repeated, respectively, until a stop

criterion was indulged.

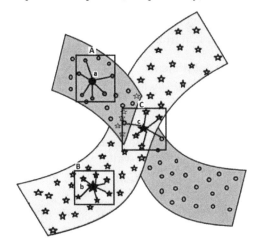

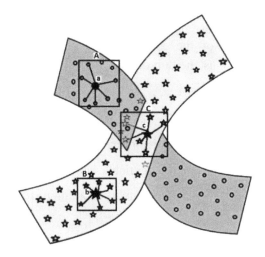

a) Representation of samples a, b, and c without Affinity constraint.

b) Representation of samples a, b, and c with Affinity constraint.

Figure 3. Effectiveness of Affinity constraint in representation of samples from overlapped manifolds.

The optimization problem in the first step can be solved by optimizing over each x_i individually.

Since (11) with $l1$-regularization is non-differentiable when x_i contains the value of 0, to solve this problem, the standard unconstrained optimization methods cannot be applied. Several approaches have been proposed to solve the problem of this form [11]. In what follows, we introduce an optimization method based upon coordinate descent to solve this problem [24]. It can easily be seen that (11) is convex, thus the global minimum can be achieved.

We updated each vector individually by holding all the other vectors constant. In order to solve the problem by optimizing over each x_i, we should re write (11) in a vector form. The reconstruction error $\left\| Y - \Phi X \right\|_F^2$ can be re written as:

$$\sum_{i=1}^{m} \left\| Y - \Phi X \right\|_F^2 \qquad (12)$$

The Laplacian regularizer $Tr(XLX^T)$ can be rewritten as:

$$Tr(XLX^T) = Tr\left(\sum_{i,j=1}^{n} L_{i,j} x_i x_j^T \right) = \\ \sum_{i,j=1}^{n} L_{ij} x_i x_j^T = \sum_{i,j=1}^{n} L_{ij} x_i^T x_j . \qquad (13)$$

Combining (11), (12), and (13), the problem can be written as:

$$\min \sum_{i=1}^{n} \left\| y_i - \Phi x_i \right\|_F^2 + \gamma \sum_{i,j=1}^{n} L_{ij} x_i^T x_j + \\ \alpha \sum_{i=1}^{n} |x_i| + \beta \left(1 - \sum_{i=1}^{n} x_i \right)^2 . \qquad (14)$$

When updating x_i, the other vectors $x_j {}_{i \neq j}$ are fixed. Thus we get the following optimization problem:

$$\min_{x_i} G(x_i) = \min \left(\begin{array}{l} \left\| y_i - \Phi X \right\|^2 + \gamma L_{ii} x_i^T x_i + x_i^T H_i + \\ \alpha \sum_{j=1}^{k} |x_i^{(j)}| + \beta \left(1 - \sum_{i=1}^{n} x_i \right)^2 \end{array} \right) \qquad (15)$$

where $H_i = 2\gamma \left(\sum_{j \neq i} L_{ij} s_j \right)$ and $x_i^{(j)}$ is the j-th coefficient of x_i.

Following the feature-sign search algorithm proposed in [25]), (15) can be solved as follows. In order to solve the non-differentiable problem, we adopt a sub-gradient strategy, which uses sub-gradients of $G(x_i)$ at non-differentiable points. Primarily we define:

$$p(x_i) = \left\| y_i - \Phi x_i \right\|^2 + \gamma L_{ii} x_i^T x_j + \\ x_i^T H_i + \beta \left(1 - \sum_{i=1}^{n} x_i \right)^2 . \qquad (16)$$

Then,

$$G(x_i) = p(x_i) + \alpha \sum_{j=1}^{k} |x_i^{(j)}|. \qquad (17)$$

Recall that a necessary condition for a parameter vector to be a local minimum in non-smooth optimizations, is that in the set containing all sub-gradients at this parameter vector, the zero-vector is an element of the sub-differential [23]. We define $\nabla_i^{(j)}|x_i|$ as the sub-differentiable value of the jth coefficient of x_i. If $|x_i^{(j)}| > 0$, then the absolute value function $|x_i^{(j)}|$ is differentiable, and therefore, $\nabla_i^{(j)}|x_i|$ is given by $sign(x_i^{(j)})$. If $x_i^{(j)} = 0$, then the subdifferentiable value $\nabla_i^{(j)}|x_i|$ is set $[-1,1]$. Thus the optimality condition for achieving the optimal value for $G(x_i)$ is:

$$\begin{cases} \nabla_i^{(j)}p(x_i) + \alpha sign(x_i^{(j)}) & if \quad |x_i^{(j)}| > 0 \\ |\nabla_i^{(j)}p \; x_i| \leq \alpha & if \quad x_i^{(j)} = 0 \end{cases} \quad (18)$$

Then we consider how to select the optimal sub-gradient $\nabla_i^j G(x_i)$, when the optimality conditions are violated, i.e.; in the case that $|\nabla_i^{(j)}p \; x_i| > \alpha$ if $x_i^{(j)} = 0$. When $x_i^{(j)} = 0$, we consider the first term in the previous expression $\nabla_i^{(j)}p(x_i)$. Suppose that $\nabla_i^{(j)}p(x_i) > \alpha$; this means that $\nabla_i^{(j)}G(x_i) > 0$, regardless of the sign of $x_i^{(j)}$. In this case, in order to decrease $G(x_i)$, we should decrease $x_i^{(j)}$. Since $x_i^{(j)}$ starts at zero, the very first infinitesimal adjustment to $x_i^{(j)}$ will make it negative. Therefore, we can let $sign(x_i^{(j)}) = -1$. Similarly, if $\nabla_i^{(j)}p(x_i) < -\alpha$, then we let $sign(x_i^{(j)}) = 1$. To update x_i, suppose that we know the signs of $x_i^{(j)}$'s at the optimal value; then we can remove the $l1$-norm on $x_i^{(j)}$ by replacing each term $|x_i^{(j)}|$ with either $x_i^{(j)}$ (if $x_i^{(j)} > 0$) or $-x_i^{(j)}$ (if $x_i^{(j)} < 0$) or 0 (if $x_i^{(j)} = 0$). Thus; (13) is converted to a standard unconstrained QP. In this case, the problem can be solved by a linear system. The algorithmic procedure of learning affine graph regularized sparse codes can be described as follows:

- for each x_i, search for signs of $sign(x_i^{(j)}); i = 1,...,k$

- solve the reduced QP problem to get the optimal x_i^* that minimizes the objective function

- return the optimal coefficients matrix

$$X^* = [x_1^*, x_2^*,...,x_n^*]$$

In the algorithm, we maintain an active set $A = \{j \mid x_i^{(j)} = 0, |\nabla_i^{(j)}p(x_i)| > \alpha\}$ for potentially non-zero coefficients and their corresponding signs $\theta = [\theta_1,...,\theta_k]$, while updating each x_i. Then it systematically searches for the optimal active set and coefficient signs that minimize the objective function (9). In each activating step, the algorithm uses the zero-value whose violation of the optimality condition $\nabla_i^{(j)}p(x_i) > \alpha$ is the largest.

The detailed algorithmic procedure of learning affine graph regularized sparse codes is stated in Algorithm 1.

Algorithm1: Learning affine graph regularized sparse codes

Input: $Y = [y_1, ..., y_n]$, $\Phi, L, \alpha, \beta, \gamma$.

1- $1 \leq i \leq n$

2- **Initializing:** $x_i = \vec{0}, \theta = \vec{0}, A = \emptyset, \theta_j \epsilon \{-1,0,1\} = sign(x_i^{(j)})$.

3- **Activating:** $j = \arg\max_j |\nabla_i^{(j)}p(x_i)|$:

    if $\nabla_i^{(j)}p(x_i) > \alpha$, $\theta_j = -1$, $A = \{j\} \cup A$
    if $\nabla_i^{(j)}p(x_i) < -\alpha$, $\theta_j = 1$, $A = \{j\} \cup A$

4- **Feature sign:** $\hat{\Phi}$ is submatrix of Φ contains only columns corresponding to A. $\hat{x}_i, \hat{p}_i$ are subvectors of x_i, p.

$$\min u(\hat{x}_i) = \|y_i - \hat{\Phi}\hat{x}_i\|^2 + \gamma L_{ii}\hat{x}_i^T\hat{x}_i + \hat{x}_i^T\hat{H}_i + \beta(1 - \sum_{i=1}^n \hat{x}_i)^2 + \alpha\hat{\theta}^T\hat{x}_i^T$$

Let $(\partial u(\hat{x}_i)/\partial \hat{x}_i) = 0$

$$-2\hat{\Phi}^T(y_i - \hat{\Phi}\hat{x}_i) + 2\gamma L_{ii}\hat{x}_i + 2\gamma\left(\sum_{j \neq i} L_{ij}\hat{x}_i\right) + 2\beta(1 - 1^T\hat{x}_i)1 + \alpha\hat{\theta} = 0$$

$$\hat{x}_i^{new} = (\hat{\Phi}^T\hat{\Phi} + \gamma L_{ii}I + \beta 11^T)^{-1}\left(\hat{\Phi}^Ty_i + \beta 1 - \frac{1}{2}(\alpha\hat{\theta} + \hat{H}_i)\right),$$

I is the identity matrix.

5- **The optimality conditions:**
    Condition(1):
    If $\nabla_i^{(j)}p(x_i) + \alpha sign(x_i^{(j)}) = 0, \forall \; x_i^{(j)} \neq 0$
    Go to condition(2).
    Else go to step 4
    Condition(2):
If $|\nabla_i^{(j)}p(x_i)| \leq \alpha, \forall \; x_i^{(j)} = 0$
Return x_i.
Else go to step 3

6- End

---

4. Experiments

In this section, for evaluating the proposed AGRSC approach, some experiments for image classification were performed. Some experiments were done on five well-known datasets including

ORL, Extended Yale B, FERET, AR, and LFW. These datasets contain several face images from distinct persons and under different conditions such as times, lighting, facial expressions and occlusions. Also some experiments were done on some noisy images with different variances for evaluating the robustness of the proposed method to noise.

4.2. Data preparation

ORL, Extended Yale B, FERET, AR, and LFW face databases are well-known datasets widely used in computer vision and pattern recognition research works. The experiments were done on these datasets. In continuation, we introduced these datasets.

Extended YaleB database [27]. This database contains 16128 images of 28 human subjects under 9 poses and 64 illumination conditions.

The images in the database were captured using a purpose-built illumination rig. This rig was fitted with 64 computer controlled strobes. The 64 images of a subject in a particular pose were acquired at camera frame rate (30 frames/second) in about 2 seconds, so there was only a small change in head pose and facial expression for those 64 (+1 ambient) images. The image with ambient illumination was captured without a strobe going off.

FERET database. The data is obtained from the UCI database [28]. It contains face images about 72 persons, and every body has 6 variations in expression.

AR database. This database consists of 126 subjects of over 4000 frontal face images [29]. These images have different illumination variations, facial expression and occlusion.

Following the standard evaluation procedure, we used a subset of the database consisting of 2600 images from 50 male subjects and 50 female subjects. For each person, we randomly selected 20 images for training and the other 6 for testing.

LFW dataset. The LFW dataset [30] contains 13233 images of 5749 individuals. The facial images in this dataset were taken in unconstrained environments. In figure 4, some examples of the datasets are shown.

4.3. Experimental setup

To evaluate the proposed AGRSC approach, the results of this method on five defined datasets were compared with some recent approaches; including LRC [2], CRC [31], SRC [8], LLC [4], FDDL [13], LH-ESRC [19], SPN-DL [14], D-KSVD [9], SVGDL [32], LC-KSVD [7], PDPL [33], and DNFC [34].

Following [17], AGRSC was performed on HOG descriptors extracted from the facial images. Before sparse code extraction from face data using the proposed method, the data dimensions were reduced using principle component analysis by keeping 98% of the information in the largest Eigen vectors. After applying the proposed algorithm to the reduced data, the SVM classifier with χ^2 kernel was applied on the sparse codes.

Under our experimental setup, we tuned the optimal parameters for the target classifier using the leave one subject out cross validation method. Therefore, we evaluated the proposed method on datasets by empirically searching the parameter space for the optimal parameter settings, and reported the best results.

Figure 4. Some samples of datasets. From top to bottom: ORL, Extended YALE B, FERET, AR And LFW datasets.

For the proposed AGRSC method, we set the trade-off parameters α, β, γ through searching. The parameter values using the ORL face dataset is shown in figure 5. As it can be seen, the parameters α, β, and γ were set to 30, 0.1 and 0.6, respectively.

At first, the value for the γ parameter was achieved for the best recognition rate, assuming $\alpha, \beta = 1$. As it can be seen in figure 5a, the highest recognition rate was achieved for $\gamma = 0.6$. In the next step, the value for α was achieved, assuming $\gamma = 0.6$ and $\beta = 1$ for the best recognition rate. As it can be seen in figure 5b, the best value for this parameter can be a number between 28 and 45. We set $\alpha = 30$, and using the same experiments, the best value for β was achieved to be 0.1.

As mentioned earlier, the dictionary learning process has been done using the method proposed in [13]. It should be noted that, the affinity constraint can be more successful when the sparsity is large enough because with the coefficients not enough sparsity, the coefficients may be selected from the hyperplane with higher dimensions than data's original dimension. In this case, if the affinity constraint is added to the objective function, it can even worsen the performance with respect to the GraphSC method.

4.4. Experimental results

In order to evaluate the proposed method, it was performed on five well-known datasets.

The classification accuracy of AGRSC on ORL dataset is illustrated in table 1 as a confusion matrix. As mentioned earlier, the ORL dataset contains 40 classes of faces. Due to the lack of space in the table, only 10 classes were depicted.

Among the whole dataset, classes 4 and 6, classes 8 and 10, classes 14 and 17, and classes 5 and 18 are very similar to each other. Therefore, we used these classes in addition to classes 1 and 2 in the

confusion matrix to show the superiority of the proposed method in classifying face datasets in table 1. The mean recognition rate was 92%. When the other 30 classes were considered as well, the mean accuracy rate was raised up to 97.2%.

4.5. Robustness to noise

For a better evaluation of the proposed method, we aimed to test the robustness of our method at the presence of noise. Some Gaussian noise added to the database images and the experiments for evaluation are repeated for noise variance levels as 10, 20, 30, 40, and 50.

Figure 7 shows some test images under different levels of noise.

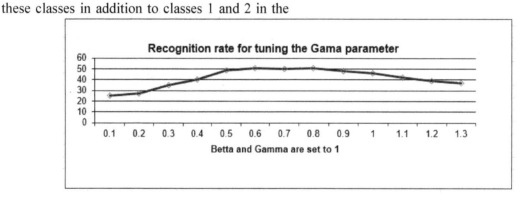

a)   **Recognition rate variations for gamma changes by setting Alpha=Beta=1.**

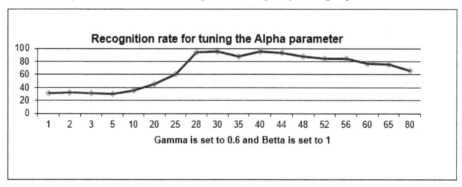

b)   **Recognition rate variations for alpha changes by setting Gamma=0.6 and Beta=1.**

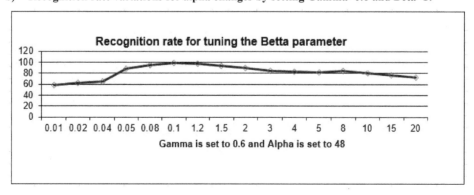

c)   **Recognition rate variations for Beta changes by setting Gamma=0.6 and Alpha=30.**

Figure 5. The parameters setting using ORL dataset.

Table 1. The confusion matrix for the proposed method on the ORL data

	C1	C2	C4	C5	C6	C8	C10	C14	C17	C18
C1	99	0	1	0	0	0	0	0	0	0
C2	0	100	0	0	0	0	0	0	0	0
C4	1	0	97	1	1	0	0	0	0	0
C5	0	0	4	87	0	3	0	1	5	0
C6	0	0	2	1	95	0	1	0	0	1
C8	0	0	0	0	0	95	4	1	0	0
C10	0	0	0	0	0	6	87	2	4	1
C14	0	0	0	0	0	0	1	90	4	5
C17	0	0	0	1	2	1	5	11	78	2
C18	0	0	0	1	1	0	2	4	0	92

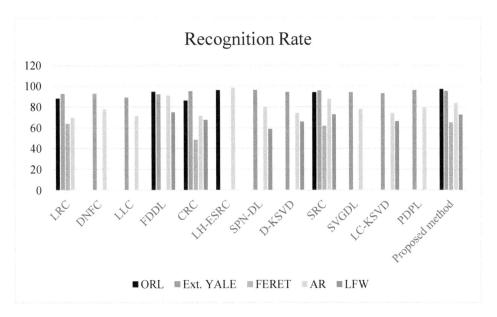

Figure 6. Recognition rate for proposed method in comparison with several other methods.

Figure 7. One test image under different levels of Gaussian noise. From left to right original image, images cluttered with Gaussian noise with variances 10, 20, 30, 40, and 50, respectively.

Table 2 shows the recognition rate of the proposed method under different noise levels for each database. It can be seen that the recognition rate of the proposed method for the ORL, Extended YALE B, FERET, AR, and LFW datasets are reduced only 3.8%, 3.24%, 3.53%, 4.02%, and 4.3%, respectively. This means that the proposed method is stable with noise.

5. Conclusion

In this paper, a novel approach was proposed for robust face recognition. In the proposed method, after extracting the HOG descriptors from the original face images, the sparse codes were extracted from the descriptors. For this purpose, the well-defined graph regularized sparse coding method was improved by adding the affinity constraint.

Using this term, until the sparsity was big enough, the manifold structure of features was better preserved. Finally, the codes obtained were classified with the SVM classifier. The results obtained indicated that the proposed AGRSC method in comparison with many other approaches had a better performance. The proposed method is efficient for face recognition for two reasons. Firstly, the dictionary atoms, because of the property of the FDDL method, has enough discriminant, and secondly, the sparse codes extracted from the descriptors, because of the affinity characteristic, can more easily choose the correct class.

Table 2. Recognition rate for noisy images.

Database	Noise Variance	Recognition Rate
ORL	10	96.8
	20	95.4
	30	94.1
	40	92.4
	50	90.3
Extended Yale	10	94.7
	20	93.6
	30	92.1
	40	90.9
	50	88.5
FERET	10	64.6
	20	63.5
	30	62.3
	40	60.1
	50	57.3
AR	10	82.8
	20	81.3
	30	80.1
	40	78.5
	50	75.4
LFW	10	71.9
	20	70.7
	30	68.1
	40	66.1
	50	63.2

References

[1] Cao, F. Hu, H. Lu, J. Zhao, J. Zhou, Z. & Wu, J. (2016). Pose and Illumination Variable Face Recognition via Sparse Representation and Illumination Dictionary, Knowledge-Based Systems, doi: 10.1016/j.knosys.2016.06.001.

[2] Naseem, I. Togneri, R. & Bennamoun, M. (2010). Linear regression for face recognition, IEEE Trans. Neural Netw. Learn. Syst. vol. 32, no. 11, pp. 2106–2112.

[3] Zhang, L. Yang, M. & Feng, X. (2011). Sparse representation or collaborative representation: which helps face recognition? in: Proceedings of IEEE International Conference on Computer Vision, pp. 471–478.

[4] Wang, J. Yang, J. Yu, K. & Lv, F. (2010). Locality-constrained linear coding for image classification, in: Proceedings of IEEE International Conference on Computer Vision, pp. 3360–3367.

[5] Shafeipour, S. Seyedarabi, H. & Aghagolzadeh, A. (2016). Video-based face recognition in color space by graph-based discriminant analysis, Journal of AI and Data Mining, vol.4, no.2, pp. 193-201.

[6] Chen, W. Zhao, Y. Pan, B. & Chen, B. (2016). Supervised Kernel Nonnegative Matrix Factorization for Face Recognition Neurocomputing, http://dx.doi. org/ 10.1016/ j.neucom.2016.04.014.

[7] Jiang, Z. Lin, Z. & Davis, L. S. (2013). Label consistent K-SVD: learning a discriminative dictionary for recognition, IEEE Trans. Pattern Anal. Mach. Intell., vol. 35, no. 11, pp. 2651–2664.

[8] Wright, J. Yang, A. Y. Ganesh, A. Sastry, S. S. & Ma, Y. (2009). Robust face recognition via sparse representation, IEEE Transactions on Pattern Analysis and Machine Intelligence, vol.31, no. 2, pp. 210-227.

[9] Liu, Y. N. Wu, F. Zhang, Z. H. Zhuang, Y. T. & Yan, S. C. (2010). Sparse representation using nonnegative curds and whey. In Proceedings of the IEEE Conference on Computer Vision and Pattern Recognition.

[10] Wen, Y. Zhang, L. von Deneen, K. M. & He, L. (2015). Face recognition using discriminative locality preserving vectors, Digit. Signal Process, http://dx.doi.org/10.1016/j.dsp.2015.11.001.

[11] Gao, S. I. Tsang, W.-H. Chia, L.-T. & Zhao, P. (2010). Local features are not lonely – laplacian sparse coding for image classification. In Proceedings of the IEEE Conference on Computer Vision and Pattern Recognition.

[12] Jiang, X. & Lai, J. (2014). Sparse and Dense Hybrid Representation via Dictionary Decomposition for Face Recognition, IEEE Transactions on Pattern Analysis and Machine Intelligence. ,DOI 10.1109/TPAMI.2014.2359453.

[13] Yang, M. Zhang, L. Feng, X. & Zhang, D. (2011). Fisher discrimination dictionary learning for sparse representation, In: IEEE International Conference on Computer Vision, pp. 543-550.

[14] Xu, Y. Li, Z. Zhang, B. Yang, J. & You, J. (2017). Sample diversity, representation effectiveness and robust dictionary learning for face recognition, Information Sciences, vol. 375, pp. 171–182.

[15] Lee, H. Battle, A. Raina, R. & Ng, A. Y. (2006). Efficient sparse coding algorithms. In Advances in Neural Information Processing Systems 20, NIPS.

[16] Zheng, M. Bu, J. Chen, C. Wang, C. Zhang, L. Qiu, G. & Cai, D. (2007). Graph Regularized Sparse Coding for Image Representation, Journal Latex Class Files, vol. 6, no. 1.

[17] Zheng, M. Bu, J. Chen, C. Wang, C. Zhang, L. Qiu, G. & Cai, D. (2011). Graph regularized sparse coding for image representation. IEEE Transactions on Image Processing, vol. 20, no.5, pp. 1327-1336.

[18] Quanz, B. Huan, J. & Mishra, M. (2012). Knowledge transfer with low-quality data: A feature extraction issue. IEEE Transactions on Knowledge and Data Engineering, vol. 24, no. 10, pp. 1789 – 1802.

[19] Zheng, C. Hou, Y. & Zhang, J. (2015). Improved Sparse Representation with Low-Rank Representation for Robust Face Recognition, Neurocomputing, http://dx.doi.org/ 10.1016/ j.neucom. 2015.07.146.

[20] Turk, M. & Pentland, A. (1991). Eigenfaces for recognition, Jornal of Cognitive Neuroscience, vol. 3, no. 1, pp. 71-86.

[21] Michiel, H. (2001). Affine transformation, Encyclopedia of Mathematics, Springer, ISBN 978-1-55608-010-4.

[22] Lu, H. Fainman, Y. & Hecht-Nielsen, R. (1998). Image manifolds, Applications of Artificial Neural Networks in Image Processing III, Proceedings of SPIE, vol. 3307, pp. 52–63.

[23] Fletcher, R. (1987). Practical methods of optimization, Wiley-Interscience.

[24] Lu, X. Yuan, Y. & Yan, P. (2014). Alternatively Constrained Dictionary Learning for Image Superresolution, IEEE Transactions on Cybernetics, vol. 44, no. 3, pp.366-377.

[25] Cand`es, E. & Tao, T. (2006). Near-optimal signal recovery from random projections: niversal encoding strategies?, IEEE transactions on information theory, vol. 52, no. 12, pp. 5406–5425.

[26] Samaria, F. & Harter, A. (1994). Parameterisation of a Stochastic Model for Human Face Identification, Proceedings of 2nd IEEE Workshop on Applications of Computer Vision, Sarasota FL.

[27] Georghiades, A. S., Belhumeur, P. N., & Kriegman, D. (2001). From few to many: illumination cone models for face recognition under variable lighting and pose, IEEE Trans. Patt. Anal. Mach. Intell., vol. 23, no. 6, pp. 643-660.

[28] The Facial Recognition Technology (FERET) Database,http://www.itl.nist.gov/iad/humanid/feret/feret_master.html (last visited January 2017).

[29] Martinez, A. M. (1998). The AR face database, CVC Technical Report.

[30] Huang, G. B. Ramesh, M. Berg, T. & Learned-Miller, E. (2008). Labeled faces in the wild: A database for studying face recognition in unconstrained environments, University of Massachusetts, Amherst, Tech. Rep.

[31] Zhang, Q. & Li, B. (2010). Discriminative K-SVD for dictionary learning in face recognition, in: Proceedings of IEEE International Conference on Computer Vision and Pattern Recognition, pp. 2691–2698.

[32] Cai, S. Zuo, W. Zhang, L. Feng, X. & Wang, P. (2014). Support vector guided dictionary learning, in: Proceedings of European Conference Computer Vision, pp. 624–639.

[33] Gu, S., Zhang, L., Zuo, W. & Feng, X. (2014). Projective dictionary pair learning for pattern classification, in: Proceedings of Advances in Neural Information Processing Systems, pp. 793–801.

[34] Xu, Y. Fang, X. Li, X. Yang, J. You, J. Liu, H. & Teng, S. (2014). Data Uncertainty in Face Recognition, IEEE Trans. Cybern., vol. 44, no. 10, pp. 1950–1961.

19

Outlier detection in wireless sensor networks using distributed principal component analysis

A. Ahmadi Livani, M. Abadi[*], M. Alikhani

Faculty of Electrical and Computer Engineering, Tarbiat Modares University, Tehran, Iran

[*]*Corresponding author: abadi@modares.ac.ir (M. Abadi)*

Abstract

Outlier detection is an important task for intrusion detection and fault diagnosis in wireless sensor networks (WSNs). Outliers in sensed data may be caused due to compromised or malfunctioning sensor nodes. In this paper, we propose a centralized and a distributed approach based on the principal component analysis (PCA) for outlier detection in WSNs. In the distributed approach, we partition the network into multiple groups of sensor nodes. Each group has a group head and several member nodes. Every member node uses a fixed-width clustering algorithm and sends a description of its local sensed data to the group head. The group head then applies a distributed PCA to establish a global normal pattern and detect outliers. This pattern is periodically updated using weighted coefficients. We compare the performance of the centralized and distributed approaches based on the real sensed data collected by 54 Mica2Dot sensors deployed in Intel Berkeley Research Lab. The experimental results show that the distributed approach reduces both communication overhead and energy consumption, while achieving comparable accuracy.

Keywords: *Wireless sensor network; Outlier detection; Principal component analysis.*

1. Introduction

Wireless sensor networks (WSNs) are composed of a large number of tiny sensor nodes deployed in an environment for monitoring and tracking purposes. Sensor nodes use ad-hoc communications and collaborate with each other to sense different phenomena that may vary in time and space, and send the sensed data to a central node for further processing and analysis [1]. WSNs are applied to various applications, ranging from military to civilian fields.

The data sensed and collected by sensor nodes are often unreliable. The quality of the sensed data may be affected by noise or missing values. The low cost and low quality sensor nodes have limitations in power supply, memory, computational capabilities, and communication bandwidth [1]. These limitations make the sensed data unreliable and inaccurate. Particularly, when power supply is exhausted, the probability of generating erroneous data will grow rapidly [2]. On the other hand, the

operations of sensor nodes are frequently susceptible to environmental effects. The vision of large scale and high density WSNs is to randomly deploy a large number of sensor nodes in harsh and unattended environments [3]. Since events occurred in the real world (*e.g.*, forest fire or earthquake) cannot be accurately detected using erroneous data, it is extremely important to ensure the reliability and accuracy of the sensed data [4], [5]. An outlier is an observation (or a set of observations) in a data set, which appears to be inconsistent with the remainder of that data set [6]. The term outlier, also known as anomaly, originally stems from the field of statistics [7]. Outlier detection, also known as anomaly detection, is one of the fundamental tasks of data mining along with predictive modeling, cluster analysis, and association analysis [8].

In WSNs, outliers can be defined as those data that have significant deviations from the normal pattern of the sensed data [9]. Potential sources of outliers include noise, actual events, or malicious attacks [8]. A straightforward approach for outlier detection in WSNs is to establish a normal pattern of the sensed data and detect data that deviate significantly from the established pattern as outliers. As environmental conditions may change over time, a predefined normal pattern will not be sufficiently representative for future outlier detection. Thus, a key challenge here is to dynamically detect outliers with acceptable accuracy while minimizing communication overhead and energy consumption.

In WSNs, the energy consumption in the radio communication is significantly greater than of that in the computation [10]-[12]. For example, in Sensoria sensors and Berkeley motes, the ratio between communication and computation energy consumption ranges from 10^3 to 10^4 [13]. Hence, we can take this advantage to prolong the network lifetime through increasing computational cost in order to reduce communication overheads.

Principal component analysis (PCA) is a powerful technique for analyzing and identifying patterns in data [14]. It finds the most important axis to express the scattering of data [15]. By using PCA, the first principal component is calculated, which reflects the approximate distribution of data.

In this paper, we propose a centralized and a distributed PCA-based approach for outlier detection in WSNs. We partition the network into groups of sensor nodes. Each group has a group head and several member nodes. In the centralized approach, every member node sends its local sensed data to the group head. The group head then applies PCA to establish a global normal pattern and detect outliers. In the distributed approach rather than sending all sensed data, every member node uses a fixed-width clustering (FWC) algorithm and sends a description of its local sensed data to the group head. The group head then applies a distributed PCA (DPCA) to establish the global normal pattern. In these two approaches, the established normal pattern is periodically updated using weighted coefficients. We compare the performance of the centralized and distributed approaches based on real sensed data collected from 54 Mica2Dot sensors deployed in Intel Berkeley Research Lab. In comparison to the centralized approach, we show that the distributed approach can achieve significant reductions in communication overhead and energy consumption, while achieving comparable accuracy.

The rest of this paper is organized as follows: Section 2 briefly reviews some related work. Section 3 formally introduces the problem of outlier detection in WSNs. Sections 4 and 5 describe the centralized and distributed outlier detection approaches, respectively, and Section 6 analyzes the communication overhead and computational cost of them. Section 7 reports the experimental results and finally Section 8 draws some conclusions.

2. Related work

In monitoring WSNs, due to the critical nature of applications in many cases, sensed data collected from various sensor nodes should be analyzed dynamically and compared to an established normal pattern in order to detect potential outliers.

Janakiram et al. [16] proposed a technique based on Bayesian belief networks (BBNs) for outlier detection in the sensed data. The technique uses BBNs to capture the spatio-temporal correlations among the observations of sensor nodes and the conditional dependencies among the observations of sensor features. Each node trains a BBN to detect outliers based on its neighbors' sensed data as well as its own sensed data. An observation is considered as outlier if it falls beyond the range of the expected class. Accuracy of a BBN depends on how the conditional dependencies among the observations of sensor features exist. This technique does not work well when the resources are limited and the network topology changes dynamically.

Rajasegarar et al. [17], [18] proposed two distributed outlier detection approaches. The first approach is based on clustering. In this approach, sensor nodes have a hierarchal topology. At the end of each time window, every sensor node clusters its sensed data and sends the statistics of the clusters to its immediate parent node. The parent node then merges its own clusters with the clusters collected from its intermediate children nodes and sends the statistics of the merged clusters to its immediate parent node. This process continues recursively up to the gateway node, where an outlier detection algorithm is applied on its merged clusters to detect outlier clusters. An outlier cluster can be determined in the gateway node, if the cluster's average inter-cluster distance is larger than one threshold value of the set of inter-cluster distances. Determining the parameter used to compute the average inter-cluster distance is not always easy. The second approach is based on one-class quarter sphere SVM. Every sensor node runs the one-class quarter-sphere SVM on its sensed data and sends its local radius to its parent node. The parent node then combines its own local radius with radii collected from its children nodes and sends the global radius to its children nodes. The children nodes use the global radius to locally detect outliers. The sensed data that lies outside the global quarter sphere are considered as outliers. This approach ignores spatial correlations of neighboring sensor nodes, which makes the results of local outliers inaccurate.

Chatzigiannakis et al. [5] proposed a centralized outlier detection approach in which PCA is applied on the sensed data of all sensor nodes in order to reduce the dimensionality of them. The first few most important derived principal components are then selected to be used in the subspace method. The goal of this method is to divide the current sensed data into normal and anomalous spaces. However, this approach has several drawbacks. It uses squared prediction error (SPE) to perform outlier detection in the residual space. Since SPE is sensitive to modeling errors, it may increase the false alarm rate. Also, sending all sensed data to a central node leads to a high communication overhead, which is a major source of energy consumption for sensor nodes.

Sheng et al. [19] proposed a histogram-based technique to detect global outliers over the sensed data. This technique attempts to reduce communication overhead by collecting hints in the form of a histogram rather than collecting all sensed data in a central node. The central node uses the hints to extract the data distribution in the network and detect the potential outliers. However, this technique does not consider the inter-feature dependencies of multi-dimensional sensed data.

Ahmadi Livani et al. [14] proposed an energy-efficient approach for detecting outliers in the sensed data. The outlier detection procedure is comprised of two phases: *training* and *outlier detection*. In the training phase, every sensor node computes a description of its local sensed data and sends it to its group head. After receiving descriptive data from all member nodes, the group head applies the approximate global PCA (AGPCA) to establish a global normal pattern and sends it to all member nodes. In the outlier detection phase, every member node detects outliers based on their projection distances from the global first principal component.

3. Problem definition

We consider a WSN composed of a set of sensor nodes deployed in a homogenous environment. The sensor nodes are synchronized and their sensed data belong to the same unknown distribution. We partition the network into multiple groups of sensor nodes. Each group has a group head and several member nodes. The sensor nodes within the same group are physically close to each other and sense a similar phenomenon. The partitioning can be static or dynamic [20]. In the dynamic partitioning, the network may be rearranged periodically, if the environmental conditions change.

Let $G = \{s_i : i = 1 \ldots s\}$ be a group of sensor nodes. At each time interval Δt_k, every member node $s_i \in G$ senses a data vector x_k^i. Each data vector is composed of features x_{kj}^i:

$$x_k^i = (x_{k1}^i, x_{k2}^i, \cdots, x_{kd}^i), \quad x_k^i \in \Re^d \ . \tag{1}$$

During each time window t, s_i senses a set of data vectors $X_i(t) = \{x_k^i(t) : k = 1 \ldots n_i\}$. An outlier in a set of data vectors is defined as a data vector that has significant deviation from the other data vectors. Our aim is to detect outliers in data vectors sensed by the member nodes.

4. Centralized outlier detection approach

In this section, we propose a centralized approach, for outlier detection in WSNs. It consists of three phases: *training, outlier detection,* and *updating*.

4.1. Training phase

The training phase involves modeling the distribution of a given set of normal data vectors. Let G be a group of sensor nodes. In this approach, every member node $s_i \in G$ sends its sensed data vectors to the group head s_G. After receiving the data vectors from all member nodes, s_G combines its own data vectors with them and forms a set of data vectors $X(0)$:

$$X(0) = \begin{bmatrix} X_1(0) \\ X_2(0) \\ \vdots \\ X_s(0) \end{bmatrix}, \tag{2}$$

where $X_i(0)$ is an $n_i \times d$ matrix of data vectors sensed by the member node s_i, $i = 1 \ldots s$. So, $X(0)$ is an $n \times d$ matrix, whose rows are the data vectors and columns are the features.

$$n = \sum_{i=1}^{s} n_i \ . \tag{3}$$

s_G first normalizes the matrix $X(0)$ to a range of [0,1]. It then computes the global column means $\bar{x}(0)$ of $X(0)$ and the global covariance matrix $S(0)$ of $X(0)$:

$$S(0) = \frac{1}{n} X^T(0)(I - \frac{1}{n} e_n e_n^T) X(0) \ , \tag{4}$$

where $e_n \equiv (1,1,\cdots,1)^T$ is a vector of length n.

To establish a normal pattern, s_G computes the global first principal component $\varphi(0)$. The principal components of $X(0)$ are given by a singular value decomposition (SVD) [21] of $nS(0)$:

$$nS(0) = V(0)\Sigma^2(0)V^T(0) , \tag{5}$$

where $V(0)$ is the matrix of principal components of $X(0)$ and $\Sigma^2(0) = \text{diag}(\lambda_1^2(0), \lambda_2^2(0), \cdots, \lambda_d^2(0))$ is the diagonal matrix of eigenvalues ordered from largest to smallest. Note that often $n-1$ is used instead of n in the above equations when the data are a sample from some larger population.

After that, as shown in Figure 1, s_G calculates the projection distance of each data vector $x_k^i(0) \in X(0)$ from $\varphi(0)$ as

$$d_p(x_k^i(0), \varphi(0)) = (\|x_k^i(0) - \bar{x}(0)\|^2 - \\ (\varphi^T(0) \cdot (x_k^i(0) - \bar{x}(0)))^2)^{\frac{1}{2}} . \tag{6}$$

The maximum projection distance of all data vectors from $\varphi(0)$ is then calculated as

$$d_{\max} = \max_{1 \le k \le n} d_p(x_k^i(0), \varphi(0)) \tag{7}$$

and the triple $(\bar{x}(0), \varphi(0), d_{\max})$ is used to establish the global normal pattern $P(0)$.

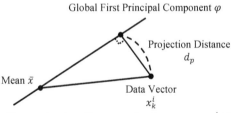

Figure 1. The projection distance of a data vector x_k^i from the global first principal component φ.

4.2. Outlier detection phase

To detect outlier data vectors, during each time window t, the group head s_G first calculates the projection distance of each data vector $x_k^i(t) \in X(t)$ from $\varphi(t-1) \in P(t-1)$. It then classifies $x_k^i(t)$ as outlier, if the calculated projection distance is greater than $d_{\max}$:

$$\begin{cases} d_p(x_k^i(t), \varphi(t-1)) > d_{\max} & : \text{Outlier} \\ d_p(x_k^i(t), \varphi(t-1)) \le d_{\max} & : \text{Normal} \end{cases} . \tag{8}$$

4.3. Updating phase

There might be changes over time in the conditions of the environment in which a WSN is deployed. Therefore, it is necessary to update the global normal pattern.

Let t be the current time window. To update the global normal pattern $P(t)$, the group head s_G first calculates the global column means and global covariance matrix of normal data vectors at the ρ previous time windows (see Figure 2):

$$\bar{x}_\rho(t) = \sum_{\tau=t-\rho+1}^{t} w(\tau)\bar{x}(\tau) , \tag{9}$$

$$S_\rho(t) = \sum_{\tau=t-\rho+1}^{t} w(\tau)S(\tau) , \tag{10}$$

where $\bar{x}(\tau)$ and $S(\tau)$ are the global column means and global covariance matrix at time window τ, respectively. $w(\tau)$ is a weighted coefficient assigned to the normal data vectors at time window τ. The Ebbinghaus' forgetting curve [15] is used to calculate the weighted coefficients. As shown in Figure 3, the purpose of using the forgetting curve is to reduce the importance of normal data vectors in the old time windows when updating the global normal pattern.

s_G then computes the global first principal component $\varphi(t)$ by a singular value decomposition of $S_\rho(t)$ and uses the triple $(\bar{x}_\rho(t), \varphi(t), d_{\max})$ to update the global normal pattern $P(t)$.

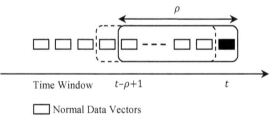

Figure 2. Updating the global normal pattern.

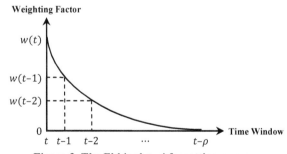

Figure 3. The Ebbinghaus' forgetting curve.

The centralized outlier detection approach has some major drawbacks. First, a large volume of data vectors should be transmitted over the network, which leads to significant decrease of the network lifetime. Second, a high communication load is imposed on the group head because all other member nodes send their data to it.

In the following section, we propose a distributed outlier detection approach employing in-network processing and sensor collaborations to prolong the network lifetime.

5. Distributed outlier detection approach

In this section, we propose a distributed approach for outlier detection in WSNs. The approach consists of three phases: *training, outlier detection,* and *updating*.

In the training phase, the distribution of normal data vectors is modeled. Let G be a group of sensor nodes. Every member node $s_i \in G$ first normalizes its local data vectors $X_i(0)$. It then applies the description procedure on $X_i(0)$ and sends the obtained descriptive data $D_i(0)$ to its group head s_G. Afterwards, s_G applies a distributed PCA (DPCA) [22] on the set of descriptive data $\mathcal{D}(0)$ received from all member nodes and then establishes a global normal pattern $P(0)$. Figure 4 shows the pseudo-code of the training phase.

In the outlier detection phase, during each time window t, s_G applies the detection procedure on the set of descriptive data $\mathcal{D}(t)$ received from all member nodes and detects outliers based upon the global normal pattern $P(t-1)$. Figure 5 shows the pseudo-code of the outlier detection phase.

In the updating phase, at the end of each time window t, s_G first applies DPCA on the set of normal descriptive data $\mathcal{D}^*(t) \subseteq \mathcal{D}(t)$ and computes the global covariance matrix $S(t)$. It then updates the global normal pattern $P(t)$ through calculating the global column means and global covariance matrix of normal data vectors at the ρ previous time windows.

Better load balancing is achieved by distributing the outlier detection process among all member nodes. Also, the communication overhead is reduced by sending the description of data vectors rather than the whole sensed data vectors. This helps to prolong the network lifetime.

5.1. Data normalization

Features of data vectors sensed by member nodes may have different ranges. Hence, when calculating the distance between data vectors, features with larger values will dominate those features with smaller values. Therefore, we normalize each feature into a range $[0,1]$ in order to ensure that all features have the same influence on the distance calculation.

In the centralized approach, all data vectors from all member nodes are sent and available at the group head. Therefore, the group head can normalize all data vectors. In the distributed approach, if every member node normalizes its local

data vectors by using the local minimum and local maximum parameters, the resulting normalized data vectors will not be exactly the same as those of the centralized approach. Hence, we perform the following operations to find the global minimum and global maximum parameters in order to normalize the local data vectors.

After each time window t, every member node $s_i \in G$ computes two vectors $x_{\min}^i(t)$ and $x_{\max}^i(t)$ of minimum and maximum values for its local data vectors $X_i(t)$ and sends them to the group head s_G. After receiving above vectors from member nodes, s_G computes the global minimum and global maximum vectors $x_{\min}^g(t+1)$ and $x_{\max}^g(t+1)$, and sends them to all member nodes. Every member node s_i uses these global parameters to normalize its local data vectors.

---

procedure Training

input:
  A group of sensor nodes $G = \{s_i : i = 1 \ldots s\}$
output:
  A global normal pattern $P(0)$
begin
  for all member nodes $s_i \in G$ **do**
    Sense a set of data vectors $X_i(0)$ and normalize it
    Apply the description procedure on $X_i(0)$ and send the
    descriptive data $D_i(0)$ to the group head s_G
  end for
  for group head s_G **do**
    $\mathcal{D}(0) := \bigcup_{i=1}^{s} \{D_i(0)\}$
    Apply DPCA on the set of descriptive data $\mathcal{D}(0)$ and
    establish a global normal pattern $P(0)$
  end for
end procedure

Figure 4. The training phase.

---

procedure Outlier Detection

input:
  A group of sensor nodes $G = \{s_i : i = 1 \ldots s\}$
  The global normal pattern $P(t-1)$
begin
  for each time window t **do**
    for all member nodes $s_i \in G$ **do**
      Sense a set of data vectors $X_i(t)$ and normalize it
      Apply the description procedure on $X_i(t)$ and send
      the descriptive data $D_i(t)$ to the group head s_G
    end for
    for group head s_G **do**
      Detect outliers based upon $P(t-1)$
    end for
  end for
end procedure

Figure 5. The outlier detection phase.

5.2. Data description

Every member node $s_i \in G$, at each time window t, computes a so-called descriptive data $D_i(t)$ of its normalized data vectors $X_i(t)$ and sends it to the group head s_G. $D_i(t)$ is represented as a ternary $D_i(t) = (\bar{x}_i(t), R_i(t), C_i(t))$, where $\bar{x}_i(t)$ is the column means of $X_i(t)$, $R_i(t)$ is the matrix obtained by the QR decomposition [22] of the column-centered matrix of $X_i(t)$, and $C_i(t)$ is the description of clusters formed by the clustering operation on $X_i(t)$. Our clustering algorithm is based on the fixed-width clustering (FWC) algorithm [23].

Figure 6 shows the pseudo-code of the algorithm FWC that takes $X_i(t)$ as input and groups its data vectors into a set of clusters $C_i(t)$ of fixed radius w_c. For each data vector $x_k^i(t) \in X_i(t)$, if $C_i(t)$ is empty, a new cluster $C_1^i(t)$ is created with $x_k^i(t)$ as its centroid. Otherwise if the distance between $x_k^i(t)$ and the centroid of $C_j^i(t)$ is less than or equal to w_c, $x_k^i(t)$ is added to the nearest cluster $C_{\min}^i(t)$ and the centroid of $C_{\min}^i(t)$ is adjusted to the mean of the data vectors it contains. Otherwise, a new cluster $C_j^i(t)$ is created with $x_k^i(t)$ as its centroid. This operation forms a set of disjoint clusters $C_i(t)$. Finally, the radius of each cluster $C_j^i(t) \in C_i(t)$ is set to the outermost data vector in the cluster.

5.3. Establishing global normal pattern

Let $\mathcal{D}(0)$ be the set of descriptive data received by the group head s_G.

$$\mathcal{D}(0) = \bigcup_{i=1}^{s} \{D_i(0)\} , \qquad (11)$$

where $D_i(0) = (\bar{x}_i(0), R_i(0), C_i(0))$ is the descriptive data of the member node s_i.

In order to establish a global normal pattern, s_G first applies DPCA on $\mathcal{D}(0)$ to compute the global first principal component $\varphi(0)$. For this purpose, s_G first computes the global column means of $X(0)$:

$$\bar{x}(0) = \frac{1}{n} \sum_{i=1}^{s} n_i \bar{x}_i(0) \qquad (12)$$

and then computes the QR decomposition of each pair of matrices $R_i(0)$ and $R_j(0)$ received from member nodes by using Givens rotations:

$$\begin{bmatrix} R_i(0) \\ R_j(0) \end{bmatrix} = Q_{(i,j)}(0) R_{(i,j)}(0) . \qquad (13)$$

Next, s_G continues this operation until $\ell = |\log_2^s|$

steps to obtain $R_{(1,2,...,s)}(0)$ and computes the QR decomposition of the following upper-trapezoidal $(s + d) \times d$ matrix:

$$\begin{bmatrix} \sqrt{n_1}(\bar{x}_1(0) - \bar{x}(0)) \\ \sqrt{n_2}(\bar{x}_2(0) - \bar{x}(0)) \\ \vdots \\ \sqrt{n_s}(\bar{x}_s(0) - \bar{x}(0)) \\ R_{(1,2,...,s)}(0) \end{bmatrix} = Q(0)R(0) . \qquad (14)$$

Next, s_G computes the global first principal component $\varphi(0)$ of $X(0)$ by a singular value decomposition of $R(0)$:

$$R(0) = U(0)\Sigma(0)V^T(0) . \qquad (15)$$

Notice that the computed global principal components are exactly the same as those computed from the centralized approach.

We can easily calculate the global covariance matrix $S(0)$ as

$$S(0) = \frac{1}{n} R^T(0)R(0) , \qquad (16)$$

---

procedure FWC

---

input:
    A set of data vectors $X_i(t) = \{x_k^i(t) : k = 1 \dots n_i\}$
    Cluster radius w_c
output:
    A set of clusters $C_i(t) = \{C_j^i(t) : j = 1 \dots l_i\}$
begin
    $C_i(t) := \emptyset$
    for each data vector $x_k^i(t) \in X_i(t)$ **do**
        if $C_i(t) = \emptyset$ **then**
            Create a new cluster $C_1^i(t)$ with centroid $x_k^i(t)$ and
            radius w_c
            $C_i(t) := \{C_1^i(t)\}$
        else
            Find the nearest cluster $C_{\min}^i(t) \in C_i(t)$ to $x_k^i(t)$
            if $d(x_k^i(t), C_{\min}^i(t)) \leq w_c$ **then**
                Add $x_k^i(t)$ to $C_{\min}^i(t)$ and update its centroid
            else
                Create a new cluster $C_j^i(t)$ with centroid $x_k^i(t)$
                and radius w_c
                $C_i(t) := C_i(t) \cup \{C_j^i(t)\}$
            end if
        end if
    end for
    for each cluster $C_j^i(t) \in C_i(t)$ **do**
        Find the outermost data vector $x_k^i(t)$ in cluster $C_j^i(t)$
        Set the radius of cluster $C_j^i(t)$ to $d(x_k^i(t), C_j^i(t))$
    end for
end procedure

Figure 6. The FWC algorithm.

Finally, s_G calculates the distance of each cluster $C_j^i(0) \in \mathcal{D}(0)$ from $\varphi(0)$:

$$d(C_j^i(0), \varphi(0)) = d_p(c_j^i(0), \varphi(0)) + r_j^i(0) \ , (17)$$

where $c_j^i(0)$ and $r_j^i(0)$ are the centroid and radius of $C_j^i(0)$, respectively. $d_p(c_j^i(0), \varphi(0))$ is the projection distance from $c_j^i(0)$ to $\varphi(0)$.

The triple $(\bar{x}(0), \varphi(0), d_{\max})$ is then used to establish the global normal pattern $P(0)$, where $d_{\max}$ is the maximum distance of all clusters in $\mathcal{D}(0)$ from $\varphi(0)$.

$$d_{\max} = \max_{1 \leq i \leq s, 1 \leq j \leq l_i} d(C_j^i(0), \varphi(0)) \ . \qquad (18)$$

It should be mentioned that $d_{\max}$ is used in the outlier detection phase to detect data vectors that have significant deviation from the global normal pattern.

5.4. Outlier detection

Let $\mathcal{D}(t)$ be the set of descriptive data received by the group head s_G at time window t and $C_i(t) \in \mathcal{D}(t)$ be the description of clusters of the member node s_i. In order to detect outliers, s_G first calculates the distance of each cluster $C_j^i(t) \in C_i(t)$ from $\varphi(t-1) \in P(t-1)$:

$$d(C_j^i(t), \varphi(t-1)) = d_p(c_j^i(t), \varphi(t-1)) + r_j^i(t) \ . \qquad (19)$$

It then classifies $C_j^i(t)$ as outlier, if the calculated distance is greater than $d_{\max}$:

$$\begin{cases} d(C_j^i(t), \varphi(t-1)) > d_{\max} & : \text{Outlier} \\ d(C_j^i(t), \varphi(t-1)) \leq d_{\max} & : \text{Normal} \end{cases} . \qquad (20)$$

If the number of outlier clusters received from a member node is greater than a threshold, the descriptive data received from that node will be discarded.

6. Complexity analysis

In this section, we analyze the communication overhead and computational cost of the centralized and distributed approaches in more detail.

In the centralized approach, at each time window, every member node s_i should communicate to the group head to send its local sensed data vectors. Hence, it incurs a communication overhead of $O(n_i d)$, where n_i is the number of data vectors sensed during the time window and d is the number of features of data vectors. Also, in order to establish or update the global normal pattern, first, the group head should calculate the global column

means and global covariance matrix of normal data vectors for several previous time windows, which has a computational cost of $O(nd^2)$, where n is the number of received data vectors. Then, it should perform a singular value decomposition to compute the updated global first principal component, which has a computational cost of $O(d^3)$.

In the distributed approach, at each time window, in order to normalize the data vectors, every member node s_i should communicate to the group head to send a pair of vectors of minimum and maximum values for its local data vectors. The group head should communicate with all the member nodes to return to them the global minimum and maximum vectors. Also, in order to compute a description of normalized data vectors, every member node s_i should perform the QR decomposition and clustering operations. Hence, it incurs a communication overhead of $O(d^2)$ and a computational cost of $O(n_i{}^2 d)$, where n_i is the number of data vectors sensed during the time window and d is the number of features of data vectors. Also, in order to establish or update the global normal pattern, first, the group head should apply DPCA on normal descriptive data and calculate the global column means and global covariance matrix of normal data vectors for several previous time windows, which has a computational cost of $O(d^3 \log_2 s)$, where s is the number of member nodes. Then, it should perform a singular value decomposition to compute the updated global first principal component, which has a computational cost of $O(d^3)$.

Table 1 shows the comparison between the communication overhead and computational costs of the centralized and distributed approaches.

Table 1. Comparing the centralized and distributed approaches for communication overhead and computational cost

	Computational Cost of the Group Head	Computational Cost of a Member Node	Communication Overhead of the Network
Centralized Approach	$O(nd^2)$	–	$O(nd)$
Distributed Approach	$O(d^3 \log_2 s)$	$O(n_i{}^2 d)$	$O(sd^2)$
$(s \ll n, d \ll n, n_i \ll n)$			

7. Experimental results

In this section, we compare the performance of the distributed outlier detection approach with that of the centralized approach.

We used the real sensed data collected from 54 Mica2Dot sensors deployed in Intel Berkeley Research Lab between February 28 and April 5, 2004. The sensed data included humidity, temperature, light, and voltage values collected once in 31 seconds. In the experiments, we first partitioned the sensor network into eight groups of sensor nodes using the grouping algorithm in [20]. We then selected data from a group that included six nodes, namely nodes 37 to 42. We also randomly selected one of nodes and added some Gaussian noise to its sensed data to simulate the malfunctioning node. The amount of noise was measured by the signal-to-noise ratio (SNR). In the experiments, the length of time window was set to 52 minutes and the parameter SNR was set to 32 dB.

Cumulative percent variance (CPV) [24] is a measure of the percent variance captured by the first few principal components. It can be used to evaluate the importance of each principal component. Figure 7 shows the percent variance captured by the global first principal component $\varphi(t)$ for time windows 0 to 10, in the centralized and distributed approaches. As shown in the Figure 7, at each time window, the global first principal component captures at least 50 percent of the total variance of normal data vectors. Hence, we can use it to establish the global normal pattern at each time window.

Figure 8 compares the behavior of the malfunctioning node with a normal node during a time window of the outlier detection phase, in the centralized and distributed approaches. As can be seen in Figure 8, the malfunctioning node behaviors significantly different from the normal node and thus it can be easily detected by considering the projection distance.

We examined the effect of varying two parameters: The cluster radius w_c ranging from 0.01 to 0.90 and the signal-to-noise ratio parameter SNR ranging from 0 to 40 dB.

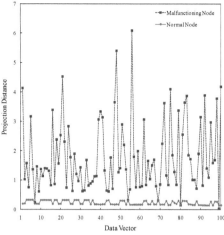

(a) Centralized approach

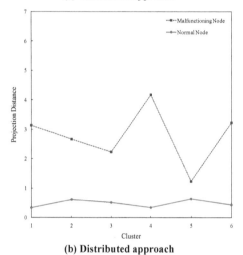

(b) Distributed approach

Figure 8. Projection distance from the global first principal component during a time window.

Table 2 compares the performance of the distributed approach for different values of w_c. For this sensed data, $w_c = 0.05$ is a better choice than other values by which the distributed approach can achieve a better trade-off between the detection rate (DR) and false alarm rate (FAR).

Table 2. Average detection and false alarm rates of the distributed approach for different values of w_c

w_c	Distributed Approach	
	Average DR	Average FAR
0.01	94.05	2.62
0.05	93.63	2.35
0.10	93.20	2.32
0.30	91.87	1.83
0.50	94.81	3.40
0.70	96.24	5.70
0.90	96.88	6.38

Table 3 compares the performance of the centralized and distributed approaches for different values of SNR. As can be seen in Table 3, the average detection and false alarm rates for the distributed approach are respectively 96.7% and 3.9%,

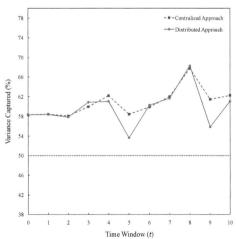

Figure 7. The percent variance captured by each principal component.

while for the centralized approach are respectively 96.4% and 2.7%. Hence, the distributed approach achieves a comparable performance to that of the centralized approach.

Table 3. Average detection and false alarm rates of the centralized and distributed approaches for different values of *SNR*

SNR	Centralized Approach		Distributed Approach	
	Average DR	Average FAR	Average DR	Average FAR
0	99.98	3.73	99.97	4.91
4	99.91	3.39	99.83	4.67
8	99.82	3.11	99.67	4.36
12	99.71	2.93	99.55	4.13
16	99.26	2.81	99.02	3.96
20	98.65	2.66	98.36	3.75
24	97.56	2.45	97.34	3.56
28	96.26	2.35	96.04	3.44
32	93.89	2.27	94.34	3.40
36	91.32	2.20	92.05	3.31
40	84.24	2.16	87.51	3.26

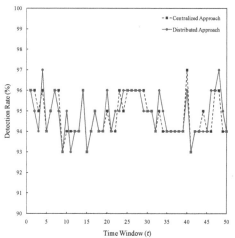

Figure 9. Detection rate of the centralized and distributed approaches during 50 time windows.

Figure 9 compares the detection rate of the centralized and distributed approaches during 50 time windows. As shown in Figure 9, the distributed approach is able to detect outlier data vectors with a rate similar to that of the centralized approach.

Table 4 compares performance of the centralized and distributed approaches for different lengths of time window, ΔT, ranging from 26 to 156 minutes. As shown in Table 4, the distributed approach is able to detect outlier data vectors with a rate similar to that of the centralized approach.

Figures 10 and 11 show reduction in communication overhead (RCO) [12] in the network for different values of w_c and ΔT, respectively. Reduction in communication overhead is calculated as

$$RCO = \frac{n - \tau}{n},\qquad(21)$$

where n and τ are the total number of data sent in the centralized and distributed approaches, respectively.

When compared to the centralized approach, the distributed approach achieves 68% to 95% reduction in communication overhead for w_c in the range of 0.01 to 0.90 and 92% to 96% reduction in communication overhead for ΔT in the range of 50 to 630 minutes.

Table 4. Average detection and false alarm rates of the centralized and distributed approaches for different values of ΔT

ΔT	Centralized Approach		Distributed Approach	
	Average DR	Average FAR	Average DR	Average FAR
26	90.92	1.65	91.43	2.22
52	93.89	2.27	94.34	3.40
78	94.48	4.70	94.53	4.89
104	94.00	5.90	94.77	5.48
130	94.46	5.96	95.49	5.94
156	95.15	6.01	95.50	6.05

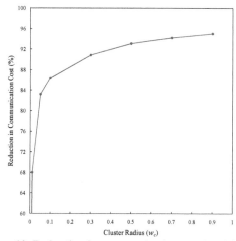

Figure 10. Reduction in communication overhead in the network for different values of w_c.

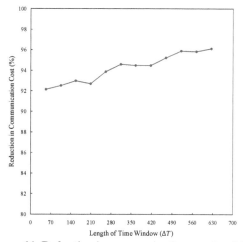

Figure 11. Reduction in communication overhead for different values of ΔT.

8. Conclusions

In this paper, we proposed a centralized and a distributed PCA-based approach to detect outliers in sensed data in WSNs. We partition the network into groups of sensor nodes. Each group has a group head and several member nodes. In the centralized approach, every member node sends its local sensed data to the group head. The group head then applies PCA to establish a global normal pattern and detect outliers. In the distributed approach, we partition the network into groups of sensor nodes. Each group has a group head and several member nodes. Rather than sending all sensed data, every member node uses fixed-width clustering (FWC) and sends a description of its sensed data to the group head. The group head then applies distributed principal component analysis (DPCA) in order to establish a global normal pattern and to detect outliers. The established normal pattern is periodically updated using a forgetting curve.

We compared the performance of the distributed approach with that of a centralized approach based on real sensed data collected from 54 Mica2Dot sensors deployed in Intel Berkeley Research Lab. The experimental results showed that the distributed approach achieves 93.09% reduction in communication overhead in comparison to the centralized approach, while achieving the similar detection and false alarm rates.

Acknowledgment

This work was supported in part by the Iran Telecommunication Research Center (ITRC).

References

[1] Akyildiz, I. F., Su, W., Sankarasubramaniam, Y., and Cayirci, E. (2002). A survey on sensor networks, IEEE Communications Magazine. 40(8), 104–112.

[2] Subramaniam, S., Palpanas, T., Papadopoulos, D., Kalogeraki, V., and Gunopulos, D. (2006). Online outlier detection in sensor data using non-parametric models, in Proceedings of the 32nd International Conference on Very Large Databases, Seoul, Korea.

[3] Zhang, Y., Meratnia, N., and Havinga, P. (2008). Outlier detection techniques for wireless sensor networks: A survey, Journal of Communications Surveys & Tutorials. 12(2), 159–170.

[4] Martincic, F. and Schwiebert, L. (2006). Distributed event detection in sensor networks, in Proceedings of the International Conference on Systems and Networks Communications, Tahiti, French Polynesia.

[5] Chatzigiannakis, V. and Papavassiliou, S. (2007). Diagnosing anomalies and identifying faulty nodes in sensor networks, IEEE Sensors Journal. 7(5), 637–645.

[6] Barnett, V. and Lewis, T. (1994). Outliers in Statistical Data, New York: John Wiley Sons.

[7] Hodge, V. and Austin, J. (2004). A survey of outlier detection methodologies, Journal of Artificial Intelligence Review. 22(2), 85–126.

[8] Tan, P.-N., Steinbach, M., and Kumar, V. (2004). Introduction to Data Mining, New York: Addison-Wesley.

[9] Chandola, V., Banerjee, A., and Kumar, V. (2007). Outlier detection: A survey, Technical Report, University of Minnesota.

[10] Ilyas, M., Mahgoub, I., and Kelly, L. (2004). Handbook of Sensor Networks: Compact Wireless and Wired Sensing Systems, London: CRC Press.

[11] Polastre, J., Szewczyk, R., and Culler, D. (2005). Telos: Enabling ultra-low power wireless research," in Proceedings of the 4th International Symposium on Information Processing in Sensor Networks, Los Angeles, CA, USA.

[12] Raghunathan, V., Schurgers, C., Park, S., and Srivastava, M. (2002). Energy aware wireless microsensor networks, IEEE Signal Processing Magazine. 19(2), 40–50.

[13] Zhao, F., Liu, J., Guibas, L., and Reich, J. (2003). Collaborative signal and information processing: An information-directed approach, Proceedings of the IEEE. 91(8), 1199–1209.

[14] Ahmadi Livani, M. and Abadi, M. (2010). An energy-efficient anomaly detection approach for wireless sensor networks, in Proceedings of the 5th International Symposium on Telecommunications, Tehran, Iran.

[15] Nakayama, H., Kurosawa, S., Jamalipour, A., Nemoto, Y., and Kato, N. (2009). Dynamic anomaly detection scheme for AODV-based mobile ad hoc networks, IEEE Transactions on Vehicular Technology. 58(5), 2471–2481.

[16] Janakiram, D., Mallikarjuna, A., Reddy, V., and Kumar, P. (2006). Outlier detection in wireless sensor networks using Bayesian belief networks, in Proceedings of 1st International Conference on Communication System Software and Middleware, New Delhi, India.

[17] Rajasegarar, S., Leckie, C., and Palaniswami, M. (2006). Distributed anomaly detection in wireless sensor networks, in Proceedings of the 10th IEEE International Conference on Communication Systems, Singapore.

[18] Rajasegarar, S., Leckie, C., Palaniswami, M., and Bezdek, J. C. (2007). Quarter sphere based distributed anomaly detection in wireless sensor networks, in Proceedings of the IEEE International Conference of Communication, Glasgow, UK.

[19] Sheng, B., Li, Q., Mao, W., and Jin, W. (2007). Outlier detection in sensor networks," in Proceedings of the 8th ACM International Symposium on Mobile Ad Hoc Networking and Computing, Montreal, Canada.

[20] Li, G., He, J., and Fu, Y. (2008). Group-based intrusion detection system in wireless sensor networks, Computer Communications, 31(18), 4324–4332.

[21] Golub, G. H. and Van Loan, C. F. (1996). Matrix Computations, Johns Hopkins University Press, Third Edition.

[22] Bai, Z.-J., Chan, R. H., and Luk, F. T. (2005). Principal component analysis for distributed data sets with updating, in Proceedings of International work-shop on Advanced Parallel Processing Technologies, Singapore.

[23] Eskin, E., Arnold, A., Prerau, M., Portnoy, L., and Stolfo, S. (2002). A geometric framework for unsuper-vised anomaly detection: Detecting intrusions in unla-beled data, Applications of Data Mining in Computer Security, Kluwer Academic Publishers.

[24] Jolliffe, I. T. (2002). Principal Component Analy-sis, New York: Springer-Verlag.

20

Protection scheme of power transformer based on time–frequency analysis and KSIR-SSVM

M. Hajian[*], A. Akbari Foroud

Department of Electrical and Computer Engineering, Semnan University, Semnan, Iran

Corresponding author: Mehdi.hajian.sem @gmail.com (M. Hajian)

Abstract

The aim of this paper is to extend a hybrid protection plan for Power Transformer (PT) based on MRA-KSIR-SSVM. This paper offers a new scheme for protection of power transformers to distinguish internal faults from inrush currents. Some significant characteristics of differential currents in the real PT operating circumstances are extracted. Multi Resolution Analysis (MRA) is used as Time–Frequency Analysis (TFA) for decomposition of Contingency Transient Signals (CTSs), and the feature reduction is done by Kernel Sliced Inverse Regression (KSIR). Smooth Supported Vector Machine (SSVM) is utilized for classification. Integration KSIR and SSVM is tackled effectively and fast technique for accurate differentiation of the faulted and unfaulted conditions. The Particle Swarm Optimization (PSO) is used to obtain optimal parameters of the classifier. The proposed structure for Power Transformer Protection (PTP) provides a high operating accuracy for internal faults and inrush currents even in noisy conditions. The efficacy of the proposed scheme is tested by means of numerous inrush and internal fault currents. The achieved results are utilized to verify the suitability and the ability of the proposed scheme to make a distinction inrush current from internal fault. The assessment results illustrate that the proposed scheme presents an enhancement of distinguished inrush current from internal fault over the method to be compared without Dimension Reduction (DR).

Keywords: *Transformer Protection Scheme, Multi Resolution Analysis (MRA), Kernel Sliced Inverse Regression (KSIR), Smooth Supported Vector Machine (SSVM).*

1. Introduction

Power transformers are the most important component of power systems and play a vital role in any power system. In the power system security, protection of power transformers is a very challenging duty [1]. Identification of errors in the power transformer is considered the key to guarantee a reliable and continuous service for electric customers. The main weakness of the differential relay stems from its potential for false tripping caused by occurring inrush current phenomenon, which flows when the power transformer is energized [2]. Two important Contingency Transient Signals (CTSs) such as inrush current and internal fault that their mis-recognition might cause to mal-function of relays is presented.

The inrush currents of power transformers are non-stationary signals, due to flux saturation in the core during energization, high magnitude currents produced. The inrush currents are often occurred during the switching of power transformers. Magnitude of inrush current depends on the switching angles, switching time, magnitude and polarity of residual flux [2]. Also it depends on type and size of transformers.

Pattern recognition is an advanced field of research familiarly link to machine learning. As a part of this literature, classification concept endeavors for constructing classifiers that can find out an input pattern class. Many studies in the last decade have focused on developing classifiers that can learn from samples to execute recognition tasks [3]. The goal of the material presented in this paper is to introduce a new identification scheme for power transformer protection by signal processing and pattern recognition methods.

In transformer protection schemes area, the novelties presented in this paper can be summarized below.

1. We have used effective extracted features that increase percentage of the correct classification.

2. The purpose of this paper is to apply an effective dimension reduction method incorporate with classifier.

3. The proposed method uses the smooth supported vector machines for classification.

Time–frequency analysis [4] methods, such as Discrete Wavelet Transform (DWT) are required to attend to non-stationary behavior of the Contingency Signals (CSs) in order to express those in the time and frequency domain. The MRA is suitable for investigation of non-stationary signals, and unlike the spectral analysis, MRA represents a main advantage. It is powerful tool for time-frequency domain localization of transient contingencies (such as inrush current) [5].

One of the first and maybe the most accepted Dimension Reduction Method (DRM) is Slice Inverse Regression (SIR) [6]. Li (1991) [7] suggested SIR to find the Effective Dimension Reduction Directions (EDRD). The reduction techniques speed up the computation and boost the numerical stability.

SIR is a well-known DRM due to provide an effectual low-dimensional linear subspace. SIR can be comprehensive to nonlinear transform via the kernel approach. This study is investigated KSIR capability to combine with SSVM for classification. Numerical results indicate that KSIR is a useful kernel tool for nonlinear dimension reduction and it can combine with SSVM to structure a commanding tool for nonlinear data analysis.

SIR adopts the class information for evaluating the projection directions (unlike Principal Component Analysis (PCA)). Resembling the PCA, SIR is a technique based on the transformation of input features x to the effective features. Nevertheless, in contradiction of PCA, SIR provides the features by modeling the relation between input x and target variables y while maintaining the majority of the information in the input data. SIR can be observed as a PCA-like method applied on the random variable $E(x|y)$ instead of on x. In other word, SIR directs to a generalized eigen-system, whilst PCA guides to an eigen-system [8]. The fundamental concept of

the kernel SIR technique [9] is at first to preprocess the data pattern by some non-linear mapping and after that to apply the same linear SIR.

Compared with other methods of classification, SVMs have demonstrated outstanding potentials in coping with classification problems [10]. This paper tested the aptitude of SSVM in making a nonlinear separating surface. Support vector machine (SVM) has been proved to be a potent tool for fault detection. Smoothing processes [11] that are comprehensively used for resolving significant arithmetical programming challenges and applications are employed here to produce and resolve an unconstrained smooth redevelop of the support vector machine for pattern recognition by kernel-based algorithm. SSVM is resolved by a very fast Newton–Armijo approach and is developed to nonlinear separation surfaces using nonlinear kernel procedures [12]. The effectiveness of this scheme is expressed by widespread simulation of different operating conditions and faults in power transformers by PSCAD / EMTDC software. In this paper, two methods, SSVM and KSIR-SSVM, are investigated and compared. The proposed scheme is performed via the framework shown in Figure 1. In this paper, MRA, KSIR and SSVM are jointly applied to differentiate internal faults from inrush currents. The schematic diagram for MRA-KSIR-SSVM method is presented in Figure 1. MRA has been applied for the TFA of fault signals for the distinguished inrush current and internal fault of power transformer using discrete wavelet coefficients (DWC). CTSs are broken down into frequency sub-bands by MRA. Then, a set of statistical features are extracted from these sub-bands to identification of CTSs. Furthermore, KSIR method is employed to decrease the dimensionality of features vector. Finally, the features vector is applied as an input to a Smooth Support Vector Machine (SSVM) with two discrete outputs: Inrush current or internal fault current.

KSIR can be employed for nonlinear dimension reduction. By combining with SSVM, we achieve a nonparametric and nonlinear classification. The effectual dimension reduction directions of the training data sets embedded in high-dimensional space is explored by KSIR. Next, the test data sets are projected onto these directions and SSVM as the classifier is more used to recognize the test data sets. PSO is adopted to optimize the parameters of SSVM. PSO is to find the optimal settings of parameters in SSVM. Compared to

GA, particle swarm optimization is powerful and easy to implement. PSO algorithm can select suitable parameters for SSVM classifier, which avoids over-fitting or under-fitting in the SSVM model occurred due to the improper determination of these parameters.

A review of the literature for distinguished fault from inrush current in power transformer is presented in the next section. Multi-resolution analysis definition and formulations are presented in section 3, and the extracted features are offered in section 4. The dimension reduction and concept of SIR and KSIR are explained in section 5, The SSVM concept and formulations are introduced in section 6 for classification of proposed protection scheme. In sections 7 and 8, modeling and simulation of various operating conditions of power system and numerical results are presented, respectively. Conclusion of the whole study is provided in section

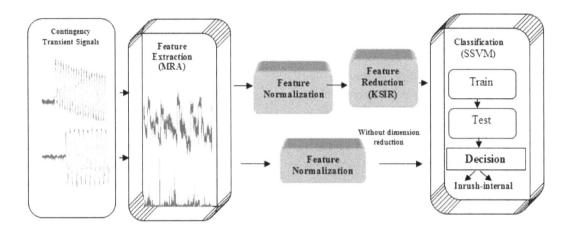

Figure 1. Framework of the proposed scheme

2. Related work

Dimension reduction has been a concentration of several main headlines of research in the statistical machine learning literature [13]. The supervised dimension reduction methods focus on the classification targets, including Linear Discriminant Analysis (LDA) [14], and Kernel Linear Discriminant Analysis (KLDA). The unsupervised dimension reduction techniques imagine that y is unidentified. PCA and kernel PCA [15], GPLVM [16] and nonlinear locality-preserving manifold learning [17] belong to this category of methods that do not control recognized target values. KSIR as a nonlinear feature reduction has been proven essential as a preprocessing stage for classification problems [18].

Many methods have been employed to distinguish inrush from internal faults in transformers. Most of them rely on an index and fixed threshold [19]. Some research has focused on to restrain tripping command of power transformer when an inrush current creates in the transformer windings. The common procedure employed to avoid false trips when inrush currents flow in windings is harmonic restraint relay [20]. These procedures

have problems, when 2nd order harmonic component makes in different operating conditions the magnitude exceeds the predefined threshold. This may be due to resonant conditions of power system, presence of a shunt capacitor and nonlinear loads or saturation of transformer [1, 2].

The different methods have been proposed to distinguish fault from inrush current based on measuring the voltage and current waveforms [21, 22]. The need to utilize voltage of transformers and increased protection strategy computational burden are disadvantage of these methods. Some other methods detect based on measuring of the time between the respective peaks of differential current [23]. Recently, several new protective schemes have been proposed to deal with the foregoing problem in power transformer protection. Most of them have focused on the applications of intelligent techniques. Neural network is applied to discriminate the internal fault current and inrush current in [24]. The MRA technique is a dominant tool for power system transient analysis. Some protective schemes were used with signal processing and machine learning techniques. [1,19]. Conventional Neural Networks

(NNs) are complicated to construct in order to require to determination a suitable number of hidden neurons. The support vector machine (SVM) is a machine-learning tool, which is generally used to data patterns [25]. Integration of WT and artificial neural fuzzy system (ANFIS) has been proposed in [26] to differentiate the faulted from unfaulted conditions.

3. Wavelet-based multi-resolution analysis

Mallat (1989) presents the Multi-resolution analysis (MRA) that it can decompose the signal into various scales of orthogonal signal component. By means of MRA, the fault signals are divided into multi-scale signals. Multi Resolution Analysis (MRA) and Quadrature Mirror Filters (QMF) are also important for evaluating the discrete wavelet decomposition. In multi-resolution strategy, a disturbance signal is decomposed into several sub-signals which have specified harmonic components. A QMF consists of two filters. One gives the average (Low Pass Filter (LPF)), while the other gives details (High - Pass Filter (HPF)). These filters are related to each other in such a way as to be able to perfectly reconstruct a signal from the decomposed components. In this strategy, the approximation sub-signal $S_j(t)$ and the detailed sub-signal $D_j(t)$, which correspond to the components of signal $x(t)$ at different scales, formulated as follows [5,27]:

$$S_J(t) = \sum_k s_{J,K} \phi_{J,K}(t) J, K \in I \qquad (1)$$

$$D_J(t) = \sum_k d_{J,K} \Psi_{J,K}(t) j, K \in I \qquad (2)$$

The $D_j(t)$ contents an approximate frequency bound of $[f_s/2^{j+1} - f_s/2^j]$ Hz and the $S_J(t)$ contents an approximate frequency bound of $[0 - f_s/2^{J+1}]$ Hz, f_s is the sampling frequency. Therefore, the better scales of $D_j(t)$ mainly capture the detailed (high-frequency) feature of $x(t)$, while the larger scales of $D_j(t)$ and $S_j(t)$ mainly reveal the whole-view (low-frequency) feature of $x(t)$. After that, the original signal $x(t)$ can be recovered in terms of these sub-signals with diverse resolutions as follow:

$$x(t) \approx S_J(t) + D_J(t) + D_{J-1}(t) + ... + D_1(t) \qquad (3)$$

MRA is normally based on Daubechies orthogonal wavelet basis. The choice of mother wavelet is important because different types of mother wavelets have different properties. This rigidly depends on the nature of the application. The most used mother wavelet in PTP diagnosis is the Daubechies wavelet with a four-coefficient filter (db4). Therefore, in this paper, the mother wavelet db4 is used, and shows that db4 has a good performance of detection of CTSs. The wavelet coefficients obtained by MRA can yield good information of CTSs. The fourth-order Daubechies' wavelet (Daublet4) was utilized as mother wavelet function to perform MRA on the CTSs.

As mentioned above, MRA permits decomposing signal into approximations (i.e. low frequency coefficients) and details (i.e. high frequency coefficients) by using a filter bank arranged of both LPF and HPF. The filtering procedure can be repeated, in order that CS is decomposed into lower resolution components and individual details. This is namely the MRA tree [27]. Figure 2 shows the MRA tree with three levels. In fact, the high frequency coefficients are ignored. So, a signal can be first decomposed into an approximation a1 and a detail d1 (that is the level 1 of the decomposition). Subsequently, a1 can be decomposed into an approximation a2 and a detail d2 (that is the level 2 of the decomposition) and so on. Taking into account n levels of decomposition, the reconstruction process consents to recovering the initial signal, summing the n details d1, d2,...,dn and the approximation an of level n [5, 27]. (According to Figure 2)

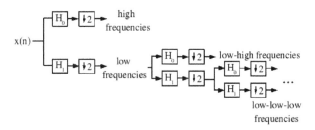

Figure 2. Three decomposed levels of MRA [27]

4. Extracted features

Feature extraction is the most important part of the intelligent system as a pattern recognition scheme. In the literature, the signal processing techniques are available for analyzing protection of power transformer signals. Some examples are Fast Fourier transforms method fractal-based method time–frequency ambiguity plane method, short time power and correlation transform method, and wavelet transforms method [28].

A signal is said to be stationary if its frequency or spectral contents are not changing with respect to time. Fourier Transform (FT) can be applied to the stationary signals. A non-stationary signal is one whose frequency changes over time. One of the major types of non-stationary signals has been identified, transient signals. Like inrush current, plenty of signals may contain non-stationary or transitory characteristics [27]. Various methods have been introduced and used to study non-stationary signals and both spectral as well as localized information has been obtained. The FT and Short Time Fourier Transform (STFT) view a signal in terms of finite time series since STFT uses a window of fixed width; they are unable to provide effective frequency relative resolution. On the other hand, the MRA is effective in providing time localized information as the information given is in both the time and frequency domains [28].

Essentially, the fault diagnosis is a pattern recognition problem, for which the key step is to extract useful fault features from vibration signals through some suitable signal processing methods [5]. In other words, the CTSs can be detected on the comparison of the extracted features from them.

Appropriate features are extracted by spectral data and statistical indicators of DWT coefficients outputs. One of the important characteristics of the selected features, are their severability for different classes. The suggested integrated feature extraction strategy has several desirable characteristics:

1. It includes the minimum number of important and effective features necessary to achieve high performance of the classification of inrush and internal fault.

2. It creates a separable feature vector.

Most useful features must be first extracted from coefficients in order to more effectively recognize the type of CTSs. For the recognition of faults, four-level MRA are applied on the measured current signals. Eight statistical features are extracted from the coefficients of different bands generated using MAR, i.e. features number from 1 to 8 are shown in Table 1.

In this paper, some statistical methods, such as mean, standard deviation, energy, shannon-entropy, log-entropy, threshold-entropy presented in Table 1 have been used as the features extractors. These features are obtained based on the practical experiments.

Table 1. Extracted features for detecting scheme

Feature number	Description
1	Standard deviation of level 2 of detail
2	Minimum value of absolute of level 5 of approximation
3	Mean of average of absolute of all level of details
4	Mean of disturbances energy (all level).
5	Energy of level 3 of detail.
6	Mean of Shannon entropy of all level of details
7	Mean of log energy of all level of details
8	Mean of threshold entropy of all level of details

Extracted feature vector should have properties, such as a variety from class to class. Also, it should not have correlation with other features. Figure 3 shows the normalized value of extracted features from inrush current and internal fault for noisy condition. As shown in Figure 3 the values of the features of each class (inrush current and internal fault) are different. So the features for any classes have different behavior. Therefore, these features create a separable feature vector. The features vector is fed to SSVM for classification.

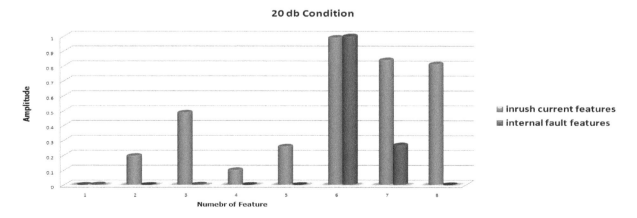

Figure 3. The values of the features of inrush current and internal fault in 20 dB noise condition.

5. Dimension reduction

Dimension reduction is a main popular strategy in analyzing multivariate input data due to visualization of the patterns of data. Also, it is a key material in data mining and machine learning. The main motivation applying dimension reduction methods are: Improve visualization, remove redundancy of data, data compression, reduce computational time and enhancement of accuracy [9]. The dimension reduction offered by KSIR can be applied as a preprocess for classification. The aim of reduction hypothesis is the high-dimensional data is projected to a lower dimensional subspace without the loss of information for separability among classes [29].

SIR finds the directions of maximum variance, with P data points collapsed into K slice means using the affinity in classes. This reduction technique will speed up the computation and increase the numerical stability.

In this paper, we employed a hybrid SIR method using a kernel machine which we call kernel SIR. The method of SIR employ to explore the EDRD from the training data embedded in high-dimensional space. The test data are then projected onto these directions and the classifier is further applied to classify the test data. In the kernel extension of SIR, input data is mapped to the Hilbert space induced from the kernel function. It means that KSIR actually finds an effective projection direction in the kernel feature space. The results show that KSIR-SSVM is an effective classification method in the structural risk minimization, non-linear characteristics, avoiding the over-fitting and strong generalization ability.

5.1. SIR method

This paper proposed an effective data-analytic tool, SIR, for reducing the dimension of the input features. The aim of below formulation is to get cut down the dimension of the input data from P to a smaller number K without losing any information. The hypothetical properties of SIR can be presented below [9].

$$\xi = \psi(\mu_1^T X, ..., \mu_K^T X, \varepsilon) \quad , \quad X \in R^P \quad (4)$$

Where the μ_K is the unknown row vector and ε is the error. For effectively reducing the dimension, we need only to estimate the EDRD generated by the μ_K. In fact, the μ_K itself is not identifiable without an exact structural shape on f. If the distribution of x has been standardized to

have the zero mean and the identity covariance, the $E(X|\xi)$, generates the EDRD.

Therefore, any supposition of ξ includes only the summary statistic S(X) that is of much lower dimension than the original data X. Linear techniques for dimension reduction concentrate on linear summaries of the data, that is,

$$S(X) = \left[\mu_1^T X, ..., \mu_K^T X \right] \quad (5)$$

The K-dimensional subspace, $s = span\{\mu_1, ..., \mu_k\}$ is mentioned as the EDRD space in [7] since S summaries all the information, we require to identify the ξ. The obtained result in [7] is that under some soft conditions the EDRD $\{\mu_j\}_{j=1}^{K}$ according to the eigenvectors of the matrix, that covariance matrix is denoted by Γ.

$$W = [\Gamma(X)]^{-1} \Gamma[E(X|\xi)] \quad (6)$$

Consequently, the EDRD or subspace can be calculated by means of an eigen-analysis of matrix W, that these directions display the major distinction in the class means relative to the within-class variance and are better for classification [9]. In other words, the output of the KSIR method permits for the evaluation of nonlinear EDRD.

5.2. Kernel process

Kernel-based algorithm [30], a non-linear transformation can map the input feature space into a high-dimensional feature space. Basically, the classification is more probable to be linearly resolved in high-dimensional space (according to Figure 4).

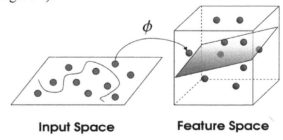

Input Space   **Feature Space**

Figure 4. Concept of non-linear kernel function

This kernel function corresponds to the inner product of $\phi(x_i)$ and $\phi(x_j)$ where ϕ is a definite mapping from input space R^d to a high-dimensional feature space F. In the other words, to train the classifier, only the kernel is required and no explicit knowledge of $\varphi(x_i)$ is needed.

$$\varphi : x \rightarrow \varphi(x), \quad k(x_i, x_j) = \varphi(x_i)^T . \varphi(x_j) \tag{7}$$

5.3. KSIR method

When the variation of data pattern is nonlinear, KSIR based visualization process has better performance than SIR. Due to overcoming several constraints, KSIR finds the linear subspace that best represents data. KSIR is a generalizing method based on linear SIR that converts into nonlinear case by the kernel approach [9]. The concept of KSIR is to transfer the original input x_i into a high-dimensional feature space $\varphi(x_i)$ firstly by kernel method and then by computing the linear SIR in $\varphi(x_i)$. The linear SIR in $\varphi(x_i)$ corresponds to a nonlinear SIR in x_i. Similarly to SIR, KSIR estimates $\Gamma[E(\Phi(x)|\xi)]$ by slicing the output.

6. Proposed classification

Classification should be considered as a significant component for the design of intelligent systems based on pattern recognition techniques. An important example of the general discriminated classifiers is the support vector machine (SVM) [31]. Support Vector Machines [32] have been widely applied to pattern classification problems [19], non-linear regressions and clustering. In years of contemporary, linear or nonlinear kernels SVMs have become one of the most hoping machine learning methods for classification. The original learning form of SVM goes ahead to a quadratic program (QP), which is a convex constrained optimization problem and therefore has a unique answer. Compared with other machine learning methods, such as the neural networks (NN), that is a great advantage [30, 32]. SVM was suggested by Vapnik [32]. After that, studies have been worked to use the SVM tool in many sciences.

6.1. Smooth support vector machine

The classification by support vector machine is defined as discovering the weights and bias parameters (separating surface) in order to maximize the margin while ensuring that the training data are well classified. This can be expressed as the QP optimization problem [32]. The optimal surface in the sense of machine learning is a balanced behavior between over fitting and under fitting. Concept of optimal

surface is based on maximizing the margin shown in Figure 5.

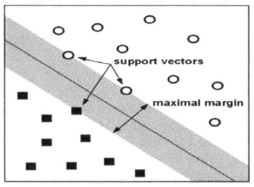

Figure 5. Concept of optimal surface based on maximize the margin

Due to convenient discussion, we first describe the linear SVM. Given a training dataset $S = \{(x_1, y_1), ..., (x_n, y_n)\} \subseteq R^d \times R$, where $x_i \in R^d$ is the input data and $y_i \in \{-1,1\}$ is the corresponding class tag, the classical SVM separating surface is modeled by resolving a convex optimization that can be defined as a mathematical problem as follows:

$$\min_{(\omega, b, \xi) \in R^{d+1+n}} \left\{ C \sum_{i=1}^{n} \xi_i + \frac{1}{2} \|\omega\|_2^2 \right\} \tag{8}$$

With non-eqilibrium constraints:

$$s.t. \{ y_i (\omega^T x_i + b) + \xi_i \geq 1$$
$$\xi_i \geq 0, \, for \, i = 1, 2, ..., n, \tag{9}$$

Where C is a cost and positive parameter that controls the trade of between the error of training process and maximizing the margin, which is got by minimizing $\|\omega\|_2^2$.

An alternative smoothing strategy has been recommended and resolved by a fast Newton–Armijo approach that converges globally and quadratically. In general, finding the global optimum of a function can be a very difficult duty. However, for a particular type of optimization problems acknowledged as convex optimization problems, and many cases can discover the global solution. A main difficulty with non-convex formulations is that the global optimal answer cannot be effectively calculated, and the behavior of a local solution is hard to evaluate. In practice, convex relaxation (such as SVM for classification) has been accepted to remedy the problem. Newton–Armijo method is applied for discovering a convex function minimum that needs neither strong convexity nor even smoothness merits on the whole space [33]. It guarantees to find global convergence when the function is not strongly convex. The smooth formulation with a nonlinear kernel retains the strong convexity and twice differentiability and as a result can be applied Newton–Armijo method to solve it [12].

The key difference between smoothing approach and that of the classical SVM [32] is that solving a linear system instead of resolving a QP as the case with the classical SVM. Furthermore, the result can be indicated that smoothing approach converges globally to the unique solution [12].

On the contrary of the basic SVM of (8), a smooth support vector machine (SSVM) minimizes the square of the slack vector ξ with weight $\dfrac{C}{2}$.

Besides, SSVM appends on the term $\dfrac{b^2}{2}$ to the objective to be minimized results in the following optimization problem:

$$\min_{(\omega,b,\xi)\in R^{d+1+n}}\left\{\frac{C}{2}\sum_{i=1}^{n}\xi_i^2+\frac{1}{2}\left(\|\omega\|_2^2+b^2\right)\right\} \quad (10)$$

$$s.t.\{y_i\left(\omega^T X_i+b\right)+\xi_i\geq 1$$
$$\xi_i\geq 0, \; for \; i=1,2,...,n, \quad (11)$$

At a solution of (10), ξ is given by $\xi_i=\{1-y_i(\omega^T X_i+b)\}+$ for all i where the *plus* function x+ is defined as $X_+=\max\{0,x\}$. Thus, we can replace ξ_i in (2) by $\{1-y_i(\omega^T X_i+b)\}+$. This will transfer the problem (10) into an unconstrained minimum optimization below:

$$\min_{(\omega,b)\in R^{d+1}}\left\{\frac{C}{2}\sum_{i=1}^{n}\{1-y_i(\omega^T x_i+b)\}_+^2+\frac{1}{2}\left(\|\omega\|_2^2+b^2\right)\right\} \quad (12)$$

This modulation decreases the variables from $d+1+n$ to $d+1$.

However, the minimization of objective function is not twice differentiable which precludes the employ of a fast Newton method. In SSVM, the plus function X_+ is estimated using a smooth p-function $p(x,\alpha)=x+\dfrac{1}{\alpha}\log(1+e^{-\alpha.x}),\alpha\succ 0$. By replacing the plus function with a very accurate smooth approximation p-function provides the smooth support vector machine strategy [34]:

$$\min_{(\omega,b)\in R^{d+1}}\left\{\frac{C}{2}\sum_{i=1}^{n}p\{1-y_i(\omega^T X_i+b),\alpha\}^2+\frac{1}{2}\left(\|\omega\|_2^2+b^2\right)\right\} \quad (13)$$

Where $\alpha\succ 0$ is the smooth parameter. The objective function in (13) is robustly convex and infinitely differentiable. Hence, it has a unique solution and can be resolved by fast Newton-Armijo approach.

For the nonlinear application, this modulation can be developed to the nonlinear SVM by the kernel trick scheme as follows:

$$\min_{(u,b)\in R^{d+1}}\left\{\frac{C}{2}\sum_{i=1}^{n}p([1-y_i\{\sum_{j=1}^{n}u_j K(X_i,X_j)+b\}],\alpha\}^2+\frac{1}{2}\left(\|u\|_2^2+b^2\right)\right\} \quad (14)$$

Where $k(x_i,x_j)$ is a kernel function.

The non-linear SSVM can be formulated in matrix form as follows:

$$\sum_{u_j\neq 0}u_j K(A_j^T,X)+b=K(X,A^T)u+b \quad (15)$$

Where $A=[x_1^T;...;x_n^T]$, $A_j=x_j^T$. The coefficient u_j is terminated by resolving an optimization problem (15) and the data points with corresponding non-zero coefficients are named support vectors. It is frequently suitable to have fewer support vectors [34].

7. Power system under study and simulation

PSCAD/EMTDC software is a graphical interface industry standard simulation instrument for simulation the transient behavior of electrical grids. The experiments of this paper are implemented through digital time-domain simulation studies in the PSCAD/EMTDC 4.2.1 software environment. To have comprehensive study, different contingency signals of inrush currents and internal faults are simulated. More than 2000 samples are generated.

For evaluation of the proposed method, a part of power system including a 160 MVA 230/63 kV real three-phase transformer is modeled (Figure 6). Different conditions of internal fault and inrush currents that may be occurred are simulated. Currents of primary and secondary sides can be saved in PSCAD/EMTDC software via output channels. By using these measured currents of both sides of power transformer, differential currents are calculated after three main stages i.e. zero sequence elimination, vector group adaptation and CT mismatch ratio correction. The sampling frequency is set 2.5 kHz. So each cycle contains 50 samples.

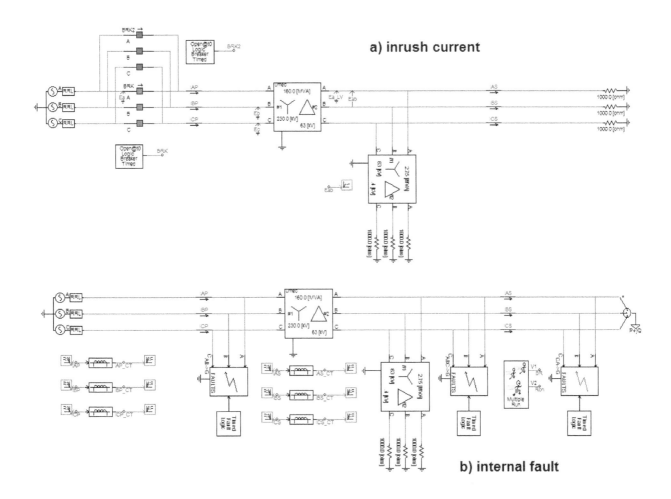

Figure 6. View of power system model, a) model of inrush current, b) model of internal fault current.

Moreover, the UMEC [35, 36] model is used for modeling of power transformer. This model considers the magnetic coupling between windings of different phases in addition to the coupling between windings of the same phase. Also, it uses the magnetization curve of transformer for considering the non-linearity of core characteristics. Thus, more accurate differential currents are obtained, specifically when transformer cores enter to saturation region. Besides, the Jiles–Atherton [37] model is applied for precise simulation of CTs' behavior. This model can yield better representation of B-H curve using a modified Langevin function and a new parameter. In the simulation process, different parameters that affect the CT saturation are considered. Remanence flux, connected burden of secondary side and magnetization curve of CT core are main parameters, which have been considered in simulation conditions.

For simulation of transformer energization, remenance flux and switching time are considered as effective parameters on magnitude of inrush currents. Usually, the maximum remenance flux in each leg is lower than 80% of the peak flux. This residual flux can be modeled by inserting a DC current source in parallel of each winding (Figure 6). Besides, the switching time interval for energization of transformer has been set 1 msec. Moreover, the similar situation occurs when transformers are energized in parallel or nearby an already energized transformer. This event that the transformers draw causes large current from the source is known as the "sympathetic inrush". Moreover, terminal faults are also simulated considering different effective parameters on fault currents like fault occurrence instant, fault resistance and fault type. For different fault types, fault resistances are considered 0, 5 and 10 ohms and the time interval of fault occurrence is set to 1 msec.

Also, the practical CTSs in an electrical power network consist of noise. Therefore, the proposed scheme has to be scrutinized under noisy condition. Due to test the sensitivity of the proposed scheme against noisy condition, white Gaussian noise with the signal-to-noise ratio (SNR) 20 dB is added with CTSs and operated with MRA for computation of features. The value of the SNR is described as follows:

$$SNR(dB) = 10 * \log\left(\frac{P_s}{P_n}\right) \qquad (16)$$

Where P_s is the power of signal and P_n is that of the noise.

The SSVM classifier is trained with training set and tested. Arbitrary parameters C, ε and kernel mainly affect on the accuracy and performance of the SSVM classifier. In this paper, PSO algorithm [38] has been used for solving the problem of choosing optimal parameters of SSVM. In order to get adequate gamma (ε) in radial basis kernel function and C parameters, a heuristic search was performed.

8. Numerical results and analysis

After obtaining differential currents, the MRA is applied for extraction of features. For normalization purpose, feature vectors are transformed to the range [0 1]. Then, the KSIR method is applied for reduction of features dimensions. Afterward, selected features are used for training and testing process. This study presents a strategy for improving SSVM performance in two aspects: Feature reduction and parameter optimization. The obtained classification accuracy shows the performance of the proposed algorithm.

In this section, we describe a sensitivity analysis of the SSVM parameters. Then, we determine the optimal parameters and employ them for pattern recognition. Finally, the results are presented.

8.1. The optimal SSVM model by PSO

For the optimization, a particle swarm optimization algorithm is proposed to improve the generalization performance of the recognizer. In this module, the SSVM classifier design is optimized by searching for the best value of the parameters that tune its kernel function parameter. Inappropriate choice of the parameters can lead to over-fitting or under-fitting. In the study, PSO is used to determine the SSVM parameters (C, ε). The obtained values of classifier parameters are

given in Table 2. These values yield maximum classification accuracy.

Particle swarms have two primary operators: Velocity update and position update. During each generation, each particle is accelerated toward its previously best position and towards its best global position. At each iteration, a new velocity value for each particle is calculated based on its current velocity, the distance from its previous best position and the distance from its best global position. The new velocity value is then used to calculate the next position of the particle [38].

Figures. 7 and 8 show the evaluated parameters of the kernel function of the SSVM classifier for MRA-KSIR-SSVM structure obtained by PSO for different runs. According to results (Figures. 7 and 8), the best classification for MRA-KSIR-SSVM structure is obtained in proper pairs of C = 0.3 and $\varepsilon = 0.01$ (see Table 2).

In this section, we mainly compare the two strategy of protection of power transformer. The concept of using pattern recognition and signal processing device for the protection of power transformer, by MRA-KSIR-SSVM scheme through training from simulation data to properly classify future data is presented. The chief goal of this study is to separate the two classes of CTSs by using MRA-KSIR-SSVM scheme. As it can be seen in Table 2, the obtained results indicate a very good classification performance and the proposed scheme showing the high robustness against noise. Also, the implementation of KSIR algorithm is concluded the fast computation and numerical stability.

As a result, the proposed method (MRA-KSIR-SSVM) can achieve better identification of internal fault and inrush current than MRA-SSVM. This comparison result implies that the proposed KSIR-SSVM strategy obviously outperforms the SSVM strategy in diagnosing different of internal fault and inrush current.

We have demonstrated the applicability of the proposed technique to the practical condition. A serious problem of practical recognition system is its low classifying speed. In the SVM classifier, the speed depends on the number of support vectors. The training points that are nearest to the separating function are called support vectors [32]. We have devised a method to overcome this problem. The KSIR-SSVM, proposed in this paper, is a new method to reduce the number of support vectors (SVs) (see Table 2). The advantages of the approach lies in the fact that the smaller the input dataset is, the fewer SVs would yield and that it would require less CPU time and memory. Experiment results demonstrate that KSIR-SSVM method can control the tradeoff between the classifying speed and the performance of SSVM. The employment of the KSIR-SSVM method to reduce the number of SVs decreases the expectation value of the probability of committing an error on a test example and enhances SSVM's generalization capability.

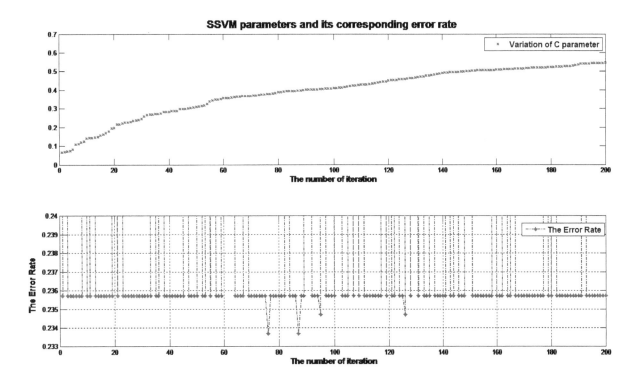

Figure 7. Sensitivity analysis of C parameter (Error rate with different C)

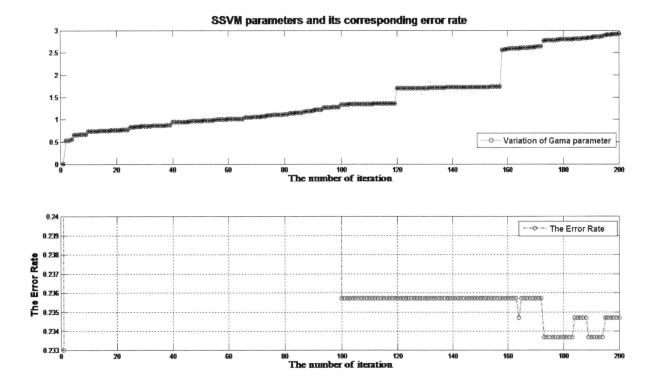

Figure 8. Sensitivity analysis of gama parameter (Error rate with different gama)

Table 2. Identification results of proposed scheme for conditions including internal fault and inrush current.

Methods	Dataset input	(C, ε)	#SVs	The error rate of testing	CPU Sec.
KSIR-SSVM	20 dB	(0.3,0.01)	41	0.233	0.0123
SSVM	20 dB	(1,0.4654)	143	0.285	0.0488

9. Conclusion

This paper has proposed and evaluated MRA-KSIR-SSVM scheme to distinguish between internal faults and inrush currents in power transformer protection. Required CSs have been attained through many simulations in PSCAD/EMTDC software. MRA has been applied to extract features. This paper is explored KSIR ability to combine with SSVM for the protection scheme. The joint KSIR and SSVM are able to efficiently decrease the feature vectors, speed up the convergence in the training of SSVM and obtain higher identification accuracy. PSO algorithm is chosen as an optimization technique to optimize the input feature subset selection and the SSVM parameters setting simultaneously. This technique will improve the SSVM performance. The KSIR–SSVM method could be a promising tool for the protection of power transformers. Also, the results show first, comparing SSVM with KSIR-SSVM obtains better generalization performance. Second, the stability of protection scheme in presence of the inrush current, internal faults signals, robust fault detection, and even in presence of a bad noisy condition may assure secure and correct performance of protection system of transformer.

References

[1] Samantaray, S.R. and Dash, P.K. (2011). Decision Tree based discrimination between inrush currents and internal faults in power transformer.Electrical Power and Energy Systems. 33, 1043–1048.

[2] Sedighi, A.R. and Haghifam, M.R. (2005). Detection of inrush current in distribution transformer using wavelet transform. Electrical Power and Energy Systems. 27, 361–370.

[3] Saxena, D., Verma, K.S. and Singh, S.N. (2010). Power quality event classification: an overview and key issues. International Journal of Engineering, Science and Technology. 2(3), 186-199.

[4] Hlawatsch, F. and Auger, F. (2008). Time-Frequency Analysis: Concepts and Methods. UK: ISTE/Wiley, London.

[5] Hossam Eldin, A.A. and Refaey, M.A. (2011). A novel algorithm for discrimination between inrush current and internal faults in power transformer differential protection based on discrete wavelet transform. Electric Power Systems Research. 81, 19–24.

[6] Scrucca, L. (2011). Model-based SIR for dimension reduction. Computational Statistics and Data Analysis. 55, 3010–3026.

[7] Li, K.C. (1991). Sliced inverse regression for dimension reduction (with discussion). Journal of the American Statistical Association. 86, 316–34.

[8] Wu, H.M. and Lu, H.H.S. (2007). Iterative sliced inverse regression for segmentation of ultrasound and MR images. Pattern Recognition. 40, 3492 – 3502.

[9] Yeh, Y.R., Huang, S.Y. and Lee, Y.J. (2009). Nonlinear Dimension Reduction with Kernel Sliced Inverse Regression. IEEE Transactions on Knowledge and Data Engineering. 21(11).

[10] Wang, Y., Chen, S. and Xue, H. (2011). Support Vector Machine incorporated with feature discrimination. Expert Systems with Applications. 38, 12506–12513.

[11] Chen, C. and Mangasarian, O.L.A. (1996). Class of Smoothing Functions for Nonlinear and Mixed Complementarity Problems. Computational Optimization and Applications. 5(2), 97-138.

[12] Lee, Y. and Mangasarian, O.L.(2001). SSVM: A Smooth Support Vector Machine for Classification. Computational Optimization and Applications. 20, 5–22.

[13] Duintjer Tebbens, J. and Schlesinger, P. (2007). Improving implementation of linear discriminant analysis for the high dimension/small sample size problem. Computer Statistic Data Analysis.

[14] Yang, J. and Yang, J.-Y. (2003). Why can LDA be performed in PCA transformed space?. Pattern Recognition. 36 (2), 563–566.

[15] Delalleau, Y. O., Le Roux, N., Paiement, J-F., Vincent, P. and Ouimet, M. (2004). Learning eigen functions links spectral embedding and Kernel PCA. Neural Computation. 16(10), 2197–2219.

[16] Lawrence, N.D. and Quiñonero Candela, J. (2006). Local distance preservation in the GP-LVM through back constraints.proceedings. of the 23rd International Conference on Machine Learning. 513-520.

[17] Roweis, S.T. and Saul, L.K. (2000). Nonlinear Dimensionality Reduction by Locally Linear

Embedding. Science. 290(22).

[18] Wu, H.M. (2008). Kernel Sliced Inverse Regression with Applications on Classification. Computational and Graphical Statistics. 17(3),590-610.

[19] Tripathy, M. (2010). Power transformer differential protection using neural network Principal Component Analysis and Radial Basis Function Neural Network. Simulation Modelling Practice and Theory. 18, 600–611.

[20] Verma, H.K. and Kakoti, G.C. (1990). Algorithm for harmonic restraint differential relaying based on the discrete Hartley transform. Electric Power Systems Research. 18 (2), 125–129.

[21] Liu, P., Malik, O. P., Chen, C., Hope, G.S. and Guo, Y. (1992). Improved operation of differential protection of power transformers for internal faults. IEEE Transaction on Power Delivery. 7(4), 1912-1919.

[22] Inagaki, K. and Higaki, M. (1998). Digital protection method for power transformers based on an equivalent circuit composed of inverse inductance. IEEE Transaction on Power Delivery. 4(4),1501-1510.

[23] Morsi, W.G. and El-Hawary, M.E. (2009). Wavelet Packet Transform-Based Power Quality Indices for Balanced and Unbalanced Three-Phase Systems under Stationary or Nonstationary Operating Conditions. IEEE Transaction on Power Delivery. 24(4).

[24] Guzman, A., Zocholl, S., Benmouyal, G. and Altuve, H.J. (2001). Acurrent based solution for transformer differential protection-part I: Problem statement. IEEE Transaction on Power Delivery. 16(5), 485-491.

[25] Chong, Z., Chong-Xun, Z. and Xiao-Lin, Y. (2009). Automatic recognition of cognitive fatigue from physiological indices by using wavelet packet transform and kernel learning algorithms. Expert Systems with Applications. 36,4664–4671.

[26] Monsef, H. and Lotfifard, S. (2007). Internal fault current identification based on wavelet transform in power transformers. Electric Power Systems Research.77, 1637–1645.

[27] Uyar, M., Yildirima, S. and Gencoglu, M.T. (2008). An effective wavelet-based feature extraction method for classification of power quality disturbance signals. Electric Power Systems Research. 78, 1747–1755.

[28] Saini, M.K. and Kapoor, R. (2012). Classification of power quality events – A review. Electrical Power and Energy Systems. 43, 11–19.

[29] Jimenez, L.O. and Landgrebe, D.A. (1997). Supervised classification in high dimensional space: Geometrical, statistical, and asymptotical properties of multivariate data. IEEE Transactions on Systems, Man and Cybernetics. 28(1), 39–54.

[30] Liang, Z. and FuLi, Y. (2009). Incremental support vector machine learning in the primal and applications. Neurocomputing. 72, 2249–2258.

[31] Ayadi, M.E., Kamel, M.S. and Karray, F. (2011). Survey on speech emotion recognition: Features, classification schemes, and databases. Pattern Recognition. 44, 572–587.

[32] Vapnik, V. (1995). The nature of statistical learning theory. Springer. New York.

[33] Zhang, T. (2010). Analysis of Multi-stage Convex Relaxation for Sparse Regularization. Journal of Machine Learning Research. 11, 1081-1107.

[34] Chang, C.C., Chien, L.J. and Lee, Y.J. (2011). A novel framework for multi-class classification via ternary smooth support vector machine. Pattern Recognition. 44, 1235–1244.

[35] Woodford, D. (2000). Introduction to PSCAD/EMTDC V3, Manitoba. Canada: Manitoba HVDC Research Center Inc.

[36] Enright, W., Nayak, O.B., Irwin, G.D. and Arrillaga, J. (1997). An electromagnetic transients model of multi-limb transformers using normalized core concept. Proceedings of the International Conference on Power Systems Transients (IPST '97), Seattle, WA, 93–98, 22–26 June 1997.

[37] Annakkage, U. D., McLaren, P.G., Dirks, E., Jayasinghe, R.P. and Parker, A.D. (2000). A current transformer model based on the Jiles–Atherton theory of ferromagnetic hysteresis. IEEE Transactions on Power Delivery. 15(1), 57–61.

[38] Liu, L., Zhuang, Y. and Xue-yong, L. (2011). Tax forecasting theory and model based on SVM optimized by PSO. Expert Systems with Applications. 38 ,116–120.

21

Data mining for decision making in engineering optimal design

A. Mosavi

University of Debrecen, Faculty of Informatics, Hungary.

Corresponding author: a.mosavi@math.unideb.hu (A. Mosavi).

Abstract
Often in modeling the engineering optimization design problems, the value of objective function(s) is not clearly defined in terms of design variables. Instead it is obtained by some numerical analysis such as finite element structural analysis, fluid mechanics analysis, and thermodynamic analyses. Yet, the numerical analyses are considerably time consuming to obtain the final value of objective function(s). For the reason of reducing the number of analyses as few as possible, our methodology works as a supporting tool to the meta-models. The research in meta-modeling for multi-objective optimization are relatively young and there is still much research capacity to further explore. Here is shown that visualizing the problem on the basis of the randomly sampled geometrical big-data of computer aided design (CAD) and computer aided engineering (CAE) simulation results, combined with utilizing classification tool of data mining could be effective as a supporting system to the available meta-modeling approaches.
To evaluate the effectiveness of the proposed method, a case study in 3D wing optimal design is proposed. Discussion focusing on how effective the proposed methodology could be in further practical engineering design problems is presented.

Keywords: *Data Mining, classification, Multi-objective Optimization, Engineering Optimization, Meta-Modeling.*

1. Introduction

The research field of considering decision problems with multiple conflicting objectives is known as multiple criteria decision making (MCDM) [1]. Solving a multi-objective optimization problem has been characterized as supporting the decision maker (DM) in finding the best solution for the DM's problem. DM and optimization typically create an interactive procedure for finding the most preferred solutions. Yet, despite the increasing level of complexity, it has been often tried to pay attention to improving all the defined objective functions instead of reducing or ignoring some of them. Although due to the increased complexity, this would apply complications where objective functions are visualized by trade-off analysis methods as well studied in [9, 10, 25, 26, 35, 37].
According to [1], the general form of the multi-objective optimization problems can be stated as;

Minimize $\mathbf{f}(x) = \{f_1(x), \dots, f_m(x)\}$, Subjected to $x \in \Omega$, where $\mathbf{x} \in \mathbb{R}^n$ is a vector of n decision variables; $\mathbf{x} \subset \mathbb{R}^n$ is the feasible region and is specified as a set of constraints on the decision variables; $\mathbf{f} : \Omega \to \mathbb{R}^m$ is made of objective functions subjected to be minimization. Objective vectors are images of decision vectors written as $\mathbf{z} = \mathbf{f}(x) = \{f_1(x), \dots, f_m(x)\}$. Yet an objective vector is considered optimal if none of its components can be improved without worsening at least one of the others. An objective vector $\mathbf{z}$ is said to dominate $\mathbf{z}'$, denoted as $\mathbf{z} \prec \mathbf{z}'$, if $z_k \leq z_k'$ for all k and there exists at least one h that $z_h \leq z_h'$. A point $\hat{x}$ is Pareto optimal if there is no other $x \in \Omega$ such that $\mathbf{f}(x)$ dominates $.\mathbf{f}(\hat{x})$. The set of Pareto optimal points is called Pareto set (PS). And the corresponding set of Pareto optimal objective vectors is called Pareto front (PF).

Solving a multi-objective optimization problem would be done by providing the DM with the optimal solution according to some certain utility criteria allowing to choose among competing PF. Such utility criteria are often inconsistent, difficult to formalize and subjected to revision.

The complete process of MCDM has two parts (1) multi-objective optimization process which tries to find the PF solutions (2) decision making process which tries to make the best decision out of the possible choices. In dealing with increased complexity, this paper focuses on the first part which mostly deals with variables, constraints and objective functions.

1.1. Computational intelligence and multi-objective optimization

Developing the methods for multi-objective optimization using computational intelligence along with real applications appeared to be quite young. However it has been observed that techniques of computational intelligence are indeed effective [3, 7, 15, 27]. On the other hand, the techniques of multi-objective optimization by themselves can also be applied to develop and to improve the effective methods in computational intelligence [2].

Currently there are many computational intelligence-based algorithms available to generate PF [1, 16, 17, 30]. However, it is still difficult to generate and visualize the PF in the cases with more than three objectives. In this situation, methods of sequential approximate optimization of computational intelligence with meta-modeling are recognized to be very effective in a series of practical problems [1, 4].

1.2 Meta-modeling and multi-objective optimization in shape optimization

Meta-modeling is a method for building simple and computationally inexpensive models, which replicate the complex relationships. However the research in meta-modeling for multi-objective optimization is relatively young and there is still much to do. So far there existed only a few standards for comparisons of methods, and little is yet known about the relative performance and effectiveness of different approaches [4, 15].

The most famous methods of Meta-modeling are known as response surface methods (RSM) and design of experiments (DOE). Although it is concluded in previous studies [16, 18, 19, 20], in the future research, scalability of MCDM models in terms of variables' dimension and objective space's dimension will become more demanding.

This is because the models have to be capable of dealing with higher computation cost, noise and uncertainties.

According to [18], the application of meta-modeling optimization methods in industrial optimization problems is discussed. Some of the major difficulties in real-life engineering design problems counted: (1) there are numerous objective functions to be involved, (2) the function form of criteria is a black box, which cannot be explicitly given in terms of design variables, and (3) there are a huge number of unranked and non-organized input variables to be considered. Additionally in engineering design problems, often the value of objective functions is not clearly defined in terms of design variables. Instead it is obtained by some numerical analyses, such as FE structural analysis [34, 37], fluid mechanics analysis [7, 16, 17, 32], thermodynamic analysis [30], chemical reactions [3]. These analyses for obtaining a single value for an objective function are often time consuming. Considering the high computation costs, the number of CAE evaluations/calculations are subjected to minimization with the aid of meta-models [18]. In order to make the number of analyses as few as possible, sequential approximate optimization is one of the possible methods, utilizing machine learning techniques for identifying the form of objective functions and optimizing the predicted objective function. Machine learning techniques have been applied for approximating the black-box of CAE function in many practical projects [1, 9, 10 ,25 ,37]. Although the major problems in these realms would be (1) how to approach an ideal approximation of the objective function based on as few sample data as possible (2) how to choose additional data effectively. The objective functions are modeled by fitting a function through the evaluated points. This model is then used to help the prediction value of future search points. Therefore, those high performance regions of design space can be identified more rapidly. Moreover the aspects of dimensionality, noise and expensiveness of evaluations are related to method selection [32]. However, according to Bruyneel et al. [18] for the multi-objective capable version of meta-modeling algorithms further aspects such as the improvement in a Pareto approximation set and modeling the objective function must be considered.

Today, numerical methods make it possible to obtain models or simulations of quite complex and large scale systems [7, 8, 20, 22]. But there are still difficulties when the system is being modeled numerically. In this situation, modeling the simplified models is an effective method, generating a simple model that captures only the relevant input and output variables instead of modeling the whole design space [3, 20, 22].

The increasing desire to apply optimization methods in expensive CAE domains is driving forward the research in meta-modeling. The RSM is probably the most widely applied to meta-modeling. The process of a meta-model from big data is related to classical regression methods and also to machine learning [4, 37]. When the model is updated using new samples, classical DOE principles are not effective. In meta-modeling, the training data sets are often highly correlated, which can affect the estimation of goodness of fit and generalization performance. Yet Meta-modeling brings together a number of different fields to tackle the problem on optimizing the expensive functions. On the other hand the classical DOE methods with employing evolutionary algorithms have delivered more advantages in this realm. Figure 1 describes the common arrangement of meta-modeling tools in multi-objective optimization processes of engineering design. It is worth mentioning that the other well-known CAD-Optimization integrations for shape optimization e.g. [24, 29, 31] would also follow the described scheme.

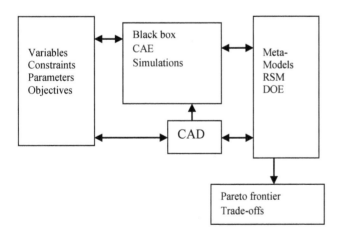

Figure 1. Meta-modeling tools in multi-objective optimization process.

2. Data mining classification in engineering design applications

The particular advantage of evolutionary algorithms (EAs) [11] in the multi-objective optimization (EMO) applications [19] is that they work with a population of solutions. Therefore, they can search for several Pareto optimal solutions providing the DM with a set of alternatives to choose from [14]. EMO-based techniques have an application where mathematical-based methods have difficulties with. EMO are also helpful in knowledge discovery related tasks in particular for mining the data samples achieved from CAE and CAD systems [29, 31]. Useful mined information from the obtained EMO trade-off solutions have been considered in many real-life engineering design problems.

2.1. Classifications

Finding useful information in large volumes of data drives the development of data mining procedure forward. Data mining classification process refers to the induction of rules that discriminate between organized data in several classes so as to gain predictive power [5]. There are some example applications of data mining classification in evolutionary multi-objective optimization available in the literature of [1, 6, 12, 19] where the goal of the classification algorithms is to discover rules by accessing the training sets. Then the discovered rules are evaluated using the test sets, which could not be seen during the training tasks [5].

In the classification procedures, the main goal is to use observed data to build a model, which is able to predict the categorical or nominal class of a dependent variable given the value of the independent variables [5]. Obayashi [12] for the reason of mining the engineering multi-objective optimization and visualization data applied self-organizing maps (SOM) along with a data clustering method. Moreover Witkowski et al. [13] and Mosavi [7, 20, 22] used classification tools of data mining for decision making supporting process to multi-objective optimization.

2.2. Modeling the problem

According to [1], before any optimization takes place, the problem must first be accurately modeled. In this case, identifying all the dimensions of the problem, such as formulation of the optimization problem with specifying decision variables, objectives, constraints, and variable bounds is an important task. Here the methodology proposes that mining the available sample data before actual modeling will indeed help to better model the problem as it delivers more information about the importance of input variables and could in fact rank the input variables. The proposed method of classification, also earlier utilized in [7, 20, 22], presented in Figure 2, is set to mine the input variables which are in fact associated with the final CAE data.

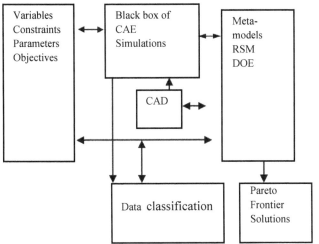

Figure 2. Supporting the meta-modeling process by mining the data

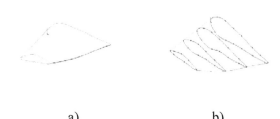

a)   b)

Figure 3. Airfoil geometry, modeled by S-plines [12, 14, 33, 34]

3. Study case; three-objective and 42-variale optimization problem

The applications in engineering optimal design have numerous disciplines to bring into the consideration. In mechanical engineering, the structural simulation is tightly integrated more than one discipline [18, 21, 22, 23, 24, 36]. Meanwhile, the trend nowadays is to utilize independent computational codes for each discipline [32]. In this situation, the aim of MCDM tools is to develop methods in order to guarantee that all physical variables are involved in the model. Bo et al. [28] in aerodynamic optimization of a 3D wing has tried to utilize the multi-objective optimization techniques in a multidisciplinary environment.

In the similar cases [20, 24, 29, 32] in order to approach the optimal shape in an aerospace engineering optimization problem, the multi-objective optimization techniques are necessary to deal with all important objectives and variables efficiently. Here the optimization challenge is to identify as many optimal designs as possible to provide a choice of better decision. However with an increased number of design variables the modeling task, in a multidisciplinary environment, is getting even ever complicated. Therefore the multi-objective optimization tasks become more difficult with the increasing number of variables [20, 35]. Although the recent advances in parametric CAD/CAE integrations [24, 29, 31] have reduced the complexity of the approach in some levels.

The airfoil of Figure 3 part (a) is subjected for shape improvement. The shape needs to be optimized in order to deliver *minimum displacement distribution* in terms of applied pressure on the surface. Figure 3, part (b) shows the basic curves of the surface modeled by S-plines. Here the proposed S-pline geometrical modeling methodology of Albers et al. [36] is successfully adapted and utilized. In the study case for modeling the 3D wing surface, four curve profiles have been with 42 points utilized. The coordinates of all points are supplied by a digitizer in which each point includes three dimensions of X, Y, and Z. Consequently the case, by adding the variable constraints, would include 126 columns plus three objectives which are going to highly increase the complexity. In fact, an optimal configuration of 42 variables supposed to satisfy the following three described objectives.

The objectives are listed as follow:

■ Objective 1: Minimizing the displacement distribution in the airfoil for constant pressure value of α.

■ Objective 2: Minimizing the displacement distribution in the airfoil for constant pressure value of 2α.

■ Objective 3: Minimizing the displacement distribution in the airfoil in constant pressure value of 4α.

In the described multi-objective optimization problem the number of variables is subjected to minimization before the multi-objective optimization modeling process takes place in order to evolve a large scale design space to the smaller and much more handy design space. Here the proposed and utilized model reduction methodology differs from the previous study Filomeno et al. [35] in terms of applicability and ease of use in general multi-objective optimization design applications.

Table 1. Training dataset including five CAE calculations' results

	Variables Configuration : V1-V42	CAD Model	Displacement Distribution	Objective Results
1	0,1,1.2,1,0.8,0.4,0.2,0,-0.4,-0.48, 0.6,-0.8,-0.72, 0,0.84,0.99,0.84,0.62,0.26,0,-0.20,-0.40,-0.36,-0.70,-0.58, 0,0.59,0.78,0.56,0.30,0,-0.21,-0.24,-0.38,-0.38 0,0.26,0.50,0.39,-0.03,-0.10,-0.12,			O1=c O2=c O3=c
2	0,1,1.21,.9,0.82,0.42,0.18,.1,-0.41,-0.46,-0.62,-0.81,-0.70, 0,0.86,0.1,0.82,0.60,0.2 5,0.01,-0.20,-0.39,-0.39,-0.70,-0.58, 0,0.58,0.76,0.57,0.32,0,-0.21,-0.23,-0.37,-0.39 0,0.26,0.54,0.40,-0.03,-0.1,-0.1,			O1=b O2=c O3=d
3	0,1,1.2,1,0.8,0.4,0.2,0,-0.4,-0.48,-0.6,-0.8,-0.72, 0,.88,0.99,0.84,0.62,0.2 6,0,-0.23,-0.35,-0.37,-0.70,-0.54, 0,0.58,0.76,0.58,0.31,0,-0.23,-0.23,-0.37,-0.37 0,0.24,0.50,0.40,-0.03,-0.13,-0.10,			O1=b O2=c O3=b
4	0,1,3,1.23,1.06,0.83,0.4 1,0.28,0.07,-0.41,-0.48,-0.6,-0.8,-0.78,0,0.84,.92,0.84,0.6 2,0.26,0,-0.23,-0.39,-0.37,-0.70,-0.54,0,0.58,0.76,0.58,0.31,0,-0.24,-0.22,-0.36,-0.38, 0,0.24,0.52,0.38,-0.02,-0.12,-0.12,			O1=d O2=c O3=b
5	0,1.01,1.21,1,0.8,0.4,0.21,0,-0.41,-0.47,-0.59,-0.79,-0.69,0,0.80,1.01,0.86,0.64,0.26,-0.01,-0.20,-0.40,-0.40,-0.72,-0.56,0,0.58,0.76,0.58,0.31,0,-0.23,-0.23,-0.37,-0.37 0,0.24,0.52,0.38,-0.06,-0.10,-0.10,			O1=c O2=d O3=e

The dataset of big data for data mining is supplied from the Table I. The table has gathered a collection of initial dataset including shapes' geometries and simulation results from five CAE calculations, based on random initial values of variables, which in the proposed method will be mined. In the next section, the discussion of how the dataset of five random CAE calculations are being utilized for creating the smaller design space for a multi-objective optimization model is made.

4. Methodology and experimental results

The effectiveness of data mining tools in multi-objective optimization problems presented by Coello et al. [2] and earlier in [5] the classification rules for evolutionary multi-objective algorithms were well implemented, in which along with the research work of Witkowski et al. [13] forms the proposed methodology working via a novel workflow. The workflow of data mining procedure methodology is described in Figure 4. In this method, the classification task is utilized to create several classifiers or decision trees. In the next steps, the most important variables, which have more effects on the objectives, are detected.

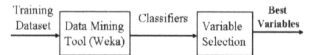

Figure 4. Proposed methodology workflow

Regressions and model trees are constructed by a decision tree building an initial tree. However, most decision tree algorithms choose the splitting attribute to maximize the information gain. It is appropriate for numeric prediction to minimize the intra subset variation in the class values under each branch.

The splitting criterion is used to determine which variable is better to split the portion T of the training data. Based on the treating the standard deviation of the objective values in T as a measure of the error and calculation the expected reduction in error as a result of testing each variable is calculated. Meanwhile the variables, which maximize the expected error reduction, are chosen for splitting. The splitting process terminates when the objective values of the instances vary very slightly, that is, when their standard deviation has only a small fraction of the standard deviation of the original instance set. Splitting also terminates when just a few instances remain. Experiments show that the obtained results are not very sensitive to the exact choice of these thresholds. Data mining classifier package of Weka provides implementations of learning algorithms and dataset which could be preprocessed and fed into a learning scheme, and analyze the resulting classifier and its performance. The workbench includes methods for all the standard data mining problems such as regression, classification, clustering, association rule mining, and attribute selection. Weka also includes many data visualization facilities and data preprocessing tools. Here three different data mining classification algorithms i.e. J48, BFTree, LADTree are applied and their performance is compared to choose attribute importance. The mean absolute error (MAE) and root mean squared error (RMSE) of the class probability is estimated and assigned by the algorithm output. The RMSE is the square root of the average quadratic loss and the MAE is calculated in a similar way using the absolute instead of the squared difference.

The comparison between importance ranking results is obtained by our experiments listed in Table II. It is concluded that in the worst case, more than 55% variable reduction is achieved. As one can see, BFTree and J48 algorithms have classified the datasets with less number of variables. While in LADTree algorithms, at least seven variables have utilized to classify dataset. The variables number 15 and 24 play much more important role in effecting the first objective (O_1).

Variables number 41 and 35 also have the more effects on third objective (O_3) as well. According to the experimental results, it is possible to optimize the model by reducing the 45% number of variables. In Table II, two types of classification error (MAE, RMSE) are shown for all algorithms corresponding to different class of objectives.

Table 2. Variables importance ranking for three classification methods

Classification Method	MAE	RMSE	Effective Variables	Objectives
BFTree	0.370	0.517	15	O_1
	0.412	0.519	23	O_2
	0.418	0.555	41	O_3
J48	0.309	0.514	15,24	O_1
	0.482	0.642	13	O_2
	0.378	0.590	35,41	O_3
LAD Tree	0.277	0.500	15,24,2,32,41,39,3 23,22,18,15,42,2,17 ,	O_1
	0.604	0.769	20	O_2
	0.365	0.584	41,35,9,17,11,38,37 , 16	O_3

5. Conclusions

In order to extract more information from the optimization variables in a reasonable way, the classification task of data mining has been applied. Variables were ranked and organized utilizing three different classification algorithms. The results show the reduced number of variables speeds up and scales up the process of optimization within a preprocessing step. The utilized data mining tool has found to be effective in this regard. Additionally, it is evidenced that the growing complexity can be handled by a preprocessing step utilizing data mining classification tools. The modified methodology is demonstrated successfully in the framework and the author believes that the process is simple and fast.

Future research should focus on the effectiveness of the proposed data reduction process. Also, trying other data mining tasks such as clustering, association rules, and comparison could be beneficial. Although in real-life applications where the optimal design problem has to be considered by inclusion of multiple criteria, a combination of the proposed method with the other developed MCDM tools [38-46] would be effective.

References

[1] J. Branke, K. Deb, K. Miettinen, R. Słowinski, Multiobjective, Optimization (Springer, Berlin, Heidelberg New York, 2008)

[2] C. Coello, S. Dehuri, S. Ghosh, Swarm Intelligence for Multi-objective Problems in Data Mining (Springer, Berlin, Heidelberg New York, 2009)

[3] A.Mosavi, "Applications of Interactive Methods of MOO in Chemical Engineering Problems," Global Journal of Researches in Engineering, Vol. 10, No. 3, p.8. (2010).

[4] J. Knowles, H. Nakayama, Meta-Modeling in Multiobjective Optimization (Springer, Berlin, Heidelberg New York, 2008)

[5] K. K. Kshetrapalapuram, M. Kirley, Mining Classificationm Rules Using Evolutionary Multi-objective Algorithms, Knowledge-Based Intelligent, Information and Engineering Systems. 3683 (Springer Berlin, Heidelberg, 2005).

[6] Alex A. Freitas, On Objective Measures of Rule Surprisingness, Principles of Data Mining and Knowledge Discovery. 1510, (2008).

[7] A. Mosavi, "The Large Scale System of Multiple Criteria Decision Making; Pre-Processing," Large Scale Complex Systems Theory and Applications, Vol. 9, 2010, pp. 354- 359.

[8] A. Adejuwon and A. Mosavi, "Domain Driven Data Mining; Application to Business," International Journal of Computer Science Issues, Vol. 7, No 2, 2010, pp. 41-44.

[9] Mosavi, M.Azodinia Abbas S. Milani, Kasun N. Hewage and M.Yeheyis, "Reconsidering the Multiple Criteria Decision Making Problems of Construction Workers with the Aid of Grapheur," International ANSYS and EnginSoft Conference, Verona, Italy, 2011.

[10] E. Foldi, A. Delavar, A. Mosavi, K. N. Hewage, A. S. Milani, A. A. Moussavi and M. Yeheyis, "Reconsidering the Multiple Criteria Decision Making Problems of Construction Projects; Using Advanced Visualization and Data Mining Tools," Conference of PhD Students in Computer Science, Szeged, Hungary, 28-30 June 2012.

[11] X. Llor, D.E. Goldberg, I. Traus, E.Bernad, Generalisation and Model Selection in Supervised Learning with Evolutionary Computation, Applications of Evolutionary Computing. 2611, (2003).

[12] S.Obayashi, evolutionary multiobjective optimization and Visualization, new developments in computational fluid dynamics (Springer, 2005)

[13] K. Witkowski, M. Tushar, Decision making in multiobjective optimization for industrial application-Data mining and visualization of Pareto, In Proceedings of 7th European LS-DYNA Conference, 416-423 (2009).

[14] K. Deb, Current Trends in Evolutionary MultiObjective Optimization, International Journal for Simulation and Multidisciplinary Design Optimization. 2, 1–8 (2007).

[15] A.Mosavi, "The Multiobjective Optimization Package of IOSO; Applications and Future Trends," In: CSCS, Conference of PhD Students in Computer Science, University of Szeged, Szeged, Hungary, 2010, p. 55.

[16] A.Mosavi, "Computer Design and Simulation of Built Environment; Application to Forest," Proceeding of ICECS'09, The Second IEEE International Conference on Environmental and Computer Science, Dubai, 28-30 December 2009, pp. 81-85.

[17] A.Mosavi, "Parametric Modeling of Trees and Using Integrated CAD/CFD and Optimization Tools: Application to Creating the Optimal Planting Patterns for New Forests," Proceedings of 2nd International Conference Wind Effects on Trees, Albert-Ludwigs-University of Freiburg, Freiburg, 2009.

[18] M. Bruyneel, B. Colson, P. Jetteur, C.Raick, A. Remouchamps, S. Grihon, Recent progress in the optimal design of composite structures: industrial solution procedures on case studies, Int. J. Simul. Multidisci. Des. Optim. 2, 283-288 (2008).

[19] S. E. Bedingfield, K. A. Smith, Evolutionary Rule Generation Classification and its Application to Multi-class Data, Computational Science, Springer. 2660, (2003).

[20] Mosavi, Multiple Criteria Decision-Making Preprocessing Using Data Mining Tools, International Journal of Computer Science Issues. 7, 26-34 (2010).

[21] V. Arularasan, Modeling and simulation of a parallel plate heat sink using computational fluid dynamics, Int J Adv Manuf Technol. 5, 172-183(2008).

[22] M. Esmaeili and A. Mosavi, "Variable Reduction for Multi-Objective Optimization Using Data Mining Tech-niques; Application to Aerospace Structures," Proceeding of ICCET, the 2nd IEEE International Conference on Computer Engineering and Technology, Vol. 5, Chengdu, 16-18 April 2010, pp. 333- 337.

[23] I. Olcer, a hybrid approach for multi-objective combinatorial optimization problems in ship design and shipping, Computers & Operations Research. 35, 2760 – 277(2007).

[24] L. Toussaint, N. Lebaal, D. Schlegel, S. Gomes, Automatic Optimization of Air Conduct Design Using Experimental Data and Numerical Results, Int. J. Simul. Multidisci. Des. Optim. 4, 77-83 (2010).

[25] A.Mosavi, M. Hoffmann and A. S. Milani, "Optimal Design of the NURBS Curves and Surfaces Utilizing Multiobjective Optimization and Decision Making Algorithms of RSO," Conference of PhD Students in Mathematics, Szeged, Hungary, Jnue 2012.

[26] Mosavi, M. Hoffmann and A. S. Milani, "Adapting the Reactive Search Optimization and Visualization Algorithms for Multiobjective Optimization Problems; Application to Geometry," Conference of PhD Students in Computer Science, Szeged, Hungary, June 2012.

[27] Mosavi, A. S. Milani, M. Hoffmann and M. Komeili, "Multiple Criteria Decision Making Integrated with Mechanical Modeling of Draping for Material Selection of Textile Composites," ECCM15, 15th Eeuropean Conference on Composite Materials, Venice, Italy, 24-28 June, 2012.

[28] Y. Bo, X. ANY, Aerodynamic optimization of 3D wing based on iSIGHT, Appl. Math. Mech. -Engl. Ed. 5, 603–610 (2008).

[29] J. B. Bluntzer, S. Gomes, D.h. Bassir, A. Varret and J.c. Sagot, Direct multi-objective optimization of parametric geometrical models stored in PLM systems to improve functional product design, Int. J. Simul. Multidisci. Des. Optim. 2, 83-90(2008).

[30] A.Mosavi, "Application of Multiobjective Optimization Packages in Design of an Evaporator Coil," World Academy of Science, Engineering and Technology, Vol. 61, 2010, pp. 25-29.

[31] P. Vik, D. Luís, P. Guilherme, J. Oliveira, Automatic Generation of Computer Models through the Integration of Production Systems Design Software Tools, Int. J. Simul. Multidisci. Des. Optim. 4, 141-148 (2010).

[32] Mosavi, "Hydrodynamic Design and Optimization: Application to Design a General Case for Extra Equipments on the Submarine's Hull," Proceeding on IEEE International Conference on Computer Technology and Development, ICCTD'09, Vol. 2, Kota Kinabalu, 13-15 November 2009, pp. 139-143.

[33] Mosavi, "Multiobjective Optimization of Spline Curves Using modeFrontier," Proceedings of Internaional Conference on Engineering Optimization

and In-ternational Mode Frontier users' Meeting, Trieste, 2010.

[34] Mosavi, "On Engineering Optimization the Splined Profiles," Proceedings of International Conference on Engineering Optimization and International modeFrontier Users' Meeting, Trieste, 2010.

[35] R. Filomeno, C. Coelho, P. Breitkopf, C. Knopf-Lenoir, Model reduction for multidisciplinary optimization - application to a 2D wing, Struct Multidisc Optim, 7, 29–48 (2008).

[36] Albers, N. Leon-Rovira, Development of an engine crankshaft in a framework of computer-aided innovation, Computers in Industry, 60, 604– 612 (2009).

[37] Mosavi, A.Vaezipour, "Reactive Search Optimization; Application to Multiobjective Optimization Problems." Applied Mathematics, 3, no.30 (2012): 1572-1582.

[38] Mosavi, "A MCDM Software Tool for the Automated Design Environments," 26th Europian Conference on Operational Research, Rome 2013, EURO - INFORMS XXVI.

[39] A.Vaezipour, A.Mosavi, U.Seigeroth, "Machine learning integrated optimization for decision making," 26th Europian Conference on Operational Research, Rome 2013, EURO - INFORMS XXVI.

[40] Mosavi, "Multiobjective Optimization package of IOSO," Mini EURO Conference EUROPT, Izmir, 2010.

[41] Vaezipour, A.Mosavi, "Managing Decision Making Within Enterprise," International CAE Conference, Verona, Italy, 22-23 Oct 2012.

[42] Vaezipour, A.Mosavi, "Enterprise Decision Management With the Aid of Advanced Business Intelligence and Interactive Visualization Tools," International CAE Conference, Verona, Italy, 22-23 Oct 2012

[43] Mosavi, "Data Mining for Business Applications," OGIK_ISBIS, Hungary, 2010.

[44] Mosavi, "Data Mining for Business Applications and Business Decision-Making: Challenges and Future Trends," OGIK_ISBIS, Hungary, 2010.

[45] Mosavi, Nage Peter, Miklos Hoffmann, "Automatic multi-objective surface design optimisation using modeFRONTIER's CAD/CAE integrated system: Application to military submarine sail," EnginSoft International Conference, CAE Technologies for Industry, Italy, 2009.

[46] Mosavi, "Recent developments and innovations in engineering optimization," Spring Wind Conference, Pecs, Hungary, 2010.

22

Prioritizing the ordering of URL queue in focused crawler

D. Koundal

University Institute of Engineering and Technology, Panjab University, Chandigarh, India

*Corresponding author: koundal@gmail.com (D. Koundal)

Abstract

The enormous growth of the World Wide Web in recent years has made it necessary to perform resource discovery efficiently. For a crawler, it is not a simple task to download the domain specific web pages. This unfocused approach often shows undesired results. Therefore, several new ideas have been proposed, and crawling is a key technique, which is able to crawl particular topical portions of the World Wide Web quickly without having to explore all web pages. Focused crawling is a technique, which is able to crawl particular topics quickly and efficiently without exploring all WebPages. The proposed approach does not only use keywords for the crawl, but also rely on high-level background knowledge with concepts and relations, which are compared with the texts of the searched page.

In this paper, a combined crawling strategy is proposed that integrates the link analysis algorithm with association metric. An approach is followed to find out the relevant pages before the process of crawling and to prioritize the URL queue from downloading higher relevant pages to an optimal level based on domain dependent ontology. This strategy makes use of ontology to estimate the semantic contents of the URL without exploring which in turn strengthen the ordering metric for URL queue and leads to the retrieval of most relevant pages.

Keywords: *WebCrawler, Importance-metrics, Association - metric, Ontology.*

1. Introduction

A crawler is a constituent of search engine that retrieves Web pages by strolling around the Internet following one link to another. A focused crawling algorithm weights a page and extracts the URLs. By rating the URLs, the crawler decides which page to retrieve next. A focused crawler fetches the page that locates on the head of its queue, examines the page and assigns a score to each URL. According to the scores inserted into the queue, the queue will organize itself in order to place URLs with higher scores in the queue head so that they first will be processed. Again, the crawler will fetch the URL on the head of the queue for new processing [1].

Intuitively, the term in-links refers to the hyperlinks pointing to a page. Usually, the larger the number of in-links, the higher a page will be rated. The assumption is made that if two pages are linked to each other, they are likely to be on the same topic. Anchor text can provide a good source of information about a target page, because it signifies how people linking to the page actually describe it. Several studies have tried to use either the anchor text or the text close to it to predict a target page's content. Researchers have developed several link-analysis algorithms over the past few years [2-11]. The most popular link-based Web analysis algorithm includes Page Rank.

A major problem of a focused crawler is to effectively order the links at the crawl frontier so that a maximum number of relevant pages are loaded, while loading only a minimum number of irrelevant pages. This is a challenging task because most of the existing focused crawlers use local search algorithms in Web searching. This may miss a relevant page if there does not exist a chain of hyperlinks that connects one of the seed pages to that relevant page.

The whole paper divides into the following sections: The section 2 discusses the related work done so far on this challenge. Section 3 gives various prioritizing algorithms. Section 4 tells about association metric based on ontology. Section 5 deals with proposed work on this challenge. The results of experimental evaluation presented in section 6. The implementation details are given in section 7. The section 8 covers conclusion.

2.Related work

Most of the focused crawling techniques use link-structures of the web to improve ordering of URLs in priority queue. A recurring problem in a focused crawling is finding relevant page that is surrounded by non-relevant pages. One remedy presented in [12] by Aggarwal et al. uses the characteristics of the linkage structure of the web while performing the crawl by introducing a concept of "intelligent crawling" where the user can specify an arbitrary predicate (e.g. keywords, document similarity, anything that can be implemented as a function which determines documents relevance to the crawl based on URL and page content) and the system adapts itself in order to maximize the harvest rate. Ehrig et al. in [13] in another approach named as CATYRPEL consider an ontology-based algorithm for page relevance computation. After preprocessing, entities (words occurring in the ontology) are extracted from the page and counted. Relevance of the page with regard to user selected entities of interest is then computed by using several measures on ontology graph (e.g. direct match, taxonomic and more complex relationships). The evaluation of the importance of the page P as $I(P)$ uses some metrics [14]. Cho et al. proposed an approach calculating the PageRank score on the graph induced by pages downloaded and then using this score as a priority of URLs extracted from a page. This may be due to the fact that the PageRank score is calculated on a very small, non-random subset of the web and also that the PageRank algorithm is too general for use in topic-driven tasks. L. page et al. in [15] proposed an approach for calculating the PageRank score on the graph induced by pages downloaded so far and then using this score as a priority of URLs extracted from a page. They show some improvement over the standard Breadth-first algorithm. Ontology based web crawler [16] estimates the semantic content of the link of the URL in a given set of documents based on the domain dependent ontology, which in turn reinforces the metric that is used for prioritizing the URL queue. The link representing concepts in the ontology knowledge path is given higher priority. However in this work, the content of the page based on the concepts is also used for

determining the relevancy of the page. An approach presented by [17] is used to prioritize the ordering of URLs through using association metric along with other importance metric. The rank or relevancy score of the URL is calculated based on the division score with respect to topic keywords available in a division i.e., finding out how many topic keywords there are in a division in which this particular URL exists and calculates the total relevancy of parent page of the relevancy score of the URL page [18]. The maximal set of relevant and quality page is to be retrieved [19].

In this proposed approach, a combination of importance metric and association metric are presented in order to obtain ordering metric for prioritizing the URLs in queue on the basis of syntactic as well as semantic nature of URL.

3. Importance Metric

For a given Webpage p, there are different types of importance metrics, which are as follow:

Back link Count

$I(p)$ is the number of links to page p that seem over the entire Web. Intuitively, a page p that is linked by many pages is more important than one that is rarely referenced. This type of "citation count" has been used widely to evaluate the impact of published papers.

Page Rank

Page Rank is the connectivity-based page quality metric suggested by Page et al. [15]. It is a static measure to rank pages in the absence of any queries. That is, PageRank computes the "global worth" of each page. Intuitively, the Page Rank measure of a page is similar to its in-degree, which is a possible measure of the significance of a page. The PageRank of a page will be high, if many pages with a high PageRank have links to it, and a page having few outgoing links contributes more weight to the pages, it links to a page containing many outgoing links. Thus, a link from the Yahoo home page counts the same as a link from some individual's home page. However, since the Yahoo home page is more important (it has a much higher IB count), it would make sense to value that link more highly. The weighted back link count of page p is given by

$$IR(p) = (1-d) + d[IR(t1)/c1 + ... + IR(tn)/cn]$$

4.Association metric with Ontology

Ontology serves as metadata schemas, providing a controlled vocabulary of concepts, each with unambiguously defined and machine-process able semantics. By defining shared and common domain theories, ontologies help people and machines to communicate succinctly - supporting semantics exchange, not merely syntax.

Ontology is a description (like a formal specification of a program) of the concepts and relationships that can be for an agent or a community of agents. The essential of an ontology is *"is-a"* hierarchy. The Reference Ontology thus created would have the following associations like "is a", "part of", "has" relationships.

The *association metric* for the URL u is estimated based on its relevancy with the reference ontology using proper text classification algorithms. Once the page p of the URL u is downloaded, the association metric for this page p is also calculated and preserved, as it will be a parent page for many links to be crawled. $AS(p)$ is the same as all links from that page p but it utilizes the Web's hyperlink structure to retrieve new pages by traversing links from previously retrieve ones.

Here an ontology-based strategy is taken into account for page relevance computation. After preprocessing, entities (words occurring in the ontology) are extracted from the page and counted and weight of the page is then calculated. With this, a candidate list of Web pages in order of increasing a priority is maintained. In next section, the core elements of proposed work are discussed in detail.

5. Proposed Work
A. System Overview

The focused crawling method consists of two interconnected cycles. The *first cycle* is ontology cycle that defines the crawling target in the form of instantiated ontology. This cycle also presents the output of the crawling process to the user in the form of a document list and proposals for enhancement of the already existing ontology to the user. The *second cycle* comprises the Internet crawler. It intermingles automatically with the data contained on the Web and retrieves them then it connects to the ontology to determine relevance. The relevance computation is used to select relevant documents for the user and to focus on links for the further search for relevant documents and metadata available on the Web. Our proposed focused crawler is based on domain dependent ontology has following components:

All_URLs queue is employed for storing the list of URLs to download.

Metric Module persistently scans through *All_URLs* to make the refinement decision. It

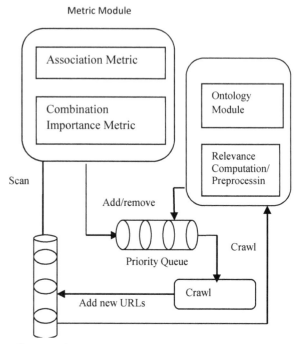

Metric Module

Scan

Add/remove

Priority Queue

Crawl

Add new URLs

Crawl

All URLs Queue

Figure 2. Prototype architecture of ontology based focused crawler

schedules for replacement of the less-important pages in priority queue with the more important page. Metric Module is a collection of Association metric and Combination Metric.

Ontology module works as background knowledge for a crawler to search in the web. It has been widely accepted that ontology is the core ingredient for the Semantic Web. This will have to be extended for the relevance measure of focused crawler. For this purpose, it is a formal and declarative representation, which includes the vocabulary (or names) for referring to the terms in that subject area and the logical statements that describe what the terms are, how they are related to each other, and how they can or cannot be related to each other. Ontology therefore provides a vocabulary for representing and communicating knowledge about some topics and a set of relationships that hold among the terms in the vocabulary. After preprocessing like HTML tag removal, stemming, lexical entries of the ontology are matched against the URLs and a relevance score is computed.

Relevance computation is a function, which tries to map the content (e.g. natural language text, hyperlinks) of a Web document against the accessible ontology to gain an overall relevance-score.

Crawl Module is started with a given set of links. The links are retrieved according to their rank.

Priority queue is used for placing the URLs to be crawled in the front. The URLs in priority queue is chosen by metric module. The processed web resources are indexed and stored in a database and then stored resources are being semantically analyzed and rated in the context of a given ontology. The crawl frontier is implemented by a standard DBMS system.

All crawling modules share the data structures needed for the interaction with the crawler. The prototype maintains a list of unvisited URLs called the frontier. This is initialized with the seed URLs specified at the configuration file. Besides the frontier, the simulator contains a queue. The scheduling algorithm fills it with the first k URLs of the frontier, where k is the size of the queue mentioned above, once the scheduling algorithm has been applied to the frontier. Each crawling loop involves picking the next URL from the queue, fetching the page corresponding to the URL from the local database that simulates the Web and determining whether the page is relevant or not. If the page is not in the database, the simulation tool can fetch this page from the real Web and store it into the local repository. If the page is relevant, the outgoing links of this page are extracted and added to the frontier, as long as they are not already in it. The crawling process stops once a certain end condition is fulfilled, usually when a certain number of pages have been crawled or when the simulator is ready to crawl another page and the frontier is empty. If the queue is empty, the scheduling algorithm is applied and fills the queue with the first k URLs of the frontier, as long as the frontier contains k URLs. If the frontier doesn't contain k URLs, the queue is filled with all the URLs of the frontier.

B. Proposed Prioritizing Algorithm:
The proposed crawler will work according to the following segment of code.
Input: seed URLs: *start_urls*
Assumption: Initially form beginning assumes Priority queue is full.
Output: Replacing "less important" pages with "more important pages" in a priority queue based on domain specific ontology.
enqueue (url_queue, start_urls);
While (not empty (url_queue) and not termination)
{
url = **dequeue** (url_queue);
page = crawl_page (url);
enqueue (crawled_pages, (url, page));
url_list = extract_urls (page);
For each page p in crawled_pages

Association_weight_page = *AS(p); // compute association weight (metric) of page*
End loop

For each u in url_list
enqueue (links, (url, u));
If [u not in url_queue] and [(u,-) not in crawled_pages]
enqueue (url_queue, u);
Association_Weight_URL = *AS(u); //compute association weight of URL*
Combination_Importance = *CI(u); //CI(u)= pagerank[u]+ backlink[p]*
End loop

Ordering_metric = O (u);
//
$O[u] = b_1 CI(u) + b_2 AS(u) + b_3[AS(p_1) + AS(p_2) + \ldots\ldots + AS(p_n)] + b_4 TD[u]$
where p1, p2 ...pn are the parent pages to this url u
reorder_queue (url_queue); //*based on O[u]*

}

C. Ordering Metric O (u)
The ordering metric O is used by the crawler for this selection, i.e., it selects the URL u such that $O(u)$ has the highest value among all URLs in the queue. In our experiments, we explore the types of ordering metrics that are best suited for either *IB* (*p*) or *IR* (*p*). The Ordering Metric O(u) used for reordering the URL queue in our crawler is a composite metric defined as follows:
CI (u) = Page Rank[u]
$O[u] = b_1 CI(u) + b_2 AS(u) + b_3[AS(p_1) + AS(p_2) + \ldots\ldots + AS(p_n)] + b_4 TD[u]$
Where, p_i is the i_{th} Parent page of URL u to be crawled and $b_1, b2, b_3, b_4$ are real constants to be evaluated from the results of our crawl.

The proposed new ordering metric will solve the major problem of finding the relevancy of the pages before the process of crawling, as well as plays an important role in estimating the relevancy of the links in the page to an optimal level.

6. Implementation details
The implementation of our ontology embedded crawler is an application with in the KAON, the Karlsruhe Ontology and Semantic Web tool suite. The underlying data structure is provided by KAON-API. The crawler is designed with the TextToOnto tool i.e. KAON Workbench. The tight integration of the crawler with the ontology and metadata management component is also important to allow for quick adaption and extension of the

structures. The proposed framework for focused crawling has been implemented in KAON framework and is written in Java.

7. Experimental Results

The results of this paper are the relevant web pages obtained from crawled pages for the different three seed URLs. The resulting comparison charts are drawn using Microsoft Excel software. Graphical interpretations of these results are also shown here.

Performance Metrics

In order to evaluate the performance of a given scheduling algorithm, the metric used is:

Harvest rate

Harvest rate is a common measure on how well a focused crawler performs. It is expressed as

$$HR = r/p,$$

Where,

HR is the harvest rate,

r is the number of relevant pages found and

p is the number of pages downloaded.

Seed URLs

For the crawler to start crawling we provide some seed URLs.

http://www.puchd.ac.in   (Panjab University),
http://www.du.ac.in (Delhi university),
http://www.ignou.ac.in/ (Indra Gandhi National Open University).

Scenario

1. **http://www.puchd.ac.in/**

In first experimental run, total 1000 pages were crawled from which 478 relevant pages were obtained. Therefore, the harvest ratio obtained for this crawler run is 48%. The harvest ratio for seed URL **http://www.puchd.ac.in:80/** is shown in Figure 4.

From first crawler run, the sample of top ten URLs of

obtained results set is shown in Table 1 as:

2. **http://www.du.ac.in/**

In second experimental run, 464 relevant pages were obtained from total crawled pages i.e. 1,000.

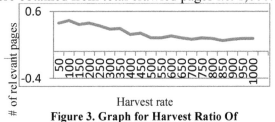

Figure 3. Graph for Harvest Ratio Of http://www.puchd.ac.in/

Table 1. Top 10 results for Panjab University

rank	Web Page
1	http://directory.puchd.ac.in:80/
2	http://exams.puchd.ac.in:80/
3	http://uiet.puchd.ac.in:80/
4	http://puchd.ac.in:80/prospectus.php
5	http://punet.puchd.ac.in:80/
6	http://forms.puchd.ac.in:80/
7	http://admissions.puchd.ac.in:80/
8	http://results.puchd.ac.in:80/
9	http://tenders.puchd.ac.in:80/
10	http://alumni.puchd.ac.in:80/

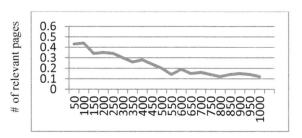

Harvest rate

Figure 5. Graph for Harvest Ratio of http://www.du.ac.in/

Therefore, the harvest ratio obtained in this second run is 46% which is shown in Figure 5.

1. **http://www.ignou.ac.in/**

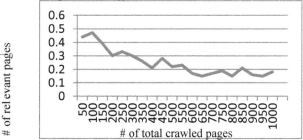

Figure 6. Graph of harvest ratio of http://www.ignou.ac.in/

In the third experimental run, 496 relevant pages are obtained from 1000 crawled pages. Therefore, the harvest ratio obtained in this third run is .49% as shown in Figure 6.

A. Average Harvest Rate Of Three Experimental Run

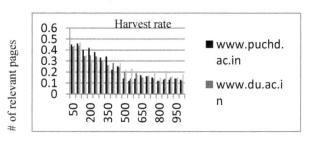

Figure 7. Average Harvest ratio of above three URLs

In above three experimental runs, total 3,000 webpages were crawled from which total of 1,434 pages were obtained. The above results of these three seed URLs i.e www.puchd.ac.in/, www.du.ac.in/, www.ignou.ac.in/ show that our ontology-based focused crawler is better than standard crawler and having average harvest ratio of 48%.

B. Comparison Of Unfocused Crawler And Ontology-Based Crawler:

The literature analysis shows that unfocused crawler with link analysis algorithm crawled 350 pages out of 1000 pages i.e. the obtained harvest ratio is 35% as shown in Table 2.

Table 2. Simulation results of different algorithm

Strategy	# of pages visited	# of relevant pages visited	Harvest Ratio
Breadth First	1,000	287	28%
PageRank	1,000	350	35%
Ontology based crawler	1,000	478	48%

Another evaluation run shows that more relevant pages were` obtained using ontology-based crawler rather than unfocused crawler is given in Figure 8. With the help of ontology-based crawler using link analysis algorithm, the harvest ratio obtained is 48%, while with unfocused crawler having link analysis algorithm, the harvest ratio obtained is 35%. This shows that more relevant pages can be retrieved by using ontology with our proposed combined strategy.

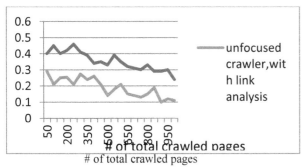

# of total crawled pages

Figure 8. Comparison of unfocused crawler, with link analysis and ontology-based crawler, with link analysis algorithm

8. Conclusion

In this paper, a combined strategy of link analysis algorithm guided by topic ontology is proposed in order to efficiently discover pages relevant to the domain of interest. The prototype uses the structured information in the ontology to guide the crawler in its search for web pages that are relevant to the topic specified in the ontology. The test results show that the use of link analysis in our prototype gives a slight increase in the harvest rate. Our crawler depends on rating the links which in turn enhance the discovery mechanism, with the introduction of combination of importance metric, this distinguishes our approach from existing approaches as the link with the higher calculated rank will be visited next. A final conclusion of this work is the realization that it is definitely worth using advanced knowledge structures when searching a specific domain on the Internet and it is possible to extract much more information from the large distributed database Internet as today's applications allow. This makes it an effective tool for the Semantic Web environment. This may result in improving the performance in the area of focused crawling and overcomes the various drawbacks of the current approaches.

References

[1] Blaz Novak, "A Survey of Focused Web Crawling Algorithms" SIKDD 2004 multi conference IS2004, 12-15 Oct 2004.

[2] Hiep Phuc Luong, Susan Gauch, Qiang Wang, 2009. Ontology-based Focused Crawling, International Conference on Information, Process, and Knowledge Management, pp. 123-128.

[3] Li, H., Peng, Q. Q., Du, Y. J., Zhao, Y., Chen, S. M., Gao, Z. Q. (2009). Focused web crawling strategy based on web semantics analysis and web links analysis. Journal of Computational Information Systems, 5(6), 1793-1800

[4] Batsakisa S, Petrakisa EGM, Milios E. Improving the performance of focused web crawlers. Data Knowl Eng 2009;68(10):1001–13

[5] Chakrabarti S, van den Berg M, Dom B. Focused crawling: a new approach to topic-specific web resource discovery. Comput Netw 1999;31(11–16):1623–40.

[6] Chakrabarti, S., M. Berg, B. Dom, Fo cused crawling: A new approach to topic-sp ecific web resource discovery, Computer Networks and ISDN Systems, 31 (11-16), 1999, 1623-1640

[7] S´anchez, D., M. Batet, D. Isern. Ontology-based information content computation. Knowledge-Based Systems, 24 (2011), 297-303

[8] Mohen Jamali, Hassan Sayyadi, Babak Bagheri, Hariri and Hassan Abolhassani, 2006. A method of focused crawling using combination of link structure and content similarity, Proceedings of the International Conference on Web Intelligence.

[9] Kozanidis L. An ontology-based focused crawler. In: LNCS 5039. Springer; 2008. p. 376–9.

[10] Liu Z, Du Y, Zhao Y. Focused crawler based on domain ontology and FCA. J Inform Comput Sci 2011;8(10):1909–17

[11] Ester M., Gro M. and Kriegel H.-P.: 2001, Focused Web crawling: A generic framework for specifying the user interest and for adaptive crawling strategies, Technical report, Institute for Computer Science, University of Munich.

[12] Aggarwal, C., F. Al-Garawi and P. Yu. "Intelligent Crawling on the World Wide Web with Arbitrary Predicates", In Proceedings of the 10th International WWW Conference, Hong Kong, May 2001.

[13] Ehrig M. and A. Maedche "Ontology-Focused Crawling of Web Documents" Proc. the 2003 ACM symposium on applied computing.

[14] Cho, J., H.Garcia - Molina, and L. Page. Efficient crawling through URL ordering. Computer Networks, 30(17):161172, 1998.

[15] Page, L., S. Brin, R. Motwani, T. Winograd. "The PageRank Citation Ranking: Bringing Order to the Web", Stanford Digital Library Technologies Project.

[16] Ganesh, S., M. Jayaraj, V. Kalyan, and G. Aghila,"Ontology-based Web Crawler," Proc. of the International Conference on Information Technology: Coding and Computing, Las Vegas, NV, USA, pp.337-341, 2004.

[17] Deepika Koundal, Mukesh Kumar, Renu Vig, "Prioritizing the URLs in Ontology based Crawler" published and presented at International Conference of IEEE- AICC '2009 at Thapar University, Patiala.

[18] Debashis Hati, Amritesh kumar, 2010. An approach for identifying URLs based on Division score and link score in focused crawler, International journal of computer applications, Volume 2 – No.3.

[19] Debashis Hati, Amritesh Kumar, Lizashree Mishra, 2010. Unvisited URL Relevancy Calculation in Focused Crawling Based on Naïve Bayesian Classification, International Journal of Computer Applications, Volume 3- No.9.

23

Solution of multi-objective optimal reactive power dispatch using pareto optimality particle swarm optimization method

S.A. Taher, M. Pakdel

Department of Electrical Engineering, University of Kashan, Kashan, Iran

*Corresponding author: sataher@kashanu.ac.ir (S.A. Taher).).

Abstract

For Multi-Objective Optimal Reactive Power Dispatch (MORPD), a new approach is proposed as a simultaneous minimization of the active power transmission loss, the bus voltage deviation and the voltage stability index of a power system are obtained. Optimal settings of continuous and discrete control variables (e.g., generator voltages, tap positions of tap changing transformers and the number of shunt reactive compensation devices to be switched) are determined. MORPD is solved using Particle Swarm Optimization (PSO). Also, Pareto Optimality PSO (POPSO) is proposed to improve the performance of the multi-objective optimization task defined with competing and non-commensurable objectives. The decision maker requires to manage a representative Pareto-optimal set provided by imposition of a hierarchical clustering algorithm. The proposed approach was tested using IEEE 30-bus and IEEE 118-bus test systems. When simulation results are compared with several commonly used algorithms, they indicate better performance and good potential for their efficient applications in solving MORPD problems.

Keywords: *Optimal reactive power dispatch, Particle swarm optimization, Multi-objective, Pareto optimality, Voltage profile, Voltage stability.*

1. Introduction

The Optimal Reactive Power Dispatch (ORPD) has played significant roles in the security and economics of power systems. Using this, the operators can select a number of control tools such as switching reactive power compensators, changing generator voltages and adjusting transformer tap settings, and achieving the Optimal Power Flow (OPF). Considering the given set of physical and operating constraints involved, the equality constraints include power flow equations and the inequality restrictions in various reactive power sources. ORPD objective is to minimize the transmission loss of the power system, keep the voltage profiles within acceptable range and improve the voltage security while satisfying certain operation constraints. However, as the transmission networks have tended to become stressed in a large number of utilities across the globe due to a variety of reasons, many voltage collapse accidents have occurred over the last few decades. Hence, voltage security has been considered in ORPD. The generator voltages are continuous variables, and the transformer ratios and shunt capacitors/inductors are discrete ones. The problem, therefore, has been defined as a non-linear, multi-uncertainty, multi-constraint, multi-minimum and multi-objective optimization (MOO) problem with a mixture of discrete and continuous variables.

A number of mathematical models for ORPD have been proposed in the literature [1–6]. Most of them adopt single-objective function and minimize it including transmission loss of the power system. Recently, minimizing voltage deviation from the desired values and improving voltage stability margin are considered as the objective function, making ORPD therefore, a MOO exercise [7–10]. In previous works, power losses and voltage deviation have received comparatively more attention than improving voltage stability. In this study, ORPD is similarly formulated as a MOO exercise with the objectives containing all three indices mentioned above as well as the operating constraints and load constraints.

Mathematical optimization techniques used to solve ORPD [1, 2, 7, 8] include gradient-based algorithms, linear programming, non-linear programming, Newton method and interior point methods. These conventional techniques require many mathematical assumptions, and hence, for problems involving non-continuous and non-linear functions, these techniques become less effective and are hardly ever used in recent years.

In recent decades, stochastic and heuristic optimization techniques, such as Evolutionary Algorithms (EAs), have emerged as efficient optimization tools [11]. EAs however, have been extensively employed for solving reactive power optimization [3-6, 9-10, 12-13]. Some of the prominent ones include Genetic Algorithm (GA) [14], particle swarm optimization (PSO) [15–19], differential evolution (DE) [20–22], seeker optimization algorithm (SOA) [23] and non-dominated sorting genetic algorithm-II (NSAGA-II) [24–25]. Theoretically, these techniques are able to converge to the near global optimum solution. PSO [26] was first suggested by Kennedy and Eberhart in 1995, and was subsequently employed successfully in power system studies for such applications as reactive power, voltage control, OPF, dynamic security border identification and state estimation [27–30].

Reviewing most studies to date, seems interesting to note that ORPD is not treated as a true multi-objective problem [18–19, 23], but instead, by linear combination of different objectives as a weighted sum, ORPD in effect has been often converted to a single objective problem. This unfortunately, requires multiple runs, as many times as the number of desired Pareto-optimal solutions. Furthermore, this method cannot be used to find Pareto-optimal solutions in problems having a non-convex Pareto-optimal front. In addition, there is no rational basis of determining adequate weights and the objective function formed might lose the significance due to combining non-commensurable objectives. To avoid this difficulty, in this study, the concept of Pareto-optimal set or Pareto-optimal front for MOO was presented as adopted in several works presented in the literature [9, 24–25]. This method is based on optimization of the most preferred objective while considering the other objectives as constraints bounded by some allowable levels. These levels are then altered to generate the entire Pareto-optimal

set. The most obvious weaknesses of this approach are time-consuming and finding weakly non-dominated solutions [31]. There are reports of Pareto optimization method being used to solve the reactive power optimization problem [9, 32], or to design the power system stabilizer [33].

In this paper, an approach is proposed based on Pareto Optimality PSO (POPSO) whose effectiveness is verified in solving a multi-objective ORPD (MORPD) by simulating results of two standard test systems, including IEEE 30-bus and IEEE 118-bus power systems. When comparing the study results with previous works, POPSO was shown to perform well in both test systems by showing the solutions near global optima.

2. Problem formulation
2.1. Objective functions
The objective functions for both ORPD and voltage control problem comprise three important terms in which technical and economic goals are considered. The economic goal is mainly to minimize the active power transmission loss. The technical goals are to minimize the load bus voltage deviation from the desired voltage and also the L-index to improve the voltage security [18].

2.1.1. Power loss
Minimizing the active power transmission loss can be described as follows [18]:

$$\textbf{Min} \quad P_{loss} = \sum_{k=1}^{N_E} Loss_k \qquad (1)$$

Where, P_{loss} is the active power transmission loss of the power system, N_E is the number of branches and $Loss_k$ is the power losses of the kth branch.

2.1.2. Voltage deviation
An effective way to improve voltage profile is to minimize the selected deviation of voltage from the desired value as follow [18]:

$$\textbf{Min} \quad \sum \Delta V = \sum_{i=1}^{N_L} \left| V_i - V_i^{ref} \right| \qquad (2)$$

Where, $\sum \Delta V$ is the sum of load bus voltage deviation, N_L is the total number of the system load buses, V_i and V_i^{ref} are actual and desired voltage magnitudes at bus i, respectively. In general, V_i^{ref} is set to be 1.0 pu.

2.1.3. Voltage stability index
There are several indices proposed for voltage stability and voltage collapse prediction, including:

voltage collapse proximity indicator (*VCPI*) [34] or voltage stability margin (*VSM*) [35]. However, *L*-index is a faster one presented by Kessel and Glavitsch [36] and developed further by Tuan et al [37]. In this paper, *L*-index is selected as the objective function for voltage stability index to improve the voltage security and keeps the operating system as far as possible from the voltage collapse point. Apart from the speedy calculation time needed to evaluate each load bus steady state voltage stability level, the chosen index can also take into account generator buses reaching reactive power limits. The *L*-index value ranges from zero to one; zero indicating a stable voltage condition (i.e. no system load) and one indicates voltage collapse. The bus with the highest *L*-index value will be the most vulnerable bus and hence, this method helps identifying the weakest areas needing critical reactive power support in the system. A summary of how *L*-index algorithm is evaluated is given below [18, 36]:

The transmission system itself is linear and allows a representation in terms of the node admittance matrix (*Y*). The network equations in this terms is:

$$\begin{bmatrix} I^L \\ I^G \end{bmatrix} = \begin{bmatrix} Y_1 & Y_2 \\ Y_3 & Y_4 \end{bmatrix} \cdot \begin{bmatrix} V^L \\ V^G \end{bmatrix} \tag{3}$$

Two categories of nodes are recognized: the load bus (PQ) set α_L and the generator bus (PV) set α_G. The hybrid matrix (*H*) can be generated from admittance matrix (*Y*) by a partial inversion as below:

$$\begin{bmatrix} V^L \\ I^G \end{bmatrix} = H \cdot \begin{bmatrix} I^L \\ V^G \end{bmatrix} = \begin{bmatrix} Z^{LL} & F^{LG} \\ K^{GL} & Y^{GG} \end{bmatrix} \cdot \begin{bmatrix} I^L \\ V^G \end{bmatrix}, \tag{4}$$

Where, V^L and I^L are vectors of voltages and currents at PQ buses; V^G and I^G are vectors of voltages and currents at PV buses; Z^{LL}, F^{LG}, K^{GL}, Y^{GG} are sub-matrices.

For any consumer node j, $j \lor \alpha_L$, the following equation for V_j can be derived from the *H*-matrix:

$$V_j = \sum_{i \in \alpha_L} Z_{ji} I_i + \sum_{i \in \alpha_G} F_{ji} V_i . \tag{5}$$

Voltage V_{oj} however, is been defined as:

$$V_{oj} = -\sum_{i \in \alpha_G} F_{ji} V_i . \tag{6}$$

Hence, the local indicator Lj becomes [36]:

$$L_j = \left| 1 - \frac{V_{oj}}{V_j} \right| = \left| 1 - \frac{\sum_{i \in \alpha_G} F_{ji} V_i}{V_j} \right| \tag{7}$$

Where, V_i and V_j are the complex voltages, and F_{ji} are the coefficients taken from a so-called *H* matrix, generated by a partial inversion of the nodal

admittance matrix and the coefficients describe the system structure.

For stable situations the condition $0 \leq L_j \leq 1$ must not be violated for any of the nodes j. Hence, a global indicator *L* describing the stability of the whole system may be described as:

$$L = \max_{j \in \alpha_L} (L_j) \tag{8}$$

The *L* value for the best individual is compared with the threshold value and if the value is less than that, it indicates a voltage secure condition. The threshold value is fixed by conducting off-line study on the system for different operating conditions, thereby, minimizing the system voltage indicator [18] that is:

$$\text{Min } f_3 = L \tag{9}$$

2.2. Constraints

Minimizing the said objective functions is subjected to a number of equality and inequality constraints as outlined below.

2.2.1. Equality constraint

This is essentially the load constraint, i.e. the active and reactive power balance described by the following set of power flow equations [18, 19]:

$$\begin{cases} 0 = P_i - V_i \sum_{j \in N_L} V_j (G_{ij} \cos \theta_{ij} + B_{ij} \sin \theta_{ij}), & i = 1, \dots, N_{B-1} \\ 0 = Q_i - V_i \sum_{j \in N_L} V_j (G_{ij} \sin \theta_{ij} - B_{ij} \cos \theta_{ij}), & i = 1, \dots, N_{PQ} \end{cases}$$
(10)

Where, V_i is the voltage magnitude at i^{th} bus, P_i and Q_i are net active and reactive power injection at bus i, G_{ij} and B_{ij} are the mutual conductance and susceptance between bus i and j respectively, θ_{ij} is the voltage angle difference between bus i and j, N_{B-1} is the total number of buses excluding slack bus, N_{PQ} is the set of *PQ* buses and N_L is the number of load buses.

2.2.2. Inequality constraint

Sometimes referred to as the operational constraint, this includes the generator voltages V_G, shunt compensations Q_C, transformer tap settings T, generator reactive power outputs Q_G and load bus voltages V_L defined as [18, 19]:

$$\begin{cases} V_{Gi\,min} \leq V_{Gi} \leq V_{Gi\,max}, & i = 1, \dots, N_G \\ Q_{Ci\,min} \leq Q_{Ci} \leq Q_{Ci\,max}, & i = 1, \dots, N_C \\ T_{i\,min} \leq T_i \leq T_{i\,max}, & i = 1, \dots, N_T \\ Q_{Gi\,min} \leq Q_{Gi} \leq Q_{Gi\,max}, & i = 1, \dots, N_G \\ V_{Li\,min} \leq V_{Li} \leq V_{Li\,max}, & i = 1, \dots, N_L \end{cases} \tag{11}$$

Where, N_G, N_C, N_T and N_L are the total number of generators, shunt compensations, transformer taps and load buses, respectively.

2.3. Problem statement

In general, considering aggregation of objectives and constraints, power loss, voltage control and voltage stability index could be mathematically formulated as a non-linear constrained MOO as described below [18]:

$$\begin{rcases} Min \quad P_{loss}(x,u) \\ Min \quad \sum \Delta V(x,u) \\ Min \quad L(x,u) \\ s.t. \\ \qquad H(x,u)=0 \\ \qquad G_{min}(x,u) \le G(x,u) \le G_{max}(x,u) \end{rcases} \quad (12)$$

Where, x is the state variable vector, consisting of load bus voltages V_L and generator reactive power outputs Q_G; u is the control variable vector including generator voltages V_G, shunt compensations Q_C and transformer tap settings T. $H(x,u)$ and $G(x,u)$ are the compact forms of Eqs. (10) and (11), respectively.

3. Pareto Optimality Particle Swarm Optimization (POPSO)

3.1. Classical particle swarm optimization

PSO is a stochastic evolutionary computation optimization technique based on the movement of swarms [26]. It was inspired by social behavior of bird flocking or fish schooling. The population is considered as swarm, and each individual is called a particle randomly initialized. Each of these particles traverses the search space looking for the global minimum or maximum. The position of each particle corresponds to a candidate solution for the optimization problem, and is treated as a point in a D-dimensional space. For a given particle P_i, its position and velocity are represented as $x_i(t)=(x_{i,1}(t),...,x_{i,d}(t),...,x_{i,D}(t))$ and $v_i(t)=(v_{i,1}(t),...,v_{i,d}(t),...,v_{i,D}(t))$, respectively. The particles have memory and each particle keeps track of its previous best position. The best previous position (the position giving the best fitness value) found so far by particle P_i is recorded as $pbest_i=(p_{i,1},...,p_{i,d},...,p_{i,D})$. The swarm remembers another value which is the best position discovered by the swarm, The best previous position among all the particles in the population (or in the neighborhood) is represented as $gbest=(g_{i,1},...,g_{i,d},...,g_{i,D})$. The velocity for particle and the their positions are updated by the following two equations [18, 26]:

$$v_{i,d}(t+1)=w \times v_{i,d}(t)+c_1 \times rand_1 \times (pbest_{i,d}(t)-x_{i,d}(t))+ \\ c_2 \times rand_2 \times (gbest_d(t)-x_{i,d}(t)) \quad (13)$$

$$x_{i,d}(t+1)=x_{i,d}(t)+v_{i,d}(t+1) \quad (14)$$

Where, w is the inertia weight, c_1 and c_2 are learning factors, $rand_1$ and $rand_2$ are two random functions in the range [0, 1]. The Eq. (13) is used to calculate the ith particle's velocity by taking three terms into consideration: the particle's previous velocity, the distance between the particle's best previous and current positions, and, finally, the distance between the position of the best particle in the swarm and the ith particle's current position. The ith particle flies toward a new searching point according to Eq. (14). In general, the performance of each particle is measured by a predefined problem-dependent fitness function.

PSO has three tuning parameters and the performance of its algorithm is influence by them. The parameters are w, c_1 and c_2 shown in Eq. (13). w is the inertia weight employed to control the impact of the previous history of velocities on the current one. Suitable selection of the inertia weight w can provide a balance between global and local exploration abilities, consequently on average less iteration is needed to find a sufficiently optimal solution [38]. The linearly decreasing w-strategy [39] decreases from w_{max} to w_{min}, according to the following equation:

$$w = w_{max} - \frac{w_{max}-w_{min}}{iter_{max}} \times iter \quad (15)$$

Where, $iter$ is the current iteration number and $iter_{max}$ is the maximum iteration number, w_{max} and w_{min} often set to 0.9 and 0.4, also c_1 and c_2 are the learning factors and determine the influence of personal best $pbest_i$ and global best $gbest$, respectively shown in Eq. (13). Most implementations [26–30] use a setting with $c_1 = c_2 = 2$, which means each particle will be attracted to the average of $pbest_i$ and $gbest$. Recently, reports show that it might be even better to choose a larger cognitive parameter c_1 than a social parameter c_2, but with this constraint $c_1 + c_2 \le 4$ [40].

The number of particles or swarm size N_{pop} is one of the most important parameters that influence results of PSO. Too few particles will cause the algorithm to become stuck in a local minimum, while too many particles will slow down the algorithm. The algorithm performance depends therefore, on the parameters and the functions being optimized, so it is important to find a set of parameters that work well in all cases [18].

3.2. Pareto optimality concept

Optimization of several objective functions simultaneously, takes place frequently in power system studies. Generally, these functions are non-commensurable and often have conflicting objectives. There are two approaches for solving MOO problems. First, is the application of the traditional algorithms aiming to convert the multi-objective to a single objective optimization problem, often carried out by aggregating all objectives in a weighted function, or simply transforming all but one of the objectives into constraints. The advantage of such an approach is application existing single-objective optimization algorithms to solve problem directly and the limitations include: 1) requiring a pre-knowledge on the relative importance of the objectives and their limitations which are being converted into constraints; 2) inability to find multiple solutions in a single run, thereby requiring it to be applied as often as the number of desired Pareto optimal solutions; 3) difficulty in evaluating the trade-off between objectives and 4) search space should be convex, otherwise the solution may not be attainable. The second approach is based on Pareto optimality (PO) concept, where a set of optimal solutions is found, instead of one optimal solution. The reason for the optimality of many solutions is that no one can be considered to be better than any other with respect to all objective functions. Compared with traditional algorithms, PO is more suitable for solving MOO not only due to the ability to obtain multiple solutions in a single run, but, a good spread of the non-dominated solutions can also be obtained [41].

The following definitions describe concept of Pareto-optimal mathematically [41]:

Def. 1 The general MOO problem consists of a number of objectives to be optimized simultaneously and is associated with a number of equality and inequality constraints. It can be formulated as follows:

$$\begin{aligned} Min \quad & \vec{y} = \vec{F}(\vec{x}) = [\vec{f}_1(\vec{x}), \vec{f}_2(\vec{x}), \dots, \vec{f}_{N_{obj}}(\vec{x})]^T \\ s.t. \quad & \vec{H}_j(\vec{x}) = 0 \\ & \vec{G}_j(\vec{x}) \leq 0, j = 1, 2, \dots, M \end{aligned} \right\} \quad (16)$$

Where, $\vec{x}^* = [\vec{x}_1^*, \vec{x}_2^*, \dots, \vec{x}_D^*] \in \Omega$ and $\vec{y}$ is the objective vector. Here, three functions are considered including: $\vec{f}_1(\vec{x}) = P_{Loss}(x, u)$, $\vec{f}_2(\vec{x}) = \sum \Delta V(x, u)$ and $\vec{f}_3(\vec{x}) = L(x, u)$.

$\vec{H}_j(\vec{x})$ is equality constraint including active and reactive power balance. $\vec{G}_j(\vec{x})$ are un-equality constraints, includes the generator voltages, shunt compensations, transformer tap settings, generator reactive power outputs and load bus voltages. $\vec{x}^*$ is a D-dimensional vector representing the decision variables within a parameter space Ω and N_{obj} is the number of objectives. The space spanned by the objective vectors is called the objective space. The subspace of the objective vectors satisfying the constraints is called the feasible space.

Def. 2 For a MOO problem, any two solutions can have one of two possibilities, one covers or dominates the other or none dominates the other. In a minimization problem, without loss of generality, a decision vector $\vec{x}_1 \in \Omega$ is said to dominate the decision vector $\vec{x}_2 \in \Omega$ (denoted by $\vec{x}_1 \prec \vec{x}_2$), if the decision vector $\vec{x}_1$ is not worse than $\vec{x}_2$ in all objectives and strictly better than $\vec{x}_2$ in at least one objective. Therefore, a solution $\vec{x}_1$ dominates $\vec{x}_2$ if the following conditions are satisfied:

$$\begin{cases} \forall i \in \{1, 2, \dots, N_{obj}\} : \vec{f}_i(\vec{x}_1) \leq \vec{f}_i(\vec{x}_2) \\ \exists j \in \{1, 2, \dots, N_{obj}\} : \vec{f}_j(\vec{x}_1) < \vec{f}_j(\vec{x}_2) \end{cases} \quad (17)$$

Def. 3 A decision vector $\vec{x}_1 \in \Omega$ is called Pareto-optimal, if there does not exist another $\vec{x}_2 \in \Omega$ that dominates it. An objective vector is called Pareto-optimal, if the corresponding decision vector is Pareto-optimal.

Def. 4 The set of all non-dominated solutions is called Pareto optimal set (POS) and the set of the corresponding values of the objective functions is called Pareto optimal front (POF) or simply Pareto front. In case of no non-dominated solution, Pareto optimal front would be non-convex.

PO is shown graphically in Figure 1 for an arbitrary two-objective minimization problem. It is apparent that for solutions contained in dominated regions, there exists at least one solution in the non-dominated region that is strictly better in terms of both objectives. Furthermore, each non-dominated solution is obviously not inferior to any solution within the entire search space.

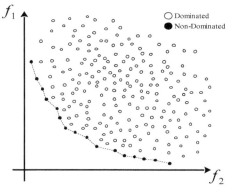

Figure 1. Depiction of domination using a two-objective minimization case

3.2.1. Best compromise solution (BCS)

From the Pareto-optimal set of non-dominated solutions, the proposed POPSO selects one solution for the decision maker as the best compromise solution. For this optimization, due to the imprecise nature of the decision making process involved, the ith objective function F_i is represented by a membership function μ_i defined as [9, 42]:

$$\mu_i = \begin{cases} 1 & F_i \leq F_{i,min} \\ \dfrac{F_{i,max} - F_i}{F_{i,max} - F_{i,min}} & F_{i,min} < F_i < F_{i,max} \\ 0 & F_i \geq F_{i,max} \end{cases} \qquad (18)$$

Where, $F_{i,min}$ and $F_{i,max}$ are the minimum and maximum value of the ith objective function among all non-dominated solutions, respectively. For each non-dominated solution k, the normalized membership function μ^k is calculated as:

$$\mu^k = \frac{\sum_{i=1}^{N_{obj}} \mu_i^k}{\sum_{k=1}^{M} \sum_{i=1}^{N_{obj}} \mu_i^k} \qquad (19)$$

Where, M is the number of non-dominated solutions. Here, the best compromise solution is the one with the maximum μ^k.

4. Solution algorithm

The difficulty in extending the original PSO to POPSO is the selection of *pbest* and *gbest* for each particle, since no single optimum solution in Pareto optimal set exist. The algorithm uses an archive, which is in essence an external repository of the population, storing non-dominated solutions. Initializing randomly the population starts the algorithm. All particles are initially compared with each other in order to store the non-dominated ones in the archive. Particles velocity and positions are updated using Eqs. (13-14) for which $gbest_d$ is randomly selected from the global Pareto archive for each particle, therefore $gbest_d$ is transformed to $gbest_{i,d}$. It means that *gbest* is exclusive for each particle. As for the $pbest_{i,d}$, the first value is set equal to the initial position of particle. In the subsequent iterations, $pbest_{i,d}$ is updated in the following stages:

(I)   if the current $pbest_{i,d}(t)$ dominates the new position $x_{i,d}(t+1)$ then $pbest_{i,d}(t+1) = pbest_{i,d}(t)$,

(II)   if the new position $x_{i,d}(t+1)$ dominates $pbest_{i,d}(t)$ then $pbest_{i,d}(t+1) = x_{i,d}(t+1)$,

(III)   if no one dominates the other, then, one of them is randomly selected to be the $pbest_{i,d}(t+1)$.

Contrary to standard PSO, where a best solution is obtained, there are several equally good non-dominated solutions stored in the POPSO archive. In every iteration t, the new positions of all particles are compared to identify the non-dominated ones, which are then compared further with all solutions stored in the archive. Following updating the archive, new non-dominated solutions are added and old solutions that have become dominated are eliminated. The size of the archive is therefore, an important parameter, which needs to be determined accordingly. Once the archive becomes full, a new non-dominated solution is found. Then this new solution replaces another non-dominated solution randomly selected in the archive. In this article, no limit has been considered for the archive size. The algorithm runs until the maximum number of iterations is reached. Below, the proposed POPSO algorithm for solving the MORPD is discretely described in steps:

Step 1: Input data

Input power system data and parameter values such as inertia weight w and learning factors c_1 and c_2 in the appropriate equations.

Step 2: Initialization

(I) Initialize randomly the position and initial velocity of the particles. Each particle in the population consists of D component, where D is the number of space dimensions indicating the number of control variables such as generator voltages, transformer taps and shunt reactive compensations. Select and verify each particle for constraints; if the particle doesn't satisfy the relevant constraints, then regenerate another one.

(II) Compute the multi-objective functions $(P_{loss}, \sum \Delta V$ and L-index) for each particle and its relevant constrains using power flow algorithm such as Newton Raphson method; then save this in a vector form.

(III) Check the PO of each particle, and store non-dominated particles in Pareto archive. If the specific constraint doesn't exist for archive, the size of the archive is assumed unlimited.

Step 3: Updating

(I) Update velocity and positions of particles according to Eqs. (13-14); $gbest_{i,d}(t)$ is randomly selected from the Pareto archive for each particle.

(II) Update $pbest_{i,d}(t+1)$ for each particle according to checking the PO of $pbest_{i,d}(t)$ and $x_{i,d}(t+1)$. If no one dominates the other, then, one of them is randomly selected to be the $pbest_{i,d}(t+1)$.

(III) If the particle doesn't remain within the feasible solution region, discard it and mutate again.

Step 4: Evaluation

Evaluate the multi-objective functions for each particle by power flow; and save it in a vector form.

Step 5: Selection and update the archive

(I) Check the PO of each particle. If the fitness value of the particle is non-dominated (compared to the Pareto optimal front in the archive), save it into the archive.

(II) If a particle is dominated from the new one in the Pareto archive, then discard it.

Step 6: Repeat

Repeat step 3 to step 5 until the maximum number of iterations is reached. The flowchart for the MORPD solution using POPSO is illustrated in Figure 2.

5. Simulation results

The proposed approach was tested with two non-linear test systems (IEEE 30-Bus and IEEE 118-Bus power system) for validation [43]. Basic information for test systems as well as control variable settings and limits are elaborated in Tables 1 and 2. The algorithm implemented in MATLAB and executed on a PC with a Pentium IV 2.1G CPU.

The following parameters are adopted in POPSO: population size = 100; inertia weight w which linearly decreases from 1 to 0.5; initial learning factors c_1 = 2.0 and c_2 = 1.6; desired number of generations = 50.

Table 1. Control variables of IEEE 30-bus and IEEE 118-bus test systems

Test system	Number of bus	Number of branch	Number of control variables		
			V_G	T	Q_C
IEEE 30-bus	30	41	6	4	4
IEEE 118-bus	118	186	54	14	9

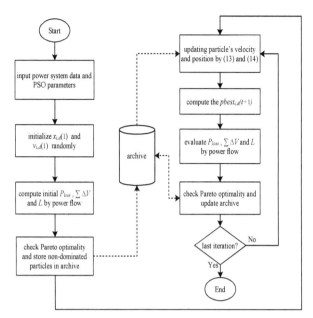

Figure 2. Flowchart for solving MORPD problem using POPSO.

Table 2. Control variable settings IEEE 30-bus and IEEE 118-bus test systems

Control variable	Control limits	variable	Step
	Min (p.u.)	Max (p.u.)	
V_G	0.9	1.1	-
T	0.9	1.1	0.01
Q_C	0	0.5	0.01

5.1. Simulation of the IEEE 30-bus test system

The proposed POPSO method was tested on the standard IEEE 30-bus system shown in Figure 3. It consists of six generator buses (bus 1 being the slack bus, while buses number 2, 5, 8, 11 and 13 are PV buses with continuous operating values), 24 load buses and 41 branches in which four branches (4–12, 6–9, 6–10 and 27–28) are tap changing transformers with discrete operating values. In addition, buses 10, 15, 19 and 24 are taken as shunt compensation buses with discrete operating values. Therefore, in total, 14 control variables are taken for MORPD in this test system. Table 3 illustrates the simulation results for the IEEE 30-bus test system, where Pareto optimal front and Pareto optimal set are listed for 36 rows of non-dominated solutions. Table 4 shows the best compromise solution (BCS) and 3 solutions in Pareto optimal front that have minimum value for each objective function individually and are similar to single objective functions (Min P_{loss}, Min $\sum \Delta V$ and Min *L-index*). The diversity of the Pareto optimal front over the trade-off surface is also shown in Figure 4.

The variation of best compromise solution power loss, voltage deviation and voltage stability index versus the number of iterations are presented in Figures. 5-7, respectively. As can be seen, the convergence characteristics are not monotonic most likely due to the existence of best compromise solution (BCS). In the each iteration, there are several non-dominated solutions and one of them has been selected as BCS considering Eqs. (18-19). In the following iteration, however, one other solutions might be selected as BCS, therefore a non-monotonic convergence may occur. Pre and post optimization for bus voltage profiles are shown in Figure 8. As can be seen after optimization, the voltage profiles are greatly improved, and voltage deviations are reduced.

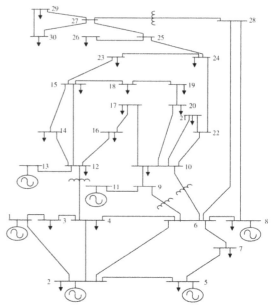

Figure 3. IEEE 30-bus test system

Table 3.The results of IEEE 30-bus test system

Pareto optimal front			Pareto optimal set													
P_{loss}	$\sum \Delta V$	L	V_{G1}	V_{G2}	V_{G5}	V_{G8}	V_{G11}	V_{G13}	T_{4-12}	T_{6-9}	T_{6-10}	T_{27-28}	Q_{C10}	Q_{C15}	Q_{C19}	Q_{C24}
5.1542	0.1080	0.1281	1.0446	1.0262	1.0190	1.0000	1.0293	0.9983	1.00	0.98	1.02	0.97	0.13	0.08	0.09	0.16
5.3292	0.0888	0.1296	1.0325	1.0400	1.0117	0.9855	1.0302	1.0024	0.99	0.98	1.04	0.95	0.10	0.09	0.09	0.20
4.5374	0.4512	0.1237	1.0974	1.0682	1.0784	1.0890	1.0154	1.0198	1.02	1.02	1.01	1.02	0.16	0.07	0.00	0.10
4.6244	0.3048	0.1207	1.0783	1.0683	1.0511	1.0502	1.0307	1.0252	1.04	1.00	1.03	1.00	0.15	0.07	0.04	0.07
4.6654	0.4320	0.1185	1.0819	1.0617	1.0757	1.0481	1.0433	1.0179	1.03	0.99	1.03	0.99	0.16	0.15	0.07	0.06
4.5190	**0.7968**	**0.1161**	**1.1000**	**1.0772**	**1.0712**	**1.0761**	**1.0499**	**1.0322**	**1.01**	**1.01**	**1.05**	**0.98**	**0.23**	**0.12**	**0.12**	**0.04**
4.9474	0.1776	0.1225	1.0542	1.0459	1.0365	1.0214	1.0283	1.0002	1.04	0.98	1.01	0.97	0.14	0.12	0.07	0.09
4.7983	0.2472	0.1216	1.0671	1.0414	1.0702	1.0545	1.0297	1.0012	1.01	1.00	1.00	0.98	0.17	0.05	0.06	0.08
5.2205	**0.0768**	**0.1339**	**1.0227**	**1.0339**	**1.0130**	**0.9977**	**1.0007**	**1.0021**	**1.02**	**1.00**	**1.00**	**0.95**	**0.21**	**0.13**	**0.07**	**0.13**
4.9473	0.1608	0.1237	1.0557	1.0304	1.0342	1.0166	1.0177	0.9889	1.00	0.99	1.02	0.97	0.12	0.10	0.09	0.15
5.1051	0.1056	0.1348	1.0430	1.0260	1.0410	1.0016	1.0257	0.9806	1.00	1.01	1.02	0.96	0.16	0.08	0.10	0.16
4.9142	0.1608	0.1247	1.0501	1.0382	1.0537	1.0197	1.0156	0.9846	1.00	1.01	1.01	0.97	0.15	0.12	0.05	0.16
4.8736	0.2472	0.1201	1.0756	1.0603	1.0543	1.0490	1.0347	1.0009	1.02	0.97	1.05	0.97	0.10	0.01	0.09	0.07
4.8666	0.1824	0.1247	1.0579	1.0360	1.0648	1.0368	1.0134	1.0027	1.02	1.00	1.02	0.99	0.16	0.14	0.01	0.12
4.8522	0.1968	0.1234	1.0541	1.0520	1.0382	1.0306	1.0217	1.0035	1.02	1.00	1.03	0.99	0.18	0.10	0.07	0.09
4.6820	0.3000	0.1210	1.0800	1.0462	1.0741	1.0494	1.0292	1.0114	1.03	1.00	1.05	1.00	0.21	0.04	0.05	0.10
4.5216	0.6048	0.1173	1.0966	1.0754	1.0952	1.0819	1.0381	1.0272	1.03	0.99	1.04	1.01	0.17	0.05	0.06	0.10
4.9216	0.1848	0.1222	1.0594	1.0522	1.0532	1.0259	1.0239	0.9950	1.03	0.98	1.03	0.98	0.12	0.11	0.08	0.10
4.6692	0.3696	0.1185	1.0779	1.0723	1.0409	1.0485	1.0474	1.0150	1.02	0.99	1.03	0.99	0.18	0.05	0.05	0.09
4.6820	0.3336	0.1207	1.0884	1.0632	1.0736	1.0517	1.0321	1.0067	1.03	1.01	1.04	1.02	0.21	0.11	0.03	0.07
4.6423	0.3888	0.1201	1.0813	1.0763	1.0448	1.0631	1.0367	1.0124	1.02	1.01	1.04	1.01	0.20	0.14	0.03	0.04
4.6362	0.3576	0.1207	1.0771	1.0536	1.0480	1.0579	1.0325	1.0391	1.00	1.00	1.03	1.00	0.13	0.07	0.03	0.08
4.7256	0.3168	0.1191	1.0854	1.0475	1.0742	1.0576	1.0505	1.0114	1.00	0.98	1.04	1.00	0.14	0.08	0.00	0.06
4.6664	0.2808	0.1225	1.0783	1.0726	1.0711	1.0498	1.0291	1.0147	1.01	1.02	1.06	1.00	0.19	0.07	0.01	0.07
4.6828	0.4200	0.1179	1.0830	1.0807	1.0668	1.0500	1.0422	1.0195	1.02	0.99	1.05	1.01	0.20	0.13	0.02	0.06
4.6703	**0.2458**	**0.1192**	**1.0713**	**1.0372**	**1.0386**	**1.0433**	**1.0318**	**1.0301**	**1.04**	**0.99**	**1.01**	**1.00**	**0.10**	**0.04**	**0.05**	**0.08**
4.6917	0.4416	0.1164	1.0808	1.0756	1.0913	1.0694	1.0557	1.0223	1.02	0.97	1.04	0.97	0.11	0.06	0.07	0.03
4.6995	0.2400	0.1250	1.0712	1.0609	1.0445	1.0482	1.0140	1.0121	1.02	1.01	1.03	0.99	0.18	0.09	0.04	0.07
4.6090	**0.5208**	**0.1151**	**1.0864**	**1.0542**	**1.0698**	**1.0695**	**1.0587**	**1.0016**	**1.02**	**0.98**	**1.04**	**1.02**	**0.14**	**0.09**	**0.07**	**0.11**
4.7586	0.2520	0.1207	1.0784	1.0632	1.0459	1.0513	1.0327	0.9987	1.04	0.99	1.02	0.99	0.14	0.10	0.07	0.09
4.6423	0.3888	0.1201	1.0813	1.0763	1.0448	1.0631	1.0367	1.0124	1.01	1.01	1.04	1.01	0.20	0.14	0.03	0.04
4.7006	0.3288	0.1179	1.0868	1.0700	1.0652	1.0430	1.0452	1.0200	1.04	0.98	1.05	1.00	0.16	0.07	0.03	0.09
4.6882	0.2880	0.1222	1.0902	1.0726	1.0711	1.0498	1.0291	1.0147	1.01	1.01	1.06	1.00	0.19	0.07	0.01	0.06
4.7531	0.3048	0.1194	1.0800	1.0740	1.0692	1.0404	1.0363	1.0095	1.03	0.99	1.05	0.99	0.21	0.05	0.01	0.12
4.7257	0.2184	0.1247	1.0677	1.0568	1.0629	1.0329	1.0157	1.0226	1.02	1.02	1.04	1.00	0.20	0.05	0.04	0.11
4.6669	0.3648	0.1191	1.0800	1.0722	1.0750	1.0743	1.0272	1.0163	1.03	0.99	1.03	1.01	0.17	0.10	0.03	0.08

Table 4. Best compromise solution (BCS) and minimum value for each objective function

	P_{loss} (MW)	$\sum \Delta V$	L
BCS	4.6703	0.2458	0.1192
Min P_{loss}	**4.5190**	0.7968	0.1161
Min $\sum \Delta V$	5.2205	**0.0768**	0.1339
Min L	4.6090	0.5208	**0.1151**

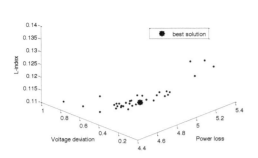

Figure 4. Pareto optimal front of the proposed approach

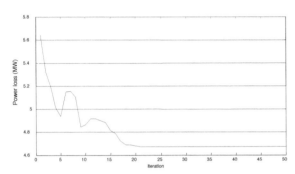

Figure 5. Convergence of best compromise solution power loss

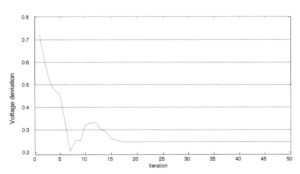

Figure 6. Convergence of best compromise solution voltage deviation

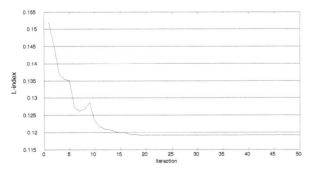

Figure 7. Convergence of best compromise solution voltage stability index

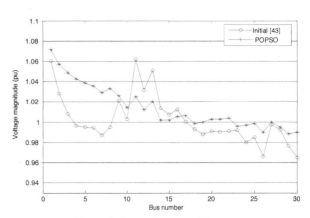

Figure 8. Bus voltage profiles

To evaluate the performance of proposed POPSO approach, the simulation results are compared with other listed algorithms in Table 5 as discussed below:

Comparing POPSO with initial case

The following points are noted: a) Active power losses before and after proposed POPSO optimization are 5.7213 (column 2 Table 5) and 4.6703 (column 11 Table 5), respectively, indicating a power loss reduction of 18.37%. b) Voltage deviation is also reduced from 0.7656 in the initial case to 0.2458, i.e. a reduction of 67.89%. c) Voltage stability index, too is reduced from 0.1563 to 0.1192 (i.e. 23.74%, improvement).

Comparing POPSO with PSO and FAPSO

The numerical results from Table 5 indicate that in the same test system, the BCS determined by POPSO is better than both PSO and FAPSO [18]. Here, the least improvement (reduction) achieved in power loss, voltage deviation and voltage stability index are 5.65%, 6.89% and 3.72%, respectively.

Comparing POPSO with CLPSO

In CLPSO technique, three cases with different objectives are considered [19]: Case 1, a single objective is defined to minimize the real power loss; Case 2, two objectives are defined in order to minimize the power loss and voltage deviation; and Case 3, where two objectives of minimizing the power loss and voltage stability index are defined. The best candidate in Pareto optimal front for comparing POPSO with CLPSO-Case 1 is Min P_{loss} in Table 4, where the solution for P_{loss} is 4.519 which compared to the latter (i.e. 4.5615) indicates slight improvement in working with POPSO. BCS is chosen in this study for comparing POPSO and CLPSO-Case 2 and CLPSO-Case 3. Only voltage deviation in CLPSO-Case 2 is slightly less than POPSO, but POPSO still illustrates better results with respect to other specification. Comparing CLPSO-Case 3 with POPSO, P_{loss} and voltage deviation are still inferior for the former. It is worth mentioning that in [19], the number of shunt compensations employed in CLPSO's is 9, while in this paper we have used 4. This may cause L index to be less than the case considered for POPSO comparisons (in CLPSO-Case 3, L index is 0.0866 against 0.1192 for POPSO).

Comparing POPSO with DE
In DE algorithm [22], three cases (Case 1: minimization of system power loss, Case 2: improvement of voltage profile and Case 3: enhancement of voltage stability) with different objectives are considered as follows: for minimizing real power loss, the best candidate at Pareto optimal front for comparison is for Min P_{Loss} in POPSO is 4.519 (column 2, Table 4) against 4.555 for DE (0.036 MW loss reduction) and as can be seen POPSO shows improvement over DE in all other specs, too (at least 78.38% improvement in $\sum \Delta V$ and L). Also, the best candidate at Pareto optimal front for comparison with DE-Case 2 and DE-Case 3 (Min $\sum \Delta V$ and Min L) are 0.0768 (column 3, Table 4) against 0.0911 for voltage deviation, and 0.1151 (column 4, Table 4) against 0.1246 for voltage stability, respectively (at least 15.69% and 7.62% improvement are observed in voltage profile and voltage stability index, respectively).

Comparing POPSO with NSGA-II and MNSGA-II
NSGA-II and MNSGA-II are algorithms that use Pareto optimality for MOO. Minimizing the power loss and voltage stability index could be defined as the two objectives of ORPD [25]. Best P_{Loss} and best L are Pareto optimal front solutions, each representing a minimum objective function for power loss and voltage stability index. The best candidates at Pareto optimal front for comparing POPSO with NSGA-II and MNSGA-II are Min P_{loss} for Best P_{Loss} and Min L for Best L. Advantage of POPSO with respect to NSGA-II and MNSGA-II are expressed in Table 5, where BCS indicate improvement in power loss and voltage stability index of at least 5.69% and 13.75%, respectively.
Figures 9-11, clearly compares the results of proposed POPSO with other methods for IEEE 30-bus test system. Therefore, as can be seen, the proposed POPSO method yields nearer global

optimal solution for both single and multi-objectives.

5.2. Simulation of the IEEE 118-bus test system
In order to evaluate the applicability of the proposed method to bigger systems, IEEE 118-bus power system is employed which consists of 54 generator buses, 64 load buses and 186 branches in which 14 branches are tap changing transformers with discrete operating values. In addition, 9 buses are taken as shunt compensation buses with discrete operating values. In this system, a total of 77 control variables are taken for MORPD.

Table 6 and Figures 12-15 show the results obtained by the proposed POPSO when compared with other methods [18, 19, 25, 43] where improvement in power loss, voltage deviation and voltage stability index are at least 1.26%, 3.3% and 8.27%, respectively, and can therefore be efficiently used for the MORPD problem. Again, it is worth noting that in [19], the number of shunt compensations employed in CLPSO's is 14, and in this paper we have used 9. The same argument for L index as outlined above applies here too (in CLPSO-Case 3, L index is 0.0965 against 0.1087 for POPSO).

6. Conclusion
In this paper, a new approach based on POPSO has been proposed and applied to MORPD problem. The problem has been formulated as MOO problem with competing power loss, bus voltage deviation and voltage stability index. A hierarchical clustering technique is implemented to provide the operator with a representative and manageable Pareto optimal set without destroying the characteristics of the trade-off front. Moreover, a proposed mechanism is employed to extract the best compromise solution over the trade-off curve. The Pareto multi-objective algorithms here implemented have the advantage of including multiple criteria without the need for introducing weights in a simple aggregating function. The results show that the proposed approach is efficient for solving MORPD problem where multiple Pareto optimal solutions can be found in one simulation run. The algorithms have been tested for standard IEEE 30-bus and 118-bus test systems and results are compared with others commonly used algorithms in the literature. Comparison shows that the proposed approach performed better than the other algorithms and can be efficiently used for the MORPD problem as near global optimum solutions reached in this study. The comparison seems to dominate other algorithms results.

Table 5. Comparison of POPSO with other techniques on IEEE 30-bus test system

	Initial [43]	PSO [18]	FAPSO [18]	CLPSO [19]			DE [22]			NSGA-II [25]		MNSGA-II [25]		POPSO
				Case 1	Case 2	Case 3	Case 1	Case 2	Case 3	Best P_{loss}	Best L	Best P_{loss}	Best L	(BCS)
P_{loss}(MW)	5.7213	5.1600[a]	4.9500[a]	4.5615	4.6969	4.6760	4.555	6.4755	7.0733	4.952	5.128	4.9454	5.102	**4.6703**
$\sum \Delta V$	0.7656	0.3840[b]	0.2640[b]	0.4773	0.2450	0.5171	1.9589	0.0911	1.4191	-	-	-	-	**0.2458**
L	0.1563	0.1307	0.1238	0.1230	0.1247	0.0866	0.5513	0.5734	0.1246	0.1393	0.1382	0.13940	0.1382	**0.1192**

[a] P_{loss}(p.u.) $\times$ 100 = P_{loss} (MW)
[b] ΔV(p.u.) $\times N_L = \sum \Delta V$

Table 6. The results of POPSO and comparison with other methods on IEEE 118-bus test system

	Initial [43]	PSO [18]	FAPSO [18]	CLPSO [19]			NSGA-II [25]		MNSGA-II [25]		POPSO
				Case 1	Case 2	Case 3	Best P_{loss}	Best L	Best P_{loss}	Best L	(BCS)
P_{loss}(MW)	133.14	117.81	115.37	130.96	132.06	132.08	119.57	132.21	119.279	132.17	**113.92**
$\sum \Delta V$	2.0150	0.7488	0.7744	1.8525	1.6177	2.8863	-	-	-	-	**0.7241**
L	0.1497	0.1295	0.1185	0.1461	0.1210	0.0965	0.4553	0.4113	0.4553	0.4074	**0.1087**

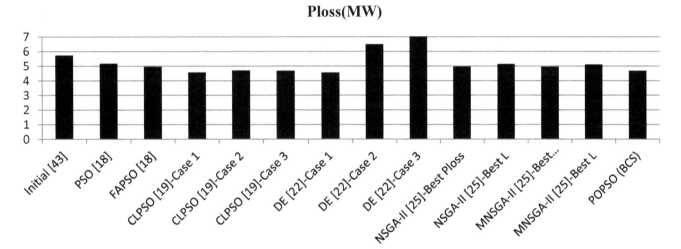

Figure 9. Comparison results of power loss in IEEE 30-bus test system

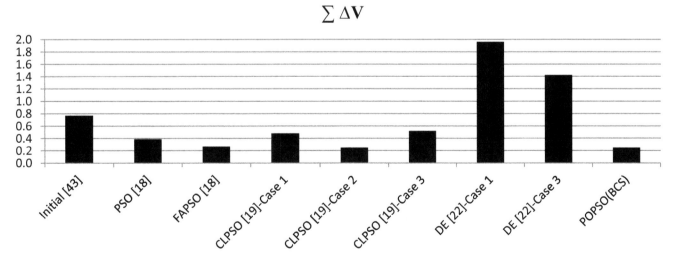

Figure 10. Comparison results of voltage deviation in IEEE 30-bus test system

L-Index

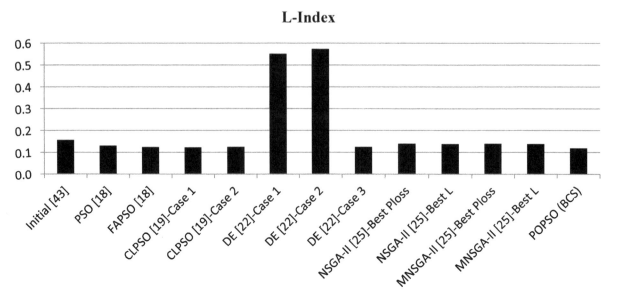

Figure 11. Comparison results of *L*-index in IEEE 30-bus test system

Ploss(MW)

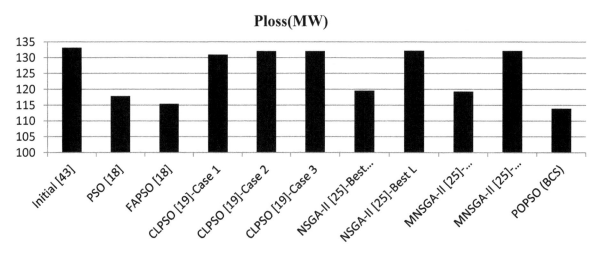

Figure 12. Comparison results of power loss in IEEE 118-bus test system

∑ ΔV

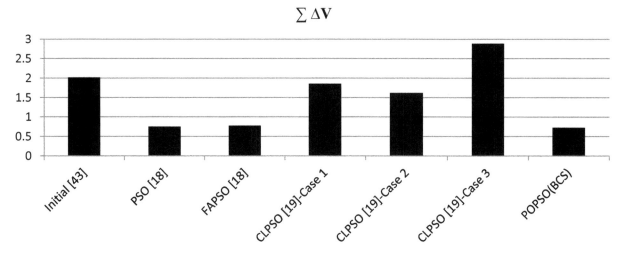

Figure 13. Comparison results of voltage deviation in IEEE 118-bus test system

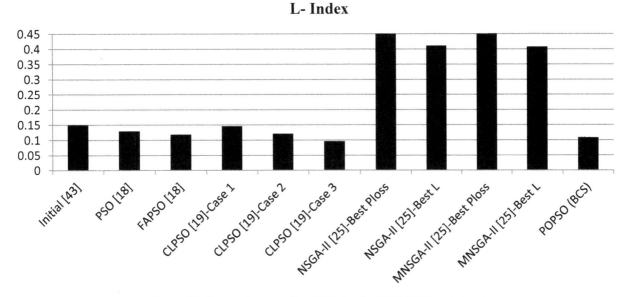

Figure 14. Comparison results of *L*-index in IEEE 118-bus test system

References

[1] Deeb, N., S. M. Shaidepour, "Linear reactive power optimization in a large power network using the decomposition approach", IEEE Trans. Power System, vol. 5, no. 2, pp. 428–35, 1990.

[2] Granville, S. "Optimal reactive dispatch through interior point methods", IEEE Trans. Power System, vol. 9, no. 1, pp. 136–46, 1994.

[3] Gomes, J. R, O. R. Saavedra, "A Cauchy-based evolution strategy for solving the reactive power dispatch problem", International Journal Electrical Power and Energy System, vol. 24, no. 4, pp. 277–83, 2002.

[4] Bhagwan, D. D., C. Patvardhan, "Reactive power dispatch with a hybrid stochastic search technique", International Journal Electrical Power and Energy System, vol. 24, no. 9, pp. 731–6, 2002.

[5] Devaraj, D., "Improved genetic algorithm for multi-objective reactive power dispatch problem", European Trans. on Electrical Power, vol. 17, no. 6, pp. 569-581, 2007.

[6] Liu, Y. T., L. Ma, J.J. Zhang, "Reactive power optimization by GA/SA/TS combined algorithms", International Journal Electrical Power and Energy System, vol. 24, no. 9, pp. 765–9, 2002.

[7] Tomsovic, K., "A fuzzy linear programming approach to the reactive power/ voltage control problem", IEEE Trans. Power System, vol. 7, no. 1, pp. 287–93, 1992.

[8] Grudinin, N. "Reactive power optimization using successive quadratic programming method", IEEE Trans Power System, vol. 13, no. 4, pp. 1219–25, 1998.

[9] Abido, M. A., J.M. Bakhashwain, "Optimal VAR dispatch using a multi-objective evolutionary algorithm", International Journal Electrical Power and Energy System, vol. 27, no. 1, pp. 13-20, 2005.

[10] Jiang, C., C. Wang, "Improved evolutionary programming with dynamic mutation and metropolis criteria for multi-objective reactive power optimization", IEE Proc Generation Transmission Distribution, vol. 152, no. 2, pp. 291–4, 2005.

[11] Zhou, A., B-Y. Qu, H. Li, S-Z. Zhao, P. N. Suganthan, Q. Zhang, "Multiobjective Evolutionary Algorithms: A Survey of the State-of-the-art", Swarm and Evolutionary Computation, vol. 1, no. 1, pp. 32-49, 2011.

[12] Aribia, H. B., N. Derbel, H.H. Abdallah, "The active–reactive – complete dispatch of an electrical network", International Journal of Electrical Power and Energy Systems, vol. 44, no. 1, pp. 236-248, 2013.

[13] Pires, D. F., C. H. Antunes, A. G. Martins, "NSGA-II with local search for a multi-objective reactive power compensation problem", International Journal of Electrical Power and Energy Systems, vol. 43, no. 1, pp. 313-324, 2012.

[14] Wu, Q. H., Y.J. Cao, J.Y. Wen, "Optimal reactive power dispatch using an adaptive genetic algorithm", International Journal Electrical Power and Energy System, vol. 20, no. 8, pp. 563–569, 1998.

[15] del Valle, Y. et al., "Particle swarm optimization: basic concepts, variants and applications in power systems", IEEE Trans. Evol. Comput., vol. 12, no. 2, pp. 171–195, 2008.

[16] Esmin, A. A. A., G. Lambert-Torres, A. C. Zambroni de Souza, "A hybrid particle swarm optimization applied to loss power minimization", IEEE Trans. Power System, vol. 20, no. 2, pp. 859–869, 2005.

[17] Vlachogiannis, J. G., K. Y. Lee, "A comparative study on particle swarm optimization for optimal steady-state performance of power systems", IEEE Trans. Power System, vol. 21, no. 4, pp. 1718–1728, 2006.

[18] Zhang, W., Y. Liu, "Multi-objective reactive power and voltage control based on fuzzy optimization strategy and fuzzy adaptive particle swarm", International

Journal Electrical Power and Energy System, vol. 30, no. 9, pp. 525–532, 2008.

[19] Mahadevan, K., P. S. Kannan, "Comprehensive learning particle swarm optimization for reactive power dispatch", International Journal Applied Soft Computing, vol. 10, no. 2, pp. 641–652, 2010.

[20] Varadarajan, M., K. S. Swarup, "Network loss minimization with voltage security using differential evolution", Electric Power System Res., vol. 78, no. 5, pp. 815–823, 2008.

[21] Varadarajan, M., K. S. Swarup, "Differential evolutionary algorithm for optimal reactive power dispatch", International Journal Electrical Power and Energy System, vol. 30, no. 8, pp. 435–441, 2008.

[22] Abou El Ela, A. A., M. A. Abido, S.R. Spea, "Differential evolution algorithm for optimal reactive power dispatch", Electric Power System Research, vol. 81, no. 2, pp. 458-464, 2011.

[23] Dai, Ch., W. Chen, Y. Zhu, X. Zhang "Reactive power dispatch considering voltage stability with seeker optimization algorithm" International Journal of Electrical Power & Energy Systems, vol. 79, no. 10, pp. 1462-1471, 2009.

[24] Zhihuan, L., L. Yinhong, D. Xianzhong, "Non-dominated sorting genetic algorithm-II for robust multi-objective optimal reactive power dispatch", IET Generation, Transmission & Distribution, vol. 4, no. 9, pp. 1000 – 1008, 2010.

[25] Jeyadevi, S., S. Baskar, C. K. Babulal, M. Willjuice Iruthayarajan, "Solving multi-objective optimal reactive power dispatch using modified NSGA-II", International Journal of Electrical Power and Energy Systems, vol. 33, no. 2, pp. 219-228, 2011.

[26] Kennedy, J., R.C. Eberhart, "Particle swarm optimization", Proc IEEE Int. Conf. Neural Networks, vol. 4, pp. 1942–8, 1995.

[27] Yoshida, H., K. Kawata, Y. Fukuyama, S. Takayama, Y. Nakanishi, "A particle swarm optimization for reactive power and voltage control considering voltage security assessment", IEEE Trans. Power System, vol. 15, no. 4, pp. 1232–9, 2000.

[28] Abido, M. A., "Optimal power flow using particle swarm optimization", International Journal Electrical Power and Energy System, vol. 24, no. 7, pp. 563–71, 2002.

[29] Kassabalidis, I. N., M. A. El-Sharkawi, R. Marks, L.S. Moulin, A.P. Alves da Silva, "Dynamic security border identification using enhanced particle swarm optimization", IEEE Trans. Power System, vol. 17, no. 3, pp. 723–9, 2002.

[30] Naka, S., T. Genji, T. Yura, Y. Fukuyama, "A hybrid particle swarm optimization for distribution state estimation", IEEE Trans. Power System, vol. 18, no. 1, pp. 60–68, 2003.

[31] Ngatchou, P., A. Zarei, A. El-Sharkawi, "Pareto multi objective optimization", Intelligent Systems Application to Power Systems, Proceedings of the 13th International Conference on 6-10 Nov. 2005, pp. 84 – 91.

[32] Montoya, F. G., et al., "Minimization of voltage deviation and power losses in power networks using Pareto optimization methods", Engineering Applications of Artificial Intelligence, vol. 23, no. 5, pp. 695-703, 2010.

[33] Yassami, H., A. Darabi, S. M. R. Rafiei, "Power system stabilizer design using Strength Pareto multi-objective optimization approach", Electric Power Systems Research, vol. 80, no. 7, pp. 838–846, 2010.

[34] Balamourougan, V., T.S. Sidhu, M. S. Sachdev, "Technique for online prediction of voltage collapse", IEE Proc. Gen. Trans. Distrib., vol. 151, no. 4, pp. 453-460, 2004.

[35] Hugang, X., C. Haozhong, L. Haiyu, "Optimal reactive power flow incorporating static voltage stability based on multi-objective adaptive immune algorithm", Energy Conversion and Management, vol. 49, no. 5, pp. 1175–1181, 2008.

[36] Kessel, P., H.Glavitsch, "Estimating the voltage stability of a power system", IEEE Trans Power Del., vol. 1, no. 3, pp. 346–54, 1986.

[37] Tuan, T. Q., J. Fandino, N. Hadjsaid, J.C. Sabonnadiere, H. Vu, "Emergency load shedding to avoid risk of voltage instability using indicators", IEEE Trans Power System, vol. 9, no. 1, pp. 341–8, 1994.

[38] Kennedy, J., "The particle swarm: Social adaptation of knowledge," in Proc. IEEE Int. Conf. Evolutionary Comp., Indianapolis, IN, pp. 303–308, 1997.

[39] Shi, Y., R.C. Eberhart, "A modified particle swarm optimizer", In: Proceedings of the IEEE international Conference Evolutionary Computation, pp. 69–73, 1998.

[40] Carlisle, A., G. Dozier, "An off-the-shelf PSO", In: Proceedings of the IEEE International Workshop Particle Swarm Optimization, USA, pp. 1–6, 2001.

[41] Sharaf, A. M., A.A.A. El-Gammal, "A multi objective multi-stage particle swarm optimization MOPSO search scheme for power quality and loss reduction on radial distribution system", International Conference on Renewable Energies and Power Quality, 2009.

[42] Dhillon, J. S., S.C. Parti, D.P. Kothari, "Stochastic economic emission load dispatch", Electric Power System Research, vol. 26, no. 3, pp. 179–86, 1993.

[43] Power System Test Case Archive, December [Online], Available: http://www.ee.washington.edu/research/pstca/, 2006.

24

Yarn tenacity modeling using artificial neural networks and development of a decision support system based on genetic algorithms

M. Dashti[1], V. Derhami[2*], E. Ekhtiyari[1]

1. Textile Engineering Department, Yazd University
2. Electrical and Computer Engineering Department, Yazd University

*Corresponding author: vderhami@yazd.ac.ir (V. Derhami).

Abstract

Yarn tenacity is one of the most important properties in yarn production. This paper focuses on modeling of the yarn tenacity as well as optimally determining the amounts of effective inputs to produce the desired yarn tenacity. The artificial neural network is used as a suitable structure for tenacity modeling of cotton yarn with 30 Number English. The empirical data was initially collected for cotton yarns. Then, the structure of the neural network was determined and its parameters were adjusted by the back propagation method. The efficiency and accuracy of the neural model was measured based on the error value and coefficient determination. The obtained experimental results show that the neural model could predicate the tenacity with less than 3.5% error. Afterwards, utilizing genetic algorithms, a new method is proposed for optimal determination of input values in the yarn production to reach the desired tenacity. We conducted several experiments for different ranges with various production cost functions. The proposed approach could find the best input values to reach the desired tenacity considering the production costs.

Keywords: *Artificial neural network, Genetic algorithm, Yarn tenacity, Modeling, Cotton yarn.*

1. Introduction

The quality and features of yarn determine possibility of using it in production of different fabrics. In this regard, tenacity is of special importance [1]. In fact, the yarn tenacity affects every next step in the processes of using it. This research was performed based on a request from Nakhchin and Nakheaftab factories, which are two distinguished textile production factories located in Yazd, Iran. This research aims at determining the best input values to produce 100% cotton yarn for a desired tenacity.

We are concerned with two constraints: first, although the effective parameters in the yarn tenacity are almost known but it is not clearly determined how these parameters affect the final yarn tenancy. In other words, there is no accurate mathematical model for this purpose. Second, optimal determination of input values to reach a desirable tenacity has not been investigated yet. In fact, nonlinearity and complexity of the relation giving the yarn tenacity in terms of the effective

parameters, have led the textile engineers to determine the values of input materials only by "trial and error" and their former experiences. Investigations show that although there is many research findings focused on modeling of tenacity but only a few of them proposed a practical approach to optimal determination of values for effective inputs. Some usual methods for the yarn tenacity modeling are mechanical models, mathematical models [2], statistical (regression) methods, fuzzy modeling [3], and artificial neural network models [7]. These primary methods (mechanical, mathematical and statistical) require highly experienced personnel as well as numerous of test steps, therefore they could not give accurate models with reasonable computational costs [8].

Artificial Neural Network (ANN) which is inspired from evolution of biological neurons of brain is a powerful method for modeling of complex phenomena. Some of its characteristics such as the ability of learning and generalization, robustness against disturbances, and information parallel processing have made ANN superior to other modeling approaches. Nowadays, ANNs are widely used for solving many engineering problems in modeling, controlling, and patterning recognition [5], [6].

Already in an ANN based yarn tenacity prediction research, the five parameters: spun fibers upper half mean length, package hardness, fineness, proportions of fiber length uniformity, and maturity of fibers content were used as neural network input parameters [7]. The accuracy of this neural model was 12%. In another study, 14 fiber properties have been used as neural network inputs to predict yarn tenacity [8]. These inputs are values of impurity, number of each package impurity (amount of trash), upper half mean length, strength and length increase to the extent on which the fiber is torn (elongation of break), fiber fineness, brightness, yellowness, fiber maturity content, standard fiber fineness (norm), length uniformity, and micronaire. The accuracy of the later neural model was 8%.

Two other papers focused on fiber properties measured by High Volume Instrument (HVI) and included upper half mean length, length uniformity, short fiber content, strength, maturity ratio, fineness, grayness, and yellowness used as neural network input [9],[10].

In this research, we use neural networks in modeling of yarn tenacity of 100% cotton with 30 Ne, where a new approach, which is based on genetic algorithms, is used for optimal determination of values of input materials. The main advantages and innovations on this research are:

　　1- Proposing an accurate neural model for predicting yarn tenacity of 100% cotton yarn. Although there are some research works concerning neural modeling, but our model is a real case study with different inputs and conditions; hence, we use a different structure of ANN.
　　2- Proposing a new idea to find the optimal values of inputs to reach desired yarn tenacity by using genetic algorithms. To the best of our knowledge, this research is the first research of its kind.

The structure of this paper is as follows. In the second section, yarn tenacity and the parameters which affect yarn tenacity are investigated and discussed. The third section deals with introducing neural networks; in the fourth section, modeling of yarn tenacity of 100% cotton with 30 NE (the most popular yarn) using neural network is presented. In the fifth section, a method to find optimal values of inputs to reach a desirable tenacity is proposed. Finally, in the last section, summary and conclusions are provided.

2. Effective parameters on yarn tenacity

The resistance of yarn against tensile forces is called yarn tenacity. It is the minimum force which is needed to tear out that yarn [1]. Several factors are involved in yarn tenancy, and the most important ones are the properties of the fibers used to produce yarn (raw materials) such as: upper half mean length, length uniformity, short fiber content, fibers strength, maturity ratio, yellowness, linear density, and fiber length increase (which is measured by HVI).

Here, the input variables have been chosen with respect to the related research [7,8,10]. The production process was set fixed for the whole time. This means, five adjustable parameters for textile machines such as spin tube, breaker speed, rotor speed, were fixed. Moreover, yarn twist and yarn counts were set constant as well. In this way, in our model, the seven mentioned parameters associated with fiber property were considered as effective parameters on yarn tenacity.

3. Artificial neural networks

Artificial neural network is a structure inspired from the human brain. It is very useful in modeling complex functions. A neural network consists of an interconnected group of artificial neurons where an artificial neuron is a mathematical function representing an abstraction of biological neurons [4].

Figure 1 shows the structure of a neuron. Vector $x = [x_1, ..., x_n]^T$ is input and the scalar y is the output of the neuron.

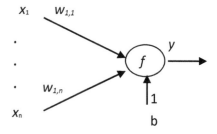

Figure 1. Model of a multi-input neuron

The influence of x_i on y is determined by $w_{1,i}$. Another input is bias parameter that its corresponding weight is 1.
The output of the neuron is computed by:

$$y = f(z) = f(Wx + b) \qquad (1)$$

$$z = \sum_{i=1}^{n} x_i w_{1,i} + b = Wx + b \qquad (2)$$

$$W = [w_{1,1}, ..., w_{1,n}] \qquad (3)$$

The activation function f could be linear or either nonlinear. Here, the designer selects a suitable activation function with respect to the problem features. Table 1 shows some widely used activation functions.

Table 1. Some activation functions

Function	Definition	Range
Linear	$f(z) = z$	$(-\infty, +\infty)$
Logistic	$f(z) = \dfrac{1}{1 + e^{-az}}$, a is slope parameter	$(0, +1)$
Hyperbolic	$f(z) = \dfrac{e^z - e^{-z}}{e^z + e^{-z}}$	$(-1, +1)$
Threshold	$f(z) = \begin{cases} 0 & if\ z < 0 \\ 1 & if\ z \geq 0 \end{cases}$	$\{0, +1\}$

In comparison with single layer networks, multilayer neural networks have more capabilities. Double layers feed forward neural networks (with sigmoid functions in first layer and that of linear in second layer) can estimate any continuous function with arbitrary precision [4].

In this research, we employed a feed forward neural network with two layers, where the first layer is known as the hidden layer. Figure 2 shows the corresponding network structure. This structure is presented as: $n{:}nh{:}o$ where n is the number of inputs, nh is the number of hidden layer neurons, and o is the number of output layer neurons. The output of network is computed by:

$$y = f_o \left(\sum_{i=1}^{nh} o_i w_i^2 + b \right) \qquad (4)$$

$$o_i = f_i \left(\sum_{j=1}^{n} x_j w_{i,j}^1 + b_i \right) \quad i = 1, ..., nh \qquad (5)$$

where, y is the final output, f_o is the activation function of output neuron, w_i^2 is the weight of link between i-th output neuron in the hidden layer and the final output, b is the bias of output neuron, o_i is the output of i-th neuron in hidden layer, $w_{i,j}^1$ is the weight of link between j-th input and i-th

neuron in hidden layer, b_i is the bias of i-th neuron in hidden layer, and f_i is the activation function in i-th neuron in hidden layer.

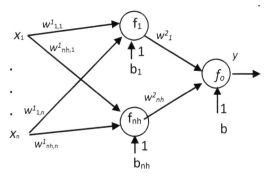

Figure 2. The feed forward neural network.

The weights $(w_{i,j}^1, w_i^2, b_i, b)$ are adjustable parameters that need to be tuned by training. In fact, the objective of network training is adjusting these parameters in such a way that the network generates desired output for different inputs.

4. Modeling

Since neural networks find and learn patterns in the training data, in the first step of modeling, we need some training data. The cotton yarn with 30 NE (Number English) is produced in tenacity range of 13 to 16. Some experiments have already been conducted on cotton fibers and the yarn 30 NE produced from them in order to collect required input data in the mentioned range. As stated in Section 2, seven properties (see Table 2) of cotton fiber are considered as effective parameters on yarn tenacity and they are selected as inputs of our model. The network output would be the yarn tenacity. The activation function for the neurons in the hidden layer is sigmoid and it is linear for the output neuron. Here, we use the obtained data from 33 cotton samples for ring carded spun yarns for input-output data.

The training data must cover the whole input range and need to have a suitable dispersion. Generally, if we use more training data, we would often be more accurate in prediction. In the primary experiments of this research, we used 100 data samples. The obtained result for this data was poor. Therefore, we had to obtain and use more data. Here, we encountered some practical constraints. For example, in measuring yarn tenacity for each sample, first we had to produce the yarn with those input materials. Finally, we totally prepared 990 experimental data for tuning our neural network. During first experiments, we observed that the major problem in training our neural model was over fitting. In fact, we could see an error which was getting smaller and smaller in the course of training (for the training data) but the magnitude of the error for the test data was not acceptable. This phenomenon was due to the fact that during training phase, the network parameters are adjusted to reduce the error for the training data; hence, the network is fitted for the training data and this is why the property of generalization of the neural network degrades considerably. As a result, network's error in the output of the network was too high for any data other than the training data. Providing a solution for the problem, we used some valid data, which are not used for training, but they are only used to stop the training properly to avoid over fitting. After each training epoch, network's error was calculated for valid data and if the training procedure was going in a way that the error was increasing the training would be stopped.

Therefore, we divided our data into three parts: Training data, valid data, and test data. They included 800, 90, and 100 samples, respectively. The test data was used in the final to assess our neural model. The statistical features of the mentioned data shown in Table 2.

4.1. Neural network structure

Previous studies focused on modeling have shown that feed forward networks are suitable for modeling. We used a two layer feed forward neural network for modeling. It consists of seven inputs and one output. The number of neurons in hidden layer is different for these networks. Activation function for neurons in hidden layer is logistic and for the last layer is linear. These networks have been trained using training data regarding the valid data. The training method was the error back propagation algorithm. Results of the experiments on different structures are shown in Table 3.

Table 2. Statistical summary of data for fiber properties

Fibers Character-istics	Fiber Tenacity (CN/Tex)	Fiber Elong-ation	%50 Average Length	length uni-formity	Micro-naire	Reflection Degree	Yellow-ness
Maximum	34	6.9	1.2	83.2	5	80.4	11.4
Minimum	26.5	5.3	0.97	79.2	3.1	73	8
Average	29.05	6.27	1.06	81.57	4.23	77.2	9.34
Standard Deviation	1.41	0.46	0.05	1.05	0.45	2.28	0.72

Table 3. Results of training on different structures of neural networks

Network Structure	7:9:1	7:10:1	7:11:1	7:12:1	7:13:1	7:14:1
Error Percentage for Training Data	3.3%	3.1%	0.8%	3.5%	2%	1.1%
Error Percentage for Test Data	12%	3.5%	10.4%	10.4%	6.4%	11.6%
R2 for Test Data	0.91	0.95	0.90	0.87	0.87	0.83

The first row in the table shows structure of the neural network. The error rate for training data has been given in the second row. The third row shows the error percent for test data, and the determination coefficient [4] has been given in the last row.

As Table 3 shows, the best results have been obtained from the neural network model consisting of 10 neurons in the hidden layer. The training stopped after 106 epochs. The percentage error for this structure in the training phase is 3.1% and 3.5% for the test data. Comparing the similar results from [2, 5] this error is acceptable. Therefore, the ANN with structure of 7:10:1 is selected as a neural model to predict yarn tenacity.

5. Optimal input values for desired tenacity

After finding the suitable neural model, we turn our attention to the determination of input parameters to reach the desired tenacity using Genetic Algorithms (GA). This is, in fact, a multi-goal problem. From one side, the production cost should be minimized and from other side the tenacity of produced yarn should be equal to or higher than the desired tenacity. If the cost reduces but the tenacity is less than the desired value, it would not be acceptable. From the other side, if the tenacity improves but the cost goes too high, it would not be acceptable too. In order to overcome this dilemma, we first convert it into an optimization problem and then propose an approach to solve it by GA. In Section 2, we introduced the seven variables which are effective in yarn tenacity. The cost production function $C(x)$ would be:

$$C(x) = \sum_{i=1}^{7} v_i x_i \qquad (6)$$

Where, v_i is the assigned weight for the *i-th* variable x_i. Weights show how effective each parameter is in the cost function. In other words, more expensive variables are expressed by higher weights.

The evaluation criterion in GA is the fitness function. Here, the algorithm looks for the responses in such a way that the fitness function decreases to a minimum value. The space of the problem is defined by all combinations of the values of variables x_i where they fall in the ranges mentioned in Table 2. Our objective is to reach the desired tenacity while the cost function (Eq. 6) is minimized. The most important challenge in using GA is defining the suitable fitness function. Here, the fitness function is defined as:

$$Fit.F = K * f(e) + C(x) \qquad (7)$$

$$e = T_{desired} - T_{actual}(x)$$

$$T_{actual}(x) \approx Output\ of\ Neural Model\ of\ Tenacity$$

$$\qquad (8)$$

$$f(e) = \begin{cases} e & e > 0 \\ 0 & Otherwise. \end{cases}$$

$$\qquad (9)$$

In the above fitness formula, the first term is the error function. The error is equal to the difference between the desired tenacity and the actual tenacity ($T_{actual}(x)$). The actual tenacity is the tenacity of produced yarn with x_i's (the amounts of input materials). We use the neural model obtained in Section 4, to predict the actual tenacity for each x and finally to compute $f(e)$ in Eq. (9). In the first relation, K serves as a weight parameter.

Each intermediate solution for a problem in GA is called a chromosome. A chromosome consists of genes, corresponding to a series of values given to the problem variables (in our case x_i's). The number of genes is equal to the number of variables; therefore in our case, each chromosome will have seven genes. Using values of genes in chromosome as the neural model input, we can get the tenacity of the yarn as well as the production cost using Eq.6. In this way, the fitness function can be computed for each chromosome.

If the predicted tenacity (output of neural model) is less than the desired tenacity, then the first term in

fitness function would be positive and its amount is error proportion. In a situation where the predicated tenacity is equal or greater than desired tenacity, the first term in fitness function would be zero. The second term stands for the production cost function. As the cost increases, the fitness function will increase, too.

Regarding the amount of K in Eq. 7, since the main objective is to reach the desired tenacity, K has to be determined in such a way that GA finds answers having first term equal to zero. Since the maximum of cost function is 1000, we set K to 1000 as well. This value for K lets one thousandth of error from the desired tenacity be equal to one unit in the second term (cost function). This will guide our GA model to find the solutions with values in first term equal to zero.

In general, a GA is inspired from evaluation theory. It looks for a chromosome that minimizes the fitness function. The algorithm begins with a random population (some chromosomes), then it uses present population to generate new population based on the following steps in each iteration [11]:

1. The value of fitness function is computed for each chromosome in the current population.
2. The algorithm selects some chromosomes based on their fitness values. These chromosomes are called parents and used to generate next generation. Some well known approaches for selection of parents are: Roulette-wheel selection, rank selection, and elitist selection.
3. The algorithm generates children with applying crossover operation on selected parents.
4. Mutation on a child is changing one or more of its properties randomly. Mutational children are produced in this step.
5. The obtained children are added to the population.

The algorithm continues until it finds a child who fits the desired criteria.

6. Experimental results

To assess the proposed approach, we performed a number of experiments with different desired tenacities and different weights (v_i's) as cost function. The objective was finding the input parameters for yarn production such that the obtained tenacity becomes greater than the desired tenacity and as a result, the production cost is minimized. In the experiments, we used one-point crossover, and mutation rate of 0.1; based on the primary results, the population size was set to 40.

The final experimental results are shown in Table 4. The first column is the desired tenacity, the second column is the obtained tenacity of the produced yarn, the third column is the final value of the fitness function at the termination of the search process in GA, and the last column is the value of V for each experiment.

For efficiency improvement of our algorithm, all input values, x_i, were normalized to be in the range of [0, 1]

Table 4. The results of the experiments

$T_{desired}$	$T_{obtained}$	$Fit.F$	V
14	14.03	660.01	[4 7 3 5 1 2 6]
15	15.01	668.81	[4 7 3 5 1 2 6]
16	16.00	679.67	[4 7 3 5 1 2 6]
14	14.04	718.26	[1 6 3 7 5 2 4]
15	15.00	720.97	[1 6 3 7 5 2 4]
16	16.01	724.81	[1 6 3 7 5 2 4]

Table 4 shows that the proposed approach was capable to find values for the input parameters in a way that the obtained tenacity is satisfactory; the amount of first term of the fitness function is equal to zero and the values of the fitness function are equal to the production cost.

Meanwhile, the obtained values for inputs depend on the amounts of v's. For example, the values in the fourth row, ($T_{desired}$=16, V=[4 7 3 5 1 2 6]), is:

x=[26.754 5.977 0.876 70.510 2.703 64.818 7.216]

and for the last row with the same desired tenacity and V=[1 6 3 7 5 2 4] is:

x=[30.966 4.558 0.855 70.236 2.713 64.890 7.233]

Comparing the two results indicates that the second case, which is the weight of first input variable in the cost function, has been decreased (changed from 4 to 1), the value of this input has been increased. In opposite, the value of forth input variable has been reduced due to its weight increase.

6. Conclusion

In this research, a neural network model of yarn tenacity for 100% yarn cotton 30 NE using empirical data is presented. The output of neural model for test data confirmed the accuracy of the proposed model. Based on the obtained results in modeling section, feed forward neural network with 10 neurons in hidden layers was a suitable structure for modeling of tenacity. We also used GA for optimal determination of values of inputs in yarn manufacturing. The results of the experiment showed that GA with the defined fitness function can find the best values for inputs such that produced yarn with the obtained values of

inputs satisfy the desired tenacity while the production cost becomes minimal. The proposed method can be used to find the best-input values for any kind of yarn production with a desired tenacity. For using the proposed method, a user determines the desired tenacity of yarn and then he/she assigns weights of input materials based on their prices. Afterwards, our proposed method presents the amounts of input materials for yarn production so that the produced yarn has the desired tenacity, and above all, the production cost has been minimized.

References
[1] Taheri, A., (1990). General Technology of Cotton Textile Industry," (in Persian) Aghabik.

[2] Majumdar, P. K., and Majumdar, A., (2004). Predicting the Breaking Elongation of Ring Spun Cotton Yarns Using Mathematical, Statistical, and Artificial Neural Network Models", Textile Research Journal, Vol.74, No.7, pp. 652-655.

[3] Shams Nateri, A. (2005). Using Neuro-Fuzzy For Prediction Ring Spun Yarn Strength From Cotton Fibers Properties", 3rd International Industrial Simulation Conference, June 9-11.

[4] M. Menhaj, (2002). Fundamental of Neural Networks," Amikabir University publication, (in Persian).

[5] Gharehaghaji, A.A., Palhang, M., and Shanbeh, M., (2006). Using Artificial Neural Network Algorithm to Predict Tensile Properties of Cotton-covered Nylon Core Yarns", Esteghlal, Vol. 24, No.2.

[6] Jackowska-Strumillo, L., Ackowski, T., Cyniak, D., Czekalski, J., (2004). Neural Model of the Spinning Process for Predicting Selected Properties of Flax/Cotton Yarn Blends", Abres & Textiles In Eastem Europe, Vol. 12, No. 4, pp. 17-21.

[7] Sette, S., Bouliart, L., Van Langenhove, L. Kiekens, P., (1997). Optimizing the Fiber to Yarn Production Process with a Combined Neural Network/Genetic Algorithm Approach", Textile Research Journal, Vol. 67, No. 2, pp. 84-92.

[8] Cheng, L., Adams, D. L., (1995). Yarn Strength Prediction Using Neural Networks, Part 1: Fiber Properties and Yarn Strength Relationship", Textile Research Journal, Vol. 65, No. 9, pp. 495-500.

[9] Majumdar, A., Majumdar, P. K. , Sarkar, B., (2004). Selecting Cotton Bales By Spinning Consistency Index And Micronaire Using Artificial Neural Networks", AUTEX Research Journal, Vol. 4, No. 1, pp.1-8.

[10] Pynckels, F., Sette, S., Van Langenhove, L., Kiekens, P., and Impe. K. (1995). Use of Neural Nets for Detemining the Spinnability of Fibres"; Journal of the Textile Institute; October Vol. 86, No. 395, pp. 425-437.

[11] Back, T. (1996). Evolutionary Algorithms in Theory and Practice", Oxford University Press, New York.

Permissions

All chapters in this book were first published in JAIDM, by Shahrood University of Technology; hereby published with permission under the Creative Commons Attribution License or equivalent. Every chapter published in this book has been scrutinized by our experts. Their significance has been extensively debated. The topics covered herein carry significant findings which will fuel the growth of the discipline. They may even be implemented as practical applications or may be referred to as a beginning point for another development.

The contributors of this book come from diverse backgrounds, making this book a truly international effort. This book will bring forth new frontiers with its revolutionizing research information and detailed analysis of the nascent developments around the world.

We would like to thank all the contributing authors for lending their expertise to make the book truly unique. They have played a crucial role in the development of this book. Without their invaluable contributions this book wouldn't have been possible. They have made vital efforts to compile up to date information on the varied aspects of this subject to make this book a valuable addition to the collection of many professionals and students.

This book was conceptualized with the vision of imparting up-to-date information and advanced data in this field. To ensure the same, a matchless editorial board was set up. Every individual on the board went through rigorous rounds of assessment to prove their worth. After which they invested a large part of their time researching and compiling the most relevant data for our readers.

The editorial board has been involved in producing this book since its inception. They have spent rigorous hours researching and exploring the diverse topics which have resulted in the successful publishing of this book. They have passed on their knowledge of decades through this book. To expedite this challenging task, the publisher supported the team at every step. A small team of assistant editors was also appointed to further simplify the editing procedure and attain best results for the readers.

Apart from the editorial board, the designing team has also invested a significant amount of their time in understanding the subject and creating the most relevant covers. They scrutinized every image to scout for the most suitable representation of the subject and create an appropriate cover for the book.

The publishing team has been an ardent support to the editorial, designing and production team. Their endless efforts to recruit the best for this project, has resulted in the accomplishment of this book. They are a veteran in the field of academics and their pool of knowledge is as vast as their experience in printing. Their expertise and guidance has proved useful at every step. Their uncompromising quality standards have made this book an exceptional effort. Their encouragement from time to time has been an inspiration for everyone.

The publisher and the editorial board hope that this book will prove to be a valuable piece of knowledge for researchers, students, practitioners and scholars across the globe.

List of Contributors

M. Shahidul Islam
Department of Computer Science, School of Applied Statistics, National Institute of Development Administration, Bangkok, Thailand

M. Vahedi, M. Hadad Zarif and A. Akbarzadeh Kalat
Faculty of Electrical & Robotic Engineering, Shahrood University of Technology, Shahrood, Iran

H. Motameni
Department of Computer Engineering, Sari Branch, Islamic Azad University, Sari, Iran

R. Ghanizadeh and M. Ebadian
Department of Electrical & Computer Engineering, University of Birjand, Birjand, Iran

A. Karami-Mollaee
Department of Electrical & Robotic Engineering, Shahrood University of Technology, Shahrood, Iran

M. Rahimi and M. Zahedi
School of Computer and IT, Shahrood University of Technology, Shahrood, Semnan, Iran

Sh. Mehrjoo
Department of Industrial Management, Islamic Azad University, Qazvin Branch, Qazvin, Iran

M. Jasemi
Department of Industrial Engineering, K.N.Toosi University of Technology, Tehran, Iran

A. Mahmoudi
Department of Industrial Engineering and Quality Assurance, Dehkhoda Sugarcane Agro Industry co, Ahvaz, Iran

M. Imani and H. Ghassemian
Faculty of Electrical and Computer Engineering, Tarbiat Modares University, Tehran, Iran

M. Askari, M. Asadi, A. Asilian Bidgoli and H. Ebrahimpour
Department of Computer Engineering, University of Kashan, Kashan, Iran

M. Fatahi and B. Lashkar-Ara
Civil Engineering Department, Jundi-Shapur University of Technology, Dezful, Iran

A. Ardakani and V. R. Kohestani
Faculty of Engineering & Technology, Imam Khomeini International University, Qazvin, Iran

A. Harimi, A. Shahzadi and Kh.Yaghmaie
Faculty of Electrical & Computer Engineering, Semnan University, Iran

A. R. Ahmadyfard
Department of Electrical Engineering and Robotics, Shahrood University of technology, Iran

M. Dehghani
Department of Computer College of Engineering, Yazd Science and Research Branch, Islamic Azad University, Yazd, Iran

S. Emadi
Department of Computer College of Engineering, Yazd Branch, Islamic Azad University, Yazd, Iran

M. Moradi Zirkohi and S. Izadpanah
Department of Electrical Engineering, Behbahan Khatam Alanbia University of Technology, Behbahan, Iran

E. Golpar-Rabooki
Department of Mathematics, University of Qom, Qom, Iran

S. Zarghamifar
Department of Computer Engineering, University of Qom, Qom, Iran

J. Rezaeenour
Department of Industrial Engineering, University of Qom, Qom, Iran

M. M. Fateh and S. Khorashadizadeh
Department of Electrical Engineering, University of Shahrood, Shahrood, Iran

S. M. Ahmadi
Department of Mechanical Engineering, University of Shahrood, Shahrood, Iran

B. Bokharaeian and A. Diaz
Facultad de Informática, Universidad Complutense de Madrid, Calle del Prof. José G! Santesmases, Madrid, Spain

M. Nikpour and M.- R Karami
Electrical and Computer Engineering Department, Babol Noushirvani University of Technology, Babol, Iran

R. Ghaderi
Nuclear Engineering Department, Shahid Beheshti University of Tehran, Tehran, Iran

A. Ahmadi Livani
Faculty of Electrical and Computer Engineering, Tarbiat Modares University, Tehran, Iran

M. Abadi
Faculty of Electrical and Computer Engineering, Tarbiat Modares University, Tehran, Iran

M. Alikhani
Faculty of Electrical and Computer Engineering, Tarbiat Modares University, Tehran, Iran

M. Hajian
Department of Electrical and Computer Engineering, Semnan University, Semnan, Iran

A. Akbari Foroud
Department of Electrical and Computer Engineering, Semnan University, Semnan, Iran

Mosavi
University of Debrecen, Faculty of Informatics, Hungary

D. Koundal
University Institute of Engineering and Technology, Panjab University, Chandigarh, India

S.A. Taher
Department of Electrical Engineering, University of Kashan, Kashan, Iran

M. Pakdel
Department of Electrical Engineering, University of Kashan, Kashan, Iran

M. Sharif Noughabi
Department of Electrical Engineering, University of Shahrood, Shahrood, Iran

V. Derhami
Electrical and Computer Engineering Department, Yazd University

E. Ekhtiyari
Textile Engineering Department, Yazd University

S.M. Hosseinirad
Department of Computer Science, Banaras Hindu University, India

S.K. Basu
Department of Computer Science, Banaras Hindu University, India

D. Darabian
Department of Electrical Engineering, University of Shahrood, Shahrood, Iran

H. Marvi
Department of Electrical Engineering, University of Shahrood, Shahrood, Iran

M. Dashti
Textile Engineering Department, Yazd University

Index

Printed in the USA
CPSIA information can be obtained
at www.ICGtesting.com
JSHW051432221024
72173JS00006B/1443